THE MINOR TRACTATES
MASSEKTOTH ḲEṬANNOTH

VOLUME I

'ABOTH D'RABBI NATHAN

*

SOFERIM

*

SEMAḤOTH

THE MINOR TRACTATES OF THE TALMUD

MASSEKTOTH ḲEṬANNOTH

IN TWO VOLUMES

TRANSLATED INTO ENGLISH
WITH NOTES, GLOSSARY AND INDICES
UNDER THE EDITORSHIP OF

REV. DR. A. COHEN
M.A., Ph.D., D.H.L.

FOREWORD BY
THE VERY REV. THE CHIEF RABBI
ISRAEL BRODIE

VOLUME ONE

THE SONCINO PRESS
LONDON

PRINTED IN GREAT BRITAIN
BY THE HOLLEN STREET PRESS LTD
LONDON, W.1

DEDICATED TO THE MEMORY OF

JACOB DAVIDSON ז״ל

FOUNDER OF THE SONCINO PRESS
WHOSE LOVE OF JEWISH LITERATURE
INSPIRED HIS VISION TO PRESENT
THE TEACHINGS OF THE RABBIS
TO THE ENGLISH-SPEAKING PUBLIC

CONTENTS

Volume One

Volume Two

FOREWORD BY THE CHIEF RABBI

It gives me great pleasure to write a brief Foreword to the first complete English translation of the *Massektoth Ḳeṭannoth.* These volumes further illustrate the notable contribution made by Anglo-Jewish scholars in the very difficult field of rendering into accurate, readable and intelligible English the great classics of Judaism. The Soncino Press, in the spirit of its founder, has displayed a characteristic courage in adding yet another important Rabbinic work to the row of publications which have brought it renown and gratitude on the part of scholars and students of Jewish literature throughout the world.

As can be seen both from the translation of the several Tractates, Introduction and Notes, the distinguished Editor and his collaborators have taken account of the research of scholars in dealing with the many problems associated with the text and dating of some of the tractates. The study of the context of these volumes must increase the student's appreciation of the variety and wealth of Israel's spiritual and ethical treasures.

ISRAEL BRODIE.

PREFACE

In many editions of the Babylonian Talmud, at the end of the fourth Order, *Seder Neziḳin,* a series of Rabbinic works is included under the heading *Massektoth Ḳeṭannoth,* 'Minor Tractates'. The number varies but the fullest collection is provided in the Wilna-Romm edition where the total is fifteen.The title is not appropriate to all of them, because *'Aboth d'Rabbi Nathan, Soferim, Semaḥoth* and *Kallah Rabbathi* are of considerable extent and the name has been attached to many more tractates than were originally intended.

Only seven appear to have formed the first collection of 'Minor Tractates'. The earliest mention of it which has so far been discovered is in a reference to *Masseketh Ẓiẓith* to be found in a work entitled *Torath 'Adam* by Naḥmanides (13th century) who speaks of *Sheba' Massektoth Ḳeṭannoth,* 'Seven Minor Tractates'. A manuscript of them in the possession of the French scholar, Eliakim Carmoly, was edited by Raphael Kirchheim in 1851 under the title *Septem Libri Talmudici Parvi Hiersolymitani,* and consists of *Sefer Torah, Mezuzah, Tefillin, Ẓiẓith* (all published by him for the first time), *'Abadim, Kuthim* and *Gerim.* L. Zunz, *Die Gottesdienstlichen Vorträge der Juden,* 1892, p. 93, gives a different enumeration, viz. *Dereḳ 'Ereẓ* (*Rabbah* and *Zuṭa*), *Soferim, Kallah, Semaḥoth, Ẓiẓith, Gerim* and *Kuthim.* He adds a tractate *Hilchoth 'Ereẓ Yisrael.*

All the fifteen tractates which are here presented in their entirety for the first time in translation may be regarded as an apocrypha to the Talmud. H. L. Strack, *Introduction to the Talmud and Midrash,* 1931, p. 73, calls them 'Extra-canonical Tractates', and the question arises whether they were excluded because they were not in existence when the Babylonian Talmud was 'closed' at the end of the fifth century or, as others hold, for the reason that they belong to the Tannaitic period and, like other halachic compendia, were superseded by the Mishnah of Rabbi Judah ha-Nasi.

Apart from *'Aboth d'Rabbi Nathan,* which is an elaboration of

Pirḳe 'Aboth, and *Kallah Rabbathi*, which is a Gemara on *Kallah*, the Minor Tractates are described by Zunz as 'Baraithoth in the form and style of the Tosefta', which means that the presentation of the material is archaic in form and style. References are met with in the Midrash and Talmud which seem to indicate that digests of certain halachic rulings existed then which correspond to some of the Minor Tractates.

The most striking occurs in the Midrash to Eccles. V, 8 on the text which is rendered, *Moreover, the profit of the earth is in all things*, and reads as follows: 'Those subjects which you deem additional to the Torah—e.g. the addenda of the School of Rabbi [Judah ha-Nasi] and of R. Nathan, *halachoth* concerning proselytes (cf. also Midrash to Ruth I, 19, Sonc. ed., p. 35) and slaves—they too were given to Moses on Sinai, and like the laws of *Ẓiẓith, Tefillin* and *Mezuzah* are an integral part of the Torah' (Sonc. ed., p. 138). The present writer makes the comment *ad loc.*: 'i.e. additions to the Mishnah (the so-called Baraithoth), *'Aboth d'Rabbi Nathan* and the tractates on Proselytes and Slaves, which were added to the official Mishnah; similarly the post-Talmudic tractates on *Ẓiẓith*, etc., which he goes on to mention. The reference can hardly be to the actual laws of these subjects, as there would be no point in mentioning that these are not superfluous, for it is obvious'.

If the interpretation is correct, the passage affords strong evidence of the existence of some of these tractates. Unfortunately the teaching is anonymous and the Midrash to Ecclesiastes is itself later; so no conclusion can be drawn from it as to their date. We are on firmer ground with respect to the tractate *Semaḥoth*, because its existence in the Talmudic period is attested by the Talmud itself. It is quoted under its alternative title, *'Ebel Rabbathi*, in M.Ḳ. 24a, 26b (Sonc. ed., pp. 148 and 172) and Keth. 28a (Sonc. ed., p. 153). The Rabbis who refer to it are Rafram b. Papa, Papa and Naḥman, who all lived in the fourth century.

Mention is also made of 'the tractate *Kallah*' in Shab. 114a (Sonc. ed., p. 558) by R. Joḥanan (3rd century), in Ta'an 10b (Sonc. ed., p. 45) and Ḳid. 49b (Sonc. ed., p. 247), but its meaning is disputed. While Rashi explains it as one of the tractates which are rarely studied, others connect *kallah* with the Babylonian assemblies twice a year for the study of the laws of the Jewish Festivals. In view of this uncertainty no sure deduction can be drawn from these passages.

The Palestinian Talmud (Shab. VI, 2, 8a end) quotes a ruling on the correct order of putting on and taking off one's shoes from '*Dereḳ 'Ereẓ*'; and the Babylonian Talmud (Ber. 22a, Sonc. ed., p. 131) has an allusion by R. Judah (2nd century) to 'the *halachoth* of *Dereḳ 'Ereẓ*'. What is intended is the tractate *Dereḳ 'Ereẓ Rabbah* which most authorities hold to be an early production; whereas *Dereḳ 'Ereẓ Zuṭa* is in all probability a much later work (cf. J.E. IV, p. 529).

While the available data may not be conclusive, they are sufficient to make it hazardous to maintain dogmatically that a pre-Gaonic date for any of the tractates must be ruled out. It is known that collections of halachic decisions were made by several *Tannaïm* before the Mishnah of Rabbi Judah ha-Nasi was accepted as the authoritative standard. Consequently the compilation of halachic manuals on various subjects in Talmudic times is not inherently impossible. Higger, in the Introduction to his edition of *The Seven Minor Tractates,* judges them to be 'the first post-Mishnaic compendia regulating specific Jewish practices and usages'. His opinion is that 'most of the Minor Tractates are Palestinian in origin, but were later modified or elaborated in Babylonia'.

A contrary view is held by such scholars as I. H. Weiss, *Dor Dor weDoreshaw,* 1904, II, pp. 216ff, and L. Ginzberg, J.E. VII, p. 640; *On Jewish Law and Lore,* 1955, pp. 166f. The latter contends: 'Among the products of the codifiers of the Gaonic period should be reckoned the seven small treatises, in the style of the Mishnah. . . . The only probable sources for these treatises are the Talmud and the halachic midrashim. The small amount of new material which they contain is not to be traced to old, lost sources, but is the work of the compiler or compilers, whose authority prominent rabbis did not rate very highly. Toward the end of the period of the Gaonim, it is probable that codifications, now entirely lost, were made of different branches of the ritual as well as of the juridical law'. Hence he regards the seven tractates as codes produced in that era which, unlike others, survived.

The translators in this volume incline to the opinion of Higger that in their original form many of the tractates belong to a comparatively early date and were subsequently revised.

* * * * * * * *

In undertaking the translation, my collaborators were faced with a difficult task. The Wilna-Romm edition has been selected as the basic text because of its availability, but it is unreliable and often in a corrupt condition. Wherever possible the invaluable notes and emendations of the Wilna Gaon were utilised, as were the editions of Schechter, Müller and Higger. Passages in one tractate not infrequently reappear in other tractates; but no attempt has been made to obtain strict uniformity in translation or even interpretation, and each translator has been allowed to give his own version. Cross-references usually indicate where the difference is material.

Biblical quotations are taken from the American-Jewish Translation with its arrangement of chapter and verse, and when a deviation is required by the Rabbinic interpretation it is noted in the Commentary. To all citations from the Babylonian Talmud and Midrash Rabbah I have added the location in the English versions published by the Soncino Press. Editorial additions to Introductions and Commentary are enclosed within square brackets.

I have, in conclusion, to thank the scholars who co-operated with me in the production of this work. The devotion with which they discharged their laborious task is deeply appreciated.

* * * * * * * *

The typescript of this work was in the hands of the Publishers when the untimely death of Mr. H. Vezey Strong caused its suspension. My long association with him in connection with the Soncino Press entitles me to acknowledge the great debt which Anglo-Jewry owes to the enthusiasm and expert knowledge of typography which he devoted to the works issued by that publishing house. On the death of its Founder, Mr. Jack Davidson, he resolved that the high traditions of the Soncino Press should not suffer by the passing of his colleague.

One consequence of the delay in publication was the appearance of J. Goldin's translation of 'The Fathers according to Rabbi Nathan' in the Yale Judaica Series before the version in this collection. The student of the Tractate may find it an advantage to have two independent renderings before him for consultation.

A. COHEN.

PUBLISHERS' NOTE

The Publishers express their gratitude to the Rev. Dr. I. W. Slotki, M.B.E., M.A., Litt.D., F.R.S.L., who agreed to undertake the preparation of the Indices although under great pressure from his many other activities.

As a further aid to reference, the pagination according to the Wilna-Romm edition has been indicated both recto *a* and verso *b*.

'ABOTH D'RABBI NATHAN

TRANSLATED INTO ENGLISH
WITH INTRODUCTION
AND NOTES

BY

ELI CASHDAN
M.A.

CONTENTS

CONTENTS

INTRODUCTION

LOCATION AND CHARACTER

The tractate *'Aboth d'Rabbi Nathan* is usually found in the editions of the Talmud at the end of Seder Neziḳin. It heads the series of 'Minor Tractates' printed after Sanhedrin and is the longest of them; though it is doubtful whether ARN is strictly to be included among the 'Minor Tractates'.

ARN may be described as a homiletical exposition and expansion of Mishnah Aboth—the collection of ethical maxims and aphorisms of the *Tannaïm* popularly entitled 'Ethics of the Fathers'. In this work the separate sentences of Mishnah Aboth are generally taken as texts which are either explained by reference to Biblical passages or illustrated by narratives and legends. Frequently long digressions are made, and subjects and stories are introduced which are connected but loosely and by a slender thread with the text. Accordingly, the five chapters of Mishnah Aboth are expounded and elaborated in the forty-one chapters of ARN. Furthermore, this work contains material which is unique in Talmudic literature, and sometimes is the only extant source for many sentences, proverbs and incidents which are quoted in the Talmud and Midrash. Indeed, the view has been strongly put forward that the *'Amoraïm* were already familiar with this work and drew from its source material in about thirty instances.

This summary description of the work suggests that ARN may be regarded as the *Tosiftha,* or perhaps as the *Gemara,* to Mishnah Aboth, and in the Middle Ages it was often quoted by these titles. Nevertheless, it must be observed that the Mishnah Aboth, which served as the basis for ARN, could not have been the present work, because of the many substantial variations in the text of the maxims of the Rabbis. An earlier version of Mishnah Aboth must have been used by the author of ARN.

VERSIONS OF THE TRACTATE

ARN has come down to us in two recensions. But there must have been other versions of this work, since the Rabbis of the Middle Ages quote passages from ARN which are not found in either of the recensions known to us. In 1887 Solomon Schechter published from manuscripts these two recensions in parallel columns, designating them Recension A and Recension B (in this work quoted as 1 ARN and 2 ARN respectively). The two recensions, though closely related to each other, are obviously independent. They are alike in method and in much of the material included, but at times differ considerably and give the impression of two distinct works. Schechter, in his comprehensive and penetrating study on this subject, has shown that Recension B is cited only by Spanish Rabbis, whereas Rashi and most of the French and German Rabbis used Recension A.

ITS COMPOSITION

The treatise ARN, like Mishnah Aboth, may be said to be a compilation of four main collections, and its chapters correspond to the following scheme:

COLLECTION A, consisting of chaps. I to XI, is in the nature of a Midrash on Aboth I, 1-11, and illustrates by text and parable the teaching of the *Zugoth* (pairs of *Tannaïm*) beginning with the men of the Great Synagogue and continuing chronologically down to Hillel and Shammai.

COLLECTION B, consisting of chaps. XII to XVIII, is likewise a Midrash elucidating the maxims contained in Aboth I, 12-15 and II, 5-21, and comprises the teachings of Hillel and Shammai, Rabban Joḥanan b. Zakkai and his five famous disciples.

COLLECTION C, consisting of chaps. XIX to XXX, is an independent mishnaic collection similar to Aboth III and IV.

COLLECTION D, consisting of chaps. XXXI to XLI is, like Aboth V, a series of anonymous statements connected by the similarity of their form. Here historical, legendary and ethical material is classified in groups of identical numbers, from ten to three.

It will be seen that the order of ARN is to a large extent identical with that of Mishnah Aboth but with one striking exception to which attention must be drawn. Mishnah Aboth I, after enumerating the *Zugoth* and their maxims down to the last pair, Hillel and Shammai, continues with the sayings of Hillel's descendants down to Rabbi Judah the Prince and his son Rabban Gamaliel III. All contemporary Rabbis and their maxims are set aside so as not to interrupt the line of the Patriarchate from Hillel to Rabbi Judah the Prince. Accordingly, the aphorisms of Rabban Joḥanan b. Zakkai, the immediate successor of Hillel, are relegated to chap. II. ARN, on the other hand, is exact in its presentation of the chain of tradition and records the sayings of Rabban Joḥanan b. Zakkai in their right place, immediately after those of Hillel, while the dicta of Rabban Gamaliel I and of his son are relegated to a later place and occur in chap. XXII.

COMPARISON WITH MISHNAH ABOTH

A comparison of the texts of the maxims of the Rabbis as found in Mishnah Aboth and in ARN is most revealing. The texts in the latter are often the informal opinions of the Rabbis, the views expressed by them in the course of conversation or discussion. These opinions, however, were edited by Rabbi Judah the Prince and his predecessors until they assumed the precise, pointed and epigrammatic style as preserved in Mishnah Aboth. Finkelstein (in his *Introduction to the Tractate Abot and Abot of Rabbi Nathan*, p. vii) comments on this feature in these words: 'While Abot of Rabbi Nathan is invaluable because it has preserved the maxims of the ancient teachers in their original informal style, the Mishnah of Abot is also invaluable because in it we discover how the Academies transformed these maxims into formal norms, to be handed down from generation to generation'.

THE TITLE OF THE TRACTATE

The title of this work, '*Aboth d'Rabbi Nathan*—with its variants 'Mishnah Aboth of Rabbi Nathan' and 'Baraitha of Rabbi

Nathan'—is problematical, particularly its attribution to Rabbi Nathan. The *Tanna'* of that name, or R. Nathan ha-Babli as he is often referred to, was a native of Babylon who migrated to the Holy Land in the middle of the second century C.E. He was at once respected for his learning and lineage—his father was the Exilarch in Babylon—and was appointed *Ab Beth Din* with his colleague, R. Meir, as *Ḥakam.* Owing to dissensions between these two scholars on the one side and the Patriarch, Rabban Simeon b. Gamaliel, on the other, they conspired to depose the Patriarch and usurp his authority. When the plot was discovered, the Patriarch had the conspirators expelled from the Academy. They were ultimately readmitted only on the condition that the name of neither should be mentioned in the Academy in connection with halachic decisions. R. Meir's authority was hidden under the style 'Others say' and R. Nathan's under 'Some say' (Horayoth 13b, Sonc. ed., p. 104). It is therefore easy to understand why the family of the Patriarch was not well disposed towards R. Nathan. No wonder, then, that Rabbi Judah the Prince, the son of the above-named Rabban Simeon, omitted as far as he could the name of R. Nathan from the Mishnah which he compiled. And though R. Nathan was the author of many ethical maxims, not once is his name found in Mishnah Aboth. R. Nathan, however, is known to have made independently a compilation of Mishnah and Baraitha; and it is reasonable to assume that ARN was originally a work which emanated from his school.

The author of the Maḥzor *Viṭri*, Rabbi Simḥah, a disciple of Rashi, in his commentary on Aboth makes the following interesting observation: 'This Baraitha is called "Aboth of R. Nathan", but I do not know the reason for it. The suggestion that it is so called because R. Nathan is the first authority mentioned therein is untenable, since R. Jose the Galilean is named first, R. 'Aḳiba second and R. Nathan only third. It must be said, however, that the Sages had a tradition that R. Nathan compiled this work. And just as we know of the Mishnah collections of R. Ḥiyya and R. Hoshaya, and also the collections of Bar Ḳappara, Samuel and Levi, so this work must have been part of the Mishnah compilation of R. Nathan referred to in Midrash Ḳoheleth and Pesiḳtha Rabbathi'.

* * * * * * * *

The present translation of ARN is based on the printed text as included in the Vilna-Romm edition of the Talmud, but constant reference has been made to Schechter's critical edition of Recension A and to the manuscripts, especially MS. E, which he quotes. The references to Mishnah Aboth are to the edition in the *Authorized Daily Prayer Book* since it is readily available. Recourse has been had to the several commentaries on this work, particularly to the brilliant and ingenious glosses and emendations of Rabbi Elijah of Vilna; to all due acknowledgment is here made. I would also express my gratitude to the many friends and scholars who so freely proffered me advice and help. And though it would be invidious to single out names, I feel that I would be failing in respect and courtesy if I did not acknowledge my deep indebtedness and gratitude to the Editor, who not only read through the manuscript with meticulous thoroughness, but discussed with me with an open mind the manifold problems and difficulties presented by this tractate. It is also with great pleasure that I express my appreciation of the invaluable assistance and advice tendered to me by my friends, Dr. L. Collins, of London and Mr. E. L. Wolfe, of Hove, with both of whom I made a thorough and minute study of the text, and together we weighed, sifted and pondered over ideas and expressions.

In conclusion, I would say how glad I am of the opportunity granted me by the Soncino Press of making this tractate available to the English-speaking world, that it might be accepted as a companion volume to that ever-popular and ever-fresh work, the 'Ethics of the Fathers'; for both are replete with eternal gems and moral treasures, and together make a positive contribution to the spiritual uplift of man.

ELI CASHDAN.

'ABOTH D'RABBI NATHAN

CHAPTER I

1. Moses was sanctified by the cloud and received the Torah at Sinai, as it is stated, *And the glory of the Lord abode upon mount Sinai, and the cloud covered him six days.*[1] [It covered Moses] in order to cleanse him, and this occurred after [the proclamation of] the Ten Commandments. So expounded R. Jose the Galilean. R. Aḳiba said: The verse *and the cloud covered him six days* refers to [the mountain and not to] Moses.[2] The continuation of the verse, *And the seventh day He called unto Moses out of the midst of the cloud,* is to single Moses out for special honour.[3]

R. Nathan said: Why was it that Moses remained on the mountain six whole days without the Word[4] descending upon him? It was that he might be purged of all food and drink which were in his bowels, until such time as he would become holy and be like the ministering angels.[5] R. Mathia b. Ḥeresh

(1) Ex. XXIV, 16, E.V. *covered it.* (2) This reading is adopted by all Commentators and has MS. support. The sense of the controversy also requires this reading. (3) The two views represented in this passage originate in the meaning given to the suffix of the verb *covered* which can signify 'him' or 'it'. R. Jose is of the opinion that immediately after the declaration of the Ten Commandments, which occurred on the sixth day of Sivan, Moses was enveloped by a Divine Cloud and thereby underwent a seven-day period of purification before he could ascend the mount and approach the Divine Presence for his forty days' stay. A similar purification was prescribed in Temple times for the High Priest before entering upon the ritual of the Day of Atonement. R. 'Aḳiba, on the other hand, holds that the Cloud covered the mountain and not Moses. Moses was not required to undergo a period of purification, because the call to him to ascend the mount came to him on the seventh day of the month counting from the day on which Israel arrived in the wilderness of Sinai (cf. Ex. XIX, 1). The call to Moses from among the assembly of Israel was merely a mark of honour, to show that he stood high above the congregation. Cf. Yoma 4aff (Sonc. ed., pp. 13ff). For the background of this controversy, cf. L. Finkelstein, *Mabo le-Massektot Abot ve-Abot d'Rabbi Nathan,* English summary, p. XXIX, note 4. (4) *Dibbur,* a Rabbinic term for Divine Revelation. (5) [For the idea of unevacuated food being a bodily defilement, cf. Semaḥot III, 10 (below, p. 338) and A. Büchler, *Studies in Sin and Atonement,* pp. 328ff.]

said to him, 'Master, surely the only purpose was to impress him so that he should receive the words of the Torah with awe and fear, with dread and trembling, as it is stated, *Serve the Lord with fear and rejoice with trembling.*[6]

It is related that R. Josiah and R. Mathia b. Ḥeresh happened to be sitting engaged in the study of the Torah, when R. Josiah departed to pursue some secular affairs. R. Mathia b. Ḥeresh said to him, 'Master, why do you forsake the words of the living God and immerse yourself in secular affairs? And though you are my teacher and I your pupil, [I venture to say that] it is not right to forsake the words of the living God and immerse oneself in secular affairs'. It was said of them that while they were engaged together in the study of the Torah they were like foes one towards the other, but when they departed they were like lifelong friends.

2. By the hand of Moses was the Torah given at Sinai, as it is stated, *And He wrote them upon two tables of stone, and gave them unto me;*[7] and in another passage it is stated, *These are the statutes and ordinances and laws, which the Lord made between Him and the children of Israel in mount Sinai by the hand of Moses.*[8] The Torah which the Holy One, blessed be He, gave to Israel was given solely through Moses, as it is stated, *Between Him and the children of Israel.* Thus Moses was worthy to become the intermediary between Israel and the All-present. Moses offered the ram of consecration[9] and prepared the anointing oil with which he anointed Aaron and his sons during the seven days of consecration. Of that same oil were anointed all subsequent High Priests and kings.[10] Eleazar burned the heifer of purification[11] from whose ashes all the unclean of later generations were made clean. R. Eliezer said: Great was this act[12] because it was effective for all future generations, since Aaron and his sons were consecrated

(6) Ps. II, 11. (7) Deut. V, 19. (8) Lev. XXVI, 46. (9) By which Aaron and his sons were initiated into the priesthood; cf. Ex. XXIX. (10) Cf. Hor. 11b (Sonc. ed., pp. 82f). (11) More commonly known as the Red Heifer (cf. Num. XIX, 3). As Eleazar, Aaron's son, acted in this matter on the instruction and under the direction of Moses, the whole ritual is referable to Moses, and on that account it was effective for all future generations. (12) lit. 'measure', of anointing oil.

with this anointing oil [and their priesthood continued for many generations], as it is stated, *And thou shalt anoint Aaron and his sons, and sanctify them, that they may minister unto Me in the priest's office.*[13]

3. Joshua received [the Torah] from Moses, as it is stated, *And thou shalt put of thy honour upon him, that all the congregation of the children of Israel may hearken.*[14]

The elders received it from Joshua, as it is stated, *And the people served the Lord all the days of Joshua, and all the days of the elders that outlived Joshua, who had seen all the great work of the Lord, that He had wrought for Israel.*[15]

The Judges received it from the elders,[16] as it is stated, *And it came to pass in the days when the judges judged.*[17]

The prophets received it from the Judges, as it is stated, *I have sent unto you all My servants the prophets, sending them daily betimes and often.*[18]

Haggai, Zechariah and Malachi received it from the [earlier] prophets.

The men of the Great Assembly[19] received it from Haggai, Zechariah and Malachi. THEY SAID THREE THINGS: BE DELIBERATE IN JUDGMENT, RAISE UP MANY DISCIPLES, AND MAKE A FENCE ROUND THE TORAH.[20]

4. BE DELIBERATE IN JUDGMENT. What does this mean? It teaches that a man should be cautious in judgment, because the more cautious a man is in judgment the more confirmed is he in his judgment, as it is stated, *These are the proverbs of Solomon, which the men of Hezekiah king of Judah copied out*[21]—they did not merely copy them out but deliberated on them.[22] Abba Saul said: [The meaning is] not that they deliberated on them

(13) Ex. XXX, 30. (14) Num. XXVII, 20. (15) Judg. II, 7. (16) So according to the MSS. and as corrected by GRA. V reads 'from Joshua'. (17) Ruth I, 1. (18) Jer. VII, 25. (19) Or, 'Great Synagogue', a legislative council of one hundred and twenty men traditionally founded by Ezra and his associates. It functioned during the Persian period and later, about 500-300 B.C.E. (20) Aboth I, 1. Quotations from Aboth are printed in capitals. (21) Prov. XXV, 1. (22) The Heb. for *copied out* (*he 'etiḳu*) may also be derived from a root meaning 'to grow old, to spend much time'; hence the suggested interpretation 'pondered over, deliberated'. The proverbs were studied for a long time and their meaning elucidated.

but brought them to light.[23] At first it was held that the books of Proverbs, Song of Songs and Ecclesiastes were to be stored away[24] since they merely contained aphorisms and were not part of the [holy] writings. Thereupon they condemned them to be stored away, [and so they remained] until the men of the Great Assembly[25] came and brought them to light again. For it is stated,[26] *And I beheld among the thoughtless ones, I discerned among the youths, a young man void of understanding. . . . And, behold, there met him a woman with the attire of a harlot, and wily of heart. She is riotous and rebellious, her feet abide not in her house; now she is in the streets, now in the broad places, and lieth in wait at every corner. So she caught him, and kissed him, and with an impudent face she said to him: Sacrifices of peace-offerings were due from me; this day have I paid my vows. Therefore came I forth to meet thee, to seek thy face, and I have found thee. I have decked my couch with coverlets, with striped cloths of the yarn of Egypt. I have perfumed my bed with myrrh, aloes, and cinnamon. Come, let us take our fill of love until the morning; let us solace ourselves with loves. For my husband is not at home, he is gone a long journey; he hath taken the bag of money with him; he will come home at the full moon.*[27] And it is written in the Song of Songs: *Come, my beloved, let us go forth into the field;* [17a] *let us lodge in the villages. Let us get up early to the vineyards; let us see whether the vine hath budded, whether the vine-blossom be opened, and the pomegranates be in flower; there will I give thee my love.*[28] And it is written in Ecclesiastes: *Rejoice, O young man, in thy youth; and let thy heart cheer thee in the days of thy youth, and walk in the ways of thy heart, and in the sight of thine eyes; but know thou, that for all these things God will bring thee into judgment.*[29] And it is further written in the Song of Songs: *I am my beloved's and his desire is toward me.*[30]

(23) Giving the Heb. verb *he'etiḳu* the sense of 'moving from a place' as in Gen. XII, 8; hence bringing out the work from its place of concealment to the light of day. The interpretation is also borne by the late Heb. verb *perash* used by Abba Saul; cf. Reifmann in *Keneset Hagedolah* I, p. 91. According to Finkelstein, *op. cit.*, p. 126, *perash* here signifies 'they put aside' for concealment and burial. (24) i.e. not regarded as canonical Scriptures. (25) All commentators rightly emend to 'the men of Hezekiah'. (26) The verses which follow are typical examples of passages from the books mentioned which ostensibly deal with erotic themes and as such are unworthy of a place in the Scriptures. (27) Prov. VII, 7, 10-20. (28) Cant. VII, 12f. (29) Eccl. XI, 9. (30) Cant. VII, 11.

Thus they did not deliberate on them but brought them to light.

Another interpretation of BE DELIBERATE IN JUDGMENT: What does it mean? It teaches that a man should speak his words calmly and should not speak in anger; for he who speaks in anger will [in the end] cause his words to be forgotten. We find it so in the case of Moses our master that he forgot his words, as it is stated, *And Eleazar the priest said unto the men of war that went to the battle: This is the statute of the law which the Lord hath commanded Moses.*[31] He commanded Moses but not me; He commanded Moses, my father's brother, but not me.[32] And where do we find that Moses had spoken in anger? It states, *And Moses was wrath with the officers of the Lord. . . . And Moses said unto them: Have ye saved all the women alive?*[33] Why does the verse state *all the women?*[34] It is because of the advice which the wicked Balaam counselled against Israel, as it is written, *And now, behold, I go unto my people; come, and I will announce to thee what this people shall do to thy people in the end of days.*[35] He said to Balak, 'This people whom you hate is hungry for food and athirst for drink, since they have nothing to eat or drink except the manna alone. Go, then, erect booths for them, set out food and drink for them, and place there beautiful girls of royal station, to the end that the people may stray after Baal of Peor, and they will fall by the hand of the All-present'. Forthwith Balak proceeded to carry out all that the wicked Balaam had counselled. See, now, what calamity that wicked Balaam brought upon Israel, since through him there fell twenty and four thousand of them, as it is stated, *And these that died by the plague were twenty and four thousand.*[36] Is there not here an argument from the greater to the less? If it happened to Moses, who was the wisest among the wise and the greatest among the great, the father of the prophets, that when he spoke in anger he forgot his words, how much more

(31) Num. XXXI, 21. (32) Although Moses received the law from God, he had forgotten it on account of his anger, and it was left to Eleazar the priest to instruct the warriors. (33) *ibid.* 14f. (34) This sentence is deleted by GRA who reads instead: 'What is meant by *through the counsel of Balaam* (*ibid.* 16)?' (35) *ibid.* XXIV, 14. (36) *ibid.* XXV, 9.

so [does this apply to us ordinary persons]! It therefore teaches that a man should speak his words calmly and not speak in anger.

Ben 'Azzai said: Beware of idle chatter in your speech.[37]

5. AND MAKE A FENCE ROUND THE TORAH. Make a fence to your words as the Holy One, blessed be He, made a fence to His words; and likewise Adam the first man, the Torah, Moses, Job, the Prophets, the Writings,[38] and the Sages all made a fence to their words.[39]

What fence did the Holy One, blessed be He, make to His words? It is stated, *Even all the nations shall say; Wherefore hath the Lord done thus unto this land?*[40] This teaches that it was already revealed to Him Who spoke and the world came into being[41] that future generations will ask: *Wherefore hath the Lord done thus unto this land?* Consequently the Holy One, blessed be He, said to Moses, 'Moses, write [down the answer] and place it on record for generations to come: *Then men shall say: Because they forsook the covenant of the Lord . . . and went and served other gods, and worshipped them, gods that they knew not, and that He had not allotted unto*

(37) Do not misuse the gift of speech with empty talk. (38) i.e. the Hagiographa, the third division of the Scriptures. The word is inserted here by GRA and is attested by the MSS. (39) The usual meaning given to the maxim 'make a fence' is that the Rabbis added restrictions and further severities to the Torah to avoid the infringement of the commandment. The examples cited, however, as illustrations of those who 'made fences', differ in character from each other and do not conform to the pattern of the traditional definition. The older and perhaps original meaning of the maxim was an injunction to the Rabbis to explain and present the reasons for their decision, thereby safeguarding it against ridicule and rejection. It is in this sense that God made a fence to His words. As a development of the original meaning of the maxim was the exhortation to the Rabbis to express the power of God in a form intelligible to human beings; this was the 'fence' adopted by the Prophets. The other examples of 'fences' are additional prohibitions in the usual sense. For a detailed discussion on this subject, cf. the essays of Finkelstein in *Journal of Biblical Literature*, vol. LVII (1938), pp. 13-50, and vol. LIX (1940), pp. 455-469. (40) Deut. XXIX, 23. (41) [For this designation of God, cf. A. Marmorstein, *The Old Rabbinic Doctrine of God*, I, p. 89.] (42) *ibid.* 24f. In this passage there is a vindication of God's

them.[42] Hence you learn that the Holy One, blessed be He, made a fence to His words, and recorded in the Torah what people would say in the future; thus bearing witness that the Holy One, blessed be He, pays His creatures their reward in full.[43]

What fence did Adam, the first man, make to his words? It is stated, *And the Lord God commanded the man, saying: Of every tree of the garden thou mayest freely eat; but of the tree of the knowledge of good and evil, thou shalt not eat of it; for in the day that thou eatest thereof thou shalt surely die.*[44] Adam was unwilling to tell this to Eve exactly as the Holy One, blessed be He, had commanded him; he therefore made a fence to his words, over and above the words which the Holy One, blessed be He, had spoken to him, and this is what he said to her, *But of the fruit of the tree which is in the midst of the garden, God hath said: Ye shall not eat of it, neither shall ye touch it, lest ye die.*[45] By so doing he meant to keep both himself and Eve away from the tree, even to the extent of not touching it. At that moment the wicked serpent reasoned to himself saying, 'Since I cannot bring about the fall of Adam, I will bring about the fall of Eve'. Thereupon he went and seated himself beside Eve and entered into much conversation with her. He said, 'If you think it is the touching [of the tree] that the Holy One, blessed be He, has forbidden us, behold I will touch it and not die; so you, too, will not die if you touch it'. What did the wicked serpent then do? He arose, touched the tree with his hands and feet, and shook it violently so that its fruit fell to the ground. There are some, however, who say that he did not actually touch it, but that as soon as the tree

actions. Lest the nations misjudge and deem them tyrannical or arbitrary, it is stated from the beginning what calamities will befall the people in the event of disobedience. Cf. the parallel passage in *'Aboth d'Rabbi Nathan*, Recension II, ed. Schechter, p. 3. (43) A difficult passage with the text in an uncertain state. The translation follows the text as emended by Finkelstein, *op. cit.*, p. 116, reading *dikthab battorah* for *dikthib bathreh* and *'edin* (i.e. *'edim*) for *'adayin*. The Meiri in his commentary on Aboth explains the last sentence to mean that God prescribed in His Torah only such laws as were acceptable to man and within the capacity of human activity, and did not lay upon His creatures impossible demands. In this way mankind was afforded an opportunity of drawing a full reward. (44) Gen. II, 16f. (45) *ibid.* III, 3.

saw him it cried out, 'O wicked one, do not touch me'; as it is stated, *Let not the foot of pride overtake me, and let not the hand of the wicked shake me.*[46]

6. Another interpretation of the verse, *Let not the foot of pride overtake me,*[47] refers it to Titus, may his bones rot! For he raised his hand in contempt and struck the altar exclaiming, 'Lukos! Lukos![48] You are a king just as I am a king, come and engage in battle with me. How many oxen have been slain upon you! How many birds have been killed upon you! How much wine has been poured out upon you! How much incense has been burned upon you! It is you who are destroying the whole world', as it is stated, *Ah, Ariel, Ariel,*[49] *the city where David was encamped! Add ye year to year, let the feasts come round!*[50]

Furthermore the serpent said to her, 'If you think it is the eating [of the fruit of the tree] that the Holy One, blessed be He, has forbidden us, behold I will eat of it and will not die; so you, too, will not die if you eat of it'. Eve then began to think to herself, 'All that my master has commanded me from the beginning is false'—for Eve used to address Adam as 'master from the beginning'. She immediately took of the fruit and ate it, and also gave some to Adam, which he ate, as it is stated, *And when the woman saw that the tree was good for food, and that it was a delight to the eyes,* etc.[51]

7. With ten curses was Eve cursed at that time, as it is stated, *Unto the woman He said: I will multiply and multiply thy pain and thy travail; in pain thou shalt bring forth children; and thy desire shall be to thy husband, and he shall rule over thee.*[52] *I will multiply and multiply*—these are the two discharges of blood [which cause pain to women], the menstrual and [at the termination of] virginity. [*Thy pain*—this is the anxiety connected with the rearing of children.][53]

(46) Cf. Ps. XXXVI, 12. E.V., *let not the hand of the wicked drive me away.* (47) This was the cry of the altar when Titus entered the Temple. (48) A Greek word meaning 'wolf', here applied opprobiously to the altar. Cf. Suk. 56b (Sonc. ed., p. 276). (49) A poetical name for the altar. (50) Is. XXIX, 1. The reference is to the countless sacrifices offered on the altars at every season because of the many sins of the people. (51) Gen. III, 6. (52) *ibid.* 16, so lit. E.V., *I will greatly multiply.* (53) Inserted by GRA in accordance with 'Erub. 100b (Sonc. ed., p. 697).

And thy travail—this is the pain associated with conception. *In pain thou shalt bring forth children*—this is to be understood in its literal meaning. *And thy desire shall be to thy husband*—this teaches that a woman particularly yearns for her husband when he is about to set out on a journey. *And he shall rule over thee*—for the man solicits by word of mouth whereas the woman solicits in her heart. [Furthermore, during her periods] she is wrapped up like a mourner, shut up as in a prison and banished from the company of all men. Now what brought about the act of touching? The answer is the fence which Adam had made to his words.[54] Hence [the Sages] said: When a man makes a fence to his words, he is not always able to stand by his words. They further said: Hence let not a man add to the words which he has heard. R. Jose said: A firm [wall] of ten handbreadths is better than a tottering [wall] of a hundred cubits.

What was in the mind of the wicked serpent at that time? 'I will go,' he thought, 'slay Adam and marry his wife; then I will be king over the whole world. I shall also walk erect and eat all the dainties of the world.' Whereupon the Holy One, blessed be He, said to him, 'You reckoned [17*b*] to slay Adam and marry Eve; therefore *I will put enmity between thee and the woman.*[55] You reckoned to be king over the whole world; therefore *Cursed art thou from among all cattle.*[56] You reckoned to walk erect; therefore *Upon thy belly shalt thou go.* You reckoned to eat all the dainties of the world; therefore *Dust shalt thou eat all the days of thy life.*

R. Simeon b. Menasia said: Alas for the most useful servant that was lost to the world! For had not the serpent been cursed, every Israelite would have been provided with two serpents for his personal use at home; one he would send to the west and the other to the east, to bring him thence gems, precious stones, pearls and every desirable thing in the world, and no creature could ever injure them.[57] Moreover, they could have been employed in the place of camels, asses and mules to provide manure for gardens and orchards.

(54) Adam's fault was that he had attached as great importance to the 'fence' as to the original command. (55) *ibid.* 15. (56) *ibid.* 14. (57) Or, according to another reading: 'could ever hold them back'.

8. R. Judah b. Bathyra said: Adam, the first man, was reclining in the Garden of Eden with ministering angels at his service, roasting meat and cooling wine for him. Then the serpent came and, seeing him in all his glory, at once grew envious of him.[58]

How was Adam, the first man, created? In the first hour his dust was gathered together, in the second his outline was shaped, in the third he was made into solid substance, in the fourth his limbs were articulated, in the fifth his orifices were opened, in the sixth a soul was infused into him, in the seventh he stood on his feet, in the eighth Eve became his mate, in the ninth he was brought into the Garden of Eden, in the tenth he received his command [concerning the tree], in the eleventh he sinned, and in the twelfth he was driven out, thus fulfilling what is stated, *Man tarrieth not overnight in his glory.*[59]

Which Psalm did Adam recite on the first day?[60] *The earth is the Lord's and the fulness thereof; the world, and they that dwell therein;*[61] because He created the world, assigned it to mankind, and is the sole Judge of the world. Which did he recite on the second day? *Great is the Lord, and highly to be praised, in the city of our God, His holy mountain;*[62] because He divided the work of creation and became Sovereign in His universe. Which did he recite on the third day? *God standeth in the congregation of God; in the midst of the judges He judgeth;*[63] because He then created the sea and the dry land, the earth was rolled[64] into position, and a place was set apart for His people. Which did he recite on the fourth day? *O Lord, Thou God to whom vengeance belongeth, Thou God to whom vengeance belongeth, shine forth;*[65] because He then created the sun, the moon, the stars and the planets, which give light on earth, and He will in the future punish those who worship them. Which did he recite on the fifth day? *Sing aloud unto God our strength;*

(58) The two paragraphs are quoted from Sanh. 59b (Sonc. ed., p. 405), but the second is there given in the name of R. Judah b. Tema. (59) Ps. XLIX, 13, indicating that Adam forfeited his glory within a day before the oncoming of night. E.V., *man abideth not in honour.* (60) Cf. R.H. 31a (Sonc. ed., pp. 145f) where the same Psalms are selected for recital by the Levites in the Temple on the successive days of the week. (61) Ps. XXIV, 1. (62) *ibid.* XLVIII, 1. (63) *ibid.* LXXXII, 1. (64) lit. 'was folded'. (65) *ibid.* XCIV, 1.

shout unto the God of Jacob;[66] because He then created the birds, the fishes and the sea-monsters, which sing aloud His praises in the world. Which did he recite on the sixth day? *The Lord reigneth; He is clothed in majesty; the Lord is clothed, He hath girded Himself with strength; yea the world is established, that it cannot be moved;*[67] because He then completed all His works, was exalted and sat enthroned in the heights of the universe. Which did he recite on the seventh day? *A Psalm, a Song. For the Sabbath day;*[68] because of the day which will be all Sabbath, when there will be neither eating nor drinking nor worldly affairs, but the righteous will sit with crowns on their heads enjoying[69] the brilliance of the Divine Presence, as it is stated, *And they beheld God, and did eat and drink,*[70] like the ministering angels. And why was this so?[71] In order that [Adam] might immediately partake of the Sabbath meal.

R. Simeon b. Eleazar said: I will expound this to you with a parable. To what might Adam be compared? To a man who married a proselyte and used to give her instruction, saying, 'My dear, do not eat bread when your hands are defiled, do not eat untithed produce, do not profane the Sabbath, do not make vows rashly, and do not associate with another man. If you break one of these rules, you will die'. Now what did a certain man do?[72] He arose and ate in her presence bread although his hands were defiled, he ate before her untithed produce—he profaned the Sabbath and made vows rashly—and also offered her some [of the food].[73] What could that proselyte have thought to herself? All that my husband forbade me in the beginning was without foundation. She thereupon went and transgressed them all.

R. Simeon b. Yoḥai said: I, too, will explain this to you by a parable. To what might Adam be compared? To a man who

(66) *ibid.* LXXXI, 2. (67) *ibid.* XCIII, 1. (68) *ibid.* XCII, 1. (69) Or, according to another reading: 'feasting on'. (70) Ex. XXIV, 11. The food and drink on that occasion were not of the material kind. (71) i.e. why was Adam created last of all, on the sixth day just before the commencement of the Sabbath? (72) So according to GRA, the reference being to a stranger who came to tempt her. V reads 'what did that man do', apparently referring to the husband. (73) Adopting the reading of MS. E, lit. 'he handed her with his hands'. V 'and brought out to her'.

had his wife at home with him. Now what did that man do? He went and brought a cask into which he put an exact number of figs and nuts. He also caught a scorpion, placed it in the mouth of the cask, covered the cask with a tight-fitting lid and put it away in a corner. He then said to his wife, 'My dear, all that I possess in this house is at your disposal except this cask which you may not touch under any circumstances'. What did this woman do? No sooner had her husband gone off to market than she arose, opened the cask, put her hand in it and was bitten by the scorpion. Immediately she went and flung herself on her bed. When her husband returned from market he asked her what had happened, and she replied, 'I put my hand in the cask and was bitten by a scorpion, and now I am dying'. He said to her, 'Did I not tell you in the beginning that everything I had in the house was at your disposal except that cask which you were not to touch under any circumstances?' He at once became furious with her and drove her out. So it was with Adam, the first man, when the Holy One, blessed be He, charged him, *Of every tree of the garden thou mayest freely eat; but of the tree of the knowledge of good and evil, thou shalt not eat of it; for in the day thou eatest thereof thou shalt surely die.*[74] No sooner had Adam eaten of it than he was driven out [of Eden], to fulfil that which is stated, *Man tarrieth not overnight in his glory; he is like the beasts that perish.*[75]

On the same one day he was formed, created, his outline was shaped, he became solid substance, his limbs were articulated, his orifices opened, a soul was infused into him, he stood on his feet, Eve became his mate, he named [all creatures], was brought into the Garden of Eden, given a command, sinned and was driven out, to fulfil that which is stated, *Man tarrieth not overnight in his glory.* On that same day two went upon the bed and four came down.[76] R. Judah b. Bathyra said: On that day two went upon the bed and six came down.[77]

(74) Gen. II, 16f. (75) Ps. XLIX, 13. See above, p. 10, n. 59 (76) The four are: Adam, Eve, Cain and Abel. (77) The six are: Adam, Eve, Cain, Abel, each of the last two with a twin sister. According to GRA and MS. E seven came down, since two twin sisters were born with Abel; cf. Midrash Rabbah, Genesis, XXII, §2 (Sonc. ed., p. 180).

On that day three decrees were pronounced upon Adam, as it is stated, *And unto Adam He said: Because thou hast hearkened unto the voice of thy wife . . . cursed is the ground for thy sake; in toil shalt thou eat of it . . . thorns and thistles shall it bring forth to thee; and thou shalt eat the herb of the field.*[78] When Adam heard that the Holy One, blessed be He, had decreed against him, *Thou shalt eat the grass of the field,* his limbs forthwith began to tremble and he exclaimed, 'Lord of the universe! Am I and my beast to eat from one manger?' Whereupon the Holy One, blessed be He, said to him, 'Since your limbs trembled [at the prospect]'[79] *In the sweat of thy face shalt thou eat bread.*[80]

Just as three decrees were pronounced upon Adam so were three decrees pronounced upon Eve, as it is stated, *I will greatly multiply thy pain and thy travail; in pain thou shalt bring forth children.*[81] [*I will greatly multiply*]—for when a woman begins to experience her monthly flow she suffers pain; *I will greatly multiply*[82] [*thy pain*]—for when a woman experiences intercourse for the first time it is painful to her; *thy pain* [*and thy travail*]—for during the first three months of pregnancy a woman's features become coarsened and pallid.

As [his first] evening set in and Adam saw the world darkening in the west, he exclaimed, 'Woe is me! Because I have sinned, the Holy One, blessed be He, is darkening the world upon me!' He was unaware that such was the course of nature; but in the morning when he saw the world becoming light in the east he was exceedingly happy. He arose and built an altar, he took a bullock whose horns came into being before its hoofs[83] and offered it as a burnt-offering, as it is stated, *And it shall please the Lord better than a bullock that hath horns and hoofs.*[84]

The bullock which Adam offered, the bull which Noah

(78) Gen. III, 17f. (79) This was considered by God as an act of penitence. (80) *ibid.* 19. (81) *ibid.* 16. (82) The Heb. is lit. 'multiply I will multiply' indicative of two pains; cf. above, p. 8, n. 53 (83) Since at the creation the first bullock came up from the ground fully grown and in erect posture (cf. Ḥul. 60a, Sonc. ed., pp. 329f), its horns necessarily appeared first and its hoofs last. (84) Ps. LXIX, 32.

offered,[85] and the ram which our father Abraham offered on the altar instead of his son, were all beasts whose horns came into being before their hoofs, as it is stated, [18a] *And Abraham lifted up his eyes, and looked, and behold behind him a ram caught.*[86]

Then and there[87] three bands of ministering angels came down with harps and lyres and other musical instruments in their hands and joined with him in a song of praise, as it is stated, *A Psalm, a Song. For the Sabbath day. It is a good thing to give thanks unto the Lord. . . . To declare Thy lovingkindness in the morning, and Thy faithfulness in the night seasons.*[88] *To declare Thy lovingkindness in the morning*—this refers to the world to come which is likened to the brightness of the morning, as it is stated, *They are new every morning; great is Thy faithfulness.*[89] *And Thy faithfulness in the night seasons*—this refers to this world which is likened to [the darkness of] night, as it is stated, *The burden of Dumah. One calleth unto me out of Seir: Watchman, what of the night? Watchman, what of the night?*[90]

At that time the Holy One, blessed be He, said, 'If I do not inflict punishment upon the serpent I will be destroying the whole world'. He also said, 'As for man whom I made lord and king over the world, how he has become entangled [in the wiles of the serpent] and eaten of the [forbidden] tree!' Thereupon He turned His attention to him and cursed him, as it is stated, *And the Lord God said unto the serpent,* etc.[91] R. Jose said: Had the curse of the serpent been deferred to later,[92] He would in the meantime have destroyed the whole world.

(85) Cf. Gen. VIII, 20. This verse, however, does not mention that Noah offered a bull. Since the word quoted from Ps. LXIX, *bullock* is lit. 'ram bullock', it has been suggested that one was Adam's and the other that of Noah. (86) Gen. XXII, 13. Tradition tells that Abraham's ram was created on the eve of the first Sabbath at twilight (Aboth V, 6, Sonc. ed., p. 64), and as all the animals of the creation were brought forth in their full-grown stature, their horns must have appeared before their hoofs. (87) Immediately Adam had brought his offering. (88) Ps. XCII, 1-3. (89) Lam. III, 23. By reason of God's faithfulness the righteous will be renewed in the morning, i.e. they will be revived in the world to come. (90) Is. XXI, 11. The faithful who watch and wait for God's deliverance cry out: How long will the sorrows and sufferings of this world continue? (91) Gen. III, 14. (92) lit. 'had the curse of the serpent been written in the end'.

When the Holy One, blessed be He, created Adam, the first man, He formed him behind and before,[93] as it is stated, *Thou hast formed me behind and before, and laid Thy hand upon me.*[94] Ministering angels descended to adore him,[95] whereupon the Holy One, blessed be He, took him up and placed him beneath His wings, as it is stated, *And laid Thy hand upon me.*

Another interpretation of *And laid Thy hand upon me:* when Adam sinned, the Holy One, blessed be He, removed one [of His hands] from him. From this it may be inferred that when Adam and the Temple were created, they were each created by His two hands. Whence do we know that man was created by His two hands? For it is stated, *Thy hands have made me and fashioned me.*[96] And whence do we know that the Temple was created by His two hands? For it is stated, *The sanctuary, O Lord, which Thy hands have established.*[97] And it is also said, *And He brought them to His holy border, to the mountain which His right hand had gotten;*[98] and further it is written, *The Lord shall reign for ever and ever.*[99]

(93) i.e. with two faces, in front and behind, from one of which Eve was formed. Cf. Ber. 61a (Sonc. ed., p. 381). (94) Ps. CXXXIX, 5. E.V., *Thou hast hemmed me in.* (95) Or, to worship him. According to MS. E: 'to destroy him', because they were jealous of him; this is also the view of GRA. (96) *ibid.* CXIX, 73. The noun is plural. (97) Ex. XV, 17. (98) Ps. LXXVIII, 54. (99) Ex. XV, 18. The last two verses which are quoted have no connection with the theme of the passage and are deleted by GRA. They are found in the original context at the conclusion of tractate Aboth.

CHAPTER II

1. What fence did the Torah make to her words? It is stated, *And thou shalt not approach unto a woman . . . as long as she is impure by her uncleanness.*[1] It might be supposed that he may embrace or kiss her, or engage with her in frivolous talk; the text therefore declares, *Thou shalt not approach.* It might be further supposed that he may sleep with her if she is clothed in the one bed; the text therefore declares, *Thou shalt not approach.* Again it might be supposed that she may wash her face and paint her eyes; the text therefore declares, *And of her that is sick with her impurity*[2]—all the days of her impurity she shall be in banishment [from society].[3] Hence [the Sages] said: Every woman who makes herself unattractive during the period of her impurity wins the approbation of the Rabbis, and she who adorns herself during the period of her impurity incurs their censure.

2. The story is told[4] of a certain man who had read much Scripture, studied much Mishnah, and had attended on many scholars, yet had died in the midst of his days. His wife used to take his *tefillin,* carry them round the Synagogues and Houses of Study, and weepingly complain, 'Masters, is it not written in your Torah, *That is thy life, and the length of thy days?*[5] Why, then, did my husband die in the midst of his days, he who read much Scripture, studied much Mishnah, and attended on many scholars?' There was no one who could answer her. One day, Elijah, of blessed memory, met her and said to her, 'My daughter, why do you weep and complain?' She replied, 'My husband had read much Scripture, studied much Mishnah and attended on many scholars; yet he died

(1) Lev. XVIII, 19. (2) *ibid.* XV, 33. (3) The Heb. נדה, 'a woman in her impurity', is here connected with its original meaning of 'cast out, banished from society'. (4) Quoted from Shab. 13a, b (Sonc. ed., p. 53) with some variants. (5) Deut. XXX, 20.

in the midst of his days'. He asked her, 'During the first three days of your impurity what was his relationship towards you?'[6] She said to him 'Master, God forbid! He did not touch me even with his little finger, but used to say to me, "Touch no vessel lest you bring me into a state of doubt" '. 'And what was his relationship towards you during the latter days of your impurity?'[7] She replied, 'Master, I ate and drank with him, slept with him[8] in the one bed with our bodies touching, but he had no other intention'. Whereupon Elijah said to her, 'Blessed be the All-present for slaying him, since it is written in the Torah, *And thou shalt not approach unto a woman . . . as long as she is impure by her uncleanness.*'[9]

It is stated, *None of you shall approach to any that is near of kin to him;*[10] hence [the Sages] said: Let no man remain alone with a woman at an inn, even though she be his sister or daughter, on account of public opinion. Let no man converse with a woman in the market-place, not even with his wife and needless to say with another woman, on account of public gossip. Let no man walk behind a woman in the market-place, not even behind his wife and needless to say behind another woman, on account of public gossip.

It is stated here,[11] *None of you shall approach,* and it is stated there, *Thou shalt not approach;*[12] do not therefore approach to any

(6) The number 'three' found in V is difficult to explain, as the woman's impurity continues, according to Biblical law, for a minimum period of seven days. Consequently there is no ground for drawing a distinction between the first three and the subsequent days. Most scholars, following GRA, substitute 'seven' for 'three', and the reference is to the monthly period of uncleanness. The 'latter days of impurity' would be, what is known in Talmudic phraseology, 'the days of white garments', i.e. the seven days of observation after the cessation of the discharge. During this period a woman is forbidden by Rabbinic law all intimacy with her husband, including acts of endearment. (7) In Shab. 13a the text reads: 'during the days of your white garments'. Cf. the preceding note. (8) V adds 'in my clothes' which is omitted in the Talmudic version and appears incompatible with the following words, 'with our bodies touching'. Some authorities retain the former phrase and alter the latter to 'without our bodies touching'. (9) Lev. XVIII, 19. (10) *ibid.* 6. (11) In the Biblical passage concerning unlawful unions. (12) *ibid.* 19. In the passage dealing with menstrual impurity.

conduct which may lead to transgression.[13] Keep aloof from anything hideous or from whatever seems hideous.[14] Accordingly the Sages said: Keep aloof from a trivial sin lest it lead you on to a grave sin. Run to perform a minor precept for it will lead you on to an important precept.

It is stated, *Thy belly is like a heap of wheat set about with lilies.*[15] *Thy belly is like a heap of wheat*—this describes the congregation of Israel;[16] *set about with lilies*—these are the seventy elders.[17]

Another interpretation of *Thy belly is like a heap of wheat* [*set about with lilies*]—these are those light precepts[18] which are as tender as a hedge of lilies and through their observance by Israel lead them to life in the world to come. How is this so? A man's wife is at home with him during the period of her impurity. He could have intimacy with her or not at his will, since no man sees him and no man knows of it to rebuke him. Hence he fears only Him Who ordained the law of [the uncleanness of women. Similarly if a man suffers a seminal emission, he may immerse himself or not as he will, since no man sees him and no man knows of it to rebuke him. Hence He fears only Him Who ordained the law of] immersion.[19] You may reason similarly with the law of the dough-offering[20] and the law of the first of the fleece.[21] Such are the light precepts which are as tender as lilies and through their observance by Israel lead them to life in the world to come.

(13) By the analogy: just as any manner of approach to a woman in her impurity is forbidden, so any approach whatsoever to a woman prohibited as being near of kin is likewise forbidden. (14) A Rabbinic rule of conduct; cf. Ḥul. 44b (Sonc. ed., p. 239). (15) Cant. VII, 3. (16) Cf. Sanh. 37a (Sonc. ed., pp. 231f). As all derive sustenance from a heap of wheat, so the whole world enjoys favour because of Israel. (17) Who constitute the Great Sanhedrin and whose duty it is to make 'fences' to safeguard the Torah. (18) i.e. the precautionary restrictions, light in themselves, but safeguarding against violation of the laws. Cf. Sanh. *loc. cit.* (19) The lines enclosed within brackets are missing in V, but have been inserted here from MS. E. The origin of the omission is due to a scribe who jumped from the first 'who ordained the law of' to the second. (20) Cf. Num. XV, 20f. (21) Cf. Deut. XVIII, 4. These are further examples of precepts observed within the privacy of the home over which no control can be exercised by other persons.

3. What fence did Moses make to his words? It is stated, *And the Lord said unto Moses: Go unto the people, and sanctify them to-day and to-morrow.*[22] Now the righteous Moses was not willing to tell it to Israel in the manner in which the Holy One, blessed be He, spoke to him, but said to them, *Be ready against the third day; come not near a woman.*[23] Thus Moses added a third day for them of his own accord, because Moses reasoned as follows, 'If a man will cohabit with his wife and on the third day the seed will issue from her they will become unclean,[24] and in consequence Israel[25] would receive the Torah from Mount Sinai in a state of defilement. I will therefore add a third day for them, so that no man will cohabit with his wife[26] and there will be no fear of the seed issuing from her. All will be clean, and in consequence [the women of] Israel will receive the Torah from Mount Sinai in a state of cleanness'.

This[27] is one of the things which Moses did of his own accord, reasoning by *a fortiori* argument, and his decision conformed to the will of the All-present.[28] He broke the tablets, and this act of his accorded with the will of the All-present; he kept away from the Tent of Meeting, and this act of his accorded with the will of the All-present; he separated from his wife, and this act of his accorded with the will of the All-present.

['He separated from his wife, and this act of his accorded with the will of the All-present.'] How was this? He reasoned as follows: If with regard to the Israelites, who were sanctified for a short period only and summoned for the sole purpose of receiving the Ten Commandments at Mount Sinai, the Holy One, blessed be He, said to me, *Go unto the people, and sanctify them to-day and to-morrow;*[29] I, who am in readiness for the purpose

(22) Ex. XIX, 10. (23) *ibid.* 15. (24) In accordance with the law that if a woman discharged semen at any time within three days of coitus she is unclean, since the semen is still potent; after three days she is clean. Cf. Shab. 86a (Sonc. ed., p. 408) where this rule is derived from the last quoted verse. (25) GRA reads 'the women of Israel', which is preferable. (26) Within these three days. (27) The addition by Moses of an extra day to the Divine command. (28) Cf. Shab. 87a (Sonc. ed., p. 411), Yeb. 62a (Sonc. ed., p. 412). (29) Ex. XIX, 10.

[of receiving] the word of God daily and hourly, since I know not when He will speak with me, whether by day or by night, must all the more separate myself from a woman! And his decision accorded with the will of the All-present.[30] R. Judah b. Bathyra said: Moses did not separate from his wife until he was ordered to do so by the Almighty, as it is stated, *With him do I speak mouth to mouth*[31]—by a *mouth-to-mouth* order I commanded him to separate from his wife, and he did so. Others interpret in this way: Moses did not separate from his wife until he was ordered to do so by the [18b] Almighty, as it is stated, *Go say to them: Return ye to your tents;*[32] and after that it is written, *But as for thee, stand thou here by Me.*[33] Moses then turned about[34] and separated from his wife, and in so doing he was in accord with the will of the All-present.

'He kept away from the Tent of Meeting.' How was this? He reasoned as follows: 'If in connection with my brother Aaron, who has been anointed with the anointing oil, clothed in the additional vestments of the High-priesthood and ministers therein in holiness, the Holy One, blessed be He, admonished, *Speak unto Aaron thy brother, that he come not at all times into the holy place;*[35] I, who have not been ordained for the purpose, must all the more keep away from the Tent of Meeting'. He kept away from the Tent of Meeting and in so doing he was in accord with the will of the All-present.[36]

'He broke the tablets.' How was this? It is related that when Moses ascended on high to receive the tablets which had been inscribed and were lying in readiness [to be revealed] since the six days of creation,[37] as it is stated, *And the tables were the work of*

(30) Proved from the fact that when the people were permitted to resume marital relations, God said to Moses, *But as for thee, stand thou here by Me* (Deut. V, 28). (31) Num. XII, 8. (32) Deut. V, 27. This was a permission to resume marital relations. (33) *ibid.* 28. (34) A strange expression in this context. The meaning seems to be that Moses extended the temporary restriction to all the days of his life, and this met with God's approval. Cf. the second recension on this passage in Schechter's ed., p. 10. (35) Lev. XVI, 2. (36) No verse or exposition is cited to prove this. In the Talmudic passages (cf. above, p. 19, n. 28) the instance of keeping away from the Tent of Meeting is not included. (37) Cf. Aboth V, 9 (Sonc. ed., V, 6, p. 63).

God, and the writing was the writing of God, graven [ḥaruth] *upon the tables*[38]—read not *ḥaruth* [graven] but *ḥeruth* [freedom], for only he is truly free who occupies himself with the Torah[39]—at that time the ministering angels arraigned Moses, saying, 'Lord of the universe! *What is man, that Thou art mindful of him? And the son of man, that Thou thinkest of him? Yet Thou hast made him but little lower than the angels, and hast crowned him with glory and honour. Thou hast made him to have dominion over the works of Thy hands; Thou hast put all things under his feet: sheep and oxen, all of them, yea, and the beasts of the field; the fowl of the air, and the fish of the sea*'.[40] They were referring disparagingly to Moses, saying, 'What virtue is there in man born of woman that he has ascended on high, as it is stated, *Thou art ascended on high, thou hast led captivity captive, thou hast received gifts?*'[41] Moses took the tablets and descended with them, rejoicing exceedingly. But as soon as he saw the depravity with which they had depraved themselves in the episode of the calf, he said to himself, 'How can I give them the tablets, thereby binding them to the performance of weighty commandments, and in consequence condemning them [if they disobeyed] to death before Heaven, for it is written therein, *Thou shalt have no other gods before Me?*'[42] He turned back, but when the seventy elders saw this they hurried after him. He seized one end of the tablets while they seized the other end, but the strength of Moses prevailed over theirs, as it is stated, *And in all the mighty hand, and in all the great terror, which Moses wrought in the sight of all Israel.*[43] He glanced at the tablets and saw that the writing had flown from them; so he exclaimed, 'How can I give Israel these worthless tablets? I will grasp hold of them and break them, as it is stated, *And I took hold of the two tables, and cast them out of my two hands, and broke them.*[44]

R. Jose the Galilean said: I will illustrate this to you by a parable. To what can the matter be compared? To a human

(38) Ex. XXXII, 16. As *the work of God* refers primarily to the six days of creation, it follows that the tablets were then prepared. (39) This incidental word-play interrupts the sequence of the passage, and is borrowed from Aboth VI, 2 (Sonc. ed., p. 80). (40) Ps. VIII, 5-9. (41) *ibid.* LXVIII, 19. E.V. refers to God. (42) Ex. XX, 3. (43) Deut. XXXIV, 12. (44) *ibid.* IX, 17.

king who ordered his agent, 'Go and betroth for me a beautiful, graceful and well-behaved maiden'. The agent went and performed the betrothal. After the betrothal he discovered that she was unfaithful with another. Thereupon he reasoned to himself, 'If I give her the contract[45] now, I will be condemning her to death[46] and depriving my master of her for all time; [I will rather tear up the contract]'. In the same way did the righteous Moses reason to himself, 'How can I now give Israel the tablets, binding them thereby to the performance of weighty commandments, and in consequence condemning them [if they disobeyed] to death, for it is written therein, *He that sacrificeth unto the gods, save unto the Lord only, shall be utterly destroyed?*[47] I will rather seize the tablets and break them, and lead Israel back to the right way. Then Israel might say,[48] "Where are the first tablets which [you say] you brought down? There were no such things at all!"'

R. Judah b. Bathyra said: Moses only broke the tablets because he was commanded to do so by the Almighty, as it is stated, *With him do I speak mouth to mouth*[49]—by a *mouth-to-mouth* order I commanded him to break the tablets. Some explain it in this way: Moses only broke the tablets because he was commanded to do so by the Almighty, as it is stated, *And I looked, and, behold, ye had sinned against the Lord your God*[50]—the expression *I looked* means that he saw that the writing had flown from off the tablets.[51] Others explain: Moses only broke the tablets because he was commanded to do so by the Almighty, as it is stated, *And there they are, as the Lord commanded me*[52]—the words *commanded me* can only mean that he was so commanded and broke them.

R. Eleazar b. Azariah said: Moses only broke the tablets

(45) Presumably the betrothal document. By destroying this document the verbal betrothal could be disclaimed, and the maiden's misbehaviour would be treated as that of an unbetrothed girl which does not involve the extreme penalty. Cf. Midrash Rabbah, Exodus, XLVI, §1 (Sonc. ed., pp. 526f). (46) Cf. Deut. XXII, 23f. (47) Ex. XXII, 19. (48) In their defence when charged with idolatry. (49) Num. XII, 8. (50) Deut. IX, 16. (51) The tablets thereby became worthless, and Moses understood it as an order to break them. (52) *ibid.* X, 5.

because he was commanded to do so by the Almighty, as it is stated, *Which Moses wrought in the sight of all Israel*[53]—as everywhere else he acted on the command of God, so here, too, he acted on the command of God.

R. 'Aḳiba said: Moses only broke the tablets because he was commanded to do so by the Almighty, as it is stated, *And I took hold of the two tables*[54]—what is it that a man takes hold of? Is it not that which he is about to break?[55]

R. Meir said: Moses only broke the tablets because he was commanded to do so by the Almighty, as it is stated, *Which* ['asher] *thou didst break*[56]—I thank [*yishar*] you for breaking them.[57]

4. Hezekiah king of Judah did four things [of his own accord] and his acts conformed to the will of the All-present. He hid the Book of Healing[58] and his act conformed to the will of the All-present, [as it is stated, *And I have done that which is good in Thy sight*].[59] He broke the brazen serpent[60] into pieces and his act conformed to the will of the All-present, [as it is stated, *And he broke in pieces the brazen serpent . . . for unto those days the children of Israel did offer to it; and it was called Nehushtan*].[61] He removed the high places and the altars and his act conformed to the will of the All-present, as it is stated, *Hath not the same Hezekiah taken away His high places and His altars, and commanded Judah and Jerusalem, saying: Ye shall worship before one altar, and upon it*

(53) *ibid.* XXXIV, 12. Cf. Shab. 87a (Sonc. ed., p. 412), Yeb. 62a (Sonc. ed., p. 412). (54) *ibid.* IX, 17. (55) A difficult sentence, the text being dubious. The meaning seems to be: since Moses held the tablets firmly he certainly had no intention of breaking them; as he did break them it must have been at the behest of the Almighty. The text varies between *leshabberan* and *lebor'an;* the latter makes no sense unless the root *bara'* be taken in the sense of 'cut down, destroy' (cf. Josh. XVII, 15, 18, and Ezek. XXIII, 47). (56) Deut. X, 2. (57) The words *'asher* (which) and *yishar* (thank) are homiletically explained as deriving from a common root. (58) A book containing remedies for various ailments believed to have been compiled by King Solomon. Hezekiah hid it so that people should pray to God for healing. Cf. Ber. 10b (Sonc. ed., p. 56), Pes. 56a (Sonc. ed., pp. 277f). In the Talmud six acts are mentioned, God approving of three and disapproving of three. (59) 2 Kings XX, 3. The words in brackets are inserted by GRA. (60) Cf. Num. XXI, 9. (61) 2 Kings XVIII, 4. The verse is omitted in V but is found in MS. E and inserted by GRA.

shall ye offer?[62] He stopped up the waters of Gihon, and his act conformed to the will of the All-present, as it is stated, *Hezekiah also stopped the upper spring of the waters of Gihon, and brought them straight down on the west side of the city of David. And Hezekiah prospered in all his works.*[63]

5. What fence did Job make to his words? It states, *A whole-hearted and an upright man, one that feareth God, and shunneth evil.*[64] This[65] teaches that Job held aloof from anything that could lead to sin, from anything improper or having the semblance of impropriety.[66] And what is the significance of the words *a whole-hearted and an upright man?* They teach that Job was born circumcised.[67]

Adam, the first man, also came into the world circumcised, for it is stated, *And God created man in His own image.*[68] Seth also was born circumcised, for it is stated, *And begot a son in his own likeness, after his image.*[69] Noah also was born circumcised, for it is stated, *In his generations a man righteous and whole-hearted.*[70] Shem also was born circumcised, for it is stated, *And Melchizedek king of Salem.*[71] Jacob also was born circumcised, for it is stated, *And Jacob was a whole-hearted man, dwelling in tents.*[72] Joseph also was born circumcised, for it is stated, *These are the generations of Jacob: Joseph.*[73] Surely Scripture should have said here, 'These are the generations of Jacob: Reuben!'[74] Why does it say *Joseph?* [To teach] that as Jacob was born circumcised so Joseph was born circumcised. Moses also was born circumcised, for it is stated, *She saw him that he was a goodly child.*[75] Now what did his

(62) 2 Chron. XXXII, 12. (63) *ibid.* 30. The last words of the verse indicate that his *works* had divine approval. (64) Job I, 8. (65) The phrase *feareth God and shunneth evil.* (66) These were the 'fences' which Job erected to safeguard him from wrong-doing. In view of the description *that feareth God,* etc., what precedes it seems superfluous. (67) The Heb. *tam,* translated 'whole-hearted', is interpreted in the sense of physically perfect, the lack of circumcision being regarded as an imperfection. (68) Gen. I, 27. 'In God's image' implies perfection. (69) *ibid.* V, 3, physically perfect like his father. (70) *ibid.* VI, 9. (71) *ibid.* XIV, 18. The Heb. *shalem* also signifies physical perfection. [On the identification of Shem with Melchizedek, cf. L. Ginzberg, *The Legends of the Jews,* V, pp. 225f.] (72) *ibid.* XXV, 28, E.V. *a quiet man* (Heb. *tam*). (73) *ibid.* XXXVII, 2. (74) Reuben was Jacob's firstborn. (75) Ex. II, 2. *Goodly* indicates physically perfect.

mother see in him finer and better than in all children? [She saw] that he was born circumcised. Even the wicked Balaam was born circumcised, for it is stated, *The saying of him who heareth the words of God.*[76] Samuel also was born circumcised, for it is stated, *And the child Samuel grew up, increased and was good.*[77] David also was born circumcised, for it is stated, *Michtam of David. Keep me, O God; for I have taken refuge in Thee.*[78] Jeremiah also was born circumcised, for it is stated, *Before I formed thee in the belly I knew thee, and before thou camest forth out of the womb I sanctified thee.*[79] Zerubbabel also was born circumcised, for it is stated, *In that day, saith the Lord of hosts, will I take thee, O Ẓerubbabel, My servant, the son of Shealtiel, saith the Lord, and I will make of thee as a signet.*[80]

Scripture states, *I made a covenant with mine eyes; how then should I look upon a maid?*[81] This teaches that Job was most strict with himself and would not even glance at a maiden. Is there not here an argument from the less to the greater? If in the case of an unmarried girl whom, if he so wish, he may marry or may give as a wife either to his son or his brother or some other relative of his, Job was most strict with himself and would not glance at her, how much more strict was he in the case of a married woman! Why was Job so strict with himself and would not even glance at a maid? Because he reasoned, 'Perhaps I look at her to-day, and to-morrow a man comes and takes her to wife; the consequence might be that I should be thinking of a married woman'.

6. What fence did the Prophets make to their words? It states, *The Lord will go forth as a mighty man, He will stir up jealousy like a man*

(76) Num. XXIV, 4. God would not have communicated with one who was uncircumcised. (77) 1 Sam. II, 26. E.V., *increased in favour.* (78) Ps. XVI, 1. The word *michtam* is interpreted in Soṭ. 10b (Sonc. ed., p. 49) as *makkatho tammah,* 'his wound was whole', i.e. the place where there should have been a wound after the operation of circumcision was sound, since he was born circumcised. (79) Jer. I, 5. Since he was consecrated even before birth he must have been formed perfect in body, i.e. already circumcised. (80) Hag. II, 23. The Heb. for 'signet', *ḥotam,* suggests the seal of circumcision. Alternatively, since the word ends with the syllable *tam* it suggests physical perfection, as above, p. 24, n. 67. (81) Job XXXI, 1. After the digression, the subject of Job making a 'fence' is resumed.

of war; He will cry, yea, He will shout aloud.[82] Surely He is not like one mighty man, but like all the mighty men of the world put together! Similarly, *The lion hath roared, who will not fear? The Lord God hath spoken, who can but prophesy?*[83] Surely He is not like one lion, but like all the lions of the world put together! Similarly, *And, behold, the glory of the God of Israel came from the way of the east, and His voice was like the sound of many waters; and the earth did shine with His glory.*[84] [We know that] the phrase *the sound of many waters* refers to the angel Gabriel, and the words *and the earth did shine* [19a] *with His glory* refer to the manifestation of the Divine Presence. Is there not here an argument from the less to the greater? If of the angel Gabriel, who is but one of the countless thousands and myriads who stand before Him, it is said that his voice reaches from one end of the world to the other, how much mightier is the voice of the King of kings, the Holy One, blessed be He, Who created the entire universe and created the celestial and terrestrial beings! But the eye of man is shown only that which it can perceive, and the ear of man is made to hear only that which it can comprehend.[85]

7. What fence did [the authors of] the Holy Writings make to their words? It states, *Remove thy way far from her, and come not nigh the door of her house.*[86] *Remove thy way far from her* refers to heresy; for a man is warned, 'Go not among heretics, nor come in to them, lest you stumble through them'. Should he, however, say, 'I am sure of myself, and even though I go among them I will not stumble through them'; or should he say, 'I will hear their words and then come away'? Scripture therefore states, *None that go unto her return, neither do they attain unto the paths of life.*[87] It is also written, *She hath prepared her meat, she hath mingled*

(82) Is. XLII, 13. (83) Amos III, 8. (84) Ez. XLIII, 2. (85) In the three examples quoted from the Prophets it is obvious that the expressions used are inadequate to describe the glory and might of God; the Prophets, however, deliberately employed them so that thereby they conveyed to the people an idea of God's majesty, using terms which could be comprehended by the limited understanding of man. This choice of expressions and similes is the 'fence' which the Prophets made to their words. (86) Prov. V, 8. (87) *ibid.* II, 19.

her wine; she hath furnished her table.[88] This verse describes the wicked [heretics].[89] When a man comes among them they give him to eat and drink, they clothe and cover him, and give him much money. But no sooner does he become one of them, than each recognizes what was his property and takes it back. Concerning these it is stated, *Till an arrow strike through his liver; as a bird hasteneth to the snare—and knoweth not that it is at the cost of his life.*[90]

Another interpretation of *Remove thy way far from her* refers to the harlot; for a man is warned, 'Go not in this square, enter not in this side-way, for a harlot is there, attractive and bedecked'. Should he, however, say, 'I am sure of myself, and even if I go there I will not stumble through her', he is again warned, 'Go not there even if you are sure of yourself, lest you stumble through her'. For the Sages have said: A man should not make it his habit to pass the door of a harlot, as it is stated, *For she hath cast down many wounded; yea, a mighty host are all her slain.*[91]

8. What fence did the Sages make to their words? They ruled that the evening *Shema*' may be recited only until midnight, although Rabban Gamaliel said: Until cockcrow.[92] How is this? When a man comes home from his work, let him not say, 'I will eat a little, drink a little, sleep a little, and then I will recite the *Shema*''; it may result in his sleeping through the whole night and he will have missed reciting it. He should rather act thus: when he comes home from his work in the evening let him go to the Synagogue or the House of Study. If he is in the habit of reading Scripture, let him read it; if he is in the habit of studying the Mishnah, let him study it; otherwise, let him recite the *Shema*' and say the *Tefillah;* and whosoever transgresses the words of the Sages is deserving of death.[93]

(88) *ibid.* IX, 2. (89) The word 'heretics' is omitted in the text, due, no doubt, to fear of the censor. It is added here by GRA. (90) *ibid.* VII, 23. (91) *ibid.* 26. (92) Cf. the opening paragraph of Mishnah Berakoth. The Sages were also of the opinion that by strict law the *Shema*' may be recited at any time until the morning, but as a precautionary measure they ruled only until midnight. This is an example of a 'fence' by the Sages. (93) Cf. Ber. 4b (Sonc. ed., p. 13).

Rabban Gamaliel said: There are times when a man recites the *Shema*' twice in one night, once before the rise of dawn and once after the rise of dawn, and he thereby fulfils his obligation both for the day and for the night.[94]

The Sages rose up and often made fences to their words.[95]

9. AND RAISE UP MANY DISCIPLES.[96] The School of Shammai said: A master should teach only those who are wise, meek, of good family and wealthy; whereas the School of Hillel said: He should teach everyone, for many sinners in Israel have in this way been brought near to the study of the Torah, and from them issued righteous, pious and worthy men.

(94) Cf. Ber. 8b (Sonc. ed., p. 44). (95) Cf. Finkelstein, *op. cit.*, pp. 26-29 for an original and interesting interpretation of this sentence. (96) Added by all commentators as the heading of the paragraph.

CHAPTER III

1. R. 'Aḳiba said: He who takes a *peruṭah* from charity when not in need of it will not depart from this world before he falls in need of his fellow-men. He also said: He who wraps rags over his eyes or about his loins, and cries, 'Help the blind! Help the leper!'[1] will in the end cry so in earnest. He also said: He who throws his bread to the ground, or scatters his money in his anger, will not depart from this world before he falls in need of his fellow-men.

2. He also said: He who tears his clothes in his anger or breaks his vessels in his rage, will in the end worship idols; for such is the device of the evil inclination: to-day it bids man, 'Tear your clothes' and to-morrow it bids him, 'Worship idols'.[2]

3. He also said: He who hopes for the death of his wife that he may inherit her property or that he may marry her sister, or hopes for the death of his brother[3] that he may marry the widow, will surely be survived by them.[4] Concerning such a person Scripture states, *He that diggeth a pit shall fall into it, and whoso breaketh through a fence, a serpent shall bite him.*[5]

4. The story is told[6] of a certain man who, in contravention of R. 'Aḳiba's teaching, unloosed a woman's hair in the market-place. When the woman came before R. 'Aḳiba he ordered the man to pay her the sum of four hundred *zuz*. The man said, 'Rabbi, give me time to pay', and he agreed. [When the man had come out] a friend of his said to him, 'I will advise you how you will not have to pay her even one *peruṭah*'. 'Do advise me', said the man; and the friend said, 'Go and take oil to the value of an *issar*, and break the jar in front of the door of that woman'. [He did so.] What did the woman do? She came out

(1) lit. 'one who is afflicted with boils (or, ulcers)'. (2) Cf. Shab. 105b (Sonc. ed., p. 510) where it is quoted by R. Simeon b. Eleazar in the name of Ḥalfa b. Agra in R. Joḥanan b. Nuri's name. (3) Without issue, so that the law of Deut. XXV, 5 might apply. (4) lit. 'in the end they will bury him during their lifetime'. (5) Eccl. X, 8. (6) Cf. B.Ḳ. 90b (Sonc. ed., p. 521).

of her house, unloosed her hair in the open street, scooped up [the oil with her hand], and then laid her hand on her head.[7] The man had arranged witnesses against her, and he proceeded before R. 'Aḳiba and said, 'To such a worthless woman must I pay four hundred *zuz?* For the sake of oil worth an *issar* she lost all self-respect, came out of her house, unloosed her hair in the open street, scooped up the oil, and then laid her hand on her head!' R. 'Aḳiba replied, 'Your words prove nothing. For he who wounds himself, though he is not permitted to do so, is free from liability, whereas if others wounded him they are liable. If this woman wounds herself she is free from liability, but you, having wounded her, must pay her four hundred *zuz*'.

5. R. Dosethai b. R. Jannai said: If you have prepared your soil[8] and sown your seed at the first rainfall[9] go and sow again at the second rainfall, lest hail fall in the world and the first sowing will be affected while the second sowing may endure, *for thou knowest not which shall prosper, whether this or that, or whether they both shall be alike good*[10] or both alike bad, as it is stated, *In the morning sow thy seed, and in the evening withhold not thy hand.* If you have prepared your soil and sown your seed at the first and second rainfalls, go and sow again at the third rainfall, lest a blight come upon the world and the early sowings will be blasted while the late sowing may endure, as it is stated, *For thou knowest not which shall prosper, whether this or that, or whether they both shall be alike good,* as it is stated, *In the morning sow thy seed,* etc.

6. R. Ishmael b. R. Jose said: Study Torah in your old age. If you have studied Torah in your youth, say not, 'I will not study in my old age'; but continue studying *for thou knowest not which shall prosper.* If you studied in a time of wealth do not leave off[11] in a time of poverty; if in a time of plenty do not leave off

(7) She rubbed the oil into her head in order not to waste it. (8) lit. 'selected' or cleared (the soil)'. MS. E reads 'set out early'; GRA suggests 'plowed'. (9) There are three periods of rain expected in the early winter: the first from the 17th to the 23rd of the eighth month (Marḥeshwan), the second from the 23rd to the end of the month, the third from the 1st of the ninth month (Kislew) and onwards. (10) Eccl. XI, 6. (11) lit. 'turn away'; according to a variant reading 'sit idle'.

in a time of famine; if in a time of ease do not leave off in a time of hardship; because one word [learnt] by a man in adversity is more precious to him than a hundred learnt in prosperity, as it is stated, *In the morning sow thy seed, and in the evening withhold not thy hand.*

R. 'Aḳiba said: If you have studied Torah in your youth, study it also in your old age, and say not, 'I will not study Torah in my old age', *for thou knowest not which shall prosper,* whether both will remain with you, *or whether they both shall be alike good,* as it is stated, *In the morning sow thy seed,* etc.

R. Meir said: If you have studied under one teacher, say not, 'It is enough for me'; but go to [another] scholar and study Torah under him. Go not, however, to anyone, but to him who is akin to you from the outset,[12] as it is stated, *Drink waters out of thine own cistern, and running waters out of thine own well.*[13] It is incumbent upon a man to attend upon three scholars [19*b*] such as R. Eliezer, R. Joshua and R. 'Aḳiba, as it is stated, *Happy is the man that hearkeneth to me, watching daily at my gates, waiting at the posts of my door*[14]—read not *my gates* but 'the door of my gates'.[15] For[16] you know not whether both will remain with you *or whether they both shall be alike good,* as it is stated, *In the morning sow thy seed,* etc.

R. Joshua said: Take a wife in your youth and take a wife in your old age; beget children in your youth and beget children in your old age. Say not, 'I will no more take a wife', but take her and beget sons and daughters and increase your

(12) i.e. whose style and manner of study approximates to your own. Alternatively *ḳarob* means 'near', i.e. who resides near your house. Another reading is *ḳarob lah* 'near to her', i.e. a scholar who is sincere and near to the Torah. (13) Prov. V, 15. The verse counsels one to learn from such sources as are similar in scope to one's own springs of learning. (14) *ibid.* VIII, 34. (15) Thus arriving at the number 'three': 'door' suggests one and 'gates' in the plural a further two; hence the need to study under three teachers. The text, however, is difficult. In the Yalḳuṭ on this verse the text reads: 'It says not *delathai* but *dalthothai*', and the explanation is that the former term, being in the plural, implies two, therefore the latter term, which is in an amplified form, implies three. (16) This is the continuation of R. Meir's dictum, explaining why it is necessary to study under more than one master.

offspring on the earth, because you know not whether both[17] will remain with you *or whether both shall be alike good,* as it is stated, *In the morning sow thy seed,* etc.

7. He used to say: If you have given a *peruṭah* to a poor man in the morning, and there comes to you in the evening another poor man asking for alms, give to him also, because you know not whether both[18] will remain with you *or whether they both shall be alike good,* as it is stated, *In the morning sow thy seed,* etc.

8. The story is told[19] of a certain pious man who, in a year of drought, gave a poor man a *dinar*. His wife scolded him for it; so he went and passed the night in a cemetery. There he overheard two spirits conversing with one another. 'Come, my dear,' said one to her companion, 'let us wander about the world and find out what calamity is about to come upon the world.'[20] The other replied, 'My dear, I cannot go forth because I am buried in a matting of reeds;[21] but you go and tell me whatever you hear'. She departed and on her return was asked, 'Did you hear from behind the curtain[22] what calamity is about to come upon the world?' She replied, 'I heard that whoever sows at the first rainfall will have his crops smitten by hail'. The man went and sowed at the second rainfall, with the result that everybody's crop was smitten but his was not. The following year he again went and passed the night in the cemetery and overheard the same two spirits conversing with one another. 'Come,' said one to her companion, 'let us wander about the world and find out what calamity is about to come upon the world.' The other replied, 'My dear, have I not previously told you that I cannot go forth because I am buried in a matting of reeds? You go, and tell me whatever you hear'. She departed and on her return her companion asked her, 'Did you hear anything from behind the curtain?' She replied, 'I heard that whoever sows at the

(17) i.e. the children of your youth and the children of your later years. (18) i.e. the two acts of charity. (19) Cf. Ber. 18b (Sonc. ed., pp. 110f). (20) According to the Talmudic version the incident happened on the eve of the New Year when the fate of the world in the coming year is decided. (21) i.e. a shroud of inferior quality and not the usual linen shroud. (22) Which screens the heavenly Court of Justice.

second rainfall will have his crops blasted'. He went and sowed at the first rainfall. When the blight came into the world, everybody's crop was blasted but his was not. His wife asked him, 'How was it that when the calamity came into the world, everybody's crops were smitten and blasted but yours were not?' He told her the whole story. After a time a quarrel broke out between that pious man's wife and the mother of the young woman,[23] and the former said to the other, 'Come and I will show you your daughter buried in a matting of reeds!' The following year the man went and spent the night in the cemetery and overheard those two spirits conversing with one another. One said, 'Come, my dear, let us wander about the world and listen to what is said behind the curtain'. But her companion replied, 'My dear, leave me alone; what has passed between you and me has in the past been overheard by the living'.

9. It is told of a certain pious man who was in the habit of dispensing charity that he was once travelling in a ship when a storm arose and the ship was sunk in the sea. R. 'Aḳiba who witnessed [the tragedy] came before the Beth Din to testify on behalf of the wife to enable her to remarry. Before the time came for him to testify, that pious man entered and stood before him. R. 'Aḳiba said to him, 'You are the man who was drowned at sea'. 'Yes, I am,' he replied. 'And who brought you up from the sea?' asked R. 'Aḳiba. He answered, 'The charity which I dispensed brought me up from the sea'. 'How do you know it?' asked R. 'Aḳiba. He replied, 'When I went down to the nethermost depths, I heard a mighty roaring of the waves calling one to the other, "Hurry and let us bring up this man from the sea because he dispensed charity all his days"'. At this R. 'Aḳiba began [to praise] saying, 'Blessed be God, the God of Israel, Who has chosen the words of the Torah and the sayings of the wise; for the words of the Torah and the sayings of the wise endure for ever and to all eternity, as it is stated, *Cast thy bread upon the waters, for thou shalt find it after many days.*[24] It is also written, *Charity delivereth from death.*[25]

(23) Who had been buried like a pauper in a reed matting. (24) Eccl. XI, 1. (25) Prov. X, 2, E.V., *righteousness delivereth.*

10. It is told[26] of Benjamin the Just, who was the overseer of the charity fund, that one day a woman came to him and said, 'Master, assist me'. He replied, 'By the Temple Service, there is nothing left in the charity fund'. She said, 'Master, if you do not assist me, I perish with my four[27] children'. He thereupon assisted her from his own purse. After a time Benjamin the Just fell ill and lay in pain on his bed. The ministering angels addressed the Holy One, blessed be He, saying, 'Sovereign of the universe, Thou hast said that whoever saves a single soul in Israel is deemed as though he had saved alive the whole world.[28] How much greater must be the merit of Benjamin the Just who saved alive a widow and her four children! He is now on his bed suffering much pain in his sickness'. Thus they sought mercy on his behalf and the decree against him was annulled, twenty-two years being added to his life.

(26) Cf. B.B. 11a (Sonc. ed., p. 52). (27) In B.B. *loc. cit.* 'seven', and so corrected here by GRA. (28) Cf. Sanh. 37a (Sonc. ed., p. 234).

CHAPTER IV

1. SIMON THE JUST WAS ONE OF THE LAST SURVIVORS OF THE GREAT ASSEMBLY. HE USED TO SAY: UPON THREE THINGS THE WORLD IS BASED: UPON THE TORAH, UPON THE TEMPLE SERVICE, AND UPON THE PRACTICE OF LOVINGKINDNESS.

UPON THE TORAH—how is this? It states, *For I desire mercy, and not sacrifice, and the knowledge of God rather than burnt-offerings.*[1] Hence one may infer that of all sacrifices the burnt-offering is the most acceptable since it is entirely consumed by fire, as it is stated, *And the priest shall make the whole smoke on the altar, for a burnt-offering.*[2] In another passage it states, *And Samuel took a sucking lamb, and offered it for a whole burnt-offering unto the Lord.*[3] Nevertheless, the study of Torah is even more acceptable to the All-present than burnt-offerings, since if a man studies Torah he knows the will of the All-present, as it is stated, *Then shalt thou understand the fear of the Lord, and find out the will of God.*[4] Hence it follows that when a scholar sits and expounds the Torah in an assembly, Scripture accounts it to him as though he had offered the fat and the blood [of a sacrifice] upon the altar.

Should[5] two scholars be sitting engaged in the study of the Torah, and a bridal procession or a cortège passes by them, if there are sufficient people present to attend to the needs of the occasion,[6] let them not interrupt their studies; otherwise it is their duty to rise and cheer[7] and applaud the bride or accompany the dead to the grave.

(1) Hos. VI, 6. (2) Lev. I, 9. (3) 1 Sam. VII, 9. Samuel's prayer was immediately answered by God on account of the acceptability of the burnt-offering. (4) Prov. II, 5. E.V., *find the knowledge of God.* (5) This and the subsequent passages are inserted here to teach that though the study of the Torah is the highest good, even that may be interrupted for a wedding ceremony or a funeral procession in the circumstances stated here. (6) As to what is considered sufficient, cf. Keth. 17a (Sonc. ed., p. 95). (7) A rare word from the root *shanan*, 'to repeat a thing', and hence 'to acclaim' or 'applaud repeatedly'. Cf. Jastrow s.v. and the next note but one.

2. It once happened that R. Judah b. Ilai was sitting and lecturing to his disciples when a bride passed before him. At once he took in his hand what was usual for the occasion,[8] and cheered[9] the bride until she had passed by.

3. On another occasion while R. Judah b. Ilai was sitting and lecturing to his disciples, a bride passed before him. 'What was that?' he asked, and they replied, 'A bridal party'. He said to them, 'My sons, arise and attend to the bride, for so we find that the Holy One, blessed be He, attended to a bride, as it is stated, *And the Lord God built up the rib.*[10] And if He attended to a bride, how much more should we do so!' Where do we find that the Holy One, blessed be He, attended to a bride? For it is stated, *And the Lord God built up the rib;* and in coastal towns a bride is referred to as *ben'itha.*[11] Hence we learn that the Holy One, blessed be He, equipped Eve, adorned her as a bride and conducted her to Adam, as it is stated, *And He brought her unto Adam.*[12]

On one occasion only did the Holy One, blessed be He, act as a groomsman to man; thereafter a man provides his own groomsman, as it is stated, *Bone of my bone, and flesh of my flesh.*[13] On one occasion only was the wife formed out of the man;[14] thereafter a man takes the daughter of his fellow to wife.

4. UPON THE TEMPLE SERVICE—how is this? As long as the Temple Service continued, the world was a source of blessing to its inhabitants and the rains fell [20a] in their seasons, as it is stated, *To love the Lord your God, and to serve Him with all your heart and with all your soul, that I will give the rain of your land in its season, the former rain and the latter rain. . . . And I will give grass in thy fields*

(8) i.e. myrtle branches. The text is uncertain, and GRA reads: 'as there were not sufficient people for her needs'. (9) In the parallel passage in *Midrash Haggadol*, ed. Schechter, p. 82, the word is not *meshannen* (var. *meshannenen*) but *mesha'anen* from a root *sha'an* 'to shake, wave about'. The text there reads: 'He took in his hand a myrtle branch and waved it until the bride had passed'. (10) Gen. II, 22; so the text lit. (11) i.e. 'with hair plaited'. The Talmud, Ber. 61a (Sonc. ed., p. 382), Shab. 95a (Sonc. ed., p. 454), connects the Heb. root for 'build' (*banah*) with *binyatha*, a word used in the coastal towns for ' plaits', and explains that God plaited Eve's hair. (12) Gen. *ibid.* (13) *ibid.* 23. (14) lit. 'was Eve taken from Adam'.

for thy cattle.[15] But when the Temple Service ceased, the world was no longer a source of blessing to its inhabitants and the rains did not fall in their season, as it is stated, *Take heed to yourselves, lest your heart be deceived . . . and He shut up the heaven, so that there shall be no rain.*[16] And it also declares in the Book of Haggai, *I pray you, consider from this day and forward—before a stone was laid upon a stone in the temple of the Lord, through all that time, when one came to a heap of twenty measures, there were but ten; when one came to the winevat to draw out fifty measures, there were but twenty.*[17] Why does not the verse also state in regard to the winevat 'to draw out twenty measures, there were but ten' as it does in regard to the wheat? Because the winevat is a significant omen, more so than wheat, thus teaching you that whenever the yield of wine is affected it is a bad omen for the whole year. [At that time] Israel said to the Holy One, blessed be He, 'Sovereign of the universe! Why hast Thou done this to us?' And the Divine Spirit replied, '*Ye looked for much, and, lo, it came to little . . . Because of My house that lieth waste, while ye run every man for his own house.*[18] But if you will devote yourselves to the service of the Temple, I will bless you as formerly, as it is stated, *Consider, I pray you . . . from the four-and-twentieth day of the ninth month, even from the day that the foundation of the Lord's temple was laid . . . Is the seed yet in the barn? Yea, the vine, and the fig-tree, and the pomegranate, and the olive-tree hath not brought forth—from this day will I bless you*'.[19] Hence you learn that no service is more precious to the Holy One, blessed be He, than the Temple Service.

5. UPON THE PRACTICE OF LOVINGKINDNESS—how is this? Scripture states, *I desire lovingkindness and not sacrifice.*[20] In the beginning the world was created by lovingkindness alone, as it is stated, *For I have said: The world is built by lovingkindness; Thou dost establish the heavens with Thy faithfulness.*[21]

It happened once that Rabban Joḥanan b. Zakkai was coming out of Jerusalem, followed by R. Joshua, and he beheld the Temple in ruins. 'Woe to us,' cried R. Joshua, 'for this house

(15) Deut. XI, 13-15. (16) *ibid.* 16f. (17) Hag. II, 15f. (18) *ibid.* I, 9. (19) *ibid.* II, 18f. (20) Hos. VI, 6. E.V., *I desire mercy.* (21) Ps. LXXXIX, 3. E.V., *For ever is mercy built; in the very heavens Thou dost establish Thy faithfulness.*

that lies in ruins, the place where atonement was made for the sins of Israel!' Rabban Joḥanan said to him, 'My son, be not grieved, for we have another means of atonement which is as effective, and that is, the practice of lovingkindness, as it is stated, *For I desire lovingkindness and not sacrifice'*. And so we find it with Daniel, the man greatly beloved, who devoted himself to acts of lovingkindness. What were the acts of lovingkindness to which Daniel devoted himself? If you say that he offered burnt-offerings and peace-offerings in Babylon, had it not been previously ordained, *Take heed to thyself that thou offer not thy burnt-offerings in every place that thou seest; but in the place which the Lord shall choose in one of thy tribes, there thou shalt offer thy burnt-offerings.*[22] What, then, were the acts of lovingkindness to which he devoted himself? He provided for the bride and made her to rejoice, he attended the dead to the grave, he gave alms to the poor, and prayed three times daily, and his prayer was accepted with favour, as it is stated, *And when Daniel knew that the writing was signed, he went into his house—now his windows were open in his upper chamber toward Jerusalem—and he kneeled upon his knees three times a day, and prayed, and gave thanks before his God, as he did aforetime.*[23]

When[24] Vespasian came to destroy Jerusalem, he proclaimed [to its inhabitants], 'Fools, why do you seek to destroy this city and burn the Temple? What do I demand of you? Merely that you deliver to me one bow or one arrow[25] and then I will depart from you'. They answered him, 'As we went forth against your two predecessors[26] and slew them, so we will go out against you and slay you'. When Rabban Joḥanan b. Zakkai heard this, he sent for the men of Jerusalem and said to them, 'My sons, why would you destroy this city and burn the Temple? What does he demand of you? Merely one

(22) Deut. XII, 13f. (23) Dan. VI, 11. (24) This passage is quoted here to indicate the active steps taken by Rabban Joḥanan b. Zakkai to preserve Judaism although the Temple was destroyed. (25) A token of submission. (26) The allusion is uncertain. The version given here differs in many respects from other passages in Rabbinic literature relating to Vespasian; cf. Giṭ. 56b (Sonc. ed., p. 258). [S. Zeitlin, *Megillat Taanit*, p. 104, writes: "The two former generals were undoubtedly Florus and Cestius", whose armies were defeated in 66 C.E., but the generals were not killed by the Jews.]

bow or one arrow, and then he will depart from you'. They answered him, 'As we went forth against his two predecessors and slew them, so we will go out against him and slay him'.

Now Vespasian had some men of his resident [within and] close to the walls of Jerusalem, and whatever they heard they wrote upon an arrow which they shot beyond the wall. [In this manner] they reported that Rabban Joḥanan b. Zakkai was among Caesar's friends. So Rabban Joḥanan b. Zakkai appealed to the men of Jerusalem. After he had pleaded with them for several days[27] and they would not agree with him, he sent for his disciples, R. Eliezer and R. Joshua, and said to them, 'My sons, arise and carry me forth from here. Make a coffin for me and I will lie in it'. [They did so, and] R. Eliezer took hold of it at the head and R. Joshua at the foot, and they carried him until sunset when they arrived at the gates of Jerusalem. The gatekeepers asked, 'What is this?' They replied, 'A dead man; do you not know that a corpse may not be kept overnight in Jerusalem?'[28] They said, 'If it is a corpse, carry it out'. They carried it out (and bore it until sunset)[29] when they arrived before Vespasian, opened the coffin and [Rabban Joḥanan] stood before him. He asked, 'You are Rabban Joḥanan b. Zakkai? Ask what I shall give you'. He replied, 'I ask for nothing but Jabneh whither I may go and teach my disciples, where I can institute prayers,[30] and observe all the commandments prescribed in the Torah'. He said to him, 'Go and do all that you wish to perform'. Rabban Joḥanan then said, 'May I be permitted to say a word to you?' 'Speak,' he said. Rabban Joḥanan then said, 'You are about to become Emperor'. 'How do you know this?' he asked, and Rabban Joḥanan replied, 'There is a tradition with us that the Temple will not be delivered into the hand of a common soldier but to a king, as it is stated, *And He shall cut down the thickets of the forest with iron,*

(27) lit. 'one day and two and three days'. (28) Cf. below XXXV, 2, p. 171. (29) The words in brackets are clearly to be deleted. (30) Or, 'a house of prayer'. A variant gives the curious reading: 'the precept of *tefillin* (phylacteries)'.

and Lebanon shall fall by a mighty one'.[31] It is related that a few days had not elapsed before there came to him a despatch[32] from his city [Rome], informing him that Caesar had died, and he had been elected Emperor. They brought to him a battering-ram which he directed[33] towards the wall of Jerusalem. Then they brought to him logs of cedar which he inserted in the battering-ram and hurled at the wall until he breached it. They then brought to him a pig's head which he inserted in the battering-ram and shot it on to the sacrificial limbs that were upon the altar. At that moment Jerusalem was captured. Rabban Joḥanan was sitting and anxiously waiting for news, as Eli had sat and waited for news, as it is stated, *Lo, Eli sat upon his seat by the wayside, watching; for his heart trembled for the ark of God.*[34] As soon as Rabban Joḥanan b. Zakkai heard that Jerusalem was destroyed and the Temple in flames, he rent his clothes, his disciples also rent their clothes, and they wept and cried out and lamented.

Scripture states,[35] *Open thy doors, O Lebanon, that the fire may devour thy cedars.*[36] This alludes to the chief priests who were in the Temple, took their keys in their hands and hurled them upwards, exclaiming before the Holy One, blessed be He, 'Lord of the universe! here are Thy keys which Thou didst entrust to us, seeing that we have not been faithful treasurers to discharge the duties imposed by the King, and we are no longer worthy to eat from the King's table'.

The patriarchs, Abraham, Isaac and Jacob, and the twelve tribes also wept and cried out and lamented, saying, *Wail, O cypress-tree, for the cedar is fallen, because the glorious ones are spoiled; [wail, O ye oaks of Bashan, for the strong forest is come down].*[37] *Wail,*

(31) Is. X, 34. Cf. Giṭ., *loc. cit.*, where *Lebanon* is identified with the Temple and *mighty one* is applied to a king. [In Jewish War III, viii, 9 Josephus relates that he made the same prediction to Vespasian.] (32) Or, 'two deputies'; so Rashi in Ta'an. 18b. [This interpretation is accepted by Krauss, *Lehnwörter*, p. 201.] (33) Reading *wesamah* as suggested by GRA. The word in V, *wetifa'*, is apparently an abbreviation which has so far defied satisfactory explanation. (34) 1 Sam. IV, 13. (35) Some attach the verse which is cited to the preceding paragraph, thus: 'and lamented saying, *Open thy doors*' etc. (36) Zech, XI, 1. (37) *ibid.* 2.

O cypress-tree, for the cedar is fallen refers to the Temple; *because the glorious ones are spoiled* refers to Abraham, Isaac and Jacob and the twelve tribes; *wail, O ye oaks of Bashan* refers to Moses, Aaron and Miriam; *for the strong forest is come down* refers to the Holy of Holies. *Hark! the wailing of the shepherds, for their glory is spoiled*[38] refers to David and his son Solomon. *Hark! the roaring of young lions, for the thickets of the Jordan are spoiled* refers to Elijah and Elisha.

6. In three things did the Holy One, blessed be He, make human beings to differ one from the other: in voice, in temperament[39] and in features.[40] Why in voice? The Holy One, blessed be He, made the voices of men different one from the other; for had He not done so, immorality would have increased in the world, since as soon as a man left his home another might enter and ravish his wife in his own house. Therefore did the Holy One, blessed be He, make men differ from each other in voice, one man's voice being different from his fellow's. Why in temperament? The Holy One, blessed be He, made the temperament of men different one from the other; because had He not done so men would be jealous of each other. Therefore did the Holy One, blessed be He, make mankind differ from one another in temperament, one man's temperament being different from his fellow's. Why in appearance? The Holy One, blessed be He, made the features of human beings different one from another; because had He not done so, the daughters of Israel would not recognize their husbands nor the husbands their wives. Therefore did the Holy One, blessed be He, make them different in facial features.

(38) *ibid.* 3. (39) lit. 'pleasantness'. (40) In the parallel passage in Sanh. 38a (Sonc. ed., p. 240) the text reads: 'in voice, in appearance, and in mind'.

CHAPTER V

1. ANTIGONOS OF SOCHO RECEIVED THE TRADITION FROM SIMON THE JUST. HE USED TO SAY: BE NOT [20*b*] LIKE SERVANTS WHO SERVE THE MASTER FOR THE SAKE OF RECEIVING A REWARD,[1] BUT BE LIKE SERVANTS WHO SERVE THE MASTER WITHOUT THE EXPECTATION OF RECEIVING A REWARD; AND LET THE FEAR OF HEAVEN BE UPON YOU, in order that your reward may be double in the world to come.[2]

2. Antigonos of Socho had two disciples[3] who repeated this doctrine to their disciples and their disciples to their disciples. They rose up and examined the matter, saying, 'Why did our predecessors say this? Is it right for a labourer to toil all day and not receive his reward in the evening? Had our predecessors known that there was another world and that there would be the resurrection of the dead they surely would not have taught thus!' So they arose and turned away from the Torah. Two sects sprang from them: the Sadducees and the Boethusians,[4] the Sadducees named after Zadok and the Boethusians after Boethus. All their lives they used vessels of silver and gold, but not[5] because they were arrogant in mind. The Sadducees said that it was a tradition of the Pharisees to subject themselves to austerity in this world,[6] and in the world to come they possess nothing at all.

(1) Or, 'gratuity'; so Maimonides *ad loc.* (2) The last clause, 'in order . . . to come', is not found in the statement of Antigonos as reported in Aboth I, 3 (Sonc. ed., p. 3), and apparently did not form part of the original teaching. It actually contradicts the doctrine of disinterested service. Moreover, if these words formed part of the teaching, there would be no foundation for the arguments of the disciples stated in the following paragraph. (3) Zadok and Boethus mentioned below. (4) For the historical origin and doctrines of these two sects, cf. J.E. under their respective headings. [On this passage, cf. Finkelstein, *The Pharisees*, p. 80 and p. 663, n. 20.] (5) GRA omits 'not'; the text is uncertain. For a recent interpretation of this passage, cf. Finkelstein, *Journal of Biblical Literature*, vol. LVII, pp. 35-37. (6) [Cf. Josephus, Antiquities XVIII, i, 3, 'The Pharisees live simply, and despise delicacies'.]

CHAPTER VI

1. JOSE B. JOEZER SAID: LET YOUR HOUSE BE A MEETING-HOUSE FOR THE WISE. What is meant by this? It teaches that a man's house should be available to the wise, their disciples, and the disciples of their disciples; in the same manner that a man might say to his fellow, 'I will wait for you at such and such a place'.[1]

Another interpretation of LET YOUR HOUSE BE A MEETING-HOUSE FOR THE WISE: this means that when a disciple comes into your presence and says to you, 'Give me instruction', if it is within your power to teach him, instruct him, but if not dismiss him at once.[2] Moreover, let him not sit before you on a couch or on a chair or on a bench, but on the ground; and every word that you utter he should accept with awe and reverence, with fear and dread.

2. AND SIT AMIDST THE DUST OF THEIR FEET. What is meant by this? When a scholar comes to a town, say not, 'I have no need of him'; but go to him, and sit not before him on a couch or on a chair or on a bench, but sit before him on the ground; and every word that he utters accept with awe and reverence, with fear and dread, in the same manner that our forefathers received the Torah at Mount Sinai with awe and reverence, with fear and dread.

Another interpretation of AND SIT AMIDST THE DUST OF THEIR FEET—as did R. Eliezer; AND DRINK IN THEIR WORDS WITH THIRST—as did R. 'Akiba.

What was the beginning of R. 'Akiba? It was said of him that at the age of forty he had learnt nothing at all. On one occasion, as he was standing by the mouth of a well, he enquired,

(1) So should your house be the rendezvous of scholars. (2) Your house should be a place for instruction and study; if therefore you are not in a position to impart knowledge, do not detain the would-be learner, but let him seek instruction elsewhere.

'Who carved out this stone?' They answered, 'The water which constantly falls on it, day in and day out'. They continued, ''Aḳiba, have you not read the verse, *The waters wear the stones?*'[3] Forthwith R. 'Aḳiba applied to himself the following *a fortiori* argument: If the soft [water] can wear away the hard [stone], how much more can the words of the Torah, which are hard like iron, carve a way into my heart which is of flesh and blood! Immediately he turned to the study of the Torah. Both he and his son went and sat down before the schoolteacher and said to him, 'Master, teach us the Torah'. R. 'Aḳiba took hold of the tablet by one end and his son by the other end, and on it the teacher wrote *'alef beth*[4] which he learnt, *'alef taw*[5] which he learnt, and then the Book of Leviticus which he also learnt.[6] So he continued to study until he had learnt the whole Torah. He then went and sat before R. Eliezer and R. Joshua and said to them, 'My masters, initiate me into the reasoning of the Mishnah'. As soon as they recited one *halakah* to him, he went away and sat down alone asking himself, 'Why is *'alef* so written? Why is *beth* so written? Why is this stated?' He thereupon returned to his masters and asked them, and held them up with his words.

R. Simeon b. Eleazar said, 'I will illustrate this to you by a parable. To what can this be compared? To a stonemason who was quarrying stones in a mountain. One day he took his pick in his hand, went out and sat on the mountain, and chipped away small stones. When people came and asked him what he was doing, he told them, "I mean to uproot the mountain and cast it into the Jordan". They said to him, "You cannot possibly uproot the whole mountain". Nevertheless, he continued chipping away until it became the size of a large boulder. He inserted himself beneath it, unloosed it, uprooted it, and cast it into the Jordan, saying, "Here is not your place but there"'.[7] In this way did R. 'Aḳiba glean

(3) Job XIV, 19. (4) The first and second letters of the Hebrew alphabet. (5) The first and last letters of the alphabet. (6) All the verbs used here are in the singular, obviously referring to 'Aḳiba; but no further information is given of the son.

the knowledge of Torah from[8] R. Eliezer and R. Joshua. R. Ṭarfon said to him, ''Aḳiba, it is of you that the verse speaks, *He bindeth the streams that they trickle not; and the thing that is hid bringeth he forth to light.*'[9] The things which were hidden from men R. 'Aḳiba brought to light.

Every day he used to gather a bundle of wood, half of which he sold to provide food for himself, and the other half he used for his personal needs. His neighbours rose up against him and cried, ''Aḳiba, you are ruining us with your smoke! Come, sell all [the wood] to us, and with the money you can buy oil, and study by the light of an oil lamp'. But he replied, 'I derive many uses from [the wood]: first I study by its light, secondly I keep myself warm by it, and thirdly I am able to sleep on it'.

In the Hereafter [the example of] R. 'Aḳiba will condemn all the poor; for when they will be charged, 'Why did you not study Torah?' and they plead, 'Because we were too poor', it will be retorted, 'Was not R. 'Aḳiba very poor and in straitened circumstances?' And if they plead, 'Because of our little children', it will be retorted, 'Did not R. 'Aḳiba have many sons and daughters for whom he had to provide as well as his wife Rachel [and yet he studied the Torah]?'[10]

He was forty years old when he started to study Torah and by the end of thirteen years he taught Torah in public. It is said that he did not depart this life before he had enjoyed the luxury of tables of silver and gold, and ascended his bed by golden steps. His wife went out dressed in fine robes[11] and

(7) The point of the parable is that by slow degrees, perseverance and skill, one can master even what seems impossible. (8) lit. 'did to, act towards'. (9) Job XXVIII, 11. (10) The text of the last sentence is far from clear and the translation follows the reading suggested by GRA; cf. Schechter *ad loc.* According to Finkelstein, *op. cit.* p. 188, the original reading is: 'many sons and daughters who were provided for by his wife Rachel'; i.e. the poor will be able to offer as defence that their wives were not like Rachel. (11) There are many variants of the word in the text and the meaning is dubious. According to Jastrow, the word is *ḳarduṭin,* 'a long-sleeved tunic'. [Krauss, *Lehnwörter*, p. 519, connects it with the Latin *scordisci,* 'leather shoes'; or in his *Talmudische Archäologie* I, p. 182 (*soleae*) *corticeae*, 'shoes with cork soles'.]

wearing a 'golden city' tiara.[12] When his disciples said to him, 'Master, you put us to shame by the [lavish] way you treat her', he replied, 'Much hardship has she endured with me for the sake of the Torah'.

3. What was the beginning of R. Eliezer b. Hyrḳanos? He was twenty-two years old and had not yet studied Torah. One day he said [to his father], 'I will go and study Torah under Rabban Joḥanan b. Zakkai'. His father Hyrḳanos replied, 'You shall not taste a morsel of food until you shall have ploughed a complete furrow'. He rose early in the morning and ploughed a complete furrow. It is said that that day was the eve of the Sabbath, so that he went and dined at the house of his father-in-law. Another version is that he tasted nothing between six hours before the Sabbath and six hours after the Sabbath. As he was walking on his way he saw a stone which he thought[13] [to be food]; he took it and put it in his mouth—some say that it was cattle dung. He walked on until he came to an inn where he spent the night. He went and sat before Rabban Joḥanan b. Zakkai in Jerusalem. Soon an offensive smell came forth from his mouth; whereupon Rabban Joḥanan b. Zakkai said, 'Eliezer, my son, have you eaten anything to-day!' He did not answer. Again the question was put to him and he still remained silent. The innkeeper was sent for and asked, 'Has Eliezer eaten with you?' He replied, 'I thought that perhaps he had eaten at your table, Master'. 'I, too, thought that perhaps he had eaten at your table,' said Rabban Joḥanan; 'between us we might have lost R. Eliezer.' He then said to Eliezer, 'Just as an offensive smell came forth from your mouth, so shall there go forth from you a distinguished name in Torah'.

When his father Hyrḳanos heard that he was studying Torah under Rabban Joḥanan b. Zakkai, he declared, 'I shall go [to Jerusalem] and prohibit my son Eliezer by vow [from deriving any benefit] from my estate'. It was said that on that

(12) An ornament of gold shaped like the city of Jerusalem worn by women; cf. Shab. 59a (Sonc. ed., p. 276). (13) An unusual word in this context. MS. E. reads *herimah* (he lifted it up).

day Rabban Joḥanan b. Zakkai was sitting and expounding the Torah in Jerusalem, and all the notables of Israel were sitting before him. On learning that Hyrḳanos had arrived, he posted watchmen and charged them, 'If Hyrḳanos comes in and wishes to sit down,[14] do not let him.'[15] When he came in and wished to sit down, they did not allow him to do so, and he was compelled to move forward[16] until he came to where Ben Ẓiẓith Hakkeseth, Naḳdimon b. Gorion, and Ben Kalba Sabua'[17] were seated, and he sat down among them trembling. It was said that on that day Rabban Joḥanan b. Zakkai turned his gaze upon R. Eliezer and bade him commence the discourse. He said, 'I cannot do so'. The master as well as the disciples urged him, whereupon he began the discourse and expounded matters about which no ear had ever heard [the like]. At every utterance that came from his lips, Rabban Joḥanan b. Zakkai stood up and kissed him on the head; but R. Eliezer exclaimed, 'My master, you have taught me the truth'. Before the time of adjournment had arrived, his father Hyrḳanos stood up and said, 'My masters, I came here for the sole purpose of depriving my son Eliezer by vow of my property, but now [I declare] all my property assigned to my son Eliezer, [21*a*] and all his brothers stand dispossessed and deprived of everything'.

Why was Ẓiẓith Hakkeseth so named? Because he used to recline upon a silver couch at the head of all the notables of Israel.[18]

It is related concerning the daughter of Naḳdimon b. Gorion that her bed had been arrayed at the cost of twelve thousand golden *dinars*, and that from one eve of the Sabbath to the next

(14) Among the scholars in the back rows. (15) He would then have to move forward to the front rows, thus coming closer to his son and witnessing his distinction. (16) lit. 'he was leaping and going forward'. (17) These three men are named as being extremely wealthy in Giṭ. 56a (Sonc. ed., p. 256). (18) On the basis of the explanation given here it has been argued that the correct form of the name is Ẓiẓith Hakkesef, i.e. 'Ẓiẓith of the silver (couch)'. This variant has some MS. authority; cf. Finkelstein, *op. cit.* p. 135. In the Talmud (Giṭ. *loc. cit.*) he was so called because his fringes (*ẓiẓith*) used to trail on cushions (*keseth*), or his seat (*kisse'*) was among those of the Roman nobility.

a Tyrian golden *dinar* was spent by her on sweetmeats. She was then a childless widow awaiting the decision of her brother-in-law.[19]

Why was Naḳdimon b. Gorion so named? Because the sun had again broken through for his sake.[20] Once[21] when all Israel had come up to Jerusalem for the festival, there was no water for them to drink. Naḳdimon went to a certain nobleman and said to him, 'Lend me twelve wells of water from now until such and such a day, and if I do not repay you twelve wells of water I will give you twelve talents of silver'. He fixed a time-limit for repayment. When the time came the nobleman sent him [the message], 'Deliver to me either twelve wells of water or twelve talents of silver'. He replied, 'There is still time during the day [for repayment]'. The nobleman sneeringly said to him, 'There has been no rain the whole year, will it rain now?' The nobleman repaired in a happy mood to the bath-house, while Naḳdimon b. Gorion entered the Temple,[22] wrapped himself in his cloak and stood up to pray. He said, 'Lord of the universe! It is revealed and known before Thee that I did not act for my own glory or for the glory of my father's house, but for Thy glory did I act that the pilgrims should have water to drink'. Immediately the sky became overcast and rain began to fall until the twelve wells were filled to overflowing. He then sent [a message] to that nobleman, 'Deliver to me the money for the extra water which you have because of me'. He replied, 'The sun has already set and the rain has fallen in my possession'. Naḳdimon returned to the Temple,[22] wrapped himself in his cloak and again stood up in prayer, saying, 'Lord of the universe! Perform for me a miracle now as Thou didst perform before'. Immediately the wind blew, the clouds dispersed, and

(19) In accordance with the law of Deut. XXV, 5ff. (20) Naḳdimon is connected with the root *naḳad* 'to pierce, break through', hence 'to shine' (of the sun). (21) Cf. Ta'an. 19b, 20a (Sonc. ed., pp. 97f). (22) So according to GRA and Ta'an. *loc. cit.* V reads: 'House of Study.' [Büchler, *Studies in Jewish History*, pp. 99f. holds that "though many legendary features are interwoven in this story, there is no ground for doubting the actual occurrence related."]

the sun shone through. When they met the nobleman said, 'I know that it was only for your sake that the Holy One, blessed be He, disorganized His world'.

Why was Kalba Sabua' so named? Because whoever entered his house hungry like a dog came out fed to the full.[23]

When the Emperor Vespasian came to destroy Jerusalem, the zealots sought to burn all his stores with fire. Kalba Sabua' said to them, 'Why do you destroy this city and seek to burn all [my] stores with fire? Wait until I go in and ascertain what I have in the house'. He went in and found that he had enough to supply food for every citizen in Jerusalem for a period of twenty-two years. He immediately gave orders and the produce was stacked and cleaned, ground and sifted, kneaded and baked into bread, so providing a food-supply for every citizen in Jerusalem for twenty-two years. They, however, paid no heed to him. What did the men of Jerusalem do? They took the loaves of bread,[24] cut them through with saws and soiled them with mud. In consequence the men of Jerusalem had to resort to cooking straw and eating it.[25] Every man of Israel who was encamped near the walls of Jerusalem called out, 'For a reward of five dates I will go down and fetch five heads of the enemy'. One man was given five dates, and he went down and brought back five heads of the men of Vespasian. When Vespasian examined the excrement of the besieged men and saw that it was without a trace of corn, he remarked to his soldiers, 'If these men who subsist on straw only can slay so many of you, how many more of you would they slay if they were to eat and drink like you!'

(23) Kalba means 'a dog' and Sabua' 'satiated'. (24) Reading *ha'iggulim* for *ha'agalim* with Jastrow, p. 1066b. (25) Because of the famine that ensued.

CHAPTER VII

1. JOSEPH B. JOḤANAN OF JERUSALEM SAID: LET YOUR HOUSE BE OPENED WIDE, AND LET THE POOR BE MEMBERS OF YOUR HOUSEHOLD; AND TALK NOT MUCH WITH A WOMAN.

LET YOUR HOUSE BE OPENED WIDE. What does this mean? It teaches that a man's house should be opened wide to the south, to the east, to the west and to the north, like Job who made four doors to his house. And why did Job make four doors to his house? So that the poor should not have the trouble of going round the entire house. He who came from the north entered straight ahead, and he who came from the south entered straight ahead, and so on all sides. For this reason Job made four doors to his house.

AND LET THE POOR BE MEMBERS OF YOUR HOUSEHOLD. This does not mean literally that they should be members of your household, but that the poor should be able to talk freely about what they ate and drank in your house, just as the poor talked freely about what they had eaten and drunk in Job's house. When the poor met, one would ask the other, 'Whence do you come?' and he would reply, 'From Job's house'. Or one would ask the other, 'Where are you going?' and he would reply, 'To Job's house'. When the great calamity befell him, he addressed the Holy One, blessed be He, saying, 'Lord of the universe! Did I not feed the hungry and give drink to the thirsty, as it is stated, *If I have eaten my morsel myself alone, and the fatherless hath not eaten thereof?*[1] And did I not clothe the naked, as it is stated, *And warmed with the fleece of my sheep?*'[2] The Holy One, blessed be He, answered him, 'For all that, Job, you have not attained to one half the standard [of hospitality] displayed by Abraham. You remained in your house waiting for guests to come to you. To him who was accustomed to eat wheaten bread you gave wheaten bread, to him

(1) Job XXXI, 17. (2) *ibid.* 20.

who was accustomed to eat meat you gave meat, and to him who was accustomed to drink wine you gave wine. Abraham, however, did not act so. He went abroad,[3] and when he met wayfarers he brought them to his home. Even to him who was unaccustomed to eat wheaten bread he gave wheaten bread, to him who was unaccustomed to eat meat he gave meat, and to him who was unaccustomed to drink wine he gave wine. Not only that; but he went and built large mansions along the roadways and placed in them a supply of food and drink, so that whoever entered ate and drank and blessed Heaven. Therefore was he granted happiness;[4] and whatever the heart desired[5] was to be found in Abraham's home, as it is stated, *And Abraham planted a tamarisk-tree in Beer-sheba'*.[6]

2. Teach the members of your household humility; for when a man is humble and the members of his household are also humble, if a poor man comes to the door and asks, 'Is your father at home?' they will reply, 'Yes, come in'. Before he even enters the house the table is already laid for him, and when he comes in he eats and drinks and blesses the name of Heaven. On this account that man is granted much happiness.[7] But when a man is not[8] humble and the members of his household are ill-tempered, if a poor man comes to the door and asks, 'Is your father at home?' they will reply, 'No', rebuke him and drive him away with harsh words.

Another interpretation of 'Teach the members of your household humility'. What does it mean? It teaches that when a man is humble and the members of his household are also

(3) lit. 'in the world'. (4) And was blessed with a child in his old age. The Hebrew phrase is frequently used in connection with the Deity and the text could be rendered, 'Therefore it afforded Him much satisfaction'. (5) lit. 'the mouth asked for'. (6) Gen. XXI, 33. The Heb. for *tamarisk-tree* is *'eshel,* which by transposition of letters can produce the verb *sha'al,* 'to ask for'. [Cf. Midrash Rabbah to Genesis *ad loc.*, LIV, 6 (Sonc. ed., p. 480): 'R. Judah said: *'Eshel* means an orchard, the word meaning ask for whatever you wish, figs, grapes or pomegranates'.] See also Rashi on Keth. 8b where the word is regarded as made of the initial letters of *'akilah* (eating), *shethiyah* (drinking) and *lewiyyah* (escorting a guest on his way), descriptive of Abraham's hospitality. (7) Or, 'and it affords Him much satisfaction'. (8) So GRA. V omits 'not'.

humble, if he sets out to a land beyond the sea, he will say [with confidence], 'I thank Thee, O Lord my God, that my wife is not engaged in strife with her neighbours'. His heart is not anxious, but his mind is at ease until the time of his return. But when a man is not humble and the members of his household are ill-tempered, if he sets out for a distant land, he will say [with apprehension], 'May it be Thy will, O Lord my God, that my wife be not engaged in strife with her neighbours nor my children in conflict'. His heart is anxious and his mind ill at ease until the time of his return.

AND TALK NOT MUCH WITH A WOMAN. This is so even though she be his wife, and needless to say if she be his fellow's wife. For when a man talks much with a woman he brings evil upon himself, neglects the study of the Torah, and in the end will inherit Gehinnom.

3. Another interpretation of AND TALK NOT MUCH WITH A WOMAN. What does it mean? When a man has come into the House of Study and has not there received the respect due to him, or he has had an argument with his fellow, let him not go and report it to his wife, saying, 'I had an argument with my neighbour; this is what he said to me and this is what I replied'. Thereby he disgraces himself, disgraces his wife and disgraces his neighbour; and his wife who previously held him in esteem [now inwardly] laughs at him. Moreover, when the neighbour hears of it, he exclaims, 'Alas! words which concerned only me and him he has gone and gossiped to his wife'. The outcome is that this man disgraces himself, his wife and his neighbour.

CHAPTER VIII

1. JOSHUA B. PERAḤIAH AND NITTAI THE ARBELITE RECEIVED THE TRADITION FROM THE PRECEDING. JOSHUA B. PERAḤIAH SAID: PROVIDE YOURSELF WITH A TEACHER, AND GET YOURSELF A COMPANION, AND JUDGE ALL MEN FAVOURABLY.[1]

PROVIDE YOURSELF WITH A TEACHER. What does this mean? It teaches that a man should provide himself with a permanent teacher from whom he may learn Scripture, Mishnah, Midrash, *halakah* and *'aggadoth*. Accordingly, points which the teacher omitted to tell him in Scripture he can teach him later in the Mishnah, [what he omitted in the Mishnah he can teach him later in the Midrash,][2] what he omitted in the Midrash he can teach him later in the *halakoth*, and finally what he omitted in the *halakoth* he can teach him in the *'aggadoth*. Consequently this man remains in his place and is replete with well-being and blessing.

2. R. Meir used to say: He who learns Torah from one teacher, to what can he be compared? To a man who has but one field; he sowed it partly with wheat and partly with barley, in another part he planted olive-trees and in still another fruit-trees. The consequence is that this man is [in one place and is] replete with well-being and blessing. When, however, a man learns from two or three teachers, he may be compared to a person who has many fields; in one he sowed wheat and in another barley, in a third he planted olive-trees and in yet another he planted fruit-trees. The result is that this man is always on the move[3] in the country and has no enjoyment of well-being and blessing.

3. AND GET YOURSELF A COMPANION. What does this mean? It teaches that a man should get a companion for himself;

(1) lit. 'in the scale of innocence'. (2) So in MS. E., omitted in V. (3) lit 'dispersed'.

one who will eat with him, drink with him, read the Scriptures with him, study Mishnah with him, lodge with him, and reveal to him all secret lore, the mysteries of the Torah and the problems of everyday life. When they sit together engaged in the study of the Torah, if one of them errs in a *halakah* or in the opening passage of a chapter, or he pronounces what is unclean to be clean or what is clean to be unclean, or he declares what is forbidden to be permitted or what is permitted to be forbidden, his companion can correct him. [21*b*] Whence do we know that when his companion corrects him and continues to read with him they both receive a good reward for their labour? Because it is stated, *Two are better than one; because they have a good reward for their labour.*[4]

4. If three sit together and are engaged in the study of the Torah, the Holy One, blessed be He, accounts it to them as though they had formed a conclave[5] before Him, as it is stated, *It is He that buildeth His upper chambers in the heaven, and hath founded His vault upon the earth; He that calleth for the waters of the sea, and poureth them out upon the face of the earth; the Lord is His name.*[6] Hence you learn that if three sit together and are engaged in the study of the Torah, it is accounted to them as though they formed a conclave before the Holy One, blessed be He.

5. If two sit together and are engaged in the study of the Torah, their reward is set aside for them on high, as it is stated, *Then they that feared the Lord spoke one with another, and the Lord hearkened . . .* [*and a book of remembrance was written before Him, for them that feared the Lord, and that thought upon His name*].[7] Who are *they that feared the Lord?* Those who decide upon a course, [and declare their intention,] saying, 'We will go to free the bound and redeem the captive'. The Holy One, blessed be He, provides them with the opportunity, and they proceed to do it

(4) Eccl. IV, 9. (5) The Heb. *'aguddah*, translated 'conclave', is frequently applied in other contexts to a collection consisting of three units, e.g. the *lulab* which is a combination of three plants: the palm, the myrtle and the willow. (6) Amos IX, 6. The Heb. for *vault* is *'aguddah*, homiletically understood as 'conclave'. (7) Mal. III, 16. The expression *one with another* suggests a group of two.

forthwith.[8] And who are *they that thought upon His name?* Those who merely think in their hearts [without declaring an intention], 'We will go to free the bound and redeem the captive'. These the Holy One, blessed be He, affords no opportunity,[9] and an angel comes and strikes them to the ground.[10]

6. If one man sits and occupies himself in the Torah, his reward is set aside for him on high, as it is stated, *Though he sit alone and meditate in stillness, yet he hath taken* [his reward] *unto himself.*[11] This may be illustrated by a parable.[12] To what can the matter be likened? To a man who had a young son. When the father went to market leaving his son on his own, the child arose, took a scroll, placed it on his lap, and began to study it. When the father returned from market he exclaimed, 'See what my young son has done! When I left him and set out to market he, of his own accord, took a scroll, placed it on his lap, and began to study it!' Hence you learn that, even if one man sits alone and occupies himself in the Torah, his reward is set aside for him on high.

7. AND JUDGE ALL MEN FAVOURABLY. It once happened that a young girl was taken captive and two pious men set out after her to ransom her. One of them entered a house of ill-fame.[13] When he came out he said to his companion, 'Of what did you suspect me?' The other replied, 'I thought that perhaps [you went there] to find out at what price she was held for ransom'. He said, 'By the Temple Service! So it was; and as you judged me favourably, so may the Holy One, blessed be He, judge you favourably.'

8. Again it happened that a young girl was taken captive and

(8) This is in accordance with the verse, *Thou shalt also decree a thing, and it shall be established unto thee* (Job XXII, 28); for God abets the good intentions of the righteous. (9) Since they did not expressly declare their course, it would seem that their original intention was not meant to be translated into action, but was to remain with them as a pious wish. (10) 'Them' in all probability refers to the captives who come to grief before their would-be deliverers decide to act. (11) Lam. III, 28. E.V., *Let him sit alone and keep silence, because He hath laid it upon him.* (12) What follows is hardly a parable, but merely an example of an individual, in this case a small child, studying alone and being praised for his act. (13) Where the girl had been taken.

two pious men set out after her to ransom her. One of them, however, was arrested on a [false] charge of robbery and was detained in prison, where his wife daily brought him bread and water. One day he said to her, 'Go to my colleague and tell him that I am detained in prison [because of my efforts to save the girl] from harlotry,[14] while he stays at home, making merry, with no concern about the girl'. She replied, 'Is it not enough for you that you are detained in prison that you must occupy yourself with futile matters?' She did not go, but occupied herself with matters of no moment. He then said to her, 'I beg of you, go and inform him'. She went and informed his colleague. Now what did that man do? He went and took with him much silver and gold as well as several men, and released the two of them. On his release he said to his companions, 'Permit this young girl to sleep with me in bed with her clothes on'.[15] [They did so.] The following morning he said to them, 'Prepare a ritual bath for me and also for her'. They did so. He then said to those who had prepared the baths, 'When I asked for a ritual bath for myself, of what did you suspect me?' They replied, 'We thought that during all the days that you were confined in prison you must have suffered hunger and thirst, and that now that you have come out into the free world your emotions were stirred and you probably suffered a pollution'. He further said to them, 'And when I asked for a ritual bath for the young girl, of what did you suspect her?' They replied, 'Seeing that all those days that she had been living among heathens she was obliged to eat of their food and drink with them, now [that she is free] you asked that a ritual bath be prepared for her in order that she may become clean'. He said to them, 'By the Temple Service! So it was; and as you judged me favourably, so may the Holy One, blessed be He, judge you favourably'.

Just as the righteous men of old were pious, so also were

(14) The phrase is strange in its present context and is deleted by GRA.
(15) His intention was to protect her from those who might take advantage of her plight.

their beasts. It was said that the camels of our father Abraham would not enter a house in which there was an idol, as it is stated, *For I have cleared the house, and made room for the camels.*[16] *I have cleared the house* of the terafim; why, then, does the verse add *and made room for the camels?* It teaches that they would not enter the house of Laban the Aramean until all the idols had been cleared out before them.

Once the ass of R. Ḥanina b. Dosa was stolen by bandits. They locked it up in a courtyard and placed before it hay, barley and water, but it would neither eat nor drink. They said, 'Why should we let it die here and befoul the courtyard with its stench?' So they proceeded to open the gate for it and let it go free. It dragged itself[17] all the way until it reached the house of R. Ḥanina b. Dosa. When it arrived, R. Ḥanina's son heard its cry and said to his father, 'Father, the sound is very similar to that of our beast.' The father said to him, 'My son, open the door for it, since it is almost dead from hunger'. He at once opened the door for it, and put before it hay, barley and water which it ate and drank. Because of this incident the Sages declared: Just as the righteous men of old were pious, so too were their beasts.

(16) Gen. XXIV, 31. (17) Because it was enfeebled by hunger and thirst. For the verb מושכת there is a variant משחקת, 'being merry', but it does not make sense here. Schechter reads מנהקת, 'braying'.

CHAPTER IX

1. NITTAI[1] THE ARBELITE SAID: KEEP FAR FROM A BAD NEIGHBOUR, ASSOCIATE NOT WITH THE WICKED, AND ABANDON NOT BELIEF IN RETRIBUTION.

KEEP FAR FROM A BAD NEIGHBOUR. It is all one whether the neighbour is within or without your house or in a [nearby] field; for leprosy affects only the house of the wicked, as it is stated, *His own iniquities shall ensnare the wicked.*[2] It teaches that leprosy is caused only through the iniquity of the wicked. Indeed, the sins of the wicked cause the righteous man's wall to be pulled down. For instance, where there is a party-wall between the house of the wicked and the righteous, and a plague-spot appears in the party-wall on the side of the wicked man's house [so that the wall must be demolished], the result is that the righteous man's wall is pulled down through the iniquity of the wicked. R. Ishmael, the son of R. Joḥanan b. Beroḳah, said: Woe to the wicked and woe to his neighbour, since the sins of the wicked cause the righteous man's wall to be pulled down.

2. With ten trials did our fathers try the Holy One, blessed be He, yet they were only punished because of their evil tongue,[3] which was but one of them. They are as follows:[4] once at the Red Sea,[5] once when the manna first fell[6] and again later on,[7] once at the [first] appearance of the quails[8] and again later on,[9] once at Marah,[10] once at Rephidim,[11] once at Horeb,[12] once

(1) In V. this chapter begins with the name of Joshua b. Peraḥiah followed by that of Nittai the Arbelite. This is an obvious error since the former's aphorism was the theme of the preceding chapter. (2) Prov. V, 22. (3) The reference is to the evil report spread by the spies; cf. Num. XIII, 32. (4) Cf. the variant list in 'Arak. 15a (Sonc. ed., pp. 85f) and below XXXIV, 1, p. 162. (5) Cf. Ps. CVI, 7, *But were rebellious at the sea, even at the Red Sea.* (6) The Israelites were commanded not to leave of the manna until the morning, but some disobeyed (Ex. XVI, 19f). (7) When they were charged not to go out and gather it on the Sabbath (*ibid.* 26f.). (8) *ibid.* 12f. (9) Cf. Num. XI, 31-33. (10) Cf. Ex. XV, 23. (11) *ibid.* XVII, 1ff.

at the episode of the golden calf,[13], and once in connection with the spies.[14] The incident of the spies was the gravest of them all, as it is stated, *Ye have put Me to proof these ten times, and have not hearkened to My voice.*[15] And it is similarly [stated], *Even those men that did bring up an evil report of the land, died by the plague before the Lord.*[16] Now is there not an inference from the less to the greater? If [for making disparaging remarks about] the Land, which can neither speak, nor blush, nor feel shame, the Holy One, blessed be He, exacted punishment from the spies for its humiliation, how much more will He exact punishment for a man's humiliation from his fellow who speaks [evil] words against him and puts him to shame!

R. Simeon said: Upon those who utter slander does the plague of leprosy fall. We find it so with Aaron and Miriam who slandered Moses and were visited with punishment, as it is stated, *And Miriam and Aaron spoke against Moses.*[17] Why does Scripture mention Miriam's name first before Aaron's? It teaches that Zipporah[18] went and spoke of it to Miriam; Miriam went and spoke of it to Aaron, and both of them arose and spoke ill of that righteous man [Moses]. Because the two of them stood speaking ill of that righteous man, Divine punishment came upon them, as it is stated, *And the anger of the Lord was kindled against them, and departed.*[19] What is the significance of the expression *and departed?* It suggests that [the leprosy] departed from Aaron[20] and attached itself to Miriam, because Aaron did not enter into the details of the matter whereas Miriam did; therefore she was immediately punished with greater severity. Miriam said, 'To me came the Word yet I did not separate myself from my husband'. Aaron said, 'To me came the Word yet I did not separate myself from my wife. The Word also came to our fathers of old and they

(12) Another name for Sinai. The temptation at Horeb is usually taken to refer to the making of the golden calf, but as this incident follows immediately in the list, the inclusion of Horeb is redundant. GRA and other commentators substitute 'Taberah' (cf. Num. XI, 1-3). (13) Cf. Ex. XXXII, 1ff. (14) Num. XIII, 1ff. (15) *ibid.* XIV, 22. (16) *ibid.* 37. (17) *ibid.* XII, 1. (18) The wife of Moses. (19) *ibid.* 9, E.V., *and He departed.* (20) Cf. Shab. 97a (Sonc. ed., p. 464).

did not separate themselves from their wives. But [Moses], in his arrogance, has separated from his wife!' They did not criticize him to his face[21] but only behind his back, and their criticism was not stated as a fact but only as a surmise; since it was a matter of doubt whether he had acted so from arrogance or not. Now is there not here an inference from the less to the greater? If Miriam, who spoke only against her brother, spoke only in [22a] secret[22] and spoke only behind Moses' back, was punished, how much greater will be the punishment of an ordinary man who speaks ill to the face of his fellow and puts him to shame!

At that time Aaron said to Moses, 'Moses, my brother, do you think that this leprosy affects only Miriam? It touches also the person of our father Amram. Let me illustrate this to you. To what can the matter be compared? To a man who had taken a glowing coal in his hand; no matter how much he shifts it about from place to place his flesh is still scorched. For so it is stated, *Let her not, I pray, be as one dead'.*[23] Thereupon Aaron began to conciliate Moses, saying, 'Moses, my brother, have we ever done evil to any person in the world?' He answered, 'You have not'. 'Well then,' he said, 'if we have never hurt anyone in the world, how could we hurt you, our brother? What can I do now? It was a misunderstanding between us; we have broken[24] the covenant between us and you, as it is stated, *And remembered not the brotherly covenant.*[25] Are we to lose our sister because the covenant which was made between us is broken?' Immediately Moses drew a small circle, stood within it and prayed for mercy on her behalf, saying, 'I shall not stir from here until my sister Miriam is healed', as it is stated, *Heal her now, O God, I beseech Thee.*[26] Forthwith the Holy One, blessed be He, said to Moses, 'If a king had rebuked her, or if her father had rebuked her, would it not be proper that she hide in shame for seven days? Surely, if I,

(21) To avoid shaming him to his face. (22) The words 'and spoke only in secret' are not found in many texts and appear to be redundant. The clause is apparently a doublet of the preceding one. (23) Num. XII, 12. (24) Adopting the variant as given in the margin of V. (25) Amos I, 9. (26) Num. XII, 13.

the King of kings, rebuke her, how much more should she hide in shame for fourteen days [at the least]! Yet for your sake I pardon her'. As it is stated, *And the Lord said unto Moses: If her father had but spit in her face,*[27] etc.

Now the man Moses was very meek.[28] It is possible [to think] he was meek but not handsome and imposing;[29] therefore Scripture states, *And he spread the tent over the tabernacle:*[30] as the tabernacle was ten cubits in height, so Moses must have been ten cubits tall. It is possible [to think] that he was as meek as the ministering angels; therefore Scripture continues, [*Moses was very meek*] *above all the men:* above all men, it is said, but not above the ministering angels. It is possible [to think] that he was as meek as those of the former generations;[31] therefore Scripture continues, *Upon the face of the earth,* implying above those of his own generation, but not above those of the former generations.

Three types of leprous condition were created in the world: the moist, the dry and the polypus;[32] but the soul of Moses was lowlier than them all.

3. R. Simeon b. Eleazar said: Also upon those who utter calumny[33] does the plague [of leprosy] fall. We find it so in the case of Gehazi; because he uttered calumny against his master leprosy clung to him until his dying day, as it is stated, *The leprosy, therefore, of Naaman shall cleave unto thee. . . . And he went out from his presence a leper as white as snow.*[34]

He further said: Also upon those who are arrogant does the plague [of leprosy] fall. We find it so in the case of Uzziah, as it is stated, *But when he was strong, his heart was lifted up so that he did corruptly, and he trespassed against the Lord his God; for he went unto the temple of the Lord to burn incense upon the altar of incense. And Azariah the priest went in after him, and with him fourscore priests of the Lord, that were valiant men; and they withstood Uzziah the king, and said unto him: It pertaineth not unto thee, Uzziah, to burn incense unto the Lord, but to the*

(27) *ibid.* 14. (28) *ibid.* 3. (29) lit. 'worthy of praise'. (30) Ex. XL, 19. (31) i.e. the patriarchs. (32) Here a type of skin disease; strictly a morbid growth in the nose. Persons so afflicted must feel very lowly. (33) GRA reads 'who utter lies'. (34) 2 Kings V, 27.

priests the sons of Aaron that are consecrated it pertaineth to burn incense; go out of the sanctuary; for thou hast trespassed; neither shall it be for thy honour from the Lord God. Then Uzziah was wroth, and he had a censer in his hand to burn incense; and while he was wroth with the priests, the leprosy broke forth in his forehead.[35] At that moment the sanctuary was split from end to end,[36] and [the chasm covered an area of] twelve square miles. The priests fled in alarm. The king also made haste to go out *because the Lord had smitten him. And he was a leper unto the day of his death, and dwelt in a house set apart, being a leper; for he was cut off from the house of the Lord; and Jotham his son was over the king's house, judging the people of the land.*[37]

4. ASSOCIATE NOT WITH THE WICKED. This teaches that a man should not associate himself either with an evil man or a wicked man. We find it so in the case of Jehoshaphat; because he associated with Ahab and went up with him to Ramoth Gilead, the wrath of the Lord came upon him, as it is stated, *Shouldest thou help the wicked, and love them that hate the Lord? For this thing wrath is upon thee from the Lord.*[38] And also later when he associated with Ahaziah, and they made themselves ships in Ezion Geber, the Lord wrecked his enterprise, as it is stated, *Because thou hast joined thyself with Ahaziah, the Lord hath made a breach in thy works. And the ships were broken.*[39] So, too, we find with Amnon who associated with Jonadab and received from him bad advice, as it is stated, *But Amnon had a friend, whose name was Jonadab, the son of Shimeah David's brother; and Jonadab was a very subtle man;*[40] he was *subtle* to do evil.[41]

Another interpretation of ASSOCIATE NOT WITH THE WICKED: even to [bring him near to] the Torah.[42]

5. AND ABANDON NOT BELIEF IN RETRIBUTION. What does this mean? It teaches that a man's heart should be daily

(35) 2 Chron. XXVI, 16-19. (36) By a violent earthquake, alluded to in Zech. XIV, 5. (37) 2 Chron. XXVI, 20f. (38) *ibid.* XIX, 2. The Biblical text is omitted in V but is found in MS. E. and inserted by GRA. (39) *ibid.* XX, 37. (40) 2 Sam. XIII, 3. (41) This unusual connotation of *ḥakam*, translated *subtle*, is quoted from Sanh. 21a (Sonc. ed., p. 114). (42) Although the purpose is laudable, there is always the danger of oneself becoming corrupt by the association. Cf., however, Finkelstein, *op. cit.*, pp. 19-22.

in fear of retribution[43] and he should say, 'Woe is me, perhaps reckoning will overtake me to-day or to-morrow'. As a consequence he is fearful every day, as it is stated of Job, *For I feared a fear.*[44]

6. Another interpretation of AND ABANDON NOT BELIEF IN RETRIBUTION. What does this mean? When a man sees that he is successful in whatever he undertakes, let him not say, 'Because I am meritorious the All-present has provided me with food and drink in this world, while the capital [of my reward] is laid up for me in the world to come'. Rather should he say, 'Woe is me, perhaps I have only one meritorious deed to my credit before Him, and as a reward for that He has granted me food and drink in this world, so as to cut me off utterly in the world to come'.

(43) The text therefore means: Do not consider yourself exempt from chastisement under the illusion of self-righteousness. (44) Job III, 25. So lit., E.V., *For the thing which I did fear.*

CHAPTER X

1. JUDAH B. ṬABBAI AND SIMEON B. SHEṬAḤ RECEIVED THE TRADITION FROM THE PRECEDING. JUDAH B. ṬABBAI SAID: ACT NOT AS THOSE THAT WOULD INFLUENCE THE JUDGES; AND WHEN THE SUITORS STAND BEFORE YOU LET THEM BE AS WRONGDOERS IN YOUR SIGHT, AND WHEN THEY HAVE DEPARTED LET THEM BE AS INNOCENT IN YOUR SIGHT, ONCE THEY HAVE ACCEPTED THE JUDGMENT.

2. ACT NOT AS THOSE THAT WOULD INFLUENCE THE JUDGES. What does this mean? It teaches that if you come to the House of Study and hear a ruling or a decision, be not hasty to dispute it, but sit and ask yourself, 'Why did they say it? On what grounds did they arrive at their decision?' Or if they stated a law, ask them first of all the fundamental principle of the law about which they were consulted.[1]

When two suitors come before you to law, one poor and the other rich, do not say, 'How can I declare the poor man innocent and the rich man guilty?' or 'How can I declare the rich man innocent and the poor man guilty?' or 'If I find against the poor man, he will become my enemy; and if I find in favour of the poor man, the rich man will become my enemy.' Furthermore, do not say, 'How dare I take the money from one and give it to the other?' For the Torah declares, *Ye shall not respect persons in judgment.*[2]

R. Meir used to say: What does Scripture intend by the words, *Ye shall hear the small and the great alike?*[3] It means that one suitor should not sit and the other stand; one should not speak all that he wishes and the other be told to be brief. R. Judah said: I have heard that if [the judges] desire both suitors to sit they may do so, and there is no objection to it.

(1) The text is in disorder although the meaning is clear. A warning is issued against a scholar's hasty criticism of a judge's decision, and unwarranted interference with a sentence of the Court. (2) Deut. I, 17. (3) *ibid.*

What is prohibited is for one to sit and the other to stand.[4]

[Another interpretation:] What is meant by *the small and the great alike?* A minor law-suit should be as important to you as a major law-suit, a law-suit involving a *peruṭah* should be as important to you as one involving one hundred *mina.*[5]

3. He[6] used to say: If anyone had said to me before I occupied high office, 'Assume that office', I would go so far as to deprive him of his livelihood.[7] But once I had assumed office, if anyone were to say to me, 'Give it up', I would pour a pot of boiling water on his head. For it is a hard thing to assume power, and hard as it is to assume power, it is harder to give it up. We find it so in the case of Saul; when he was asked to assume the regal dignity he hid himself, as it is stated, *And the Lord answered: Behold, he hath hid himself among the baggage.*[8] But when he was told to surrender the crown, he pursued David to kill him.

4. SIMEON B. SHEṬAḤ SAID: EXAMINE THE WITNESSES THOROUGHLY; and when examining them BE CAREFUL WITH YOUR WORDS, lest through your words those who are listening may add falsehood to them: [a necessary precaution] on account of dishonest persons.

(4) Cf. Shebu. 30a (Sonc. ed., p. 167). (5) Cf. Sanh. 8a (Sonc. ed., p. 32). (6) In the parallel passage, Men. 109b (Sonc. ed., p. 678), the author of this statement is R. Joshua b. Peraḥiah. Here it might be attributed to Judah b. Ṭabbai, the author of the aphorism at the beginning of the chapter. (7) In Men. the reading is: 'I would bind him and put him in front of a lion'. In both versions the threat is, of course, not meant to be taken seriously. (8) 1 Sam. X, 22.

CHAPTER XI

I. SHEMAIAH AND ABṬALYON RECEIVED THE TRADITION FROM THE PRECEDING. SHEMAIAH SAID: LOVE WORK AND HATE PUBLIC OFFICE, AND BECOME NOT KNOWN TO THE RULING POWER.

LOVE WORK. What does this mean? It teaches [22b] that a man should love work and not hate it; for just as the Torah was given [to man] by a covenant, so work too was given by a covenant, as it is stated, *Six days shalt thou labour and do all thy work; but the seventh day is a sabbath unto the Lord thy God.*[1]

R. 'Aḳiba said: There are times when a man does work [on the Sabbath] and escapes the penalty of death, and there are times when a man does no work [on the Sabbath] and incurs death by Heaven. How can this be? If a man sat the whole week doing no work and on the eve of the Sabbath, having nothing to eat, took of the sacred money which is in his possession and used it for his needs, he thereby incurred the penalty of death by Heaven.[2] On the other hand, if he is at work on the Temple building, although he receives sacred money in payment which he uses for his needs, he escapes the penalty of death.

R. Dosethai said: Whence is it that if a man does no work all the six days he will eventually have to work all the seven days? If he is idle all the days of the week doing no work, when the Sabbath eve arrives he will have nothing to eat. He then goes forth and joins a band of robbers; he is caught and put in chains, and is now compelled to work [also] on the Sabbath. All this is the sequel of his not working during the six days of the week.

(1) Ex. XX, 9f. This verse, however, does not contain the word 'covenant' required for the purpose of the analogy, and the commentators substitute Ex. XXXI, 15, *Six days shall work be done; but on the seventh day is a sabbath of solemn rest,* etc., concluding with *a perpetual covenant (ibid.* 16). (2) For misappropriating Temple funds.

R. Simeon b. Eleazar said: Even Adam, the first man, did not taste a morsel until he had done some work, as it is stated, *And He put him into the garden of Eden to dress it and to keep it,*[3] and only then [is it recorded], *Of every tree of the garden thou mayest freely eat.*[4]

R. Ṭarfon said: Even the Holy One, blessed be He, did not cause His Presence to dwell in Israel until they had performed some work, as it is stated, *And let them make Me a sanctuary, that I may dwell among them.*[5]

R. Judah b. Bathyra said: What should a man do when he has no work to undertake? If he has a dilapidated courtyard or a waste field let him go and attend to it;[6] for it is stated, *Six days shalt thou labour, and do all thy work.*[7] Why does the verse add the words *and do all thy work?* To include the case of a man who has dilapidated courtyards or waste fields, that he should go and occupy himself with them.

R. Jose[8] said: No man dies except in idleness, as it is stated, *And he expired, and was gathered unto his people.*[9] Hence if a man had a seizure, came under the care of his physician and died, he only died because he was in idleness.[10] If a man was standing [idly] on the top of a roof or a castle or a building or by the river's edge and fell and died, he only died because he was in idleness.

We have heard this[11] in connection with men, but whence in connection with women? As it is stated, *Let neither man nor woman make any more work for the offering of the sanctuary.*[12] And whence in connection with children? As it is stated, *So the people were restrained from bringing.*[13]

R. Nathan said: At the time that Moses was engaged upon

(3) Gen. II, 15. (4) *ibid.* 16. (5) Ex. XXV, 8. (6) Rather than be idle. (7) *ibid.* XX, 9. (8) So in all MSS.; V reads: R. Ṭarfon. (9) Gen. XLIX, 33. The term *he expired* is interpreted as 'he ceased to work', and when idleness set in death follows. Schechter suggests that the proof-text should read, *And they shall die without knowledge* (Job XXXVI, 12) which follows immediately on *If they hearken and work* [E.V., *serve Him*], *they shall spend their days in prosperity* (*ibid.* 11). This is Scriptural proof that work leads to prosperity, idleness to death. (10) i.e. through inability to work. (11) The duty to work. (12) Ex. XXXVI, 6. (13) *ibid.*; the term *people* includes the young.

the work of the Tabernacle, he declined to consult with the princes of Israel. Consequently they sat in silence, thinking to themselves, 'The time will soon come when Moses will have need of us'. When they heard the proclamation made in the camp which declared, *The stuff they had was sufficient,*[14] they exclaimed, 'Alas, we have had no share in the work of the Tabernacle!' They arose and added a large contribution of their own accord, as it is stated, *And the rulers brought the onyx stones.*[15]

2. AND HATE PUBLIC OFFICE. What does this mean? It teaches that no man should himself put a crown on his head, but others should put it on him; as it is stated, *Let another man praise thee and not thine own mouth; a stranger, and not thine own lips.*[16]

R. 'Aḳiba said: Whoever exalts himself by his knowledge of Torah, to what is he like? To a carcase which lies in the road, anybody passing by puts his hand to his nose and moves far away from it; as it is stated, *If thou hast done foolishly in lifting up thyself, or if thou hast planned devices, lay thy hand upon thy mouth.*[17] Ben 'Azzai said to him, 'Interpret the text in this sense: If a man debases himself for the sake of Torah, eats dry dates, wears shabby clothes, and sits and keeps guard at the door of the wise, though every passer-by may think him a fool, in the end you will find that the whole Torah is within him'.

R. Jose said: Go down and you will be up,[18] go up and you will be down. He who exalts himself by his knowledge of Torah will in the end be brought low; he who humbles himself by his knowledge of Torah will in the end be exalted.

3. AND BECOME NOT KNOWN TO THE RULING POWER. What does this mean? It teaches that a man should not wish to have a reputation [for wealth] with the ruling powers,[19] because if this happens they will eventually have their eyes upon him, put him to death and confiscate all his wealth. [Similarly, a man should not cause a reputation for wealth to

(14) *ibid.* 7. (15) *ibid.* XXXV, 27. (16) Prov. XXVII, 2. (17) *ibid.* XXX, 32. (18) A fine pithy saying. The more humble a man is, the higher he stands in the estimation of his fellows. (19) The harsh sentiments expressed here refer particularly to the cruel and despotic rule of the Roman local governors in the Herodian era.

be spread abroad about his neighbour among the ruling powers.][20] Thus if a man meets his friend in the market and exclaims, 'May the Holy One, blessed be He, bless that man [still more]! Only to-day there came from his establishment a hundred oxen, a hundred sheep and a hundred goats!', an inspector may hear it and proceed to inform the governor, who has the man's house surrounded and confiscates all his wealth. Of such a man Scripture says, *He that blesseth his friend with a loud voice . . . it is counted a curse to him.*[21]

Another interpretation of AND BECOME NOT KNOWN TO THE RULING POWER. A man's friend is sitting in the market and the former exclaims, 'May the Holy One, blessed be He, bestow still more blessings upon him! To-day he brought into his house so many *kors* of wheat and so many *kors* of barley!' Robbers hear of it and come and surround his house, taking away all his wealth, so that in the morning he is left with nothing. Of such a man Scripture says, *He that blesseth his friend with a loud voice*, etc.

Another interpretation of AND BECOME NOT KNOWN TO THE RULING POWER. What does it mean? It teaches that a man should not intend [to occupy office] in order to say, 'I am the city's governor', or 'I am the deputy-governor', because they rob Israel.[22]

4. Another interpretation: A man should not have the intention [to occupy] a governmental position, for though in the beginning they show him favour, ultimately they trouble him sorely.[23]

5. ABṬALYON SAID: WISE MEN, BE HEEDFUL OF YOUR WORDS, lest men teach doctrines in your name not in accord with the Torah, and YOU THEREBY INCUR THE PENALTY

(20) Inserted by GRA. This is the maxim for the illustration that follows. (21) *ibid.* XXVII, 14. E.V., *it shall be counted.* (22) A curious passage and its meaning is obscure. Perhaps the explanation is to be sought in Midrash Rabbah, Genesis LXXVI, §6 (Sonc. ed., p. 706), which tells that the Romans used to offer petty local governorships to wealthy Jews in order to hold them responsible for the collection of the taxes and other impositions. As in many cases the taxes were unjustly levied, they who occupied these offices were assisting in robbing their own brethren.

OF EXILE, AND ARE EXILED TO A PLACE OF EVIL WATERS.[24] Moreover, the disciples who come after you may also teach doctrines in your name not in accord with the Torah, and they too incur the penalty of exile and are exiled to a place of evil waters.[25] What is to be understood by 'evil waters'? That which is implied in the verse, *But they mingled themselves with the nations, and learned their works.*[26] Others say: The phrase 'evil waters' bears its literal significance.[27] Another view is: [The meaning is] lest they be exiled for hard labour.

(23) lit. 'they open to him a door that is pleasant . . . a door that is harsh'. (24) i.e. exiled among the nations where pernicious and heretical ideas are current. (25) V repeats 'and you thereby incur', etc. (26) Ps. CVI, 35. 'Evil waters' has to be interpreted metaphorically. (27) Unhealthy waters, productive of physical ills.

CHAPTER XII

1. HILLEL AND SHAMMAI RECEIVED THE TRADITION FROM THE PRECEDING. HILLEL SAID: BE OF THE DISCIPLES OF AARON, LOVING PEACE AND PURSUING PEACE, promoting peace between man and wife, LOVING MANKIND AND BRINGING THEM NEAR TO THE TORAH.

HE USED TO SAY: WHOEVER MAKES HIS NAME GREAT LOSES HIS NAME; WHOSOEVER INCREASES NOT HIS KNOWLEDGE DECREASES IT; HE WHO DOES NOT STUDY DESERVES DEATH; AND HE WHO MAKES USE OF THE CROWN[1] WILL PASS AWAY.

2. HE FURTHER USED TO SAY: IF I AM NOT FOR MYSELF WHO IS FOR ME? AND IF I AM ONLY FOR MYSELF, WHAT AM I? AND IF NOT NOW, WHEN?

3. LOVING PEACE. What does this mean? It teaches that a man should love [to foster] peace in Israel between man and man, just as Aaron loved [to foster] peace in Israel between man and man, as it is stated, *The law of truth was in his mouth, and unrighteousness was not found in his lips; he walked with Me in peace and uprightness, and did turn many away from iniquity.*[2] R. Meir said: What is meant by *and did turn many away from iniquity?* Whenever Aaron walked along the road and met a wicked man, he would offer him greetings. On the following day when that man was about to commit a transgression, he would say, 'Woe is me! How can I raise my eyes after doing that and look Aaron in the face? I should be ashamed before him, since he greeted me'. Consequently that man withholds himself from transgression.

Similarly, when two men had quarrelled one with the other, Aaron would go and sit with one of them and say, 'My son, see what your companion is doing![3] He beats his

(1) Usually explained: he who makes worldly use of the crown of the Torah; but cf. the end of this chapter. (2) Mal. II, 6. (3) So according to GRA; V reads 'saying'.

breast and tears his clothes, exclaiming, "Woe is me! how can I raise my eyes and look my companion in the face? I am ashamed before him since it is I who offended him"'. Aaron would sit with him until he had removed all enmity from his heart. Then Aaron would go and sit with the other and say likewise, 'My son, see what your companion is doing! He beats his breast and tears his clothes, exclaiming, "Woe is me! how can I raise my eyes and look my companion in the face? I am ashamed before him since it was I who offended him"'. Aaron would sit with him until he had removed all enmity from his heart. Later when the two met, they embraced and kissed each other. Therefore it is stated, *They wept for Aaron thirty days, even all the house of Israel.*[4]

4. Another interpretation—why was it that for Aaron *all the house of Israel* wept thirty days, i.e. the men as well as the women? Because Aaron judged everyone favourably,[5] for he never said to any man or any woman, 'You have done wrong'. Therefore it is written of him that *all the house of Israel* wept for him. Of Moses, on the other hand, who rebuked the people with harsh words, it is stated, *And all the children of Israel wept for Moses.*[6] Moreover, many thousands in Israel were given the name Aaron, since but for him they would not have come into the world, because he was the peacemaker between husband and wife. When [after being reconciled] they were united, they would name the child who was born after him. [23a]

Others say that for this reason it is stated, *And they wept for*

(4) Num. XX, 29. (5) The usual and literal connotation of the phrase is: 'he judged a judgment of truth according to its truth', i.e. he dealt out justice strictly and in all its severity. This quality, however, is inapplicable to Aaron in this context where he is described as overlooking faults. In the parallel passage in the Yalḳuṭ on the verse in Num. *ibid.*, this phrase is descriptive of Moses and not of Aaron; consequently the commentators have resorted to emendation here in order to make the passages correspond (cf. GRA and the Glosses of J. Bachrach). The translation given in the text retains the original reading and is to be interpreted: he regarded every matter in the light of truth, i.e. he considered every person's action as right (he 'gave him right'), or at least endeavoured to see justification in every person's action, taking a favourable view of it. Cf. the expression in Aboth I, 6, 'Judge all men in the scale of merit'.

Aaron thirty days, even all the house of Israel—because who could look upon Moses our teacher sitting and weeping and himself not weep? Others express it in this way: Who could look upon Eleazar and Phinehas,[7] the two High Priests, standing and weeping and himself not weep?

At that time Moses wished to die in the same manner as Aaron had died; because he saw Aaron's couch arrayed in great splendour, and hosts of ministering angels lamenting him. Did Moses express this desire in the hearing of another person? No, he only expressed the wish to himself and the Holy One, blessed be He, heard his whisper [and granted his wish,] as it is stated, *And die in the mount whither thou goest up, and be gathered unto thy people; as Aaron thy brother died in mount Hor.*[8] From this you may infer that Moses wished to die the same death as Aaron.

At that hour [when Moses was to die], He said to the angel of death, 'Go and bring Me the soul of Moses'. The angel of death went and stood before him and said, 'Moses, deliver your soul to me'. Moses rebuked him saying, 'In the place where I am seated you have not the right to stand,[9] yet you say to me, "Deliver your soul to me"'. He rebuked him and drove him away in anger. At length the Holy One, blessed be He, [intervened and] said to Moses, 'Moses, you have had enough of this world; the world to come awaits you since the six days of creation', as it is stated, *And the Lord said: Behold there is a place by Me, and thou shalt stand upon the rock.*[10] The Holy One, blessed be He, took the soul of Moses and stored it under the Throne of Glory, as it is stated, *The soul of my lord shall be bound in the bundle of life with the Lord thy God.*[11] When He took his soul it was with a kiss, as it is stated, *By the mouth of the Lord.*[12]

Not only the soul of Moses is stored under the Throne of Glory but the souls of the righteous are also stored there, as it is stated, *The soul of my lord shall be bound in the bundle of life with*

(6) Deut. XXXIV, 8. (7) The son and grandson of Aaron respectively. (8) Deut. XXXII, 50. (9) For Moses was engaged in the study of the Torah, and the angel of death cannot approach one who is so engaged; cf. Shab. 30b (Sonc. ed., p. 134). (10) Ex. XXXIII, 21. (11) 1 Sam. XXV, 29. (12) Deut. XXXIV, 5. So lit.; E.V., *according to the word of the Lord.*

the Lord thy God. It is possible [to think that] it is the same with the souls of the wicked; therefore Scripture declares, *And the souls of thine enemies, them shall He sling out as from the hollow of a sling.*[13] To what may this be compared? To a man who took a stone and placed it in a sling; though he hurls it from place to place he knows not where it will come to rest. Similarly, the souls of the wicked are held fast [as in a vice],[14] and driven about aimlessly in the world, knowing not whereon to rest.

Again said He to the angel of death, 'Go and bring Me the soul of Moses'. He went and searched for him in his usual place but could not find him. He went to the Great Sea and asked, 'Has Moses been here?' The Sea replied, 'Since the day Israel passed through me I have not seen him'. He went to the mountains and hills and asked, 'Has Moses been here?' They replied, 'Since the day Israel received the Torah on Mount Sinai we have not seen him'. He then went to Sheol and Abaddon[15] and asked, 'Has Moses been here?' They replied, 'We have heard his name but have not seen him'. He went to the ministering angels and asked, 'Has Moses been here?' They replied, '*God understandeth his way, and He knoweth his place.*[16] God has hidden him away for life in the world to come, and no creature knows his whereabouts', as it is stated, *But wisdom, where shall it be found? And where is the place of understanding? Man knoweth not the price thereof; neither is it found in the land of the living. The deep saith: It is not in me; and the sea saith: It is not with me.*[17] *Destruction and Death say: We have heard a rumour thereof with our ears.*[18] Joshua also was sitting and grieving over Moses, because he did not know where he was, until the Holy One, blessed be He, said to him, 'Joshua, why do you grieve for Moses? *Moses My servant is dead*'.[19]

5. PURSUING PEACE. What does this mean? It teaches that a man should pursue peace in Israel among all men in the same

(13) I Sam. *ibid.* (14) lit. 'muzzled'; cf. Shab. 152b (Sonc. ed., p. 779) and Rashi's comment *ad loc.* (15) lit. '[place of] Destruction'; used in the Bible as a term for Sheol (Job XXVI, 6) death (*ibid.* XXVIII, 22) and the grave (Ps. LXXXVIII, 12). (16) Job XXVIII, 23, E.V., *the way thereof . . . the place thereof.* (17) *ibid.* 12-14. The passage is related to Moses who possessed the wisdom of the Torah. (18) *ibid.* 22. (19) Josh. I, 2.

way that Aaron pursued peace in Israel among all men; as it is stated, *Depart from evil, and do good; seek peace, and pursue it.*[20] R. Simeon b. Eleazar said: If a man stays at home in quietude, how can he pursue peace in Israel among all men? He should rather leave his home and go about the world so that he can pursue peace in Israel, as it is stated, *Seek peace, and pursue it*: meaning *seek peace* in your own place, *and pursue it* by going elsewhere.

Even the Holy One, blessed be He, made peace on high.[21] What manner of peace did He make on high? By not naming ten [angels] 'Gabriel', ten 'Michael', ten 'Uriel', or ten 'Raphael', after the manner of men who name ten [persons] 'Reuben', ten 'Simeon', ten 'Levi', or ten 'Judah'. Had He done as men do, on summoning one [angel, all bearing that name] would come before Him and they would be envious of one another. He therefore named one [angel] 'Gabriel' and one 'Michael', so that when He summons an angel [by name] only one appears before Him and is sent wherever He wishes. And whence do we know that [the angels] reverence one another, respect one another, and are more humble than human beings? When they are about to open their mouths to sing hymns, one says to the other, 'You begin, for you are greater than I'; and the other replies, 'No, you begin, for you are greater than I'. This is quite unlike the behaviour of human beings, everyone saying to his fellow, 'I am greater than you'. According to another view [the courteous remarks are made by] groups of angels, one group saying to the other, 'You begin, for you are greater than we'; as it is stated, *And one called unto another, and said.*[22]

6. LOVING MANKIND. What does this mean? It teaches that a man should love his fellow-creatures and not hate them; for so we find it among the men of the generation of the Dispersion. Since they loved one another,[23] the Holy One, blessed be He, did not wish to destroy them, but dispersed

(20) Ps. XXXIV, 15. (21) Cf. Job XXV, 2. (22) Is. VI, 3 where the reference is to groups of seraphim. (23) This is inferred from the statement that they were *of one language and of one speech* (Gen. XI, 1).

them to the four corners of the earth.[24] Because the men of Sodom, on the other hand, hated one another, the Holy One, blessed be He, destroyed them from this world and the world to come; as it is stated, *The men of Sodom were wicked and sinners against the Lord exceedingly.*[25] [*Wicked* signifies that they hated one another;][26] *sinners,* that they offended against morality; *against the Lord,* that they profaned the Name; *exceedingly,* that they sinned with premeditation. Hence you learn that because they hated one another, the Holy One, blessed be He, destroyed them from this world and from the world to come.

7. AND BRINGING THEM NEAR TO THE TORAH. What does this mean? It teaches that a man should prevail upon his fellows and bring them beneath the wings of the Divine Presence, as our father Abraham used to prevail upon men and bring them beneath the wings of the Divine Presence. Not only Abraham did this, but also Sarah, as it is stated, *And Abram took Sarai his wife, and Lot his brother's son, and all their substance that they had gathered, and the souls that they had made in Haran.*[27] Is it not a fact that all mankind cannot create even a gnat? How, then, can Scripture declare, *And the souls that they had made in Haran!* It teaches that the Holy One, blessed be He, accounted it to them as though they had created them.

[28] Just as a man does not share his fellow's reward in this world, so a man does not share his fellow's reward in the world to come; as it is stated, *And behold the tears of such as were oppressed, and they had no comforter; and on the side of their oppressors there was power, but they had no comforter.*[29] Why does the verse repeat *they had no comforter?* It speaks of those men who in this world eat and drink and are fortunate in their sons and daughters, but in the world to come have nothing[30] and are without a comforter. In this world, if a man has been robbed or suffered a bereavement, his sons, brothers and kinsmen come to com-

(24) *ibid.* 8. (25) *ibid.* XIII, 13. (26) Inserted by GRA; it is also found in all the parallel passages. (27) *ibid.* XII, 5; so lit.; E.V., *had gotten in Haran.* [Midrash Rabbah, Genesis, XXXIX, 14 (Sonc. ed., p. 324) explains it of the proselytes made by Abraham and Sarah.] (28) This paragraph is clearly out of place here; it is inserted by GRA after the first sentence in the paragraph which follows. (29) Eccl. IV, 1.

fort him. It is possible [to imagine] that it is the same in the world to come; therefore Scripture declares, *He hath neither son nor brother.*[31] Similarly, if a man sins and begets an illegitimate child, they say to him, 'Fool that you are! You have harmed yourself and also the child'. For that illegitimate son may be desirous of studying Torah together with the scholars who sit and study in Jerusalem. He joins their company until they reach Ashdod; there he halts and cries, 'Woe is me! Had I not been of illegitimate birth, I should now be studying with those who were hitherto my fellow-students; but being illegitimate I may not sit and study with them because an illegitimate is not allowed to enter Jerusalem; as it is stated, *And a bastard shall dwell in Ashdod, and I will cut off the pride of the Philistines.*[32]

8. HE USED TO SAY: IF I AM NOT FOR MYSELF, WHO IS FOR ME? If I do not win merit for myself in my lifetime, who will do so for me?[33] AND IF I AM ONLY FOR MYSELF, WHAT AM I? If I have won merit for myself alone, what have I achieved?[34] AND IF NOT NOW, WHEN? If I do not win merit for myself in my lifetime, who will do so for me after my death? As Scripture declares, *For a living dog is better than a dead lion.*[35] *A living dog is better* refers to a wicked man while he exists in this world;[36] *than a dead lion* refers to the patriarchs Abraham, Isaac and Jacob who sleep in the dust.[37]

Another interpretation: *A living dog is better* refers to a wicked man while he exists in this world, because if he repents the Holy One, blessed be He, receives him; whereas a righteous man, once dead, cannot add to his merits.

9. He used to say: If you will come to my house I will go to yours. Wheresoever my heart desires [to go] there my feet lead me.[38]

(30) Because they did not live a good life but a life of self-centred pleasure. (31) *ibid.* 8. (32) Zech. IX, 6. (33) According to GRA the preceding paragraph should follow here. (34) V reads 'If I do not win merit for myself, who will do so for me?' This cannot be correct because it merely repeats the preceding sentence. The translation in the text is based on a suggestion by Schechter *ad loc.* (35) Eccl. IX, 4. (36) Because as long as he is alive there is hope that he may repent. (37) And all their achievements have come to an end. (38) Quoted as a saying of Hillel in Suk. 53a (Sonc. ed., p. 253).

'If you will come to my house I will go to yours.' What does this mean? It refers to the persons who are found in the Synagogues and Houses of Study early in the morning and late at night. The Holy One, blessed be He, will bless them in the world to come, in accordance with what is stated, *In every place where I cause My name to be mentioned I will come unto thee and bless thee.*[39]

'Wheresoever my heart desires [to go] there my feet lead me.' What does this mean? It refers to the persons who leave their silver and gold behind and go up [to Jerusalem] for the Festival to appear before the Divine Presence in the Temple. The Holy One, blessed be He, stands on guard for them in the midst of their homesteads, as it is stated, *Neither shall any man covet thy land, when thou goest up to appear before the Lord thy God.*[40]

10. He used to say: If I am here, all are here; if I am not here, who is here?[41] Turn it[42] and turn it again, for everything [23*b*] is in it. And with regard to all things [the rule applies]: according to the labour so is the reward.[43]

11. The story is told of Hillel the Elder that he was walking along the road when he met some men carrying wheat. He asked them, 'How much a *se'ah?*' They replied, 'Two *dinars*'. Later he met other men [carrying wheat] and he asked them, 'How much a *se'ah?*' They replied, 'Three *dinars.*' He said to them, 'But those who were in front of you only asked two *dinars*'. They rejoined, 'You stupid Babylonian, do you not know the rule: according to the labour so is the reward?'[44] He said to them, 'You foolish and empty-headed persons! Because I ask you [a civil question], do you answer me [rudely]?' Nevertheless Hillel the Elder so affected them that he turned them on to the good path.

(39) Ex. XX, 21. (40) *ibid.* XXXIV, 24. (41) A continuation of the passage quoted from Suk. 53a. (42) The Torah. (43) The last two maxims are quoted from Aboth V (end) in the names of Ben Bag Bag and Ben He He respectively, who were reputed to have been Hillel's disciples. [In Ḳid. 10b (Sonc. ed., p. 40) the full name appears as Joḥanan b. Bag Bag. Some scholars interpret 'Bag' as an abbreviation of 'Ben Ger' (son of a proselyte) and conjecture that 'Bag' and 'He' are identical, the numerical value of BG, being five, indicated by the letter *he*.] (44) Since the latter had brought the wheat from a longer distance their charge was higher.

MOREOVER, HE SAW A SKULL FLOATING ON THE SURFACE OF THE WATER; HE SAID TO IT, 'BECAUSE YOU DROWNED OTHERS THEY DROWNED YOU, AND THEY THAT DROWNED YOU WILL THEMSELVES BE DROWNED'.[45]

13. He also said the following four [aphorisms] in Aramaic: WHOSOEVER MAKES GREAT HIS NAME LOSES HIS NAME; HE WHO DOES NOT WAIT UPON SCHOLARS DESERVES DEATH; HE WHO DOES NOT INCREASE HIS KNOWLEDGE LOSES WHAT HE HAS; AND HE WHO MAKES USE OF THE CROWN WILL PASS AWAY AND PERISH.[46]

WHOEVER MAKES GREAT HIS NAME LOSES HIS NAME. What does this mean? It teaches that a man should not spread abroad of himself a reputation [for wealth] in the kingdom, because if he does so, before long the authorities will cast their eyes upon him, kill him, and confiscate his wealth.[47]

HE WHO DOES NOT WAIT UPON SCHOLARS DESERVES DEATH. What does it mean? The story is told of a certain man of Beth-Ramah[48] who used to conduct himself in the strictest piety, that Rabban Joḥanan b. Zakkai once sent a disciple to him to test him in his conduct.[49] When he arrived, he found that the man took some oil and set it on the oven-range [to be warmed], then he removed it from the range and poured it into a dish of crushed beans. On being asked what he was doing, the man replied, 'I am a High Priest[50] and I always eat *terumah* in conditions of cleanness'. 'Is this oven-range clean or unclean?' [the disciple] asked him, and he answered, 'Is it ever mentioned in the Torah about an oven-range being

(45) Quoted from a maxim of Hillel in Aboth II, 7 (Sonc. ed., II, 6, p. 16). It is in Aramaic, not Hebrew. (46) A quotation from Aboth I, 13, with variants, the most important being in the third saying which reads in the Mishnaic version, 'he who does not study deserves death'. [The version given here, 'he who does not wait', etc., occurs in Nazir VII, 1, 56b, where it is attributed to R. 'Aḳiba.] (47) Cf. XI, 3, above, p. 68. (48) The modern Beit Rima, about 20 miles north-west of Jerusalem. (49) Since, as stated later, the man was the High Priest, who generally belonged to the Sadducean party, Rabban Joḥanan investigated a report that he followed Pharasaic teaching and practice (cf. Finkelstein, *op. cit.*, pp. 152f). (50) Not necessarily the High Priest in office at the time, but who had served at one time in that office and had therefore retained the title.

unclean? Surely the Torah speaks only of a common oven as being unclean; as it is stated, *Whatsoever is in it shall be unclean'*.[51] The other retorted, 'Just as the Torah speaks of a common oven as being unclean, so it likewise speaks of an oven-range as being unclean; for it is stated, *Whether oven, or range for pots, it shall be broken in pieces; they are unclean'*.[52] He added, 'If that is what you were accustomed to do, you have never eaten clean *terumah* in your life'.

HE WHO DOES NOT INCREASE HIS KNOWLEDGE LOSES WHAT HE HAS. What does it mean? It teaches that if a man has studied one tractate, or even two or three tractates, and does not add anything thereto, eventually he will forget what he learnt in the beginning.

AND HE WHO MAKES USE OF THE CROWN WILL PASS AWAY AND PERISH. What does this mean? It teaches that he who makes use of the Expressed Name[53] has no portion in the world to come.

(51) Lev. XI, 33, where the reference is to an *earthen vessel.* (52) *ibid.* 35. (53) Generally identified with the Tetragrammaton, and synonymous with the 'Unique Name'. It was commonly held that by pronouncing the Name of God as it is written, one could work miracles, and Hillel's saying is interpreted as a warning against the practice.

CHAPTER XIII

1. SHAMMAI SAID: MAKE YOUR STUDY OF THE TORAH A FIXED HABIT; SAY LITTLE AND DO MUCH; AND RECEIVE ALL MEN WITH A CHEERFUL COUNTENANCE.

2. MAKE YOUR STUDY OF THE TORAH A FIXED HABIT. What does this mean? It teaches that if a man hears a theme from a Sage in the House of Study, he should not treat it as something casual, but should regard it as a fixed norm. Moreover, what a man learns he should perform and teach to others that they, too, may perform it; as it is stated, *That ye may learn them, and observe to do them.*[1] It similarly states of Ezra, *For Ezra had set his heart to seek the law of the Lord, and to do it,*[2] the verse continuing, *And to teach in Israel statutes and ordinances.*

3. SAY LITTLE AND DO MUCH. What does this mean? It teaches that the righteous say little and do much, whereas the wicked say much and do not even a little. Whence do we know that the righteous say little and do much? We find it so with Abraham our father who said to the angels, 'You will eat with me to-day a morsel of bread'; as it is stated, *And I will fetch a morsel of bread, and stay ye your heart.*[3] But in the end, see how much Abraham prepared for the ministering angels—he went and prepared for them three oxen and nine measures of fine flour! Whence do we know that he prepared for them nine measures of fine flour? For it is stated, *And Abraham hastened into the tent unto Sarah, and said: Make ready quickly three measures of fine meal.*[4] Now the word *three* signifies literally what it says; *fine* also implies three making six; and *meal* implies a further three, making nine in all. And whence do we know that he prepared for them three oxen? For it is stated, *And Abraham ran unto the herd and fetched a calf tender [and good].*[5] Now the word *herd* implies one, *calf* implies another making two, and *tender* implies a third, thus making three in all. Some say that

(1) Deut. V, 1. (2) Ezra VII, 10. (3) Gen. XVIII, 5. (4) *ibid.* 6. (5) *ibid.* 7.

the word *good* implies a fourth. *And he gave them unto the servant, and he hastened to dress them:*[6] he gave them to his son Ishmael in order to train him in the performance of good deeds.

The Holy One, blessed be He, likewise said little and did much; as it is stated, *And He said unto Abram: Know of a surety that thy seed shall be a stranger in a land that is not theirs, and shall serve them; and they shall afflict them four hundred years; and also that nation whom they shall serve, will I judge; and afterward shall they come out with great substance.*[7] [In His announcement] He only used a word of two letters, *daleth* and *nun*; eventually when the Holy One, blessed be He, inflicted punishment upon the enemies of Israel, He did so with seventy-two letters; as it is stated, *Or hath God assayed to go and take Him a nation from the midst of another nation, by trials, by signs, and by wonders, and by war, and by a mighty hand, and by an outstretched arm, and by great terrors?*[8] Hence you learn that when He inflicted punishment upon Israel's enemies He only did so with seventy-two letters.

And whence do we know that the wicked say much and do not even a little? We find it so with Ephron who said to Abraham, *A piece of land worth four hundred shekels of silver,* [*what is that betwixt me and thee*]*?*[9] Eventually when Abraham weighed out the silver for him, it is stated, *And Abraham hearkened unto Ephron; and Abraham weighed to Ephron the silver . . .* [*current money with the merchant*].[10]

4. AND RECEIVE ALL MEN WITH A CHEERFUL COUNTENANCE. What does this mean? It teaches that if a man presents the most precious gifts in the world to his fellow but gives them with a sullen countenance, Scripture regards him as having

(6) *ibid.* E.V., *gave it . . . dress it.* (7) *ibid.* XV, 13f. The Heb. for *judge* is *dan*, a word of only two letters. (8) Deut. IV, 34. There are 75 letters in the Heb. text quoted, beginning with *to go*. The Midrash Rabbah, Leviticus, XXIII, §2 (Sonc. ed., p. 293) and Song of Songs II, §2 (Sonc. ed., p. 95), suggests that the second *nation*, a word of three letters in Heb. (*goï*), should be omitted from the enumeration. The virtue of the number 72 lies in the fact that one of the sacred Names consists of 72 letters. (9) Gen. XXIII, 15. This verse suggests that the land is of so little value that it is unworthy of their further discussion. (10) *ibid.* 16. Ephron insisted upon the fullest value of the money although at first he regarded the transaction as of little significance.

presented him with nothing. On the other hand, he who receives his fellow with a cheerful countenance, though he give him nothing, Scripture accounts it to him as though he had presented him with the most precious gifts in the world.

CHAPTER XIV

1. RABBAN JOḤANAN B. ZAKKAI RECEIVED THE TRADITION FROM HILLEL AND SHAMMAI.

Hillel the Elder had eighty disciples:[1] thirty of them were worthy that the Divine Presence should rest upon them as upon Moses our teacher, but their generation was not worthy of it; thirty of them were worthy that the intercalation of the years[2] should be determined by them; and twenty were average. The greatest of them all was Jonathan b. 'Uzziel,[3] and the least of them all was Rabban Joḥanan b. Zakkai. It was said of Rabban Joḥanan b. Zakkai that he mastered[4] Scripture, Mishnah, Gemara, *halakoth, 'aggadoth, toseftoth,* the minutiae[5] of the Torah, the minutiae of the Scribes, and all the hermeneutical rules of the Sages. Not a word in the Torah did he not master, fulfilling the text, *That I may cause those that love me to inherit substance, and that I may fill their treasuries.*[6]

2. HE USED TO SAY: IF YOU HAVE OBSERVED[7] MUCH TORAH CLAIM NO MERIT FOR YOURSELF, FOR TO THIS END YOU WERE CREATED; inasmuch as human beings were created solely for the purpose of occupying themselves with the Torah.

3. Rabban Joḥanan b. Zakkai had five disciples whom he described in these terms: Eliezer b. Hyrḳanos as 'a cemented cistern that loses not a drop' and 'a glazed pitcher that preserves its wine'; Joshua b. Ḥananiah as '*a threefold cord that is not quickly broken*';[8] Jose [24*a*] the priest as 'the saint of the generation';

(1) Cf. the parallel passage in Suk. 28a (Sonc. ed., p. 123) and B.B. 134a (Sonc. ed., p. 563). (2) The calculations were made only by the leading members of the Sanhedrin. (3) [Meg. 3a (Sonc. ed., p. 9) names him as the author of an Aramaic translation of the Prophets. The extant Targum is not by him.] (4) lit. 'he had not left (unstudied)'. (5) The subtle points of exposition. (6) Prov. VIII, 21. (7) In Aboth II, 9 (Sonc. ed., II, 8, p. 17) 'learnt'. (8) Eccl. IV, 12. This is no doubt intended as alluding to three virtues of Joshua b. Ḥananiah, but they are not specified.

Ishmael b. Ḥananiah[9] as 'an oasis[10] in the desert which retains its waters'. Happy the disciple whose teacher acknowledges and describes him [in such terms]! Eleazar b. 'Arak he described as 'a swift-running stream and a vigorous fountain whose waters increase and overflow abroad', thus fulfilling the verse, *Let thy springs be dispersed abroad, and courses of water in the streets.*[11]

4. HE USED TO SAY: IF ALL THE SAGES OF ISRAEL WERE IN ONE SCALE OF THE BALANCE AND R. ELIEZER B. HYRḲANOS IN THE OTHER, HE WOULD OUTWEIGH THEM ALL. ABBA SAUL SAID IN HIS NAME: IF ALL THE SAGES OF ISRAEL WERE IN ONE SCALE OF THE BALANCE, INCLUDING R. ELIEZER B. HYRḲANOS, AND R. ELEAZAR B. 'ARAK WAS IN THE OTHER, HE WOULD OUTWEIGH THEM ALL.

5. HE SAID TO THEM: GO FORTH AND SEE WHICH IS THE GOOD WAY TO WHICH A MAN SHOULD CLEAVE so that thereby he may enter the world to come. R. ELIEZER came forward, and SAID: A GOOD EYE.[12] R. JOSHUA came forward and SAID: A GOOD FRIEND.[13] R. JOSE came forward and SAID: A GOOD NEIGHBOUR,[14] a good impulse and a good wife. R. SIMEON SAID: ONE WHO FORESEES THE CONSEQUENCES OF AN ACTION.[15] R. ELEAZAR came forward and SAID: A HEART THAT IS GOOD[16] towards Heaven and is good towards [all] creatures. THEREUPON HE SAID TO THEM: I PREFER THE WORDS OF R. ELEAZAR B. 'ARAK TO YOUR WORDS, BECAUSE IN HIS WORDS YOURS ARE INCLUDED.

HE THEN SAID TO THEM: GO FORTH AND SEE WHICH IS THE EVIL WAY THAT A MAN SHOULD SHUN so that he may enter the world to come. R. ELIEZER came forward and

(9) In conformity with Aboth II, 10 (Sonc. ed. II, 8, p. 18) GRA emends to 'Simeon b. Nathaniel'. This paragraph corresponds to Aboth II, 10f, but with several variants. (10) A doubtful word; some emend it to *'arugah*, 'a garden bed' or 'grove', a term applied to a scholar in DEZ I, p. 567 below. (11) Prov. V, 16. (12) Denoting generosity, freedom from envy which is termed 'an evil eye'. (13) Indicating the quality of friendliness. (14) Implies sympathy and goodwill. 'A good impulse', etc., is omitted in Aboth II, 13 (Sonc. ed., II, 9, p. 19). (15) The virtue of foresight and prudence. V inserts in brackets, 'As, for instance, Mordecai the Jew who foresaw the consequences of an action'. (16) i.e. unselfishness.

SAID: AN EVIL EYE. R. JOSHUA came forward and SAID: AN EVIL FRIEND. R. JOSE came forward and SAID: AN EVIL NEIGHBOUR, an evil impulse and a bad wife.[17] R. SIMEON came forward and SAID: ONE WHO BORROWS AND DOES NOT REPAY, SINCE HE WHO BORROWS FROM MAN IS AS ONE WHO BORROWS FROM THE ALL-PRESENT, as it is stated, *The wicked borroweth, and payeth not; but the righteous dealeth graciously, and giveth.*[18] R. ELEAZAR came forward and SAID: A HEART THAT IS EVIL towards Heaven and is evil towards [all] creatures. THEREUPON HE SAID TO THEM: I PREFER THE WORDS OF R. ELEAZAR B. 'ARAK TO YOUR WORDS, BECAUSE IN HIS WORDS YOURS ARE INCLUDED.

6. When the son of Rabban Joḥanan b. Zakkai died, his disciples came in to console him. R. Eliezer came and sat before him and said, 'My master, is it your wish that I say a word in your presence?' He replied to him, 'Speak'. Thereupon he said, 'Adam, the first man, had a son who died, and he allowed himself to be comforted in his loss. And whence do we know that he accepted condolence? For it is stated, *And Adam knew his wife again.*[19] Therefore do you also accept condolence'. He retorted, 'Is it not sufficient for me to bear my own grief that you have to mention Adam's grief?' Then R. Joshua[20] entered and said, 'My master, is it your wish that I say a word in your presence?' He replied to him 'Speak'. Thereupon he said, 'Job had sons and daughters who all died in one day and he allowed himself to be comforted; you too accept condolence. And whence do we know that Job accepted condolences? For it is stated, *The Lord gave, and the Lord hath taken away; blessed be the name of the Lord.*[21] He retorted, 'Is it not sufficient for me to bear my own grief that you have to mention Job's grief?' Next R. Jose entered, sat before him and said, 'My master, is

(17) So according to GRA, giving the reverse of R. Jose's previous statement. V reads, 'An evil eye, an evil neighbour, and an evil wife'. (18) Ps. XXXVII, 21. (19) Gen. IV, 25. (20) 'One must assume that the disciples came in one by one, each ignorant that his line of approach had been previously tried without success. Joḥanan's irritation must have increased with each successive attempt' (Montefiore and Loewe, *Rabbinic Anthology*, p. 672). (21) Job I, 21.

it your wish that I say a word in your presence?' He replied, 'Speak'. Thereupon he said, 'Aaron had two grown sons and both died in one day, yet he allowed himself to be comforted, as it is stated, *And Aaron held his peace,*[22] the phrase *held his peace* implying that he accepted condolence. Therefore do you also accept condolence'. He retorted, 'Is it not sufficient for me to bear my own grief that you have to mention Aaron's grief?' Then R. Simeon entered and said, 'My master, is it your wish that I say a word in your presence?' He replied, 'Speak'. Thereupon he said, 'King David had a son who died, and he allowed himself to be comforted; do you also accept condolence. And whence do we know that David accepted condolence? For it is stated, *And David comforted Bathsheba his wife, and went in unto her; and she bore a son, and called his name Solomon.*[23] Therefore do you also accept condolence'. He retorted, 'Is it not sufficient for me to bear my own grief that you have to mention King David's grief?' Finally R. Eleazar b. 'Arak[24] entered. When [Rabban Joḥanan saw him approaching] he said to his attendant, 'Take my clothes and follow me to the bath-house, because this man is distinguished and I cannot appear before him as I am'.[25] Then R. Eleazar came in and sat before him and said. 'Let me tell you a parable. To what is the matter like? To a man with whom a king had deposited an article of value. Daily the man wept and exclaimed, "Woe is me! when will I be free from the responsibility of this trust?" You, too, my master, had a son versed in the Torah, who had studied the Pentateuch,[26] Prophets and Hagiographa, Mishnah, *halakoth* and *'aggadoth*. He has departed sinless from this world. Surely you should derive comfort from having returned your trust intact!' Rabban Joḥanan said to him, 'Eleazar my son, you have comforted me as men can comfort'.[27]

When they left his presence, R. Eleazar said [to his col-

(22) Lev. X, 3. (23) 2 Sam. XII, 24. (24) In V the name is incorrectly printed as 'R. Eleazar b. Azariah'. (25) i.e. in the clothes of a mourner. (26) The usual connotation of this word, מקרא, is 'Scripture', but in this context the Pentateuch is intended. (27) i.e. as far as lies within the power of human beings to comfort.

leagues], 'I will go to Dimsith,[28] a delectable spot with excellent and refreshing waters'. The others said, 'We will go to Jabneh,[29] a place abounding with scholars and lovers of Torah'. Because he went to Dimsith, a delectable spot with excellent and refreshing waters, his fame in the Torah waned;[30] whereas they who went to Jabneh, a place abounding with scholars and lovers of the Torah, their renown in Torah increased.

(28) In Shab. 147b (Sonc. ed., pp. 749f) the name is given as Diomsith which Jastrow identified with Emmaus, a town in the plain of Judah renowned in Talmudic days for its warm springs and luxurious life. [On this passage, cf. Bacher, *Ag. d. Tannaiten*, I, p. 71, n. 3, who thinks that Tiberias is meant.] (29) Or Jamnia, a town north-west of Jerusalem, near the coast, the seat of the Sanhedrin after the destruction of Jerusalem. (30) Cf. Shab. *loc. cit.* (Sonc. ed., p. 750).

CHAPTER XV

1. THEY EACH SAID THREE THINGS. R. ELIEZER SAID: LET THE HONOUR OF YOUR FELLOW BE DEAR TO YOU AS YOUR OWN; BE NOT EASILY MOVED TO ANGER; REPENT ONE DAY BEFORE YOUR DEATH.

LET THE HONOUR OF YOUR FELLOW BE DEAR TO YOU AS YOUR OWN. What does this mean? It teaches that as a man regards his own honour, so should he regard the honour of his fellow; and as a man would not wish to see an ill report spread about his own honour, so should he not wish to see an ill report spread about the honour of his fellow.

Another interpretation of LET THE HONOUR OF YOUR FELLOW BE DEAR TO YOU AS YOUR OWN: Thus if a man once possessed a million and is now deprived of all his wealth, he should not lose his self-respect even to the slightest degree.[1]

2. BE NOT EASILY MOVED TO ANGER. What does this mean? It teaches that a man should be meek like Hillel the Elder and not impatient like Shammai the Elder.

What was the meekness of Hillel the Elder? It is related[2] that two men once wagered with each other the sum of four hundred *zuz*, saying, 'Whoever will succeed in provoking Hillel to anger will take the four hundred *zuz*'. One of them went [to call on Hillel]. The day was the eve of the Sabbath towards dusk, and Hillel was then washing his head. He came, knocked at the door, and called out, 'Where is Hillel? Where is Hillel?' Hillel wrapped himself in his robe and went to him, asking, 'My son, what do you require?' 'I have a question to ask,' he said. 'Ask it,' said Hillel. Thereupon he

(1) lit., 'to the value of a *peruṭah*'. Though he is destitute his self-esteem should remain high; cf. Sanh. 92b (Sonc. ed., p. 621): 'Even in times of danger one should not lay aside his insignia of office'. Honour is a precious possession. (2) Cf. Shab. 31a (Sonc. ed., pp. 138ff) for variants of this passage.

asked, 'Why are the inhabitants of Palmyra bleary-eyed?' He answered, 'Because they live in sandy deserts, and the winds scatter the sand over their eyes; for that reason their eyes are bleary'. The man departed, waited a while, returned, again knocked at the door, and called out, 'Where is Hillel? Where is Hillel?' Hillel wrapped himself in his robe and went out to him, asking, 'My son, what do you require?' 'I have a question[3] to ask,' he said. 'Ask it,' said Hillel. Thereupon he asked, 'Why have the Africans flat feet?' He answered, 'Because they live in marshy places and constantly walk in the water;[4] for that reason their feet are flat'. The man departed, waited a while, returned, again knocked at the door and called out, 'Where is Hillel? Where is Hillel?' He wrapped himself in his robe, and went out to him, asking, 'What do you wish to ask?' 'I have a question to ask,' he said. 'Ask it,' said Hillel. The man then wrapped himself in his cloak and sat down before him. 'What do you wish to ask?' said Hillel. The other rejoined, 'Is that the manner in which a President[5] replies? May there not be many like you in Israel!' 'Heaven forfend!' exclaimed Hillel, 'mind your temper. What is it you require?' He asked, 'Why have the Babylonians long heads?'[6] He answered, 'My son, you have asked an important question. Because they lack skilful midwives there, as soon as a child is born it is placed in the arms[7] of male and female slaves; for that reason their heads are long. Here [in the Holy Land] there are expert midwives, and as soon as a child is born it is placed in a cot and its head is massaged; for that reason their heads are round'. Then said the man to him, 'Through you I have lost four hundred *zuz*'. Hillel retorted, 'Hillel is worthy that you should lose [twice] four hundred *zuz* on his account, and Hillel should not lose his temper'.

3. What was the impatience of Shammai the Elder? It is related

(3) The Heb. *halakah,* the term for a legal decision, cannot have this meaning here. (4) They therefore walk barefoot, and so their feet are broad because of not having been cramped by shoe or sandal. (5) The Heb. is in the plural, referring to the Presidents of the Sanhedrin. (6) An insulting remark since Babylon was Hillel's birthplace. (7) The Heb. is *'ebarim,* 'limbs', a peculiar word in the context. A variant is *ḥeḳ,* 'bosom'.

that a man[8] once came and stood before Shammai and said to him, 'Master, how many Torahs have you?' He answered, 'Two, one written and one oral'. The man said, 'I believe you regarding the written, but I do not believe you regarding the oral'. Shammai rebuked him and [24*b*] angrily drove him away. The man then came before Hillel and asked, 'Master, how many Torahs were given [to Israel]'. He answered, 'Two, one written and one oral'. He said, 'I believe you regarding the written, but I do not believe you regarding the oral'. Hillel said to him, 'My son, take a seat'. He then wrote the alphabet for him. Hillel asked him, 'What is this letter?'[9] 'An *alef*,' he replied. Hillel said, 'It is not an *alef* but a *beth*'. He asked, 'And what is this letter?'[10] 'A *beth*,' he replied. Hillel said, 'It is not a *beth* but a *gimel*'. 'Moreover, how do you know that this letter is *alef*, that *beth*, and the other *gimel?*' continued Hillel. He replied, 'So it has been handed down to us by our forebears: this is *alef*, that *beth*, and the other *gimel*'. 'Just as you have accepted this[11] on trust, so accept the other[12] on trust.'

Once a gentile was passing behind a Synagogue when he heard a child reciting the verse, *And these are the garments which they shall make: a breastplate, and an ephod, and a robe.*[13] He came to Shammai and asked him, 'Master, for whom is all that finery?' He answered, 'For the High Priest who stands and ministers at the altar'. The gentile said to him, 'Make me a proselyte on condition that you appoint me High Priest'. Shammai retorted, 'Is there no priest in Israel and have we no High Priests in Israel to serve in the High-priesthood, except this insignificant proselyte who comes with staff and scrip only and wishes to minister as High Priest?' He rebuked him and angrily drove him away. The gentile then came to Hillel and said to him, 'Master, make me a proselyte on condition that you appoint me High Priest, so that I may stand and minister at the altar'. Hillel said to him, 'Take a seat, and I will tell you something. If a man wishes to have an audience of a

(8) In Shab., *loc. cit.*, he was 'a Gentile', but in the context a Jew is clearly intended. (9) Pointing to an *alef*. (10) Pointing to a *beth*. (11) The letters of the alphabet. (12) The existence of two Torahs. (13) Ex. XXVIII, 4.

human king, is it not proper for him to learn how to make his entrance and his exit?' 'Certainly,' answered the gentile. Hillel continued, 'As you are desirous to have an audience of the King of kings, the Holy One, blessed be He, is it not all the more incumbent upon you to learn how to enter the Holy of Holies, how to trim the lamps, how to approach the altar, how to order the table, how to arrange the altar-pile?' 'Do whatever seems good to you,' said the gentile. Hillel then wrote the alphabet for him which he soon learnt, and then [he studied] the Book of Leviticus. So he continued until he reached the verse, *And the common man that draweth nigh shall be put to death.*[14] Then the proselyte reasoned within himself thus, 'If Israelites who are designated sons of the All-present,[15] of whom the Divine Presence declares, *Ye shall be unto Me a kingdom of priests, and a holy nation,*[16] are warned by Scripture, *And the common man that draweth nigh shall be put to death,* how much more so does it apply to me, an insignificant proselyte, who am come with nothing but my scrip!' In this manner the proselyte was reconciled of his own accord. He came to Hillel the Elder and said to him, 'May all the blessings of the Torah alight on your head! Had you been like Shammai the Elder, I would never have entered the assembly of Israel. The impatience of Shammai sought to destroy me out of this world and out of the world to come; your gentleness brought me to life in this world and in the world to come'. It is reported that that proselyte became the father of two sons; one he named Hillel and the other Gamaliel. They were called 'Hillel's proselytes'.

4. REPENT ONE DAY BEFORE YOUR DEATH. The disciples asked R. Eliezer.[17] 'Does, then, a man know on which day he will die that he should repent [the day before]?' He replied, 'All the more reason that he repent to-day lest he die to-morrow, or that he repent to-morrow lest he die the day after; as a consequence his whole life is spent in repentance'.

R. Jose b. Judah said in the name of R. Judah b. R. Ilai, who

(14) Num. I, 51. (15) Cf. Deut. XIV, 1. (16) Ex. XIX, 6. (17) Cf. Shab. 153a (Sonc. ed., p. 781).

said it in the name of his father R. Ilai, who reported it in the name of R. Eliezer the Great: REPENT ONE DAY BEFORE YOUR DEATH; WARM YOURSELF BEFORE THE FIRE OF THE SAGES, BUT BEWARE OF THEIR GLOWING COALS LEST YOU BE SCORCHED, FOR THEIR BITE IS THE BITE OF A FOX, AND THEIR STING IS THE STING OF A SCORPION; YEA ALL THEIR WORDS ARE LIKE COALS OF FIRE.[18]

(18) From Aboth II, 15 (Sonc. ed., II, 10, pp. 20f).

CHAPTER XVI

1. R. JOSHUA SAID: THE EVIL EYE, THE EVIL INCLINATION, AND THE HATRED OF MANKIND DRIVE A MAN OUT OF THE WORLD.

THE EVIL EYE. What does this mean? It teaches that as a man regards his own house, so he should regard the house of his fellow; and as a man would not wish an evil report spread about his wife and children, so he should not wish an evil report spread about his fellow's wife and children.

Another interpretation. What is meant by THE EVIL EYE? It teaches that no man should begrudge the learning of his fellow. The story is told of a man who looked with a grudging eye upon his colleague's learning that his life was cut short and he departed [prematurely from the world].

2. THE EVIL INCLINATION. What does this mean? It has been said that the evil inclination is senior to the good inclination by thirteen years,[1] for it grows with and accompanies the child from the moment it comes forth from the mother's womb. If the child begins to profane the Sabbath it[2] does not deter him; if he is about to take life it does not deter him; if he is about to commit an immoral act it does not deter him. After thirteen years, however, the good inclination is born in him. If then he is about to profane the Sabbath it[3] warns him, 'You fool! Scripture states, *Every one that profaneth it shall surely be put to death*'.[4] If he is about to take life, it warns him, 'You fool! Scripture states, *Whoso sheddeth man's blood, by man shall his blood be shed*'.[5] If he is about to commit an immoral act, it warns him, 'You fool! Scripture states, *Both the adulterer and the adulteress shall surely be put to death*'.[6] When a man's passions are stirred and he is about to commit an act of lewdness, all his limbs are

(1) The evil inclination, it was held, entered the human body even before birth, whereas the good inclination was acquired at the age of thirteen, the age of religious responsibility. (2) i.e. the evil inclination; the child has no sense of wrongdoing. (3) i.e. the good inclination. (4) Ex. XXXI, 14. (5) Gen. IX, 6.

ready to obey him, because the evil inclination is king over the two hundred and forty-eight limbs of man. On the other hand, when a man is about to perform an act of piety, all his limbs become sluggish,[7] because the evil inclination which is within him bears sway over the two hundred and forty-eight limbs of his body, whereas the good inclination is like one who is confined in prison, as it is stated, *For out of prison he came forth to be king*,[8] which verse has been interpreted as referring to the good inclination.[9]

Others interpret this verse as referring to the righteous Joseph. When that wicked woman[10] came [to tempt him] she afflicted him with her words, saying, 'I will have you imprisoned'; and he replied, '*The Lord looseth the prisoners*'.[11] She said, 'I will have your eyes plucked out'; and he replied, '*The Lord openeth the eyes of the blind*'.[12] She said, 'I will bend your stature'; and he replied, '*The Lord raiseth up them that are bowed down*'.[13] She said, 'I will accuse you of sin';[14] and he replied, '*The Lord loveth the righteous*'.[15] She said, 'I will make you a stranger';[16] and he replied, '*The Lord preserveth the strangers*'.[17] Finally he said, '*How then can I do this great wickedness*'.[18]

Marvel not at the [virtue of the] righteous Joseph, for consider the case of R. Zadok, the greatest man of his generation. When he was taken captive, a certain matron acquired him [as a slave] and sent in a beautiful maid-servant to him. As soon as he saw her, he turned his eyes to the wall so as not to look upon her, and sat absorbed in study the whole night long. In the morning the girl went and complained to her mistress, saying, 'I would rather die than be given to that man!' [The matron] sent for him and asked, 'Why did you not treat this woman as men usually act?' He replied, 'What else could

(6) Lev. XX, 10. (7) The Heb. *mith'annin* is unusual in this sense, but might be derived from the verb *'innah*, 'to delay' (cf. *'innuï haddin*, 'the delay of justice', Aboth V, 8). Schechter suggests the reading *mith'azzlin*, 'are slothful'. (8) Eccl. IV, 14. (9) Cf. Midrash Rabbah, Ecclesiastes, *ad loc.* (Sonc. ed., p. 123). (10) Potiphar's wife (Gen. XXXIX, 7ff). (11) Ps. CXLVI, 7. (12) *ibid.* 8. (13) *ibid.* (14) lit. 'I will make you wicked'. (15) *ibid.* (16) The word in the text *'armai*, 'a heathen', makes no sense. The translation follows the version quoted by the Baalë Tosafoth on Gen. XXXIX, 12. Joseph is threatened with banishment. (17) *ibid.* 9. (18) Gen. XXXIX, 9.

I do, seeing that I belong to the High-priestly line? I am from a noble family and said to myself, "[I must refrain] lest I cohabit with her and increase the number of illegitimate children in Israel"'. On hearing his words, she ordered [his release] and set him free with great honour.

Do not marvel at [the virtue of] R. Zadok, for consider the case of R. 'Aḳiba who was greater than he. When R. 'Aḳiba came to a certain land,[19] a malicious accusation was laid against him before the Ruler. The latter sent in two beautiful women to him who had bathed, anointed and adorned themselves like brides for their grooms. They importuned him throughout the night, each saying, 'Turn to me'. He sat between them, spat [in disgust], and turned to neither of them. They went and complained to the Ruler, saying, 'We would rather die than be given to that man!' He sent for him and asked, 'Why did you not treat these women as men usually act towards women? Are they not beautiful? Are they not human like yourself? Did not He Who created you create them?' He answered, 'I could not do otherwise; their odour seemed to me like the odour of carrion, torn beasts and creeping things'.

Do not marvel at [the virtue of] R. 'Aḳiba, for consider the case of R. Eliezer the Great who was more distinguished than he. R. Eliezer brought up his sister's daughter, and for thirteen years she [slept] with him in one bed until she reached puberty. Then he said to her, 'Go and get married'. She replied, 'Am I not your maid, [even contented] to be a servant to wash the feet of your disciples?'[20] He said to her, 'My daughter, I am now an old man; go and marry a young man of your own age'. She replied, 'Have I not already told you that I am your maid, [even contented] to be a servant to wash the feet of your disciples?' When he heard her words, he obtained her consent to a betrothal and married her.

3. R. Reuben b. Iẓtroboli said: How can a man keep far away from the evil inclination which is within his body? For the

(19) MS. E. reads 'to Rome'. (20) By this expression she implied her desire to marry him. The parallel passage in j.Yeb. XIII, 2, 13c reads, 'I am your handmaid to wash the feet of my master's slaves'.

first drop which a man injects into a woman is the evil inclination.[21] Moreover, the evil inclination dwells at the entrances of the heart, as it is stated, *Sin coucheth at the door.*[22] It already speaks to the human being while he is an infant in the cot, saying, 'That man seeks to kill you', and [in consequence the infant] is ready to pluck out his hair.[23] When an infant lies in his cot and places his hand upon a snake or a scorpion so that he is bitten, this was caused by none other than the evil inclination which is within his body. Or when he lays his hand on glowing coals and is burnt, this was caused by none other than the evil inclination which is within his body, since the evil inclination it is that drives him headlong [to destruction]. Observe, however, a kid or lamb: when it sees a well it turns back, since there is no evil inclination in a beast [to lead it into harm].

R. Simeon b. Eleazar said: I will explain it to you by a parable. To what is the evil inclination like? [25*a*] To a piece of iron which is cast into the fire. As long as it is in the fire one can make of it whatever vessel he wishes. So it is with the evil inclination: there is no other remedy for it but the study of the Torah which is likened to fire;[24] as it is stated, *If thine enemy be hungry, give him bread to eat, and if he be thirsty, give him water to drink; for thou wilt heap coals of fire upon his head, and the Lord will reward thee.*[25] Read not *will reward* [*yeshallem*] *thee* but 'will make him at peace [*yashlim*] with thee.'

R. Judah the Prince said: I will explain it to you by a parable. To what is the evil inclination like? To the case of two men who entered an inn and one of them was arrested on a charge of robbery. When asked, 'Who was with you [as an accomplice]?' he could reply, 'There was no one with me'; but he

(21) i.e. the first seed, the result of man's passion, creates the evil inclination in the unborn child. (22) Gen. IV, 7. Cf. Ber. 61a (Sonc. ed., p. 384). (23) The aggressive tendencies in a child are accordingly explained as incitement by the evil inclination, the latter creating the fear that persons wish to do him harm. (24) Cf. Jer. XXIII, 29, homiletically explained as teaching that by a man's devotion to Torah, God will cause the enemy (i.e. the evil inclination) to be at peace with him and cease assailing him. (25) Prov. XXV, 21f.

says to himself, 'Since I am to be executed, let my fellow be executed along with me'. In the same way the evil inclination speaks, 'Since I am doomed in the world to come, I will drag the entire body with me to destruction'.

R. Simeon b. Yoḥai said: By this reasoning Israel will never see Gehinnom. This may be explained by a parable. To what is the matter like? To a mortal king who had a field of poor quality. Certain men came and leased it at a rental of ten *kors* of wheat annually. They manured it, hoed it, watered it and weeded it; but they could only make it yield one *kor* of wheat during the year. The king asked them for an explanation and they replied, 'Our sovereign lord! You know that the field which you leased to us originally yielded nothing to you; now after manuring it, weeding it and watering it, we made it yield us no more than one *kor* of wheat'. In like manner Israel will in the future plead with the Holy One, blessed be He, 'Lord of the universe! Thou knowest that it is the evil inclination that incites us, as it is stated, *For He knoweth our impulse*'.[26]

4. AND THE HATRED OF MANKIND. What does this mean? It teaches that a man should not adopt the rule: Love the Sages and hate the disciples, or Love the disciples and hate the '*Am ha'areẓ*. Let his rule be: Love them all, and hate [only] heretics, apostates, seducers and informers. So said David, *Do not I hate them, O Lord, that hate Thee? And do not I strive with those that rise up against thee? I hate them with utmost hatred; I count them mine enemies.*[27] But does not Scripture declare, *Thou shalt love thy neighbour as thyself: I am the Lord?*[28] And why? Because I created him. If he acts as *thy people* should act,[29] then you must love him, but if not, then you must not love him. R. Simeon b. Eleazar said: With a great oath[30] was this command said, *Thou shalt love thy neighbour as thyself. I the Lord have created him*[31]—if you love him, I am trustworthy to give you a good reward; but if you do not, I am a Judge to punish you.[32]

(26) Ps. CIII, 14. E.V. *our frame*, the Heb. being the same as for 'inclination, impulse'. (27) *ibid.* CXXXIX, 21f. (28) Lev. XIX, 18. (29) Cf. Ex. XXII, 27, *Thou shalt not ... curse a ruler of thy people*, and B.Ḳ. 94b (Sonc. ed., p. 549). (30) So according to the MSS.; V reads 'in a great hour' which makes no sense. (31) Is. XLV, 8. E.V., *created it.* (32) On this passage, cf. Finkelstein, *op. cit.*, pp. 47-52.

CHAPTER XVII

1. R. JOSE SAID: LET THE PROPERTY OF YOUR FELLOW BE AS DEAR TO YOU AS YOUR OWN; FIT YOURSELF FOR THE STUDY OF THE TORAH, SINCE IT DOES NOT COME TO YOU BY INHERITANCE.

2. What does this mean? It teaches that as a man regards his own property, so he should regard the property of his fellow; and as a man would not wish to see an evil report spread about his own property, so he should not wish to see an evil report spread about the property of his fellow.

Another interpretation of LET THE PROPERTY OF YOUR FELLOW BE AS DEAR TO YOU AS YOUR OWN. What does it mean? When a disciple comes to you and asks for instruction, if it is within your power to teach him, do so; but if not, dismiss him at once and take no money from him;[1] as it is stated, *Say not unto thy neighbour: Go and come again, and to-morrow I will give; when thou hast it by thee.*[2]

3. FIT YOURSELF FOR THE STUDY OF THE TORAH, SINCE IT DOES NOT COME TO YOU BY INHERITANCE. Thus when Moses our teacher perceived that his sons had not the knowledge of the Torah to be able to succeed him in leadership, he wrapped himself in his robe and stood up to pray. He said, 'Sovereign of the universe! Make known to me who will come in and go out at the head of this people, as it is stated, *And Moses spoke unto the Lord, saying: Let the Lord, the God of the spirits of all flesh, set a man over the congregation, who may go out before them, and who may come in before them.*[3] Thereupon the Holy One, blessed be He, said to him, 'Moses, *take thee Joshua*'.[4] The Holy One, blessed be He, further said to Moses, 'Go and appoint for him an interpreter[5] that he may expound [the

(1) As remuneration for teaching; cf. Ned. 37a (Sonc. ed., p. 113) where the taking of a fee is prohibited. (2) Prov. III, 28. (3) Num. XXVII, 15-17. (4) *ibid.* 18. (5) Also called *'Amora*, 'speaker'; he was the scholar who attended on the Rabbi during the lecture and expounded at length and in popular style the subject-matter given to him by the instructor.

Torah] in your presence at the head of the notables of Israel'. At that time Moses said to Joshua, 'Joshua, as for this people that I am delivering into your charge, they are not he-goats but kids; I am not delivering to you sheep but lambs, because as yet they have not occupied themselves with the commandments, and so have not reached the stage of he-goats;[6] as it is stated, *If thou know not, O thou fairest among women, go thy way forth by the footsteps of the flock and feed thy kids, beside the shepherds' tents.*[7]

4. Rabban Joḥanan b. Zakkai[8] was once walking in the market place when he observed a young woman picking grains of barley from under the feet of the cattle of the Arabs. He said to her, 'My daughter, who are you?' She remained silent. Again he asked her, 'My daughter, who are you?' She continued silent [for a time], and then said to him, 'Wait a moment'. She wrapped herself in her hair, sat down before him and said, 'I am the daughter of Naḳdimon b. Gorion'.[9] He asked, 'My daughter, what became of your father's wealth?' She replied, 'Master, is not the proverb current in Jerusalem, "The salt[10] of wealth is its diminution [by charitable use] (or, according to another version, "[The salt of wealth is] benevolence")?' 'And what became of the wealth of your father-in-law?' he asked. She replied, 'The one swallowed up the other'.[11] Then Rabban Joḥanan b. Zakkai turned to his disciples and said, 'All my life I have read the verse, *If thou know not, O thou fairest among women, go thy way forth by the footsteps of the flock,* but did not understand its significance until to-day when I have realized its meaning, viz. that Israel will come under the domination of the lowest of the nations, and not merely under the domination of the lowest of the nations but will be among the dung of their cattle'. The young woman then asked him, 'Master, do you remember when you put your signature to my marriage contract?' 'I do,' he replied; and turning to his disciples he said, 'By the Temple Service! I signed this

(6) And must be treated with care and consideration; cf. Sifre to Deut., §305. (7) Cant. I, 8. (8) Cf. Sifre *ibid.* and Keth. 66b (Sonc. ed., p. 405). (9) Cf. above VI, 3, p. 47. (10) A preservative. The difference in the two versions is in one letter, the former having חסר and the latter חסד. (11) The fortunes of the two men were interlocked.

young woman's marriage contract, and it mentioned a settlement of one million Tyrian golden dinars'. [It is related that] the members of the family to which the young woman belonged never set out from their house to go to the Temple until the finest woollen rugs were spread before them.

5. The story[12] is told of a young woman who was taken captive together with her ten maids. A Gentile acquired her and she grew up in his house. One day he handed her a jug and said, 'Go and fetch me some water'. One of her maids arose and took it from her. 'What is this?' he asked; and she replied, 'By your life, master! I was one of five hundred maids of this young woman's mother.' When he heard these words, he at once set her free together with her ten maids.

6. Another story is told of a young woman who was taken captive. A Gentile acquired her and she grew up in his house. The Angel of Dreams[13] appeared to him and said, 'Send the young woman from your house'. His wife said to him, 'Do not send her away'. Again the Angel of Dreams appeared to him and said, 'If you do not send her away I will kill you', and he let her go. He followed her, saying [to himself], 'I must go and see what will befall this young woman'. On her journey she became thirsty and went down to drink at a spring, When she placed her hand on the wall, a snake came and bit her so that she died, [her body] floating on the surface of the water. He went down, took her out and buried her. On his return home he remarked to his wife, 'This people whom you behold bear the anger of none other than their Father in heaven'.

7. AND LET ALL YOUR DEEDS BE DONE FOR THE SAKE OF HEAVEN.[14] That means, for the sake of the Torah, as it is stated, *In all thy ways acknowledge Him, and He will direct thy paths.*[15]

8. R. SIMEON SAID: BE CAREFUL TO READ THE SHEMA' AND

(12) Further anecdotes of the wretched plight of even the wealthiest families in Israel during the siege of Jerusalem and after. (13) lit. 'the master of the dream'; cf. Ber. 10b (Sonc. ed., p. 55, n. 5) where another explanation is suggested. (14) The conclusion of R. Jose's teaching in Aboth II, 17 (Sonc. ed., II, 12, p. 22). (15) Prov. III, 6. By following the ways of the Torah one arrives at a knowledge of God.

THE 'AMIDAH; AND WHEN YOU PRAY LET NOT YOUR PRAYER BE A CONVERSATION[16] BUT SUPPLICATION BEFORE THE HOLY ONE, BLESSED BE HE, AS IT IS WRITTEN, FOR HE IS GRACIOUS AND FULL OF COMPASSION, SLOW TO ANGER AND ABUNDANT IN MERCY, AND REPENTETH HIM OF THE EVIL.[17]

R. ELIEZER SAID: BE EAGER TO STUDY THE TORAH, AND KNOW HOW TO ANSWER AN UNBELIEVER. Let not one word of the Torah be forgotten by you. KNOW BEFORE WHOM YOU TOIL, AND WITH WHOM YOU HAVE ENTERED INTO A COMPACT.[18]

(16) The reading in Aboth II, 18 (Sonc. ed., II, 13, p. 23) is 'a fixed task'. (17) Joel II, 13. A variant text is the verse from Jon. IV, 2. (18) The phrase *Ba'al berith* as a designation for God is not found elsewhere in Rabbinic literature. GRA substitutes *Ba'al melakteka,* 'thy Employer', in conformity with Aboth II, 19 (Sonc. ed., II, 16, p. 25).

CHAPTER XVIII

1. Likewise[1] R. Judah the Prince used to recount the praises of the following Sages: R. Ṭarfon, R. 'Aḳiba, R. Eleazar b. Azariah, R. Joḥanan b. Nuri and R. Jose the Galilean.

R. Ṭarfon he described as a heap of stones (another version: a heap of nuts). When a man removes one, they all topple and fall over each other. So it was with R. Ṭarfon; whenever a disciple came to him and said, 'Teach me', he would produce for him [instruction in] Scripture, Mishnah, Midrash, *halakoth* and *'aggadoth*. When that disciple departed, he left laden with blessing and [intellectual] wealth.

R. 'Aḳiba he described as a treasury with compartments.[2] To what may [25*b*] R. 'Aḳiba be compared? To a pedlar who takes his sack and goes into a field. When he finds wheat he drops it in the sack; similarly when he finds barley, spelt, beans and lentils he drops them all in the sack. On returning home he sorts them all out, putting the wheat apart, the barley apart, the spelt, the beans, the lentils all apart. Such was the practice of R. 'Aḳiba: he sorted all the Torah [he amassed] into its various compartments.[3]

(1) This passage links up with the dictum in Aboth II, 11 (Sonc. ed., II, 8, p. 18) where Rabban Joḥanan b. Zakkai recounts the distinctive qualifications of his five foremost disciples. (2) The translation follows the view of Rashi, given in Giṭ. 67a (Sonc. ed., p. 317), where he explains בלום as 'divided into several compartments'. Jastrow, *s.v.* בלם, defines it 'a packed treasury' (of knowledge), but explains the variant, בלוס (*s.v.* בלס) as 'a mind full of knowledge'. [Bacher, *Ag. d. pal. Amoräer*, II, p. 65, n. 6, gives בלום as the correct reading which he understands as 'locked up' or 'packed'.] (3) The text varies between *ṭaba'oth*, 'rings' and *maṭbe'oth*, 'coins'. Rashi, *loc. cit.*, adopts the latter according to which the meaning is: As coins are put into a box according to their various denominations, so did R. 'Aḳiba systematize the whole of the oral tradition. [Bacher, *Ag. d. Tannaiten* I, p. 267, n. 1, accepts the former reading, and explains that R. 'Aḳiba sorted out the heterogeneous material and arranged it like 'a chain of connected links'.]

R. Eleazar b. Azariah he described as a perfumer's chest. To what may R. Eleazar be compared? To a perfumer who takes his chest with him and enters a city. The townsfolk come out and enquire, 'Have you fine oil? Have you spikenard oil? Have you balsam oil?' and find that he has everything [they require]. So it was with R. Eleazar b. Azariah. When a disciple came to him and enquired about Scripture he enlightened him, about Mishnah he enlightened him, about Midrash or *halakoth* or *'aggadoth* he enlightened him. When the disciple departed he left laden with [intellectual] wealth and blessing.

2. When R. Joshua was an old man, his disciples came to visit him.[4] He said to them, 'My sons, what new interpretation was there at the House of Study to-day?' They replied, 'We are your disciples and drink your waters'.[5] He said to them, 'Heaven forfend! No generation is orphaned of its Sages.[6] Whose Sabbath[7] was it?' They replied, 'It was the Sabbath of R. Eleazar b. Azariah'. He asked, 'And what was the theme of his discourse to-day?' They answered, 'It was the section [beginning], *Assemble the people, the men and the women and the little ones*'.[8] He further asked, 'What exposition did he give in connection with it?' They said, 'His comment was as follows: The men came to learn, the women to listen, but why had the little ones to come? In order to grant a good reward to those who brought them'. He said to them, 'You had such a precious pearl in your possession and sought to withhold it from me! Had you visited me only for the purpose of imparting this to me, it would have been sufficient'. They said to him, 'He also gave this exposition: *The words of the wise are as*

(4) Cf. Ḥag. 3a (Sonc. ed., pp. 8f). This passage is inserted as an example of the skill of R. Eleazar b. 'Azariah in *'aggadoth*. (5) We cannot possibly have anything to teach you. (6) He deprecated the suggestion that there were no other great teachers. (7) Rabban Gamaliel, the President of the College, had been deposed because of his high-handed treatment and humiliation of R. Joshua, and R. Eleazar b. 'Azariah had been elected in his place. When Rabban Gamaliel had been reinstated it was arranged that he should give the discourse three Sabbaths in the month and R. Eleazar b. 'Azariah one Sabbath (cf. Ber. 27b, 28a; Sonc. ed., pp. 166ff). This explains the question asked by R. Joshua. (8) Deut. XXXI, 12.

goads, and as nails well fastened are the words of masters of assemblies:[9] as the goad guides the heifer along its furrows, so do the words of the Torah guide a man along the paths of life. But [should you contend,] As the goad is movable so the words of the Torah are likewise movable,[10] the text adds, *And as nails well fastened:* As nails well fastened cannot be pulled out, so the words of the Torah cannot be dislodged. *Masters of assemblies:* these are the disciples of the wise who enter [the House of Study] and sit in several groups; some declare a thing forbidden others declaring it permitted, some pronounce a thing unclean others pronouncing it clean, some rule a thing unfit others ruling it fit. Now lest a man say to you, "I will sit idle and not study", the text continues, *They were given from one shepherd,* i.e. one God created them,[11] one leader[12] gave them, the Lord of all creation uttered them. Therefore make your ear like a funnel and allow to enter therein the words of those who forbid and those who permit, the words of those who pronounce unclean and of those who pronounce clean, the words of those who rule it unfit and of those who rule it fit'.

3. R. Joḥanan b. Nuri he described as a chest [filled with] *halakoth.*

R. Jose the Galilean he described as a collector of the finest, devoid of arrogance; because he held fast to the rule of the Sages[13] derived from Mount Sinai, and diligently taught all the wise men of Israel.

4. Issi b. Judah used to describe certain Sages in these terms:[14] R. Meir was a wise man and a scribe;[15] R. Judah was a wise man when he desired to be such;[16] the Mishnah of R. Eliezer b. Jacob was little and good;[17] R. Jose always had his reasons; R. Joḥanan b. Nuri was a chest [filled with] *halakoth;* R. Jose the

(9) Eccl. XII, 11. E.V., . . . *fastened are those that are composed in collections.* (10) i.e. not of permanent authority. (11) [Cf. what 'a heavenly voice' declared of the controversies between the Schools of Hillel and Shammai, 'They both speak the words of the Living God' ('Erub. 13b, Sonc. ed., pp. 85f). (12) i.e. Moses. (13) That a man should be humble. (14) Cf. Giṭ. 67a (Sonc. ed., pp. 317f.) from which the following annotations are quoted. (15) That was his profession. (16) i.e. when he was not too hasty, he could be even wiser than R. Meir.

Galilean was a collector of the very finest, devoid of arrogance; R. Simeon b. Gamaliel was a shop stocked with the best purple; R. Simeon studied much and forgot little. Later when R. Simeon met Issi b. Judah he said to him, 'Why do you prate about me before the Sages?' He replied, 'I merely said that you study much and forget little, and the little you do forget is but the bran of your learning'.[18]

(17) lit. 'a *ḳab* (little in quantity) but fine (well-sifted)'. So that whenever he gives an opinion, the *halakah* follows him. (18) i.e. those statements which were not followed by the *halakah*.

CHAPTER XIX

1. 'Aḳabya b. Mahalalel said: Whosoever takes four things to heart[1] will never sin: whence he came, whither he is going, what he is destined to become, and who is his Judge. 'Whence he came'—from a place of darkness; 'whither he is going'—to a place of thick darkness; 'what he is destined to become'—dust, worms and maggots; 'and who is his Judge'—the King of kings, the Holy One, blessed be He.

2. R. Simeon said: Man came from a place of darkness and returns to a place of darkness. He came from a fetid drop, from a place which no eye can behold. And what is he destined to become? Dust, worms and maggots, as it is stated, *How much less man, that is a worm! and the son of man, that is a maggot!*[2] R. Eleazar b. Jacob said: *Man that is a worm* when alive, *and the son of man that is a maggot* when dead. In what sense is he a worm when alive? By reason of the lice [which infest him]. And a maggot when dead? By reason of the creeping things which he generates when dead.

3. R. Simeon b. Eleazar said: I will illustrate it to you by a parable. To what can the matter be compared? To a king who built a large palace in which he resided,[3] but the waste-pipe of a tannery ran through it and emptied itself at the entrance. Every passer-by exclaimed, 'How beautiful and magnificent would that palace be if the waste-pipe of the tannery did not run through it!' Just so is it with man; and if in his present state, when from his entrails issue fetid streams,[4] he lords it

(1) Cf. Aboth III, 1 (Sonc. ed., p. 26) where the more popular version reads: 'Consider three things', etc., omitting the third item, 'what he is destined to become—dust, worms and maggots' as being heterodox in outlook; cf. Finkelstein, *Akiba: Scholar, Saint and Martyr*, pp. 159f, where the maxim of 'Aḳabya is described as 'this unequivocal denial of personal immortality'. See also DER III, 1 (below, p. 543) where the saying is quoted as in the present text in the name of Ben 'Azzai. (2) Job XXV, 6. (3) According to a variant reading: 'which he elaborately adorned'. GRA reads 'magnificent in every detail'. V has 'large palaces'. (4) The natural secretions.

over all creatures, how much more would he lord it over all creatures if there were to issue from him streams of fine oil, balsam and spikenard!

4. When R. Eliezer fell ill, his disciples came to visit him. They sat before him and said, 'Master, tell us in one word what you have taught us'.[5] He replied, 'What shall I tell you? Go forth and be mindful of the honour of your fellow-man, and when you pray know before Whom you are standing and praying. Then will you merit the life of the world to come'.

R. Eleazar said: Five things did we learn from R. Eliezer [on that day], and they afforded us greater pleasure than all that we had enjoyed from him in his lifetime, and they are as follows: If a round cushion, a ball, a shoemaker's last, an amulet or a phylactery, about which you spoke to us, were torn, what would be the law?[6] The answer he gave was: They can contract uncleanness so be careful with them; and [if unclean] they may be immersed as they are. These laws are well established, for they were communicated to Moses on Mount Sinai.[7]

(5) lit. 'teach us one word of what you have taught us'. In the master's last hours the disciples enquire of him the epitome of his wisdom and experience. In the parallel passage, Ber. 28b (Sonc. ed., p. 173), the text reads: 'Teach us the ways of life'. (6) The five articles enumerated have in common that they are made of leather and are permanently filled with stuffing. It is established law that an article of leather can contract defilement only if it is a receptacle, i.e. it has a cavity in which it can hold things. Since the articles here listed are *permanently* filled, the Sage held the view that they are not considered to be vessels with receptacles and consequently cannot be ritually defiled. R. Eliezer, however, was of the opinion that since the filling was removable, they were to be considered vessels with receptacles and could contract defilement. Furthermore, if any one of the enumerated articles were torn the opinion was unanimous that it could contract defilement, because some of the filling must have fallen out and in consequence a receptacle was formed. If, in the circumstances stated, the article became unclean, there was a further argument between R. Eliezer and the Sages whether it was necessary to remove *all* the filling before immersion took place. The Sages held the view that this must be done otherwise the immersion would be invalid, since the filling interposed between the vessel and the water. R. Eliezer, on the other hand, ruled that it could be immersed as it was without the removal of the filling. R. Eliezer here put forward his views as ancient traditional rulings. Cf. Kel. XXIII, 1 (Sonc. ed., p. 110). (7) For textual variants of this passage, cf. below XXV, 2 (p. 171), Sanh. 68a (Sonc. ed., pp. 462f) and DER III, end (below p. 544).

CHAPTER XX

1. R. Ḥananiah, the deputy High Priest,[1] said: He who lays the words of the Torah to his heart will be freed from the anxieties of the sword, hunger, madness, lust, the evil inclination, adultery, vain thoughts, and of the yoke of human cares; for so it is written in the Book of Psalms by David king of Israel, *The precepts of the Lord are right, rejoicing the heart; the commandment of the Lord is pure, enlightening the eyes.*[2] And he who does not lay the words of the Torah to his heart will be burdened with the anxieties of the sword, hunger, madness, lust, the evil inclination, adultery, vain thoughts, and of the yoke of human cares; for so it is written in the Book of Deuteronomy by Moses our master, *And they shall be upon thee for a sign and for a wonder, and upon thy seed for ever; because thou didst not serve the Lord thy God with joyfulness, and with gladness of heart, by reason of the abundance of all things; therefore shalt thou serve thine enemy whom the Lord shall send against thee in hunger, and in thirst, and in nakedness, and in want of all things.*[3] *In hunger:* what does this mean? When a man longs to eat barley bread and cannot afford even that, his enemies demand of him white bread and rich meat. *And in thirst:* what does this mean? When a man longs to drink a drop of sour wine or a drop of beer and cannot afford even that, his enemies demand of him the best wine of all the lands. *And in nakedness:* what does this mean? When a man wishes to wear a woollen or linen shirt and cannot afford even that, his enemies demand of him the finest silks and satins of all the lands. *And in want of all things:* he will be without a lamp, [26*a*] without a knife and without a table. Another interpretation of *And in want of all things:* he will be without vinegar and salt. When people curse

(1) In Aboth III, 2 (Sonc. ed., p. 27) there is a different saying attributed to 'R. Ḥanina, the deputy High Priest', and in III, 6 (Sonc. ed., III, 5, p. 29) a statement of R. Neḥuniah b. Ha-Ḳanah bears some resemblance to what is quoted here. (2) Ps. XIX, 9. (3) Deut. XXVIII, 46-48.

one another they say, 'May there be no vinegar or salt in your house!'

He used to say: [It is written:] *Look not upon me, that I am swarthy, that the sun hath tanned me; [my mother's sons were incensed against me]:*[4] these are the councillors[5] of Judah who cast from themselves the yoke of the Holy One, blessed be He, and set a human king over them.[6]

Another interpretation of *My mother's sons were incensed against me:* this refers to Moses when he killed the Egyptian,[7] as it is stated, *And it came to pass in those days, when Moses was grown up, that he went out unto his brethren, and looked on their burdens . . . and he looked this way and that way, and when he saw that there was no man, he smote the Egyptian, and hid him in the sand.*[8] What do the words *that there was no man* imply? They teach that Moses had set up a Sanhedrin of ministering angels[9] and said to them, 'Shall I kill this man?' They replied, 'Kill him'. And do you think that he killed by the sword? No, he killed him with speech, as it is stated, *Dost thou* say *to kill me as thou didst kill the Egyptian,*[10] proving that he killed him by [pronouncing] the Name.

Another interpretation of *My mother's sons were incensed against me:* this refers to Moses when he fled to Midian; as it is stated, *When Pharaoh heard this thing, he sought to slay Moses. But Moses fled from the face of Pharaoh, and dwelt in the land of Midian; and he sat by a well. Now the priest of Midian had seven daughters . . . and the shepherds came and drove them away; but Moses stood up and helped them and watered their flocks.*[11] Moses came forward and sat in judgment upon [the men]. He said to them, 'In the ordinary way men draw[12] the water and women give the flocks to drink, but here women draw the water and men [take it and] give their flocks

(4) Cant. I, 6. (5) Reading *bula'oth.* Cf. Giṭ. 37a (Sonc. ed., p. 151, n. 5, where the word is explained as the Greek for 'city councils'). V has *banoth* (daughters) which does not make sense. [On the passage, cf. Büchler, *Studies in Sin and Atonement*, pp. 63f and *The Economic Conditions of Judaea*, p. 28, n. 2.] (6) The lords of Judah were so incensed against God that in their exasperation they acted to their own hurt. (7) Moses was so incensed at the injustice which he witnessed that he acted zealously 'for Me', i.e. on God's behalf. (8) Ex. II, 11f. (9) Since no human beings were about, he had no alternative but to call upon angels to form a court of justice. (10) *ibid.* 14. E.V., *thinkest thou to kill me.* (11) *ibid.* 15-17. Moses was incensed by the action of the shepherds.

to drink! This is an injustice; you are guilty in law'. Thereupon he rose up and helped [the women].[13] Some report the matter as follows: So long as Moses was standing by the edge of the well the waters surged up towards him, but when he moved away the waters receded. At that moment he exclaimed, 'Woe is me! I have abandoned my people and am come to dwell with strangers!'

Another interpretation of *My mother's sons were incensed against me:* this refers to the people of Israel when they made the golden calf.[14] At first they said, *All that the Lord hath spoken will we do and obey,*[15] but later they said, *This is thy god, O Israel.*[16]

Another interpretation of *My mother's sons were incensed against me*: this refers to the spies when they spread an evil report about the land, and in consequence caused the carcasses of Israel to fall in the wilderness; as it is stated, *Your carcasses shall fall in this wilderness.*[17]

They made me keeper of the vineyards.[18] The Holy One, blessed be He, declared, 'Who was it that caused Me to show favour to the Gentiles, if not Israel? For so long as the Gentiles dwell at ease, the people of Israel are oppressed, rejected and tossed about'.

Another interpretation of *They made me keeper of the vineyards:* this refers to the people of Israel when they were exiled to Babylon. The prophets in their midst arose and bade them, 'Set apart your *terumah* and your tithes.' They replied, 'It was because we did not separate *terumah* and tithes that we were exiled from our land, and now you bid us to set apart *terumah* and tithes [in exile]?' Scripture therefore states, *They made me keeper of the vineyards; [but mine own vineyard have I not kept].*[19]

(12) Or 'fill' according to a variant. (13) Following the emendation of GRA and Schechter. V reads 'you are guilty at the hour'. (14) The people here showed their resentment against God by making a golden calf, and the spies (next §) by spreading an evil report about the land. (15) *ibid.* XXIV, 7. (16) *ibid.* XXXII, 4. (17) Num. XIV, 29. (18) Cant. I, 6. The verse concludes, *but mine own vineyard have I not kept*. Israel, God's vineyard, was unkept by Him because of the people's shortcomings. (19) *ibid.* Because Israel had not observed the laws relating to fields and vineyards, they were driven into captivity where they had to labour in the vineyards of strangers.

CHAPTER XXI

I. R. DOSA B. HARKINAS SAID: MORNING SLEEP, AND MIDDAY WINE, [AND CHILDREN'S TALK, AND SITTING IN THE MEETING-HOUSES OF THE IGNORANT] DRIVE A MAN OUT OF THE WORLD.

MORNING SLEEP—what does this mean? It teaches that a man should not wilfully sleep late so that the time-limit for the recital of the *Shema'* passes; for if he sleep late so that the time-limit for reciting the *Shema'* passes he consequently neglects the study of the Torah,[1] as it is stated, *The sluggard saith: There is a lion in the way; yea, a lion is in the streets. The door is turning upon its hinges, and the sluggard is still upon his bed.*[2]

MIDDAY WINE—what does this mean? It teaches that a man should not form the habit of drinking wine at midday; for when he drinks wine at midday, the consequence is that he neglects the [study of the] whole Torah, as it is stated, *Woe to thee, O land, when thy king is a boy, and thy princes feast in the morning.*[3] And it continues, *Happy art thou, O land, when thy king is a free man,* [*and thy princes eat in due season!*].[4] And when is that *due season?* You must say that it is in the time to come, as it is stated, *I the Lord will hasten it*[5] *in its due season.*[6] Scripture also states, *Like the time it will be said of Jacob and of Israel: What hath God wrought!*[7] Thus said the Holy One, blessed be He, to Balaam: *Like the time* (*ka'eth*), and not 'in the time' (*ba'eth*)—not in the time in which you live, but *like the time* when I am about to bring deliverance to Israel.

CHILDREN'S TALK—what does this mean? It teaches that a man should not make a practice of sitting and studying at

(1) By reciting the *Shema'* one fulfils a dual obligation: the duty of proclaiming the unity of God and that of Torah-study; cf. Yalkuṭ on Ps. I, 2, §614. (2) Prov. XXVI, 13f. In V. the order of the verses is reversed. (3) Eccl. X, 16. (4) *ibid.* 17. (5) The coming salvation. (6) Is. LX, 22, E.V., *in its time.* (7) Num. XXIII, 23, E.V., *now it is said of Jacob.* The reference in the verse is to the time to come when Israel will enjoy close relationship with God, knowing what He is about to do.

home;[8] because when a man sits and studies at home and engages in conversation with his children and members of his household, the outcome is that he neglects the Torah; and it is stated, *This book of the law shall not depart out of thy mouth, but thou shalt meditate therein day and night.*[9]

AND SITTING IN THE MEETING-HOUSES OF THE IGNORANT—what does this mean? It teaches that a man should not sit with idlers in the market-place;[10] [for when a man sits with idlers in the market-place] it follows that he neglects the Torah, as it is stated, *Happy is the man that hath not walked in the counsel of the wicked nor stood in the way of sinners, nor sat in the seat of the scornful. But his delight is in the law of the Lord.*[11]

R. Meir said: What does the verse mean by *nor sat in the seat of the scornful?* It refers to the theatres and circuses[12] of the Gentiles[13] where men are condemned to death, and it is written, *I hate the gathering of evil-doers (mere'im), and will not sit with the wicked.*[14] By *mere'im* the wicked are meant, as it is stated, *For evil-doers (mere'im) shall be cut off.*[15] And what will be their punishment in the hereafter? Even as it is stated, *For behold the day cometh, it burneth as a furnace; and all the proud, and all that work wickedness shall be stubble.*[16] And by *the proud* none other are intended but the scorners, as it is stated, *A proud and haughty man, scorner is his name.*[17]

2. It is related of R. 'Aḳiba that once when he was sitting and lecturing to his disciples he recalled the conduct of his youth,[18] and offered up the prayer, 'I thank Thee, O Lord my God, that Thou hast set my portion with those who sit in the House of Study, and hast not set my portion with the idlers in the market-place'.

(8) So according to the MSS. V. reads: 'a man should not make a practice, while studying at home, of engaging in conversation with his wife and children, because all the time he sits at home and studies and converses with his children and members of his household, the outcome is', etc. The proper place for study is the house of learning where his family will not distract him. (9) Josh. I, 8. (10) [On the identity of 'idlers in the market-place' with 'the ignorant', cf. Büchler, *The Economic Conditions of Judaea*, p. 31n.] (11) Ps. I, 1f. (12) 'and circuses' is inserted from the MSS. (13) V. 'scorners'. (14) *ibid.* XXVI, 5. (15) *ibid.* XXXVII, 9. (16) Mal. III, 19. (17) Prov. XXI, 24. (18) Until the age of forty, R. 'Aḳiba was wholly unlearned in the Torah; cf. VI, 2, p. 43.

CHAPTER XXII

I. R. ḤANINA B. DOSA SAID: HE WHOSE FEAR OF SIN COMES BEFORE HIS WISDOM, HIS WISDOM SHALL ENDURE; [BUT HE WHOSE WISDOM COMES BEFORE HIS FEAR OF SIN, HIS WISDOM SHALL NOT ENDURE,] as it is stated, *The fear of the Lord is the beginning of wisdom.*[1]

HE USED TO SAY: HE WHOSE DEEDS EXCEED [HIS WISDOM, HIS WISDOM SHALL ENDURE; BUT HE WHOSE WISDOM EXCEEDS HIS DEEDS, HIS WISDOM SHALL NOT ENDURE,] as it is stated, *We will do and obey.*[2]

Rabban Joḥanan b. Zakkai was asked, 'How would you describe the man who is both learned and sin-fearing?' He replied, 'He is a craftsman who has the tools of his craft in his hand'. 'And the man who is learned but not sin-fearing?' He replied, 'He is a craftsman who has not the tools of his craft in his hand'. 'And the man who is sin-fearing but not learned?' He replied, 'He is no craftsman though he has the craftsman's tools in his hand'.

R. ELEAZAR B. AZARIAH SAID: WHERE THERE IS NO TORAH THERE ARE NO MANNERS,[3] etc. He used to say: A man who has good deeds to his credit and has learnt much Torah, to what is he like? To a tree planted by the waters, whose branches are few but whose roots are many, so that even if the four winds of the world come and blow against it they cannot move it from its place; as it is stated, *For he shall be as a tree planted by the waters,*[4] etc. But he who has no good deeds to his credit and yet has learnt much Torah, to what is he like? To a tree planted in the desert, whose branches are many

(1) Ps. CXI, 10. (2) Ex. XXIV, 7. Credit was ascribed to Israel that, at the time of the Revelation at mount Sinai, they declared their readiness 'to do' even before they had heard the commandments; cf. Shab. 88a (Sonc. ed., p. 418). (3) Quoted from Aboth III, 21 (Sonc. ed., III, 17, p. 40). The next saying is from *ibid.* 2 with variants and in the reverse order. (4) Jer. XVII, 8.

but whose roots are few, so that when the wind blows against it, it uproots and overturns it; as it is stated, *For he shall be like a tamarisk in the desert,*[5] etc.

Rabban Gamaliel said: Provide yourself with a teacher and get a companion:[6] a teacher for wisdom and a companion for study. Remove yourself from all doubt, and do not make a habit [26*b*] of tithing by guesswork.[7]

2. Simeon his son said: All my days I have grown up among the wise and have found nothing better for a man than silence.[8] If silence is good for the wise, how much more so for fools!

3. Wisdom does not produce words, nor do words produce wisdom; [the chief thing] is doing.[9] He who multiplies words brings about sin, as it is stated, *In the multitude of words there wanteth not transgression;*[10] and it further states, *Even a fool, when he holdeth his peace, is counted wise.*[11]

(5) *ibid.* 6. (6) This is a maxim of Joshua b. Peraḥiah in Aboth I, 6 (Sonc. ed., p. 5). (7) cf. *ibid.* 16 (Sonc. ed., p. 9). (8) From *ibid.* 17 (Sonc. ed., p. 9). (9) A comment on the maxim in Aboth I, 17 (Sonc. ed., p. 9): 'Study is not the chief thing but deed'. (10) Prov. X, 19. (11) *ibid.* XVII, 28.

CHAPTER XXIII

1. BEN ZOMA SAID: WHO IS WISE? HE THAT LEARNS FROM ALL MEN, AS IT IS STATED, FROM ALL MY TEACHERS HAVE I GOT UNDERSTANDING.[1] Who is the humblest among the humble? He who is humble like Moses our teacher, as it is stated, *The man Moses was very meek.*[2] WHO IS THE RICHEST AMONG THE RICH? HE WHO REJOICES IN HIS PORTION, AS IT IS STATED, WHEN THOU EATEST THE LABOUR OF THY HANDS, HAPPY SHALT THOU BE, AND IT SHALL BE WELL WITH THEE.[3] WHO IS THE MIGHTIEST AMONG THE MIGHTY? HE WHO SUBDUES HIS PASSIONS, AS IT IS WRITTEN, HE THAT IS SLOW TO ANGER IS BETTER THAN THE MIGHTY; AND HE THAT RULETH HIS SPIRIT THAN HE THAT TAKETH A CITY.[4] Whosoever subdues his passions is accounted as though he conquered a city filled with mighty men, as it is stated, *A wise man scaleth the city of the mighty;*[5] and[6] *the mighty* are none other than those who are strong in [the performance of the] Torah, as it is stated, *Ye mighty in strength, that fulfil His word.*[7] Some say: They are the ministering angels, as it is stated, *Bless the Lord, ye angels of His, ye mighty in strength.*[8] Others say: [Who is mighty?] Who turns an enemy into his friend.

2. R. NEHORAI SAID: WANDER FORTH TO A PLACE OF THE TORAH,[9] etc. [10]He used to say: Despise no man and consider nothing impossible, as it is stated, *Whoso despiseth the word shall*

(1) Ps. CXIX, 99, E.V., *I have more understanding than all my teachers.* (2) Num. XII, 3. (3) Ps. CXXVIII, 2. In Aboth IV, 1 (Sonc. ed., p. 43) the question reads, 'Who is rich?'. (4) Prov. XVI, 32. In Aboth *loc. cit.* the question reads, 'Who is mighty?' (5) *ibid.* XXI, 22. (6) GRA inserts here 'Another interpretation' which is to be preferred, because what follows is an exposition substantially different from the preceding. (7) Ps. CIII, 20. The verse therefore means: the wise man is raised to the category of 'the mighty' who fulfil God's word. (8) *ibid.* The verse is thereby interpreted to mean that the wise man is raised above the level of the angels. (9) From Aboth IV, 18 (Sonc. ed., IV, 14, p. 51). (10) A saying of Ben 'Azzai, *ibid.* 3 (Sonc. ed., pp. 44f.). [Cf. Bacher, *Ag. d. Tannaiten* I, p. 410, n. 1.]

suffer thereby; but he that feareth the commandment shall be rewarded.[11]

[12]He used to say: He who learns Torah in his youth, to what is he like? To a heifer which has been broken in while young, as it is stated, *Ephraim is a heifer well broken, that loveth to thresh.*[13] But he who learns Torah in his old age is like a heifer which was broken in only in its late years, as it is stated, *For Israel is stubborn like a stubborn heifer.*[14]

He used to say: He who learns Torah in his youth is like dough which a woman kneads with warm water;[15] but he who learns Torah in his old age is like dough which a woman kneads with cold water.

3. R. Eliezer b. Jacob said: He who learns Torah in his youth is like writing which is written on new paper; but he who learns Torah in his old age is like writing which is written on old paper.[16]

4. Rabban Simeon b. Gamaliel added to the former's saying: He who learns Torah in his youth is like a young man who married a virgin: they suit one another and desire one another. But he who learns Torah in his old age is like an old man who married a virgin: she suits him but he does not suit her; she desires him but he withdraws from her, as it is stated, *As arrows in the hand of a mighty man, so are the children of one's youth,*[17] and in the following verse it is written, *Happy is the man that hath his quiver full of them.*

He who learns [Torah] and forgets it is like a woman who bears children and buries them, as it is stated, *Though they bring up their children, yet I will bereave them till none is left.*[18] Read not *I will bereave them* but 'I will make them forget'.[19]

(11) Prov. XIII, 13. (12) GRA inserts here: 'Elisha b. 'Abuyah used to say: If one learns as a child, what is it like? Like ink written on clean paper, etc. (Aboth IV 25, Sonc. ed., IV, 20, p. 55). Cf. §3 below. (13) Hos. X, 11. Trained from its early days to thresh, the animal welcomes the task. So, too, the scholar, initiated in his youth to Torah-study, finds it a welcome duty. (14) *ibid.* IV, 16. (15) Following the emendation of GRA. (16) i.e. paper which has once been written on and rubbed out, so that any further writing would be blurred and indistinct. (17) Ps. CXXVII, 4. (18) Hos. IX, 12, E.V., *that there be not a man left.* (19) The two verbs differ in only one letter, ושכלתים, 'and I will bereave them', and ושכחתים, 'and I will make them forget'. The lesson is derived by drawing upon both verbs: bereavement is the result of forgetting the Torah.

R. Simeon b. Eleazar said: He who learns Torah in his youth is like a surgeon who, even when confronted with a growth, possesses a knife for the operation and remedial drugs to cure; but he who learns Torah in his old age is like a surgeon who, when confronted with a growth, possesses a knife for the operation but has no drugs to cure.

Therefore[20] let the words of the Torah be distinguished so that one thing [may be derived] from another and one thing [may be equated] with another, as it is stated, *Bind them upon thy fingers, write them upon the table of thy heart;*[21] and Scripture also states, *Bind them continually upon thy heart, tie them about thy neck.*[22]

(20) This paragraph follows logically on the last but one, and suggests means whereby the words of the Torah shall not be forgotten; cf. 'Erub. 54b (Sonc. ed., pp. 381ff). The preceding paragraph, the maxim of R. Simeon b. Eleazar, is manifestly out of place where it stands, and is transferred by GRA to the end of chap. XXII. It could very well be inserted between §§3 and 4 of this chapter. (21) Prov. VII, 3. (22) *ibid.* VI, 21.

CHAPTER XXIV

1. Elisha b. 'Abuya said: [1]A man who has good deeds to his credit and has also studied much Torah, to what is he like? To one who builds [a structure and lays] stones below [for the foundation] and bricks above, so that however much water may collect at the side it will not wash it away.
2. But a man who has no good deeds to his credit, though he has studied Torah, to what is he like? To one who builds [a structure and lays] bricks first [for the foundation] and then stones above, so that even if only a little water collects it at once undermines it.[2]
3. He used to say: A man who has good deeds to his credit and has also studied Torah, to what is he like? To a coating of lime spread on stone,[3] so that however much rain falls on it, it will not wash it away. But a man who has no good deeds to his credit, though he has studied much Torah, is like a coating of lime spread on bricks, so that even if the lightest rain falls on it, it will immediately dissolve and fall away.
4. He used to say: A man who has good deeds to his credit and has also studied much Torah is like a cup which has a square base[4] to it, so that when it is set down, though it is

(1) This chapter is devoted entirely to the teachings of Elisha b. 'Abuyah, a great scholar of the second century C.E. and teacher of R. Meir, who entered too deeply into theosophical speculations and eventually abandoned Judaism. Thereafter he was always referred to as *'Aḥer*, 'That other one'; cf. Ḥag. 15a (Sonc. ed., pp. 93ff). For a recent and learned study of this 'outcast' scholar, cf. Travers Herford in *Essays Presented to J. H. Hertz*, 1944, pp. 215-225. (2) The study of the Torah can become a permanent blessing only if it is founded on the good life. This is the theme of all the illustrations quoted. (3) So according to the MSS. and GRA. V. reads 'bricks', an obvious error since the contrast is between lime spread on stone and lime spread on bricks, the former enduring whilst the latter flakes off quickly. (4) The Heb. noun is the Greek for 'a stone', here a solid base with four polished sides (cf. below XXVIII, 9, p. 137). Since the cup has a wide four-square base, even if it be shaken and pushed, it will retain its balance and not lose its contents.

turned on its side, all its contents will not be spilt. But a man who has no good deeds to his credit, though he has studied much Torah, is like a cup which has not a square base, so that when it is set down it will at once turn on its side and all its contents will be spilt.

He used to say: A man who has good deeds to his credit and has also studied much Torah is like a horse with a bridle;[5] but he who has no good deeds to his credit, though he has studied much Torah, is like a horse without a bridle,[6] and as soon as a man attempts to mount it he is thrown headlong.

He used to say: He who learns Torah in his youth, its words are absorbed in his blood and issue from his mouth with clarity; but he who learns Torah only in his old age, its words are not absorbed in his blood and do not issue from his mouth with clarity. Accordingly the proverb runs, 'If thou hadst no delight in them in thy youth, how canst thou attain them in thy old age?'

5. He used to say: The words of the Torah are hard to acquire as vessels of gold, and are easily destroyed as glassware; as it is stated, *Gold and glass cannot equal it.*[7] A comparison is drawn between gold and glass: a golden vessel can be repaired when it is broken, but vessels of glass cannot be repaired when broken unless they are reduced to their original element.[8] And how am I to interpret, *Neither shall the exchange thereof be vessels of fine gold?*[9] It teaches that he who toils in [the words of the Torah] and fulfils them, his face shines like fine gold; but he who toils in them and does not fulfil them, his face is dark like glass.[10]

6. He used to say: A man may study the Torah for twenty years and forget it in two years. How can this be? If he sits idle for six months and does not revise his studies, he will in consequence pronounce the unclean to be clean and the clean to be unclean. [If he continues idle for] twelve months

(5) Reading כלינוס, as found in the MSS. and 'Aruk. V. reads 'fine trappings'. (6) Here, too, reading *kalinos* in accordance with the authorities quoted in the preceding note. V. has 'a bridle to curb it'. (7) Job XXVIII, 17. (8) i.e. melted by fire and then reshaped. (9) *ibid.* (10) The meaning is either opaque glass which is dull, or glass which quickly darkens.

without revision, he will then confuse [the names of] the Sages;[11] if for eighteen months without revision, he will forget the opening words of the chapters; and if twenty-four months without revision, he will forget even the titles [27a] of the Tractates.[12] And so, having pronounced the unclean to be clean and the clean to be unclean, having also confused [the names of] the Sages, and forgotten the chapter headings and even the titles of the Tractates, he will eventually sit in silence. Of him Solomon said, *I went by the field of the slothful, and by the vineyard of the man void of understanding; and, lo, it was all grown over with thistles, the face thereof was covered with nettles, and the stone wall thereof was broken down.*[13] When the wall of a vineyard collapses the entire vineyard is soon destroyed.

7. He used to say: He who causes another to perform a commandment is regarded by Scripture as if he had performed it himself. . . . [14]This may be illustrated by a parable. To what can it be compared? To a human king who caught a bird and gave it to one of his servants saying, 'Be careful with the bird. If you guard it, well and good; but if not I will take your life for it'. So, too, did the Holy One, blessed be He, say to Israel, 'I have entrusted the words of the Torah to you. If you guard them, well and good; but if not I will take your lives for them'. For it is stated, *Only take heed to thyself, and keep thy soul diligently, lest thou forget the things which thine eyes saw.*[15] [And it is also stated,] *For it is no vain thing for you, because it is your life.*[16]

(11) Attributing a teaching to the wrong authority. (12) This is the more logical order and is supported by MSS., cf. Schechter *ad loc.* V. reverses the order, putting 'the titles of the Tractates' before 'the opening words of the chapters'. (13) Prov. XXIV, 30f. (14) There seems to be a lacuna here, because the parable which follows has no relation to the preceding statement. GRA inserts here the teaching of R. Dostai b. Yannai in Aboth III, 10 (Sonc. ed., III, 8, p. 32): 'Whosoever forgets one word of his study, him Scripture regards as though he was guilty against his soul.' This dictum is well illustrated by the parable. Cf. Men. 99b (Sonc. ed., p. 607). (15) Deut. IV, 9. In Aboth *loc. cit.* this verse is quoted in support of R. Dostai's teaching mentioned in the preceding note. (16) *ibid.* XXXII, 47.

CHAPTER XXV

1. Ben 'Azzai said: He whose mind is at ease because of his learning,[1] it is a good omen for him; and he whose mind is ill at ease because of his learning, it is a bad omen for him. He whose mind is at ease with his inclination,[2] it is a good omen for him; and he whose mind is ill at ease with his inclination, it is a bad omen for him. Whoever holds the good opinion of the Sages at the hour of his death, it is a good omen for him; but whoever does not hold the good opinion of the Sages, it is a bad omen for him. Whoever [dies] with his face directed upwards[3] it is a good omen; if it is turned downwards it is a bad omen. If his eyes look straight towards the people [about him] it is a good omen; if they do not look towards the people [about him] it is a bad omen. Whoever [dies] with a cheerful countenance it is a good omen; if with a frowning countenance it is a bad omen.

When Rabban Joḥanan b. Zakkai was about to depart from this world,[4] he wept aloud. His disciples said to him, 'Master! Exalted pillar! Light of the world! Mighty hammer! Why do you weep?' He replied, 'Is it into the presence of a human king that I am going? If he be angry with me his anger endures only in this world; if he imprison me the imprisonment endures only in this world; and if he kill me my death is only in this world. Moreover, him I can appease with words and bribe with money. Behold, I am going into the Presence of the King of kings, the Holy One, blessed be He. If He be angry with me His anger endures in this world and in the world to come; and Him I cannot appease with words or bribe with

(1) The knowledge which he acquired did not make him overbearing, but confirms him in his faith and helps him to live the good life. Cf. Tosif. Ber. III, 5. (2) i.e. his desires are not in constant conflict within him. A variant reading has 'his Creator' for 'his inclination'. (3) Indicating that he is prepared to meet his Maker with a clear conscience. Cf. on this passage, Keth. 103b (Sonc. ed., p. 661). (4) Cf. Ber. 28b (Sonc. ed., p. 173).

money. Furthermore, before me lie two ways, one leading to the Garden of Eden and the other to Gehinnom, and I know not whether I will be condemned to Gehinnom or conducted to the Garden of Eden; and concerning this[5] Scripture declares, *All they that go down to the dust shall kneel before Him.*[6] Of Moses Scripture states, *And he expired, and died, and was gathered to his people.*[7] And it further states, *And I will take away My hand.*[8] It also states, *And He spread it before me, and it was written on its face and on its back*[9]—*face* refers to this world and *back* to the world to come. According to another interpretation *face* refers to the suffering of the righteous on earth and the prosperity of the wicked in this world, and *back* to the reward of the righteous in the hereafter and the punishment of the wicked in Gehinnom. *And there was written therein lamentations, and sweet music, and woe*[10]—*lamentations* [*ḳinim*] refers to the punishment of the wicked[11] in this world, as it is stated, *This is the lamentation* [*ḳinah*] *which shall be chanted; the daughters of the nations shall chant it.*[12] *Sweet music* [*hegeh*] refers to the reward of the righteous in the hereafter, as it is stated, *With an instrument of ten strings, and with the psaltery; with sweet music* [*higgayon*] *upon the harp.*[13] *Woe* [*he*] refers to the punishment of the wicked in the world to come, as it is

(5) The day of his death. (6) Ps. XXII, 30. This verse is interpreted in Midrash Rabbah, Numbers, XIV, 22 (Sonc. ed., p. 640), as indicating that at death all are led into the Presence of God. (7) This verse is not found of Moses, but only of Abraham (Gen. XXV, 8) and Isaac (*ibid.* XXXV, 29). The text is in disorder, and the verses which follow have but a slender connection with the theme of the passage (cf. GRA and Schechter's notes *ad loc.*). The verse in the text suggests that the righteous are 'gathered' to God and are shown the reward which has been stored up for them. Cf. Midrash Rabbah, Gen. LXII, 2 (Sonc. ed., p. 549). (8) Ex. XXXIII, 23. This verse also suggests that at the hour of death God 'takes away His hand' and reveals their reward to the righteous. (9) Ezek. II, 10, E.V., *written within and without.* The scroll which was spread before the prophet apparently contained the doctrine of retribution; cf. 'Erub. 21a (Sonc. ed., p. 147). (10) *ibid.*, E.V., *lamentations, and moaning, and woe.* (11) In the parallel passage in 'Erub. *loc. cit.*, as well as in Rashi's commentary on the verse of Ezek., *lamentations* refers to the sufferings of the righteous on earth. (12) *ibid.* XXXII, 16, E.V., *lamentation wherewith they shall lament . . . shall lament therewith.* This verse proves that the term *ḳinah*, the singular of *ḳinim*, signifies a dirge of misery and suffering.

stated, *Calamity [howah] shall come upon calamity, and rumour shall be upon rumour.*[14]

[In his last utterance] he[15] said, 'Remove all vessels from the house that they be not defiled, and prepare a throne for Hezekiah king of Judah'.[16]

2. He used to say: He who dies in a tranquil frame of mind it is a good omen for him;[17] if in a state of delirium it is a bad omen for him. [If he dies] while speaking it is a good omen; if while silent it is a bad omen. If while conversing about the Torah it is a good omen, about business affairs it is a bad omen; if while engaged upon a religious act it is a good omen, upon a worthless pursuit it is a bad omen. [If he dies] in the midst of a joyous atmosphere it is a good omen, amidst sadness it is a bad omen; [if he dies] smiling it is a good omen, if weeping it is a bad omen. Should a man die on the Sabbath-eve it is a good omen,[18] if at the termination of the Sabbath it is a bad omen. If he dies on the eve of the Day of Atonement it is a bad omen,[19] if at the termination of the Day of Atonement it is a good omen.

3. The day when R. Eliezer fell ill was, according to tradition, the Sabbath-eve. R. 'Aḳiba and his colleagues came to visit him, and he was sitting in his canopied four-poster[20] while they waited in an anteroom. His son Hyrḳanos went in to remove his father's *tefillin,*[21] but he would not allow him to do so. Hyrḳanos came out weeping and said to the Sages, 'My masters, it seems that my father's mind is deranged'.

(13) Ps. XCII, 4, E.V., *with a solemn sound.* The words *hegeh* and *higgayon* are related in meaning, suggesting melodious song. (14) Ezek. VII, 26. The words הי and הוה are here brought together, each signifying 'sorrow, woe'. (15) viz. of Rabban Joḥanan b. Zakkai. (16) Who will accompany him into the next world. Rabban Joḥanan, like king Hezekiah, had acted zealously for the spread of Torah-study and the observance of the commandments; cf. Sanh. 94b (Sonc. ed., p. 637). (17) Because he is able to put his affairs in order with calmness and deliberation. (18) He will enter immediately into rest. (19) He dies with his sins unexpiated. (20) So according to a variant reading and the parallel passage in Sanh. 68a (Sonc. ed., p. 461). V. reads: 'he was sleeping in his room'. (21) Which are not worn on the Sabbath.

[Thereupon R. Eliezer] called out, 'My son, it is not my mind that is deranged but yours, because you put off kindling the Sabbath lamp for which you incur the penalty of death at the hand[22] of Heaven and occupied yourself with the *tefillin* for which you incur only the penalty of transgressing a Rabbinic precept concerning the Sabbath rest'.[23] When the Sages perceived that his mind was clear, they entered, sat at a distance of four cubits away from him,[24] and enquired of him, 'Master, if a round cushion, a ball, a shoe-last, an amulet or a phylactery were torn, can they contract uncleanness?'[25] He replied, 'They can, and [if they are unclean] they may be immersed as they are. Be careful about these laws, because they are important laws which were communicated to Moses at Sinai'. They continued to question him on matters concerning cleanness and uncleanness and the regulations of ritual immersion. They said to him, 'Master, what is the law in this case?' and he answered, 'It is unclean'. 'And what is the law in that case?' and he answered, 'It is clean'. Throughout he pronounced the unclean to be unclean and the clean to be clean. After that R. Eliezer said to the Sages, 'I am concerned about the disciples of the present generation lest they be punished with death at the hand of Heaven'. They asked him, 'Master, what is the reason?' He replied, 'Because they did not come and attend upon me'.[26] He then said to 'Aḳiba b. Joseph, ''Aḳiba, why did you not come and attend upon me?' He replied, 'Master, I had no leisure'. He retorted, 'I wonder whether you will die a natural death'. Some say that R. Eliezer did not make that rejoinder, but as R. Eliezer spoke to his disciples in this manner, R. 'Aḳiba at once felt his blood

(22) To light the Sabbath lamp after the Sabbath had begun constitutes a profanation of the holy day involving the death penalty. (23) Wearing the *tefillin* on the Sabbath is comparable to the wearing of an adornment, which is forbidden only by Rabbinic law. (24) R. Eliezer had been placed under the ban of excommunication (cf. B.M. 59b, Sonc. ed., p. 353) and all intercourse with him by his colleagues was carried out at a distance of four cubits. (25) On the questions and the ritualistic principles involved, cf. above XIX, 4 (p. 108, n. 6). (26) On account of the ban imposed upon him, the scholars had not sought his instruction.

melt within him and exclaimed, 'Master, what will my death be?' and he replied, 'Yours will be the most cruel of all'.

R. 'Aḳiba then approached, sat down before him and said, 'Master teach me now'. He began and taught him three hundred *halakoth* on the subject of 'the bright spot'.[27] At that time R. Eliezer raised his two arms and, laying them upon his breast, exclaimed, 'Alas for these two arms of mine, [the equal of] two scrolls of the Torah, which must leave this world! For though all the seas were ink, all reeds quills and all men scribes, they could not set down all the Scripture which I read, all the Mishnah which I studied, and all that I had gained by attending upon the scholars at their sessions. And I took from my teachers no more than a man takes of the sea when he dips his finger in it; and my disciples took no more from me than a paint-stick takes of the paint in the tube.[28] Moreover, I can recite three hundred (another version: three thousand) *halakoth* on the prohibition, *Thou shalt not suffer a sorceress to live,*[29] yet no one ever questioned me about them except 'Aḳiba b. Joseph. For on one occasion he said to me, "Master, teach me how cucumbers are planted"[30]. So I pronounced a word and the entire field [about us] was filled with cucumbers. He then said to me, "You have taught me how they are planted, now teach me how to uproot them". I again pronounced a word and all the cucumbers were gathered in one place'.

R. Eleazar b. Azariah enquired of him, 'Master, what is the law if the shoe is still on the shoemaker's last?'[31] He answered, 'It is clean'. He made reply [to many questions] declaring the

(27) A symptom, as well as a type, of leprosy; cf. Lev. XIII. (28) The text is evidently faulty and the translation follows the emendation of GRA which accords with the parallel passage in Sanh. 68a (Sonc. ed., p. 462). V is lit., 'I withheld not of all that my eyes desired only to the extent of a man dipping his finger in the sea, and I no more lost of my learning than a paint-stick removes paint from a tube'. (29) Ex. XXII, 17. (30) The reference to the planting and uprooting of cucumbers has a magical connotation; cf. Sanh. *loc. cit.* V adds in brackets, 'and how they are uprooted'. (31) Since the shoe is still on the last, it could be regarded as unfinished, and consequently should not contract defilement.

unclean to be unclean and the clean to be clean until with the word 'clean' [on his lips] his soul departed. At once R. Eleazar b. Azariah rent his clothes and wept. He went out to the Sages and said, 'Come, my masters, and behold R. Eliezer who is clean for the world to come, because his soul departed with the word "clean" [upon his lips]'. After the Sabbath, R. 'Aḳiba set out and encountered [his master's] bier as it proceeded from Caesarea to Lydda. Forthwith he rent his garments and plucked his hair, and [beat his breast until] his blood flowed to the ground. He wept and cried, 'Woe is me! I grieve for you, my master! Woe is me! I mourn for you, my teacher who left his whole generation orphaned!' As they stood in a row[32] he began his funeral oration and said, '*My father, my father, the chariots of Israel and the horsemen thereof.*[33] I have many coins, but there is no money-changer to exchange them'.[34] [27b]

4. BEN 'AZZAI SAID: RUN TO FULFIL EVEN A LIGHT PRECEPT.[35] He used to say: If you have performed a precept and have no regrets with regard to it, it will in the end draw many precepts in its train. And if one has committed a transgression and has no regrets about it, it will in the end draw many transgressions in its train; FOR ONE PRECEPT LEADS TO ANOTHER PRECEPT, AND ONE TRANSGRESSION TO ANOTHER TRANSGRESSION; FOR THE REWARD OF A PRECEPT IS ANOTHER PRECEPT, AND THE REWARD OF A TRANSGRESSION IS ANOTHER TRANSGRESSION.

He used to say: Desist[36] of your own accord and you will reap the reward for desisting; but let not others make you desist, because they will then reap the reward for making you desist.

He used to say: Step down from your place two or three

(32) Which was formed around the bier. (33) 2 Kings II, 12. (34) Many difficult questions of law will now be left unanswered because none but R. Eliezer, with his vast accumulation of traditional rulings, could have solved them. (35) [This passage is discussed in Büchler, *Studies in Sin and Atonement*, pp. 311f.] (36) From committing a transgression (Emden). Alternatively: 'Allocate charity of your own accord' (B.Y.), or 'Keep silent of your own accord and wait not for others to silence you' (Meiri).

degrees and sit there, because it is better for you to be told to ascend than to be told to descend; as it is stated, *For better is it that it be said unto thee: Come up hither, than that thou shouldest be put lower in the presence of the prince, whom thine eyes have seen.*[37]

5. There are three whose life is not worth living, and they are: He who must look to the table of another [for sustenance], he who lives in an attic, and whoever is dominated by his wife. Others add: he whose body is afflicted with sufferings.[38]

He used to say: It is easier to rule over the whole world than to sit and teach[39] people who are wrapped in linen robes.[40]

(37) Prov. XXV, 7. (38) Cf. Beẓah 32b (Sonc. ed., p. 165). [Cf. also Bacher, *Ag. d. Tannaiten*, I, p. 414, n. 4.] (39) Or, 'to study in the presence of'. (40) A term for hypocrites, who wrap themselves in a mantle of piety but inwardly are of evil mind. Cf. Midrash Tehillim on XVIII, 44. [Buber, *ad loc.*, defines the phrase as 'judges'. Bacher, *op. cit.*, n. 1, holds the meaning to be doubtful. He quotes Midrash Rabbah, Ecclesiastes, to I, 7 (Sonc. ed., p. 24) where it refers to two Sages who were humble men.]

CHAPTER XXVI

1. R. 'Akiba said: A fence[1] to honour is [the avoidance of] jesting,[2] a fence to wisdom is silence, a fence to vows is self-restraint,[3] a fence to purity is holiness, a fence to humility is the fear of sin.

2. He used to say: Come not among scoffers lest you learn of their ways. Eat not bread with a priest who is an *'am ha-'arez* lest you trespass in hallowed things. Be not free with vows lest you trespass in oaths.[4] Be not in the habit of feasting sumptuously lest in the end you will have to eat the bread of charity.[5] Bring not yourself to a state of doubt lest you come up against a certain [transgression]. Do not leave the land [of Israel] lest you serve idols; for so David said, *For they have driven me out this day that I should not cleave unto the inheritance of the Lord, saying; Go, serve other gods.*[6] Can it, however, enter your mind that king David would serve idols? But this is what David meant: Whosoever leaves the land of Israel and goes abroad, Scripture regards him as an idolater.

He used to say: Whoever is buried in other lands is considered as though he were buried in Babylon;[7] whoever is

(1) The 'fence' is here taken in the sense of a safeguard or an aid to. With this paragraph, cf. Aboth III, 17. (2) That this is the true meaning of the saying is proved by the wording in Schechter's second version of ARN XXXIII (beg.) ,'a fence to honour is not to jest'. Cf. Finkelstein's translation of this maxim in his *Akiba: Scholar, Saint and Martyr,* p. 111, 'Laughter protects one's honour'. (3) By practising abstinence the making of vows becomes unnecessary. (4) The breaking of an oath is a more serious matter than the breaking of a vow. Cf. Ned. 20a (Sonc. ed., p. 56) and R. Nissim *ad loc.* (5) Reading *hakkuppah,* lit. '[the charity] chest' which is found as a variant. The word in the text *hakkanim,* 'the reeds', makes no sense. The emendation of GRA is attractive, *hazziknin,* 'the scrapings of the pot'. (6) 1 Sam. XXVI, 19. (7) Death being an expiation, when a person dies and is interred, he is brought one degree closer to the Divine Presence which manifests its greatest concentration and brilliance in the Throne of Glory which is directly above the altar in Jerusalem. The degrees in ascending scale which lead to the Divine Glory are: other lands, Babylon, the land of Israel, Jerusalem (this is omitted in the text), the altar, and the Throne of Glory. Cf. Kel. I, 6ff (Sonc. ed., pp. 10ff).

buried in Babylon is as though he were buried in the land of Israel; whoever is buried in the land of Israel is as though he were buried beneath the altar, because all the land of Israel is fit [to be the site of] the altar; and whoever is buried beneath the altar[8] is as though he were buried beneath the Throne of Glory; as it is stated, *The throne of glory, on high from the beginning, is the place of our sanctuary.*[9]

3. HE USED TO SAY: AN IGNORANT MAN CANNOT BE PIOUS, THE BASHFUL MAN CANNOT LEARN, AND THE IMPATIENT MAN CANNOT TEACH.[10] He used to say: Why do disciples of the Sages [often] die young? It is not because they are immoral or because they rob; but because they interrupt their study of the Torah to indulge in idle talk. Moreover, [when returning to their studies] they do not begin where they left off.

4. R. Simeon b. Eleazar said: The Israelites who live outside the land of Israel serve idols in all innocence.[11] How is this? For example, a Gentile prepares a banquet for his son and invites all the Jews of his town to it; although they eat and drink [of their own], and their own attendant waits on them and serves them with drink, Scripture accounts it to them as though they had eaten of the sacrifices of the dead; as it is stated, *And they call thee and thou eat of their sacrifice.*[12]

R. ELIEZER OF MODIN SAID: IF A MAN PROFANES THE SABBATHS,[13] SLIGHTS THE FESTIVALS, MAKES VOID THE COVENANT IN THE FLESH,[14] OR MISINTERPRETS THE TORAH, EVEN THOUGH HE POSSESSES TORAH AND GOOD DEEDS, HE HAS NO SHARE IN THE WORLD TO COME.

(8) This is a strange statement. GRA substitutes 'in Jerusalem' for 'beneath the altar'. Cf. Keth. 111a (Sonc. ed., p. 714). (9) Jer. XVII, 12. E.V., *Thou throne . . . thou place of our sanctuary*. (10) A saying ascribed to Hillel in Aboth II, 10. (11) lit. 'in purity'. Cf. 'A.Z. 8a (Sonc. ed., p. 38). [The word for 'in purity' is omitted in the Tosiftha to 'A.Z. IV, 6, and Büchler, *Studies in Sin and Atonement*, p. 319, n. 2, explains it as 'without evil intention'. (12) Ex. XXXIV, 15. (13) In Aboth III, 15: 'the hallowed things'. (14) i.e. disregards the rite of circumcision. Aboth, *loc. cit.*, reads, 'the covenant of Abraham our father . . . the Torah contrary to the *halakah*'. [Some Jewish scholars have detected here a polemic against the early Christians; cf. Bacher, *Ag. d. Tannaiten* I, p. 190, n. 1.]

R. 'Aḳiba said: Whoever marries a wife who is unsuited to him transgresses five commandments, namely: *Thou shalt not take vengeance;*[15] *Thou shalt not bear a grudge;*[16] *Thou shalt not hate thy brother in thy heart;*[17] *Thou shalt love thy neighbour as thyself;*[18] and *That thy brother may live with thee*[19]—because since he hates her, he wishes her dead, and, in consequence, he abstains from fulfilling the duty to be fruitful and multiply in the world.[20]

5. He used to say: If a man eats food which is unsuitable for his constitution,[21] he transgresses three commandments: he disgraces himself, he disgraces his food, and he recites a benediction to no purpose.[22]

6. R. Judah b. Ilai said: If a man died and left a son, and that son, who had learnt no Torah from his father, now seeks to learn Torah from others, he is obviously insincere in his quest.[23]

R. Eleazar ha-Ḳappar said: Be not like the top lintel of a doorway which is out of reach of a man's hand, nor like the top of the door-frame which can injure the face, nor like the middle of the door-frame which can hurt the legs; but be like the threshold below upon which all tread, and when the entire building is demolished it remains in its place.[24]

(15) Lev. XIX, 18. (16) *ibid.* (17) *ibid.* (18) *ibid.* (19) *ibid.* XXV, 36. (20) Gen. I, 28. (21) A variant reading is: 'over which no blessing should be recited'. Cf. R. Judah's opinion in Ber. VI, 3 (Sonc. ed., p. 251). (22) lit. 'that is not in accordance with the regulation'. Since the food is harmful to health, no blessing is to be recited, and one who does so pronounces the name of God in vain. (23) Since he missed the opportunity of being instructed by his own father. The passage, however, is obscure (cf. the commentaries *ad loc.*). (24) A maxim stressing the importance of humility with its enduring virtue, and the harmfulness of pride and arrogance in whatever degree.

CHAPTER XXVII

1. R. JOSE SAID: HE WHO HONOURS THE TORAH IS HIMSELF HONOURED BY MANKIND, as it is stated, *For them that honour Me I will honour, and they that despise Me shall be lightly esteemed.*[1]

Another interpretation[2] of *For them that honour Me I will honour:* this refers to Pharaoh king of Egypt who paid honour to Him Who spoke and the world came into being by going out at the head of his council of ministers. His servants said to him, 'Usually kings go out behind their ministers, but you go out at their head!' He replied, 'Am I going out to meet a [28*a*] king of flesh and blood? No, I go to meet the Presence of the King of kings, the Holy One, blessed be He'. Therefore the Holy One, blessed be He, paid Pharaoh honour, and He Himself meted out retribution to him, as it is stated, *I have compared thee, O my love, to a steed in Pharaoh's chariots.*[3]

2. R. Pappias said: The congregation of Israel praised the horses and chariots of Pharaoh, as it is stated, *Thou hast trodden the sea with Thy horses.*[4]

R. Joshua b. Ḳorḥah said: When Pharaoh came to the Red Sea he was riding on a stallion, and the Holy One, blessed be He, appeared to him on a mare,[5] as it is stated, *To a steed in*

(1) 1 Sam. II, 30. 'Me' is here identified with the Torah, a doctrine frequent in the Zohar and other mystical literature. (2) Omitted in V, but inserted by GRA. (3) Cant. I, 9. This verse in no wise proves the point that God Himself inflicted punishment upon Pharaoh. GRA substitutes for this verse Hab. III, 15, quoted in the preceding paragraph. This latter verse suggests that God set forth on His horses in order to requite Pharaoh; cf. Sanh. 94b (Sonc. ed., p. 634). (4) Hab. *ibid.* This verse too offers no proof for R. Pappias' statement, and it has been suggested that Cant. I, 9 should be read here as indicating the high esteem in which Pharaoh's steeds were held, since God likens His love for Israel to a highly prized mare among Pharaoh's chariots. The text of the passage is evidently in disorder and Schechter gives it up as hopeless. [Bacher, *Ag. d. Tannaiten* I, p. 319, n. 3, thinks that the appropriate quotation is Hab. III, 8.] (5) To lure Pharaoh's stallion to follow headlong into the sea; cf. Midrash Rabbah, Song of Songs, on I, 9 (Sonc. ed., p. 71).

Pharaoh's chariots. But did He not ride upon a cherub, as it is stated, *And He rode upon a cherub, and did fly; yea, He did swoop down upon the wings of the wind?*[6] The cherub appeared to the steeds of Pharaoh in the form of a mare, and they followed her into the sea.

And they that despise Me shall be lightly esteemed: this refers to Sennacherib who behaved contemptuously before Him Who spoke and the world came into being, as it is stated, *By thy servants hast thou taunted the Lord, and hast said: With the multitude of my chariots am I come up to the height of the mountains, to the innermost parts of Lebanon; and I have cut down the tall cedars thereof, and the choice cypress-trees thereof; and I have entered into his farthest height, the forest of his fruitful field. I have digged and drunk water, and with the sole of my feet have I dried up all the rivers of Egypt.*[7] Therefore the Holy One, blessed be He, meted out punishment to him by an angel who shaved his head and beard,[8] so that he returned shamefacedly to his land.[9]

R. ISHMAEL THE SON OF R. JOḤANAN B. BEROKA SAID: HE WHO LEARNS IN ORDER TO TEACH, etc.[10] He used to say: It is not incumbent upon you to undertake to finish the whole of the Torah, yet you are not free to keep aloof from it.[11] But he who greatly amasses [knowledge of the Torah] accumulates abundant reward.

R. ELEAZAR B. ḤISMA SAID: THE LAWS CONCERNING BIRD-OFFERINGS AND THE PURIFICATION OF WOMEN ARE THE ESSENTIAL ORDINANCES.[12] R. Joḥanan b. Nuri said: The *halakoth*, the laws of ritual purity and of menstrual women and bird-offerings are the essentials of the Torah. He used to say: The arranging of the table[13] and the establishment of a *Beth Din*[14] as well as its upkeep bring welfare to the world.

(6) Ps. XVIII, 11. (7) Is. XXXVII, 24f. (8) Cf. Sanh. 96a (Sonc. ed., p. 646). (9) In the MSS. quoted in Schechter's edition the words 'who shaved . . . land' are omitted, and in their place is quoted the appropriate verse from Is. XXXVII, 36, *And the angel of the Lord went forth and smote in the camp of the Assyrians*, etc. (10) From Aboth IV, 6 (Sonc. ed., IV, 5, p. 46). (11) An adaptation of R. Ṭarfon's dictum in Aboth II, 21 (Sonc. ed., II, 16, p. 24). (12) From Aboth III, 23 (Sonc. ed., III, 18, p. 41). (13) To set out the Shewbread (cf. Lev. XXIV, 5ff). According to GRA, the provision of a large and lavish table to feed the scholars and the needy. (14) To administer justice and establish law and order in the community.

3. R. Joḥanan b. Dehabai said: If a man says, 'This law is not acceptable',[15] he has no share in the world to come. He used to say: Keep not aloof from a pursuit which is limitless or from a task which is endless.[16] [This may be illustrated by] a parable. To what is the matter like? To a man who was [hired] to carry away the waters from the sea and pour them out on the dry land. The sea did not grow less nor was the dry land filled up; so the man became dispirited. Whereupon people said to him, 'You fool! why are you dispirited? Continue to draw your pay of one golden *dinar* daily'.

4. R. ELIEZER B. SHAMMUA' SAID: LET THE HONOUR OF YOUR DISCIPLE BE AS DEAR TO YOU AS YOUR OWN, AND THE HONOUR OF YOUR COLLEAGUE AS THE REVERENCE FOR YOUR TEACHER, AND THE REVERENCE FOR YOUR TEACHER AS THE REVERENCE OF HEAVEN. Whence do we know that the honour of a disciple should be as dear as one's own honour?[17] All may derive it from Moses our teacher who said to Joshua, *Choose for us men.*[18] It is not stated, 'Choose for me' but *Choose for us,* proving that he regarded Joshua as an equal, although he was the master and Joshua his disciple.

Whence do we know that the honour of a colleague should be as dear as [the reverence for] one's teacher? As it is stated, *And Aaron said unto Moses: Oh my lord.*[19] But was not Moses his younger brother? Yet he acknowledged Moses as his master.[20]

And whence do we know that the reverence[21] for a teacher should be as dear to one as the reverence of Heaven? As it is stated, *And Joshua the son of Nun, the minister of Moses from his youth up, answered and said: My lord Moses, shut them in.*[22] He then considered his teacher's honour as equal to that of the Divine.[23]

(15) Reading נראית for נבראת. The statement is a denial of the authenticity and Divine origin of the Torah; cf. Sanh. 99a (Sonc. ed., pp. 671f). (16) i.e. the study of the Torah. This is an exposition of R. Ṭarfon's dictum in Aboth II, 21 (Sonc. ed., II, 16, p. 24). The author may well be R. Ṭarfon himself. (17) As corrected by the Commentators. V. reads, 'It teaches that . . . as the honour of his colleague'. (18) Ex. XVII, 9. E.V., *choose us out men.* (19) Num. XII, 11. (20) By addressing him as *my lord.* (21) The text has 'honour', but the intent is 'reverence' as set out at the beginning of the passage. (22) *ibid.* XI, 28. (23) Joshua regarded disobedience to his teacher Moses as disobedience to the Divine command.

For[24] at first they said, 'Corn [is plentiful] in Judah, straw in Galilee, and chaff beyond the Jordan'. Later, however, they said, 'In Judah there is no corn [only straw], in Galilee there is no straw but only chaff, and beyond the Jordan there is neither the one nor the other'.[25]

(24) This word is deleted by GRA as the passage has no connection with what has gone before; but cf. the commentary of B.Y. (25) The passage describes in metaphor the state of learning which prevailed in Judah and the provinces, and proceeds to contrast the attainments of the early generations with the later, showing how the standard had deteriorated in the course of the years. Cf. 'Erub. 53a (Sonc. ed., pp. 370ff). Schechter considers this passage out of place here and suggests its transference to XXVIII, 2.

CHAPTER XXVIII

1. R. Nathan said: There is no love like the love for the Torah, no wisdom like the wisdom of the land of Israel,[1] no beauty like the beauty of Jerusalem, no wealth like the wealth of Media, no might like the might of Persia, no immorality like that of the Arabs, no arrogance like the arrogance of Elam, no hypocrisy like the hypocrisy of Babylon, as it is stated, *And he said unto me: To build her a house in the land of Shinar,*[2] and no magic like the magic of Egypt.[3]

2. R. Simeon b. Eleazar said: If a sage who has been living in the land of Israel leaves it for a foreign country, he has lost merit;[4] and he who remains there is more worthy than he. But although he has lost merit, he is still far more worthy than the meritorious of other lands. [This may be illustrated by] a parable. To what can the matter be compared? To Indian iron[5] which has been exported to a land[6] beyond the sea; even when it has deteriorated it is still superior to the best of other lands.

3. R. Simeon b. Gamaliel said: Whoever makes peace in his house, Scripture ascribes it to him as though he made peace for every individual in Israel; but whoever brings jealousy and strife into his house, Scripture ascribes it to him as though he brought these among Israel; because each person is a king in his home, as it is stated, *That every man shall bear rule in his own house.*[7]

4. Rabban Gamaliel said: By four methods heathen States devour [their inhabitants]: by their taxes, bath-houses, theatres and annual levies.[8]

(1) So MSS. and GRA; V, 'worldly affairs'. (2) Zech. V, 11. (3) On this passage, cf. Ḳid. 49b (Sonc. ed., pp. 248f). (4) Cf. B.B. 158b (Sonc. ed., p. 691): 'The climate of the land of Israel makes one wise'. (5) Iron from India was highly prized for the making of armour. Cf. 'A.Z. 16a (Sonc. ed., p. 79). (6) So GRA. V. reads, 'which has come from a land'. (7) Esth. I, 22. (8) The exorbitant taxes, and the life of ease, sport and luxury indulged in by the upper classes, contributed largely to the disintegration of the Roman Empire.

5. He used to say: The words of the Torah are as difficult to acquire as fine woollen clothes, but are as easily lost as linen garments. Foolish and frivolous words are easily acquired, but are as hard to lose as a sack. Often a man buys a sack in the market for a *sela'* and continues using it for four or five years.

R. Judah the Prince said: Whoever indulges in the pleasures of this world will be withheld from the pleasures of the world to come; but whoever denies himself the pleasures of this world will be granted the pleasures of the world to come.

6. He used to say: To what can the righteous who are unfortunate in this world be compared? To a chef who prepares a meal for himself; for though it cost him much effort, he prepares it for none other than himself; but to what can the wicked who are unfortunate in this world be compared? To a chef who prepared a meal for others; for though it cost him much effort, he has prepared nothing for himself but only for others.

7. He used to say: Let your private life be open to full view;[9] and what is not meant to be heard[10] tell not to your fellow.

8. HILLEL SAID: DO NOT SEPARATE YOURSELF FROM THE CONGREGATION, etc.[11]

9. He used to say: The more one eats the more he discharges; the more flesh one puts on the more worms and maggots he breeds; the more good deeds [28b] one does the more peace he provides for his body.

R. Eleazar b. Shammua' said: There are three types of disciple: a cut stone, a corner-stone and a plinth. 'A cut stone'—what does this describe? The disciple who has studied *Midrash*[12] only, so that whenever a scholar comes to consult him on a Midrashic subject he can enlighten him. Such a one is like a cut stone which has only one polished surface. 'A corner-stone'—what does this describe? The disciple who has studied *Midrash* and *halakoth*, so that whenever a scholar comes

(9) i.e. act in private as you would in public. The phrase used is equivalent to the more usual expression *toko kebaro*, 'whose inside is as his outside', i.e. sincere; cf. Ber. 28a (Sonc. ed., p. 168). (10) i.e. a confidential matter. (11) From Aboth II, 5 (Sonc. ed., II, 4, p. 14). (12) Laws derived from the text of the Torah by exegesis.

to consult him either on a Midrashic or halakic subject he can enlighten him. Such a one is like a corner-stone which has two polished surfaces. 'A plinth'—what does this describe? The disciple who has studied *Midrash, halakoth, 'aggadoth* and *tosephoth*, so that whenever a scholar comes to consult him on a subject in the *Midrash*, in the *halakoth*, in the *'aggadoth* or in the *tosephoth* he can enlighten him. Such a one is like a plinth which has four polished surfaces on its four sides.

10. R. Judah b. Ilai said: He who treats the words of the Torah as of primary importance and worldly affairs as secondary will himself be of primary importance in the world;[13] but he who treats worldly affairs as of primary importance and the words of the Torah as secondary will himself be of secondary importance in the world.[13] [This may be illustrated by] a parable. To what is the matter like? To a public roadway which runs between two paths, one formed of fire and the other of snow. If a man walks close to the path of fire he will be scorched by the heat, and if he walks close to the path of snow he will be frost-bitten; so what should he do? He should walk in the middle of the roadway and so protect himself from being scorched by the fire or bitten by the frost.[14]

(13) V. prints 'this' with 'world' in brackets. MS. E. has 'in the world to come'. (14) The view expounded by this parable is that of the *via media*, a wholesome combination of Torah-study and worldly affairs.

CHAPTER XXIX

1. R. SIMEON B. ELEAZAR SAID IN THE NAME OF R. MEIR: DO NOT APPEASE YOUR FELLOW IN THE TIME OF HIS ANGER; DO NOT COMFORT HIM IN THE TIME OF HIS MOURNING;[1] DO NOT QUESTION HIM IN THE HOUR OF HIS VOW; DO NOT ENTER HIS HOUSE IN THE DAY OF HIS CALAMITY; AND DO NOT STRIVE TO SEE HIM [IN THE HOUR OF HIS DISGRACE].

He used to say:[2] If among your colleagues there are some who rebuke you and others who praise you, love him who rebukes you and hate him who praises you; because it is the one who rebukes you that leads you to the life of the world to come, while he who praises you drives you out of the world.

He used to say: Wherever a man goes his heart goes there too; wherever he stands his heart stands there too; and wherever he sits his actions confront him.[3]

2. He used to say: Whoever is diligent in the study of Torah is afforded many opportunities for being diligent, and whoever is neglectful of the study of Torah is likewise afforded many causes for neglect; e.g. a lion, wolf, leopard, tiger, a snake or a band of troops or robbers will come and encircle him and inflict punishment upon him; as it is stated, *Verily there is a God that judgeth in the earth.*[4]

(1) Aboth IV, 23 (Sonc. ed., IV, 18, pp. 53f) where the text reads: 'when his dead lies before him'. This is the meaning required here; at that hour silence is the greatest kindness. The phrase 'do not enter . . . calamity' is omitted. (2) The reading of GRA instead of V. 'some say'. (3) lit. 'words (or, actions) are settled before him'. The thought seems to be that it is wholly within the power of man to guide his heart on the course which he chooses for himself; and once the choice is made he cannot escape the consequences. [Bacher, *Ag. d. Tannaiten* II, p. 427, n. 4, suggests the following interpretation based on the use of 'heart' for 'mind' in Hebrew psychology: When a man walks about his mind is active; when he stands still his mind is passive; when he sits his mind is settled and not agitated.] (4) Ps. LVIII, 12. God offers man the opportunity for the performance of good or evil, but he has the power to determine his step. Cf. Yoma 38b (Sonc. ed., p. 181): 'If a man goes to defile himself, they open the door for him; and if he goes to purify himself, they assist him.'

3. Abba Saul b. Nanos said: There are four types of scholars: he who studied but did not teach others; he who taught others but did not teach himself; he who studied and taught others; and he who neither studied nor taught others. 'He who studied but did not teach others'—how is this? A man learnt a chapter or two or three [of the Mishnah] but did not rehearse them with another and occupy himself with them so as not to forget them—he is one who studied but did not teach others. 'He who taught others but did not teach himself'—how is this? A man learnt an Order[5] or two or three [of the Mishnah] several times and taught them to others, but he did not occupy himself with them so that he forgot them—he is one who taught others but did not teach himself. 'He who studied and taught others'—how is this? A man learnt an Order or two or three [of the Mishnah] and rehearsed them with others, occupied himself with them so that he did not forget them, and both he and they grasped them firmly—he is one who studied and taught others. 'He who neither studied nor taught others'—how is this? A man learnt an Order or two or three [of the Mishnah] several times but did not teach them to others or occupy himself with them so that he forgot them—he is one who neither studied nor taught others.

R. Ḥananya b. Jacob said: He who keeps awake at night by reason of Torah-study, it is a good omen for him; if by reason of general conversation,[6] it is a bad omen for him.

R. Jacob b. Ḥananya said: He who keeps awake at night and does not utter any words of Torah, for him it were better —and indeed he would deserve it—had his mother's afterbirth been turned upon his face [and suffocated him], and he had not come forth into the atmosphere of the world or ever seen its light.

4. R. Eliezer ha-Ḳappar said: Whoever honours his fellow for the sake of gain[7] will in the end depart from him in shame; and whoever slights his fellow in connection with a religious cause[8] will in the end depart from him in honour. Whence

(5) One of the six divisions of the Mishnah. (6) A variant reading is: 'business affairs'. (7) He flatters him in the hope of personal gain. (8) He rebukes him for his shortcomings, in accordance with the precept in Lev. XIX, 17.

do we know that whoever honours his fellow for the sake of gain will in the end depart from him in shame? We find it so with the wicked Balaam who honoured Balak for the sake of gain, as it is stated, *And Balaam answered and said to the servants of Balak: If Balak would give me his house full of silver and gold.*[9] And whence do we know that he departed from him in shame? For it is stated, *Now flee thou to thy place . . . but, lo, the Lord hath kept thee back from honour.*[10] Whence do we know that whoever slights his fellow in connection with a religious cause will in the end depart from him in honour? We find it so with Moses our teacher who slighted Pharaoh in connection with a religious cause, as it is stated, *And all these thy servants shall come down unto me, and bow down unto me, saying.*[11] But was Pharaoh standing on the roof[12] and Moses on the ground? It was rather this that Moses said to Pharaoh, 'Even if all your servants, who stand before you and prostrate themselves before you on your dais, were to stand and implore me, I would not hearken to them'. And whence do we know that he departed from him in honour? For it is stated, *And he called for Moses and Aaron by night.*[13] They said to Pharaoh, 'Are we thieves that we should leave [Egypt] by night? You must wait until the Holy One, blessed be He, will produce the seven clouds of glory for us, that we may go forth in them joyfully and with head uncovered,[14] as it is stated, *On the morrow after the Passover the children of Israel went out with a high hand.*[15]

5. To enquire about the four different forms of atonement[16] R. Matthia b. Ḥeresh paid a visit to R. Ishmael b. Eleazar ha-Ḳappar at Laodicea. He said to him, 'Have you heard [a tradition] concerning the four different forms of atonement which R. Ishmael expounded?' He replied, 'I have heard [a tradition] and there are only three forms, and repentance is imperative

(9) Num. XXII, 18. (10) *ibid.* XXIV, 11. (11) Ex. XI, 8. Moses slighted Pharaoh and his court by declaring that he would refuse to listen to their appeals and supplications. (12) Implied in the verb *come down.* (13) *ibid.* XII, 31. Pharaoh thus honoured Moses by personally calling upon him with the appeal to depart. (14) An expression meaning 'defiantly, fearlessly', equivalent to the Biblical idiom *with a high hand* (Ex. XIV, 8). (15) Num. XXXIII, 3. (16) On this paragraph, cf. Yoma 86a (Sonc. ed., p. 426).

with each. One verse states, *Return, ye backsliding children (saith the Lord) I will heal your backslidings.*[17] A second verse states, *For on this day shall atonement be made for you, to cleanse you.*[18] A third verse states, *Then I will visit their transgression with the rod, and their iniquity with strokes.*[19] And a fourth verse states, *Surely this iniquity shall not be expiated by you till ye die.*[20] How are these verses [to be reconciled]? If a man transgressed a positive command and repented, before he stirs from his place he is forthwith forgiven; and concerning him it states, *Return, ye backsliding children.* If a man transgressed a negative command and repented, the repentance suspends [the punishment] and the Day of Atonement effects atonement; and concerning him it states, *For on this day shall atonement be made for you.* If a man transgressed a prohibition punishable by *kareth* or by death at the hands of the court and repented, the repentance and the Day of Atonement together suspend [the punishment] and sufferings in the course of the year will purge the sin;[21] and concerning him it states, *Then will I visit their transgression with the rod.* But if a man profaned the Name of Heaven[22] [and repented], there is no power in the repentance to suspend [punishment], or in sufferings to purge the sin, or in the Day of Atonement to effect atonement; but repentance [with the Day of Atonement and][23] with sufferings together suspend [the punishment], and death purges the sin; and concerning him it states, *Surely this iniquity shall not be expiated by you till ye die.*

6. Isi b. Judah said: Why do scholars [sometimes] die before their time? It is not because they are immoral or because they rob, but because they make themselves contemptible.[24]

7. R. Isaac b. Phinehas said: Whoever is versed in *Midrash* [25]and not in *halakoth*[26] has never experienced the taste of wisdom;

(17) Jer. III, 22. *Saith the Lord* is not in the Biblical text. (18) Lev. XVI, 30. (19) Ps. LXXXIX, 33. (20) Is. XXII, 14. (21) The text is in some disorder; the translation follows Schechter's text and is required by the context. (22) 'By sinning himself and causing others to sin' (Rashi, Yoma *loc. cit.*). (23) Inserted by GRA and required by the context. (24) By neglecting their appearance. Cf. XXVI, 3, p. 130. (25) Here the word seems to be a synonym of *'aggadah*, the ethical and moral expositions of the Bible. (26) Here the analytical reasoning and exegetical argument on the Biblical law.

and he who is versed in *halakah* and not in *Midrash* has never experienced the taste of the fear of sin.

He used to say: Whoever is versed in *Midrash* and not in *halakoth* is like a strong man without weapons; whoever is versed in *halakoth* and not in *Midrash* is like a weak man with a weapon; but whoever is versed in both is like a strong man with a weapon.

He used to say: Be careful to greet your fellow-man;[27] enter not into a quarrel nor be eager to see it; sit in the company of your fellows,[28] AND BE RATHER A TAIL TO LIONS THAN A HEAD TO FOXES.[29]

(27) In Aboth IV, 20 (Sonc. ed., IV, 15, p. 52) the reading is 'be beforehand in greeting all men'. (28) Or, your equals. (29) From Aboth *loc. cit.*

CHAPTER XXX

1. R. NATHAN[1] B. JOSEPH SAID: WHOEVER NEGLECTS THE STUDY OF THE TORAH IN THE MIDST OF WEALTH SHALL IN THE END NEGLECT IT IN POVERTY; AND WHOEVER FULFILS THE WORDS OF THE TORAH IN POVERTY SHALL IN THE END FULFIL THEM IN THE MIDST OF WEALTH. [29*a*]

He used to say: Comforting mourners, visiting the sick, and the practice of lovingkindness bring welfare into the world.

2. R. Meir said: Whoever is in doubt whether he has transgressed or not is regarded by Scripture [more gravely than][2] if he transgressed of a certainty. How is this? If a man sinned [in error] and then became aware of his sin, he must bring a sin-offering of the value of one *sela*,[3] or a tenth of an ephah [as a meal-offering][4] of the value of one *pondion*;[5] whereas if he was in doubt whether he had sinned or not, he must bring a trespass-offering with the 'added fifth',[6] or a guilt-offering of the value of two *selas*.[7] Now which Divine attribute is the greater, that of reward[8] or that of punishment? You must agree that the attribute of reward is the greater;[9] so is there not here an argument from the lesser to the greater? For if

(1) Aboth IV, 11 (Sonc. ed., IV, 9, pp. 48f) where the dictum is given in reverse order in the name of R. Jonathan. GRA emends to R. Jonathan b. Joseph, a disciple of R. 'Aḳiba. (2) So according to B.Y. and required by the context. (3) The usual price of a sin-offering; cf. Ker. 10b (Sonc. ed., p. 81). (4) If the sinner is poor and unable to afford an animal offering. (5) Cf., however, Ker. *loc. cit.*, where a tenth of an ephah of fine flour is priced at one *peruṭah* (i.e. a sixteenth of a *pondion*). (6) If his doubt referred to an inadvertent misappropriation of Temple property (cf. Lev. V, 15f). (7) This is the minimum price of a ram for a guilt-offering (Lev. *ibid.*). Consequently the cost of the sacrifice in the case where a man sinned in error is less than that of the sacrifice where a man was in doubt whether he had sinned in error; in the former the cost is one *sela*, in the latter two *selas*. (8) lit. 'goodness'. (9) For God's lovingkindness extends to thousands of generations, while punishment for sin reaches only to the third and fourth generation (Ex. XX, 5f).

with regard to the attribute of punishment, which is the lesser, he who is in doubt whether he has transgressed or not is regarded by Scripture [more gravely[10] than] if he had transgressed of a certainty, how much more is it so with the attribute of reward, which is the greater![11]

R. Nathan b. Joseph said: Whoever transgressed in error is regarded by Scripture as if he had acted wantonly. How is this? If a man killed a person unintentionally and fled to a city of refuge,[12] and the avenger of blood found him[13] and killed him, the avenger of blood is not culpable;[14] whereas if a man killed wantonly and the avenger of blood found him and killed him, he is put to death.[15] Now which of the Divine attributes is the greater, that of reward or that of punishment? Surely that of reward. And if with regard to the attribute of punishment, which is the lesser, it is held that he who transgressed in error is regarded by Scripture as if he had acted wantonly, how much more so is it with the attribute of reward, which is the greater!

3. R. 'Aḳiba said: [16]Whoever joins himself to those that commit a transgression, even though he does not act like them, is punished as they are; and whoever joins himself to those that fulfil a commandment, even though he does not act like them, is rewarded as they are. How is this? If two testify of another saying, 'That man killed a person', and they are found to be false witnesses[17] so that sentence of death is passed upon them, and as they are being led to the place of execu-

(10) Since he has to bring a more costly sacrifice. (11) Thus a man who is not sure whether he has performed a meritorious deed will receive a reward as if he had done it of a certainty. (12) In accordance with Num. XXXV, 11f. (13) Outside the city of refuge. (14) Num. *ibid.* 27. (15) So MS. E. and GRA. V. reads, 'he must escape into exile because of him'; but this is not established law. It is, however, evident that the avenger of blood may in certain circumstances exercise his right of vengeance against the unintentional killer but not against the wanton killer, so proving the thesis that the transgressor in error is in a graver position than the deliberate transgressor. (16) Cf. Mak. I, 7 (Sonc. ed., p. 29). (17) lit. 'plotters'; i.e. they were proved by the evidence of two subsequent witnesses to have been absent at the time of the alleged crime. Their punishment is on the principle of retaliation (cf. Deut. XIX, 19).

tion[18] a third man comes running after them calling out, 'I know something concerning this testimony', they say to him, 'Come and offer your testimony'. This man also is found to be a false witness, so that sentence of death is passed upon him. As he is led to the place of execution, he exclaims, 'Woe is me! had I not come, I would not have been sentenced to death; but now that I came and joined them I am sentenced to death'.[19] They say to him, 'Fool that you are, even if one hundred men were to come after you and found to be false witnesses, they would all be put to death!' Now which Divine attribute is the greater, that of reward or that of punishment? Surely that of reward. And if with regard to the attribute of punishment, which is the lesser, it is held that he who joins himself to those who commit a transgression, even though he does not act like them, is punished [as they are], how much more is it so with the attribute of reward which is the greater!

4. R. Simeon said: Such is the penalty of a liar, that even when he speaks the truth he is not believed;[20] for we find it so with the sons of Jacob. When they first lied to their father he believed them, as it is stated, *And they took Joseph's coat, and killed a he-goat;*[21] and it is written, *And he knew it, and said: It is my son's coat.*[22] But finally, although they spoke the truth to him, he did not believe them, as it is stated, *And they told him, saying: Joseph is yet alive . . . And his heart fainted, for he believed them not.*[23] Some say that the Holy Spirit, which had departed from our father Jacob [during his grieving for Joseph], now settled upon him, as it is stated, *The spirit of Jacob their father revived.*[24]

(18) lit. 'house of stoning'. (19) Though his evidence alone would be worthless since two witnesses at least are required. (20) Cf. Sanh. 89b (Sonc. ed., p. 596). This passage follows naturally on the preceding which deals with perjured witnesses. (21) Gen. XXXVII, 31. (22) *ibid.* 33. Jacob believed their story. [Cf., however, *Soferim* XXI, below p. 332.] (23) *ibid.* XLV, 26. (24) *ibid.* 27. It was only the return of the Divine Spirit to him that convinced him of the fact that Joseph was alive, but he did not accept the word of his sons on this occasion when they spoke the truth.

CHAPTER XXXI

1. [1]R. Aḥai b. Josiah said: He who buys grain in the market,[2] to what may he be compared? To a child whose mother has died; though it is taken around to the homes of nursing mothers, it is not satisfied. And he who buys bread in the market, to what may he be compared? To a man who digs his own grave.[3] But he who eats of his own produce is like a child reared at his mother's breast.

He used to say: When a man eats of his own labour his mind is at ease. Even when he is dependent upon his father or mother or children, his mind is not at ease; and needless to say when he is dependent upon strangers.

2. BY TEN SAYINGS WAS THE WORLD CREATED. What need is there for mankind to [know] this? It is to teach that if a person performs one precept, or keeps one Sabbath, or saves one life, Scripture imputes it to him as though he had saved a whole world which was created by ten sayings.[4] And if a person commits one sin, or profanes one Sabbath, or destroys one life, Scripture imputes it to him as though he had destroyed a whole world which was created by ten sayings. We find it so with Cain who slew his brother Abel; as it is stated, *The voice of thy brother's bloods crieth unto Me.*[5] He shed the

(1) This paragraph has no connection with the theme of this chapter, which is an extensive commentary on Aboth V. Such commentary begins with §2. Accordingly it has been suggested that this paragraph should be joined to the previous chapter. This arrangement has been adopted by Schechter. (2) Not having land of his own, he must resort to the market for grain for his household. This was considered a precarious existence; cf. Men. 103b (Sonc. ed., p. 637). (3) lit. 'is dug and buried'. His is a wretched existence; cf. the statement in Men. *loc. cit.*: '*And shalt have no assurance of this life* (Deut. XXVIII, 66): this refers to one who has to rely upon the bread dealer [for his daily needs]' (Sonc. ed., p. 638). (4) The importance of the world is enhanced by the fact that God, in view of His omnipotence, took so much trouble with its creation, for instead of a single fiat He resorted to ten utterances to perfect the world. (5) Gen. IV, 10, E.V., *brother's blood.* The Heb. noun is plural.

blood of one person, yet Scripture speaks of many bloods! But it teaches you that the blood of his sons, of his sons' sons and of his descendants to the end of all generations that were destined to issue from him, all stood and cried to the Holy One, blessed be He. Hence you learn that one man is equal in worth to the entire creation.[6]

3. R. Nehemiah said: Whence do we know that one man is equal in worth to the entire creation? For it is stated, *This is the book of the generations of Adam. [In the day that God created man, in the likeness of God made He him]*;[7] and elsewhere it states, *These are the generations of the heaven and of the earth when they were created, [in the day that the Lord God made earth and heaven]*.[8] As in the one verse [which describes the creation of the world] the terms *created* and *made* are used, so in the other verse [which describes the creation of man] the terms *created* and *made* are used. This teaches that the Holy One, blessed be He, showed Adam all the future generations that were to issue from him standing and sporting, as it were, before him. Some say that He showed him only the righteous [of every generation], as it is stated, *Every one that is written unto life in Jerusalem*.[9]

R. Joshua b. Ḳorḥa said: It states, *Thine eyes did see mine unformed substance, and in Thy book they were all written*.[10] This teaches that the Holy One, blessed be He, showed Adam, the first man, every generation and its teachers, every generation and its administrators, every generation and its leaders, every generation and its prophets, every generation and its heroes, every generation and its transgressors, every generation and its pious men, and that in a certain generation such a king will arise and in a certain generation such a Sage will live.

R. Eliezer the son of R. Jose the Galilean said: Nine hundred and seventy-four generations before the creation of the world

(6) Cf. Sanh. IV, 5 (Sonc. ed., pp. 233f.). (7) *ibid.* V, 1. (8) *ibid.* II, 4. (9) Is. IV, 3. The verse refers to the righteous, God's elect, whose names are inscribed in the 'Book of Life', which is identical with *the book of the generations of Adam*. (10) Ps. CXXXIX, 16. *Thy book* is interpreted as *the book of the generations*.

the Torah was already written[11] and lay in the bosom of the Holy One, blessed be He, singing praises together with the ministering angels; as it is stated, *Then I was by Him as a nursling; and I was daily all delight, [playing always before Him,] playing in His habitable earth.*[12]

[R. Jose the Galilean said: All that the Holy One, blessed be He, created in the world, He also created in man.[13]] This may be illustrated by a parable. To what can it be compared? To a man who takes a piece of wood intending to engrave many designs on it; but as he has insufficient space for his designs, he is dejected. He, however, who draws his designs on the ground can do so interminably, and keep everything distinct and apart. On the other hand,[14] the Holy One, blessed be He, —may His great name be blessed for ever and to all eternity— in His wisdom and understanding created the whole world: He created the heaven and the earth, the celestial beings and terrestrial creatures. He likewise fashioned in man all that He had created in His world: He created forests in the world and forests in man, viz. his hairs; He created wild beasts in the world and wild beasts in man, viz. the intestinal worms;[15] He created destructive agents[16] in the world and destructive

(11) The Divine plan, as intimated *ibid.* CV, 8: *The word* (i.e. the Torah) *which He commanded to a thousand generations,* was that a thousand generations were to pass before the giving of the Torah to man. Since, in fact, Moses received the Torah and he lived in the twenty-sixth generation from the creation, it follows that the Torah must have been in existence for nine hundred and seventy-four generations before the creation. Cf. Ḥag. 13b, 14a (Sonc. ed., p. 82, n. 7). (12) Prov. VIII, 30f. (13) This sentence is omitted in V. It is found in the Oxford MS. of this work [cf. Bacher, *Ag. d. Tannaiten,* I, p. 365, n. 1] and serves as a fine introduction to the parable and the extensive paragraph which follow. (14) So according to Schechter's text which has MS. authority. V reads 'so too'. The contrast in the thought is this: whereas man requires the whole surface of the earth to draw his designs, God formed within the confined space of his body everything which He had created in the world. This is the concept of the 'microcosm': that man is regarded as an epitome of the universe, a world in miniature. (15) The text varies between 'the intestines of man' and 'the worms in man'. Both readings apparently refer to the same thing, the intestinal worms. (16) Heb. *ḳorẓin,* a difficult word with doubtful meaning. According to Jastrow 'destructive insects', but he emends the end of the line to 'intestines' in place of 'ears'. Bacher, R.E.J. XXXVII, pp. 301f, compares this word with the Aramaic expression in Dan. III, 8: *wa'akalu ḳarẓehon,* 'and they brought accusations' and translates here 'accusers', 'slanderers'.

agents in man, these [act via] the ears of man;[17] He created odours[18] in the world and odours in man, these are [sensed by] the nose of man; He created a sun in the world and a sun in man, viz. the light of [the countenance of] man;[19] fetid water in the world and also in man, viz. his nasal discharge; salt water in the world and also in man, viz. his tears; streams in the world and also in man, viz. the secretions;[20] ramparts[21] in the world [29*b*] and also in man, viz. his lips;[22] doors in the world and also in man, viz. his teeth; vaults in the world and also a vault in man, viz. his tongue;[23] sweet water in the world and also in man, viz. his sputum; contours[24] in the world and also in man, viz. his jaws; towers in the world and a tower in man, viz. his neck;[25] riggings[26] in the world and also in man, viz. his arms; pegs in the world and also in man, viz. his fingers; a king in the world and also in man, viz. his head; [wine-bearing] clusters in the world and also in man, viz. his blood;[27] counsellors in the world and also in man, viz. his kidneys;[28] grinding mills in the world and also in man, viz. his stomach; crushing mills in the world and also in man, viz. his spleen; refuse bins in the world and also in man, viz. the belly; pits in the world and also in man, viz the navel;[29]

(17) Which are the receptacles of slanderous and malicious talk. (18) Another reading is 'wind'. (19) Another reading is 'his forehead'. (20) lit. 'tears'; but as tears have just been mentioned with the qualification 'of the eyes', the word might mean 'secretions'. GRA reads 'the urine'. (21) Another reading is 'seals'. (22) Cf. 'Arak. 15b (Sonc. ed., p. 87) where it is stated that the tongue is surrounded by two walls, one of bone (the teeth) and one of flesh (the lips), to guard it from speaking evil. (23) Or, the palate, which is the vault of the mouth. (24) lit. 'jaws'. GRA reads 'stars'; cf. Shab. 151b (Sonc. ed., p. 774) where the stars represent man's cheeks. (25) Cf. Cant. VII, 5 where the neck is likened to *a tower of ivory*. (26) The word is unique in Heb. literature and the meaning is a matter of conjecture. Jastrow's translation is adopted here. [Krauss, *Lehnwörter*, p. 413, suggests a connection with סרדיוטות, 'officers', which is also found in the commentary *Tummath Yesharim*.] (27) The red juice of the grape is designated 'blood' in Deut. XXXII, 14. In the MSS. 'his breasts' is read in place of 'his blood'; for this cf. Cant. VII, 8. (28) For this and the following two comparisons, cf. Ber. 61a, b (Sonc. ed., p. 384): 'the kidneys prompt [thought]'. (29) Which forms a slight depression on the body.

running waters in the world and also in man, viz. the urine; life in the world and also in man, viz. his blood; trees in the world and also in man, viz. the bones; hills in the world and also in man, viz. the hips; a pestle and mortar in the world and also in man, viz. his knees;[30] horses in the world and also in man, viz. his shanks;[31] the angel of death in the world and also in man, viz. his heels;[32] hills and valleys in the world and also in man, for erect he is like a hill, fallen he is like a valley. Hence you learn that all that the Holy One, blessed be He, created in His world He also created in man.

(30) These articulate in ball and socket fashion, i.e. like a pestle and mortar. (31) [GRA reads 'deers in the world and also in man, viz. his legs'.] (32) Man can crush to death beneath his heel.

CHAPTER XXXII

I. THERE WERE TEN GENERATIONS FROM ADAM TO NOAH. What need is there for mankind to [know] this? It is to teach you that although those generations provoked Him continually, the Holy One, blessed be He, did not bring the waters of the flood upon them on account of the righteous and pious who were among them. Some say that as long as Methuselah was alive the flood did not descend upon the earth; and even when Methuselah died the flood was yet suspended for them for seven days after his death, as it is stated, *And it came to pass after the seven days.*[1] What special feature was there about those seven days? They were the days of mourning for that righteous man which stayed the retribution; therefore it is stated, *And it came to pass after the seven days.*[2]

Another interpretation of *And it came to pass after the seven days*: it teaches that the Holy One, blessed be He, granted them this further respite after the original period of one hundred and twenty years, in which time they might repent;[3] but they did not do so, therefore it is stated, *And it came to pass after the seven days.*

Another interpretation is: the words teach that the Holy One, blessed be He, reversed for them the order of the universe, the sun rising in the west and setting in the east, perchance they would notice it, be awestruck and repent; but they did not do so, therefore it is stated, *And it came to pass after the seven days.*[4]

(1) Gen. VII, 10. (2) Cf. Sanh. 108b (Sonc. ed., p. 744). (3) The verse in Gen. VI, 3, *Therefore shall his days be a hundred and twenty years,* is interpreted by the Rabbis as a period of warning which God granted to that generation in which to repent. When this ended, He allowed them a further seven days' grace. (4) The words *the seven days* recall the days of the creation and suggest that God interfered with the order of nature, as laid down at the creation, in the hope that mankind would be awestruck at the phenomenon and repent.

Another interpretation: The words teach that the Holy One, blessed be He, spread His table before them and showed them His bounty of the kind to be enjoyed in the world to come, so that they might scrutinize themselves and say, 'Woe to us for all this good which we shall have lost!' But they corrupted their way upon the earth,[5] as it is stated, *And God saw the earth, and, behold, it was corrupt; [for all flesh had corrupted their way upon the earth]*.[6]

2. R. Eleazar b. Parṭa said: It is written, *My spirit shall not judge man for ever.*[7] The Holy One, blessed be He, said, 'I shall not judge them until I shall have first doubled their reward',[8] as it is stated, *They spend their days in prosperity, and peacefully they go down to the grave.*[9]

R. Jose the Galilean said: Scripture states, *Shall not judge.* The Holy One, blessed be He, said, 'I shall not regard the evil impulse as equal to the good impulse'. When is this so? Before the decree has been sealed; but once the decree has been sealed, both impulses bear equal responsibility for sin.[10]

3. He used to say: From the righteous the evil impulse is removed[11] and they are left with[12] the good impulse only, as

(5) The text is in disorder and the translation follows Schechter's text which gives the MS. reading. V reads 'and [woe to us] for having destroyed our seed from the earth'. (6) *ibid.* VI, 12. (7) *ibid.* 3. The verb *yadon,* translated in the Versions as 'abide' or 'contend', is here given the meaning 'judge'. (8) This is in agreement with the Rabbinic doctrine (cf. Ḳid. 40b, Sonc. ed., p. 202) that God bestows prosperity upon the wicked in this world, paying them a double reward for the few good deeds to their credit in this world (cf. B.B. 15b, Sonc. ed., p. 75), in order to deny them the world to come. (9) Job XXI, 13. Their reward is thus double: they live in prosperity and die in tranquillity without suffering; cf. Sanh. 108a (Sonc. ed., p. 739) where the verse is explained as referring to the generation of the flood. (10) The intention of this passage is obscure. Perhaps the meaning is: because the evil impulse enters man at birth (Gen. VIII, 21) and the nature of man is prone to fall under its sway (*ibid.* VI, 5), God will not judge it on the same footing as the good impulse, but make allowance for human frailty. Once man has been sentenced at the seat of judgment, both impulses are on equal footing as regards responsibility for sin. Cf. the somewhat similar statement by the same author in Midrash Rabbah, Genesis, XXVI, §6 (Sonc. ed., pp. 216f). (11) lit. 'he takes away from them'. (12) lit. 'and he gives them'.

it is stated, *My heart is slain within me.*[13] From the wicked the good impulse is removed and they are left with the evil impulse only, as it is stated, *Transgression speaketh to the wicked, methinks—there is no fear of God before his eyes.*[14] Average people are left with both impulses: he who draws near to the evil impulse is swayed by it, and he who draws near to the good impulse is swayed by it, as it is stated, *Because He standeth at the right hand of the needy, to save him from them that judge his soul.*[15]

R. Simeon b. Eleazar said: Scripture states, *Shall not judge.* The Holy One, blessed be He, said, 'I will not judge them until I have rewarded the righteous'. This is so only in this world;[16] but as for the world to come Scripture declares, *His breath goeth forth, he returneth to his dust.*[17]

R. 'Aḳiba said: Scripture states, *My spirit shall not judge man for ever.* The Holy One, blessed be He, said, 'They did not scrutinize themselves as mortals,[18] but displayed an arrogant spirit towards the Most High', [as it is stated,] *Yet they said unto God: Depart from us.*[19]

R. Meir said: Scripture states, *Shall not judge.* The Holy One, blessed be He, said, 'That generation declared, "The Lord shall not judge" [meaning,] there is no Judge in the world; the All-present has abandoned the world'.

(13) Ps. CIX, 22, E.V., *is wounded.* By *heart* is meant the desires of the heart, i.e. the evil impulse. [According to Bacher, *Ag. d. Tannaiten*, I, p. 361, n. 3, the interpretation is based on the use of *leb* for *heart* instead of *lebab* both here and in the next quotation. The latter is explained by the Rabbis as the two impulses while the former denotes only one of them.] (14) *ibid.* XXXVI, 2. *Transgression speaketh* is interpreted as 'the evil impulse prompts'. (15) *ibid.* CIX, 31. The *needy* are the average persons who are lacking in good deeds. *Them that judge his soul* are the two impulses in man which control him. On the passage, cf. Ber. 61b (Sonc. ed., p. 385). (16) The punishment of the wicked will be the more poignant when they see the bliss of the righteous. This, however, can only happen in this world and not in the world to come, because the generation of the flood will not stand in the judgment in the world to come; cf. Sanh. 107b (Sonc. ed., p. 737). (17) *ibid.* CXLVI, 4. Consequently the wicked will not see anything of the reward granted to the righteous in the hereafter. (18) According to this interpretation the subject of *yadon*, here understood as 'they did not judge themselves', is the generation of the flood. (19) Job XXI, 14.

Rabbi [Judah the Prince] said: Scripture states, *Shall not judge.* The Holy One, blessed be He, said, 'They do not set up courts of justice on earth, so I will set up[20] against them courts of justice on high'.

(20) There is a variant, 'I, too, will not set up'; i.e. I will punish them without recourse to judicial procedure.

CHAPTER XXXIII

I. THERE WERE TEN GENERATIONS FROM NOAH TO ABRAHAM. What need is there for mankind to [know] this? It is to teach that all those generations were provoking Him, and there was not one man who would walk in the ways of the Holy One, blessed be He, until Abraham our father came and walked in His ways; as it is stated, *Because that Abraham hearkened to My voice, [and kept My charge, My commandments, My statutes, and My laws.]*[1] The verse does not say 'law' but *laws*. But whence did he learn them?[2] It teaches you that the Holy One, blessed be He, provided Abraham with two reins which, like two Sages, instructed him, counselled him, and taught him wisdom all the night long, as it is stated, *I will bless the Lord who hath given me counsel; yea, in the night seasons my reins instruct me.*[3] Moreover, our father Abraham was wont to practise righteousness first and justice afterwards, as it is stated, *For I have known him, to the end that he might command [his children and his household after him, that they may keep the way of the Lord, to do righteousness and justice].*[4] Whenever two disputants came before our father Abraham with a lawsuit, the one claiming a *mina* from the other, he would take out a *mina,* give it to the defendant, and say to him, 'Argue your case before me'. After their case had been argued, if [he found that] one was in debt to the other, he would say to the defendant in whose hand was the *mina*, 'Pay the *mina* to your companion'; but if [the claim was] not [proved], he would say to them, 'Divide it between you and depart in peace'. King David, on the other hand, did not act so; he was wont to do justice first and righteousness afterwards, as it is stated, *And David executed justice and righteousness unto all his people.*[5] When disputants

(1) Gen. XXVI, 5. (2) In the plural. So according to a variant reading. V reads, 'Did he keep one law? Surely he kept many laws!' (3) Ps. XVI, 7. Cf. above XXXI, 3, p. 148f., where the kidneys are said to act as counsellors. (4) Gen. XVIII, 19. In this description of Abraham *righteousness* precedes *justice*. (5) 2 Sam. VIII, 15.

came before king David with a lawsuit, one claiming a *mina* from the other, he said to them, 'Argue your case'. After their case had been argued, if [he found that] one owed a *mina* to the other, he would take out a *mina* of his own and give it to the claimant; but if [the claim was] not [proved] he would say to them, 'Depart in peace'.[6]

2. WITH TEN TRIALS WAS ABRAHAM OUR FATHER TRIED BY THE HOLY ONE, BLESSED BE HE, AND HE WAS FOUND STEADFAST IN THEM ALL.[7] They are: twice when he had to leave his home,[8] twice with his two sons,[9] twice with his two wives,[10] once [when he fought] against the kings,[11] once at the Covenant between the Pieces,[12] once in Ur of the Chaldees[13] and once at the Covenant of Circumcision.[14] [30*a*] Why [was he subjected to these trials]? So that when our father Abraham will come to claim his reward, the angels[15] will say, 'Far more than all of us is our father Abraham worthy of claiming his reward'; as it is stated, *Go thy way, eat thy bread with joy, and drink thy wine with a merry heart.*[16]

Corresponding to the ten trials with which our father Abraham was tried, in all of which he was found steadfast, the

(6) In V the text reads, as with Abraham, 'Divide it between you and depart in peace'. This is an obvious error, because where the case was not proved, king David made no gift of money. Consequently the words 'divide it between you' are incorrectly interpolated. (7) The version in Aboth V, 4 (Sonc. ed., V, 3, p. 59) is 'and he stood firm in them all'. (8) The first time when he was bidden to leave his native land (Gen. XII, 1), and the second time when he set out for Egypt because of a famine in the land (*ibid.* 10). (9) First when he was induced to drive his son Ishmael out of the house (*ibid.* XXI, 10), and then in the supreme test of the binding of Isaac (*ibid.* XXII). (10) When Sarah was taken to Pharaoh's palace (*ibid.* XII, 15), and when he was induced to send Hagar from his home (*ibid.* XXI, 10). Alternatively, the second trial was the occasion when Sarah was taken by Abimelech (*ibid.* XX, 2). (11) *ibid.* XIV. (12) *ibid.* XV, 7ff. (13) According to a tradition, Abraham had been thrown by Nimrod into a fiery furnace because of his belief in God, from which he came forth unharmed. The name *Ur* means 'fire' in Heb. (14) Cf. *ibid.* XVII, 10. (15) GRA reads 'all will say'. There is a variant 'the nations of the world will say'. (16) Eccl. IX, 7. Midrash Rabbah, Ecclesiastes, *ad loc.*, applies the verse to Abraham when, after his many trials, he was steadfast in his faith.

Holy One, blessed be He, performed ten miracles for his children in Egypt.[17] On account of them He brought ten plagues [upon the Egyptians]; so, too, on account of them ten miracles were wrought for Israel at the Red Sea;[18] and also on account of them He brought ten plagues upon the Egyptians at the Red Sea.[19]

The Egyptians thundered against Israel with their voices; so did the Holy One, blessed be He, thunder against them with His voice at the Red Sea, as it is stated, *God thundereth marvellously with His voice.*[20] The Egyptians advanced towards the Red Sea with bow and arrow; and the Holy One, blessed be He, likewise revealed Himself to them with bow and arrow, as it is stated, *Thy bow is made quite bare,*[21] and it is also stated, *And He sent His arrows, and scattered them.*[22] The Egyptians advanced towards the Red Sea with swords; and the Holy One, blessed be He, also came against them with swords and spears, as it is stated, *And He sent out His arrows, and scattered them; and He shot forth lightnings and discomfited them;*[23] 'lightning' indicates nothing else than the sword, as it is stated, *A sword, a sword, it is sharpened, and also furbished; it is sharpened that it may make a sure slaughter, it is furbished that it may be as lightning.*[24] The Egyptians gloried in shield and buckler; and the Holy One, blessed be He, did likewise, as it is stated, *Take hold of shield and buckler, and rise up to my help.*[25] The Egyptians advanced with spears; so, too, did the Holy One, blessed be He, as it is stated, *At the shining of Thy glittering spear.*[26] The Egyptians advanced with stones and slings; and the Holy One, blessed be He, triumphed over them with great hailstones, as it is stated, *At the brightness before Him, there passed through His black clouds, hailstones and coals of fire.*[27]

At the time when our ancestors stood at the Red Sea, Moses

(17) The children of Israel were immune from the ten plagues which afflicted the Egyptians. (18) These are enumerated in the passage which follows, each miracle being introduced by the formula 'we will not cross until'. (19) Implied in the ten expressions used in Ex. XV describing the complete destruction of the Egyptians. (20) Job XXXVII, 5. (21) Hab. III, 9. (22) Ps. XVIII, 15. (23) *ibid.* (24) Ez. XXI, 14f. The last words of the quotation are rendered as in the Revised Version. (25) Ps. XXXV, 2. (26) Hab. III, 11. (27) Ps. XVIII, 13.

said to them, 'Rise up and cross'; but they replied, 'We will not cross until the Sea appears to us as yawning holes'.[28] Moses took his staff and struck the Sea so that it became like yawning holes, as it is stated, *Thou hast stricken through with his own rods the head of his rulers.*[29] Moses said to them, 'Rise up and cross'; but they replied, 'We will not cross until the Sea will become before us like a valley'. Moses struck the Sea and it became before them as a valley, as it is stated, *He cleaved the sea and caused them to pass through;*[30] and it is also stated, *As the cattle that go down into the valley.*[31] Moses said to them, 'Rise up and cross'; but they replied, 'We will not cross until it will be divided before us into parts'.[32] [Moses struck the Sea so that it was divided into parts,] as it is stated, *To Him who divided the Red Sea into parts.*[33] Moses said to them, 'Rise up and cross'; but they replied, 'We will not cross until it will become for us like clay'.[34] Moses took his staff and struck the Sea so that it became for them like clay, as it is stated, *Thou hast trodden the sea with Thy horses, the clay of the mighty waters.*[35] Moses said to them, 'Rise up and cross'; but they replied, 'We will not cross until it will become for us as a wilderness'. Moses took up his staff and struck the Sea [and it became for them as a wilderness], as it is stated, *And He led them through the depths, as through a wilderness.*[36] Moses said to them, 'Rise up and cross'; but they replied, 'We will not cross until it will crumble into pieces before us.' Moses took his staff and struck the Sea [so that it crumbled into pieces], as it is stated, *Thou didst break the sea in pieces by Thy strength.*[37] Moses said to them, 'Rise up and cross'; but they replied, 'We will not cross until it will turn into rocks for us'. Moses took his staff and struck the Sea [and it turned into

(28) Here are enumerated ten miracles which God wrought for Israel at the Red Sea. Cf. on this passage Mekilta, *Beshallaḥ*, on Ex. XIV, 16. (29) Hab. III, 14. The verb *naḳabta, Thou hast stricken through*, is of the same root as *neḳabim*, 'holes'. (30) Ps. LXXVIII, 13. The verb *baḳa', He cleaved*, is of the same root as *biḳ'ah*, 'valley'. (31) Is. LXIII, 14. (32) i.e. into lanes, a separate lane for each tribe. (33) Ps. CXXXVI, 13. E.V., *in sunder*. (34) Or, 'like a heap'. (35) Hab. III, 15. E.V., *the foam of the mighty waters*. The noun, *ḥomer*, is the same as for 'clay'. According to the alternative rendering, 'heap', the end of the verse should read, 'the heap of the mighty waters'. (36) Ps. CVI, 9

rocks], as it is stated, *Thou didst shatter the heads of the sea-monsters on the waters,*[38] and you must say that the heads of sea-monsters can only be shattered on rocks. Moses said to them, 'Rise up and cross'; but they replied, 'We will not cross until it will become dry land for us'. Moses took his staff and struck the Sea [and it became dry land], as it is stated, *He turned the sea into dry land,*[39] and it further states, *But the children of Israel walked upon dry land in the midst of the sea.*[40] Moses said to them, 'Rise up and cross'; but they replied, 'We will not cross until it will stand up before us like walls'. Moses took his staff and struck the Sea [so that it stood up like walls], as it is stated, *And the waters were a wall unto them on their right hand, and on their left.*[41] Moses said to them, 'Rise up and cross'; but they replied, 'We will not cross until it will stand up for us [as in] bottles'. Moses took his staff and struck the Sea [so that it stood up as in bottles], as it is stated, *The floods stood upright as in bottles.*[42] And whence do we know that from between the several divisions a fire came forth which licked them up?[43] For it is stated, *As when fire kindleth melting waters, and the fire causeth the waters to boil; to make Thy name known to Thine adversaries.*[44] The bottles produced a flow of oil and honey into the mouths of the infants from which they drew nourishment, as it is stated, *And He made him to suck honey out of the crag.*[45] Some say that fresh water issued for them from the Sea which they drank when they were in the sea-lanes, because sea-water is salty, as it is stated, *the floods* [*nozelim*],[46] and by *nozelim* sweet water is meant, as it is stated, *A well of living waters, and flowing streams* [*nozelim*] *from Lebanon.*[47] Above them were clouds of glory that the sun should not overpower them, and so Israel passed through that they might suffer no discomfort. R. Eliezer said: He arched the deep over them like a vault, and Israel passed through that

(37) *ibid.* LXXIV, 13. (38) *ibid.* (39) *ibid.* LXVI, 6. (40) Ex. XIV, 29. (41) *ibid.* (42) *ibid.* XV, 8. E.V., *as a heap.* The noun נד is homiletically read as נאד, 'bottle'. (43) The sea lanes were licked dry by the fire so that Israel might walk in comfort along the paths. (44) Is. LXIV, 1. E.V., *kindleth the brushwood.* (45) Deut. XXXII, 13. (46) Ex. *ibid.* The Heb. word signifies 'flowing streams'. (47) Cant. IV, 15.

they should suffer no discomfort. R. Eliezer and R. Simeon said: The upper and lower waters [combined] to overthrow the Egyptians, as it is stated, *And the Lord overthrew the Egyptians in the midst of the sea.*[48]

(48) Ex. XIV, 27.

CHAPTER XXXIV

1. WITH TEN TRIALS DID THE HOLY ONE, BLESSED BE HE, TEST OUR FATHERS,[1] and in all of them they were not found perfect. They are: *In the wilderness, in the Arabah, over against Suph, between Paran and Tophel, and Laban, and Hazeroth, and Di-zahab.*[2] *In the wilderness:* where they made the golden calf, as it is stated, *They have made them a molten calf.*[3] *In the Arabah:* [where they murmured] for water, as it is stated, *And the people thirsted there for water.*[4] *Over against Suph:* because they rebelled at the Red Sea.[5] Some say that it refers to Micah's graven image.[6] R. Judah said: They rebelled at the Sea and also while in the Sea, as it is stated, *They were rebellious at the sea, even in the Red Sea.*[7] *Between Paran*: in the episode of the spies, as it is stated, *And Moses sent them from the wilderness of Paran.*[8] *And Tophel:* this refers to the disparaging remarks which they made regarding the manna.[9] *And Laban:* this refers to Korah's revolt.[10] *And Hazeroth:* in the

(1) According to the MSS. and Aboth V, 7 (Sonc. ed., V, 4, p. 60) the statement is reversed: 'With ten trials did our fathers try the Holy One, blessed be He'. (2) Deut. I, 1. (3) Ex. XXXII, 8. This verse, however, does not mention 'the wilderness'. Cf. Pseudo-Jonathan on Num. XXIV, 1: 'And he (Balaam) set his face toward the wilderness, in order to call to mind against them the golden calf which they had made there'. In Schechter's ed. Ps. CVI, 19 is quoted here: *They made a calf in Horeb.* (4) Ex. XVII, 3. This occurred at Rephidim, which might be described as 'Arabah', i.e. a desert, a waterless region. (5) Which is called in Heb. *Yam Suf.* (6) Micah was an Ephraimite who had set up a private idolatrous shrine (cf. Judg. XVII). He had made his graven image while yet in Egypt, and took it with him when Israel crossed the Red Sea. Cf. Sanh. 103b (Sonc. ed., p. 704) where the verse from Zech. X, 11, *And there passed through the Sea a rival* (E.V., *and over the sea affliction shall pass*) is interpreted as a reference to Micah's idol. (7) Ps. CVI, 7, so lit. E.V. *even at the Red Sea.* (8) Num. XIII, 3. (9) There is a play upon words between the place-name תפל and תפלות, 'disparaging remarks'. (10) Cf. Num. XVI. It is difficult to see how *Laban*, meaning 'white', can allude to Korah's revolt. The commentators suggest that the allusion is based on the Midrash (Tanḥuma, Num. XVI, 1) where it is related that Korah was prompted to question the authority of Moses by a specious argument about the law of *ẓiẓith* which provides for 'white' threads as well as a blue one.

matter of the quails.[11] Here are seven [trials], and elsewhere it states, *And at Taberah, and at Massah, and at Kibroth-hattaavah,*[12] [thus making ten]. *And Di-zahab:*[13] Aaron [14] said to them, 'Sufficient unto you is this sin of the gold which you provided for the calf'. R. Eliezer b. Jacob said: This sin [of the golden calf] is sufficient [in gravity] for Israel to suffer on its account from now until the resurrection.[15]

2. By ten terms of praise is the Holy One, blessed be He, designated: viz. the Name beginning with *alef-daleth,*[16] *YHVH,*[17] *'Elohim,*[18] *'Eloah, 'Eloheka,*[19], *'Elohekem,*[20] *'El, 'Ehyeh 'asher 'eheyeh,*[21] *Shaddai,*[22] and *Ẓeba'oth.*[23] R. Jose said: I disagree with regard to *Ẓeba'oth,* since it is stated, *Captains of hosts [ẓeba'oth] shall be appointed at the head of the people.*[24]

3. By ten terms of opprobium are idols designated: viz. detestable things, abominations, molten images, graven images, things of naught, *'asherim,* sun-pillars, carved figures, wickedness, and *teraphim.*[25]

4. Two distinguishing marks are inserted in the Torah at a short section.[26] Which is that short section? The verses, *And it came to pass, when the ark was set forward, that Moses said . . . [And when it rested, he said,* etc.].[27] Rabban Simeon b. Gamaliel said: It would have been appropriate for this section to have been taken from its place here and written elsewhere.[28] [30*b*]

Similarly [a peculiarity occurs in the verse], *And Jonathan, the*

(11) Cf. Num. XI, 31ff. A variant is 'in the matter of forbidden sexual relationship'; cf. Yoma 75a (Sonc. ed., p. 361). (12) Deut. IX, 22. (13) These are the concluding words of Deut. I, 1 and are interpreted not as place-names but according to the meaning of the words: 'sufficient of gold'. (14) Since it was through his agency that the golden calf was made (Ex. XXXII, 35). (15) Cf. Sanh. 102a (Sonc. ed., p. 694). (16) The name *'Adonai,* 'the Lord'. (17) The Tetragrammaton, but pronounced *'Adonai.* (18) Usually rendered 'God'. So also *'Eloah* and *'El.* (19) 'Thy God'. (20) 'Your God'. (21) Ex. III, 14, rendered 'I am that I am'. (22) 'The Almighty'. (23) 'Hosts'. As a name of God it is always preceded by 'God' or 'the Lord'. (24) Deut. XX, 9. Here the word has a secular meaning. (25) All these terms are of frequent occurrence in the Bible. For 'wickedness' a reading 'Baalim' has been suggested. (26) The marks are in the form of an inverted *nun,* one being placed at the beginning and the other at the end of the section. They serve to put the section in parentheses. (27) Num. X, 35f. (28) Cf. Shab. 116a (Sonc. ed., p. 568).

son of Gershom, the son of Manasseh.[29] But was he the son of Manasseh? Surely he was the [grand]son of Moses![30] But since his deeds were unlike those of his [grand]father Moses, his descent is traced to Manasseh.[31]

Similarly we find in the verse, *These are the two anointed ones that stand by the Lord of the whole earth:*[32] these are Aaron and the Messiah.[33] I know not which of the two is the more beloved; when, however, Scripture states, *The Lord hath sworn and will not repent: Thou art a priest for ever [after the manner of Melchizedek],*[34] I know that king Messiah is more beloved than the righteous priest.[35]

Scripture states, *The boar out of the* wood *doth ravage it,*[36] although as written [the Hebrew means], *The boar of the* river *doth ravage it. The boar of the* wood *doth ravage it*—because when Israel do not perform the will of the All-present, the heathen nations are like a boar of the wood to them: as the boar of the wood kills persons, attacks beasts[37] and injures human beings, so when Israel do not perform the will of the All-present, the heathen nations kill, attack and injure them. But when Israel perform the will of the All-present, the heathen nations have no power over them [and are harmless] like the boar of the river: as the

(29) Judg. XVIII, 30. In M.T. the *nun* of מנשה is suspended; without that letter the name reads משה, 'Moses'. (30) This Jonathan was the grandson of Moses. 'Son' is commonly used in the Heb. Bible for 'grandson'. (31) lit. 'they suspend him with Manasseh'. He was one of the most wicked kings of Judah (cf. 2 Kings XXI, 1-17). Out of respect for Moses, Scripture associates the idolatrous priest Jonathan with the wicked Manasseh. Cf. B.B. 109b (Sonc. ed., p. 453). (32) Zech. IV, 14. The allusion is to Joshua the High Priest and to Zerubbabel of the royal line of David. (33) Representing the priesthood and monarchy. This passage is inserted here in contrast to the preceding exposition: as the wicked are traced back to the wicked, so the righteous are traced back to, or named after, the righteous. Accordingly, Joshua the High Priest, is here designated 'Aaron' and the leader Zerubbabel 'king Messiah'. (34) Ps. CX, 4. (35) The first element in the name Melchizedek signifies 'king'. The verse therefore implies that the priest is *after the manner of* the king, i.e. he ranks second to the king, thus proving that king Messiah has precedence over the High Priest. (36) *ibid.* LXXX, 14. In M.T. the *'ain* of מיער, 'of the wood', is suspended; without this letter the word is מיר which might be equated with מיאר 'of the river'. (37) According to the MSS, 'mankind'.

boar of the river neither kills persons nor injures human beings, so when Israel perform His will no nation or tongue can kill, attack or injure them. Therefore it is written *the boar of the* river.

5. In ten places in the Torah [certain words or letters] have dots over them:[38] viz. (*i*) In *The Lord judge between me and between thee*,[39] there is a dot over the [second] *yod* in the word *ubeneka* [*and between thee*]—it teaches that she spoke to him so only about Hagar.[40] Others say that [she intended her words] against those who stir up strife 'between me and thee'.[41] (*ii*) In *And they said unto him: Where is Sarah thy wife*,[42] there are dots over the letters *alef*, *yod* and *waw* of the word *'elaw* [*unto him*]—because they knew where she was but made [courteous] enquiry about her.[43] (*iii*) In *And He knew not when she lay down, nor when she arose*,[44] there is a dot over the [second] *waw* in the first occurrence of *ubeḳumah* [*when she arose*]—it teaches that he was not aware at all when the younger daughter arose.[45] (*iv*) Similarly in *And Esau ran to meet him, and embraced him, and fell on his neck and kissed him*,[46] there are dots over every letter of the word *wayyishshaḳehu* [*and kissed him*]—it teaches that he did not kiss him with sincerity.

(38) On the whole passage, cf. the parallels in Sifrë on Num. IX, 10, Midrash Rabbah, Numbers, III, 13 (Sonc. ed., pp. 91ff) and Soferim VI, below pp. 238; also L. Blau, *Masoretische Untersuchungen*. Among the many theories put forward in explanation of these dots two may be mentioned: (*i*) they were intended to call attention to important homiletical teachings which the early Rabbis had connected with the dotted words; (*ii*) they indicate that the words or letters are doubtful and are to be deleted. Cf. J.E., VIII, p. 368. (39) Gen. XVI, 5. (40) Sarah reproached Abraham because he did not check Hagar's haughtiness towards her. (41) Words 'between me and thee' should be of no concern to others. (42) *ibid.* XVIII, 9. (43) Since they were angels they had knowledge of her whereabouts; but they asked a rhetorical question out of courtesy and in order to endear her to her husband. (44) *ibid.* XIX, 33. In M.T. it is the last word of this verse which has the dot; the reference might be to *ibid.* 35. (45) The text is in disorder and various corrections have been proposed. The reading adopted is that of MS. E, בה for אלא. The exposition seems to be this: the word ובקומה in verse 33, which speaks of the elder daughter, has a dot over it suggesting the deletion of the word. Accordingly Lot did know she rose up, in contrast with the younger daughter, of whose rising he was unaware. (46) *ibid.* XXXIII, 4.

R. Simeon b. Eleazar said: The kissing on this occasion was sincere, though at all other times it was insincere.[47] (*v*) Similarly in *And his brethren went to feed their father's flock in Shechem,*[48] there are dots over the word *'eth*[49]—it teaches that they did not go to feed the flock but to eat, drink and indulge in pleasures. (*vi*) Similarly in *All that were numbered of the Levites, whom Moses and Aaron numbered,*[50] there are dots over the letters of the word *weAharon* [*and Aaron*]—why is this so? It teaches that Aaron was not included in the number.[51] (*vii*) Similarly in *Or be in a journey afar off,*[52] there is a dot over the *he* in the word *reḥoḳah* [*afar off*]—it teaches that a journey afar off means no more than beyond the threshold of the Temple court.[53] (*viii*) Similarly in *And we have laid waste even unto Nophah, which reacheth unto Medeba,*[54] there is a dot over the *resh* in the word *'asher* [*which*]: why is this so? It teaches that they destroyed the people but not the lands. [Others say that] they did not destroy the people but only the lands.[55] (*ix*) In *And a separate tenth part,*[56] in connection with [the sacrifices offered on the] first Festival day of Tabernacles, there is a dot over the *waw* in the word *we'issaron* [*and a tenth*]. Why is this so? It teaches that there was to be only one tenth-measure.[57] (x) Similarly in *The secret things belong unto the Lord our God; but the things that are revealed belong unto us and unto our children for ever,*[58] there are dots over every letter in the words *lanu ulebanenu* [*unto us and unto our children*] and over the *ayin* in the word *'ad* [*for*]. Why is this so? [It teaches that He did not punish them for any sin until they had crossed the Jordan.][59] And why all these dots? Thus said Ezra, 'If Elijah

(47) Cf. Rashi *ad loc.* (48) *ibid.* XXXVII, 12. (49) This word indicates the accusative and is not reproduced in translation. (50) Num. III, 39. (51) Although a Levite, Aaron was not included in the census of the Levites; cf. Bek. 4a (Sonc. ed., p. 18). (52) *ibid.* IX, 10. (53) Cf. Pes. 93b (Sonc. ed., p. 500). (54) *ibid.* XXI, 30. (55) The two sentences are in contradiction. Hence the insertion of 'Others say that' (cf. B.Y.). The text has 'idolaters' for 'peoples' which is the reading of GRA and others. (56) *ibid.* XXIX, 15. (57) For all occasions the tenth-measure had to be used, even when it was necessary to measure three-tenths as for the meal-offering for a bullock; cf. Men. 87b (Sonc. ed., p. 529). (58) Deut. XXIX, 28. (59) Lacking in V but added by GRA; cf. Sanh. 43b (Sonc. ed., p. 285, n. 4).

will come and say to me, "Why have you written these words?" I will reply, "But I have already placed dots over them". And if he will say to me, "You have written them correctly", then I will remove the dots from them'.

Eleven times in the Torah the word *he'*[60] is spelt with a *yod:* (i) *The king of Bela, the same is [he'] Ẓoar;*[61] (ii) *Said he not himself unto me: She is my sister? And she [wehe'], even she herself said: He is my brother.*[62] (iii) *When she was brought forth, she [wehe'] sent to her father-in-law, saying.*[63] (iv) *And if any beast, of which [he'] ye may eat, die.*[64] (v) *And it [wehe'] have turned the hair white.*[65] (vi) *But if the priest look on it . . . but it [wehe'] be dim.*[66] (vii) *And she [wehe'] see his nakedness.*[67] (viii) *She [he'] profaneth her father.*[68] (ix) In connection with the meal-offering of jealousy, *She [wehe'] being defiled secretly.*[69] (x) *Neither she [wehe'] be taken in the act.*[70] (xi) *Or if the spirit of jealousy come upon him, and he be jealous of his wife, and she [wehe'] be not defiled.*[71]

6. Ten descents did the Divine Presence make upon the earth. The first time in the Garden of Eden, as it is stated, *And they heard the voice of the Lord God walking in the garden.*[72] Again in the generation of the Tower of Babel, as it is stated, *And the Lord came down to see the city and the tower.*[73] Again in Sodom, as it is stated, *I will go down now, and see whether they have done altogether according to the cry of it.*[74] Again in Egypt, as it is stated, *And I am come down to deliver them out of the hand of the Egyptians.*[75] Again at the Red Sea, as it is stated, *He bowed the heavens also, and came down.*[76] Again at Sinai, as it is stated, *And the Lord came down upon mount Sinai.*[77] Again in the Temple, as it is stated, *And the Lord said unto me: This gate shall be shut, it shall not be opened . . . for the Lord,*

(60) Meaning 'she' or 'it'. The pronoun is regularly spelt with a *waw* (*hu'*) in the Pentateuch but pronounced *he'*. In vowelless texts it is indistinguishable from the masculine pronoun pronounced *hu'*. (61) Gen. XIV, 2. (62) *ibid.* XX, 5. (63) *ibid.* XXXVIII, 25. (64) Lev. XI, 39. (65) *ibid.* XIII, 10. (66) *ibid.* 21. (67) *ibid.* XX, 17. (68) *ibid.* XXI, 9. (69) Num. V, 13. (70) *ibid.* This is not in agreement with M.T. GRA therefore omits this verse and substitutes Lev. XVI, 31, *It is [he'] a sabbath of solemn rest unto you.* (71) Num. V, 14. (72) Gen. III, 8. This verse does not mention a descent; so GRA substitutes Cant. VI, 2, *My beloved is gone down to his garden,* the Rabbis explaining *my beloved* as God. (73) Gen. XI, 5. (74) *ibid.* XVIII, 21. (75) Ex. III, 8. (76) 2 Sam. XXII, 10; Ps. XVIII, 10. (77) Ex. XIX, 20. The text continues 'in the sight of the people', but there is no such verse.

the God of Israel, hath entered by it.[78] Again in the pillar of cloud,[79] as it is stated, *And the Lord came down in the cloud.*[80] And once more when it will come down in the future in the days of Gog and Magog,[81] as it is stated, *And His feet shall stand in that day upon the mount of Olives.*[82]

7. By ten stages did the Divine Presence depart [from Israel], moving from place to place:[83] from the ark-cover to the cherub, from the cherub to the threshold of the house, from the threshold of the house to the two cherubim, from the two cherubim to the roof of the Sanctuary, from the roof of the Sanctuary to the wall of the Temple court, from the wall of the Temple court to the altar, from the altar to the city, from the city to the mountain, from the mountain to the wilderness, [and finally it ascended to its abode on high].[84] 'From the ark-cover to the cherub', as it is stated, *And He rode upon a cherub, and did fly.*[85] 'From the cherub to the threshold of the house', as it is stated, *And the glory of the Lord mounted up from the cherub to the threshold of the house.*[86] 'From the threshold of the house to the two cherubim', as it is stated, *And the glory of the Lord went forth from off the threshold of the house and stood over the cherubim.*[87] 'From the cherubim to the roof of the Sanctuary', as it is stated, *It is better to dwell in a corner of the housetop.*[88] 'From the roof of the Sanctuary to the wall of the Temple court', as it is stated, *And, behold, the Lord stood beside a wall made by a plumbline.*[89] 'From the wall of the Temple court to the altar', as it is stated, *I saw the Lord standing beside the altar.*[90] 'From the altar to the city', as it is stated, *Hark! the Lord crieth unto the city.*[91] 'From the city

(78) Ez. XLIV, 2. To enter the gate God must have descended from heaven. (79) Another reading is 'in the Tent of Meeting'. (80) Num. XI, 25. (81) In Jewish eschatology the Messianic era will be preceded by a final combat between Israel and the nations led by Gog and Magog; cf. Ez. XXXVIII, 2ff. (82) Zech. XIV, 4. The list of 'descents' is incomplete; cf. Pirḳë d'Rabbi Eliezer XIV for a fuller and variant list. (83) Cf. R.H. 31a (Sonc. ed., pp. 147f). (84) The words in brackets are added by GRA. (85) 2 Sam. XXII, 11; Ps. XVIII, 11. GRA precedes this quotation with, *And there I will meet with thee, and I will speak with thee from above the ark-cover* (Ex. XXV, 22) to indicate the starting-point of the ascent. (86) Ez. X, 4. The words in the text are not found as a verse in the Bible. (87) *ibid.* 18. (88) Prov. XXI, 9. (89) Amos VII, 7. (90) *ibid.* IX, 1. (91) Micah VI, 9.

to the mountain', as it is stated, *And the glory of the Lord went up from the midst of the city, and stood upon the mountain.*[92] 'From the mountain to the wilderness', as it is stated, *It is better to dwell in a desert land.*[93] 'And finally it ascended to its abode on high', as it is stated, *I will go and return to My place.*[94]

8. By ten terms is a prophet designated, viz. ambassador, the faithful one, servant, messenger, visionary, watchman, seer, dreamer,[95] prophet, and man of God.

9. By ten terms is the Holy Spirit designated, viz. proverb, parable, riddle, speech, oracle, triumphant song,[96] command, burden, prophecy, and vision.

10. By ten terms is joy described, viz. joy, gladness, happiness, song, exultation, pleasure, delight, rejoicing, triumph, and jubilation.

11. Ten are distinguished by the expression 'living',[97] viz. the Holy One, blessed be He, [as it is stated], *The Lord God is the true God, He is the living God.*[98] The Torah is termed living, as it is stated, *She is a tree of life to them that lay hold upon her.*[99] Israel are described as living, as it is stated, *But ye that did cleave unto the Lord your God are alive every one of you this day.*[100] The righteous are termed living, as it is stated, *The fruit of the righteous is a tree of life.*[101] The Garden of Eden is described by the term living, as it is stated, *I will walk before the Lord in the lands of the living.*[102] A tree is described as living, as it is stated, *The tree of life also in the midst of the garden.*[103] [31*a*] The land of Israel is designated living, as it is stated, *And I will set glory in the land of the living.*[104] Jerusalem is described by the expression living, as it is stated, *Every one that is written unto life in Jerusalem.*[105] The practice of lovingkindness is termed living, as

(92) Ez. XI, 23. (93) Prov. XXI, 19. (94) Hos. V, 15. (95) GRA reads 'messenger'. (96) There is a variant reading סוכה, 'foreseeing', which Schechter emends to סופה, 'tempest'. GRA reads 'calling'. (97) The list enumerates eleven, but the obvious intruder is 'a tree' which is not found in the parallel passage in Yalḳuṭ, Psalms, 874. (98) Jer. X, 10. (99) Prov. III, 18. (100) Deut. IV, 4. (101) Prov. XI, 30. GRA reads 'good deeds' for 'the righteous'. (102) Ps. CXVI, 9. (103) Gen. II, 9. (104) Ez. XXVI, 20. (105) Is. IV, 3. So according to GRA; V repeats the quotation from Ps. CXVI, 9. GRA's continuation is: the world to come is called living, quoting Dan. XII, 2, *some to everlasting life*; righteousness is called living (cf. Prov. XII, 28); wisdom is called living (*ibid.* XIII, 14); light is called living (Job XXXIII, 30).

it is stated, *For Thy lovingkindness is better than life; my lips shall praise Thee.*[106] The wise are termed living, as it is stated, *The teaching of the wise is a fountain of life.*[107] Waters are described as living, as it is stated, *And it shall come to pass on that day, that living waters shall go out from Jerusalem.*[108]

(106) Ps. LXIII, 4. (107) Prov. XIII, 14. (108) Zech. XIV, 8.

CHAPTER XXXV

1. TEN MIRACLES WERE WROUGHT FOR OUR FATHERS IN JERUSALEM:[1] THE HALLOWED FLESH NEVER TURNED PUTRID; NO WOMAN MISCARRIED THROUGH THE SMELL OF THE HALLOWED FLESH; no man was ever injured in Jerusalem, no man was ever attacked in Jerusalem; no man ever stumbled in Jerusalem; never did fire break out in Jerusalem; never did a building collapse in Jerusalem; no man ever said to his fellow, 'I cannot find an oven in which to roast the Passover-offering in Jerusalem'; no man ever said to his fellow, 'I cannot find a bed to sleep on in Jerusalem'; AND NO MAN EVER SAID TO HIS FELLOW, 'THE PLACE IS TOO STRAIT FOR ME TO LODGE OVERNIGHT IN JERUSALEM'.

2. [The[2] houses of] Jerusalem cannot become defiled by leprosy.[3] [Jerusalem] cannot be condemned as an apostate city.[4] No juttings, balconies or gutters in it were allowed to overhang the public thoroughfare lest they form a tent for defilement by a corpse.[5] No dead bodies were kept in it overnight,[6] and no human bones were carried through it. A resident alien was not permitted to settle in it. No graves

(1) The current editions read 'in the Temple'. This is an error, because the list of miracles wrought in the Temple is given later in the chapter, §5, and the name 'Jerusalem' is specified in the last eight items. It would seem that the first two were common to the Temple and Jerusalem. Cf. Aboth V, 8 (Sonc. ed., V, 5, pp. 61f). Furthermore, in the current editions the first two items are followed by, 'Ten miracles were wrought for our fathers in Jerusalem'. It is suggested that these words were a marginal correction for the opening line of the chapter, intended to replace it, but by mistake it was inserted in the text in addition to the opening line. Cf. Schechter's note in his ed. (2) Here is enumerated a list of special regulations which applied to Jerusalem. Cf. B.Ḳ. 82b (Sonc. ed., pp. 468f) and Maimonides, Yad, *Beth Habbeḥirah*, VII, 14. (3) Cf. Lev. XIV, 34-53. The law of leprosy of houses did not apply to the buildings in Jerusalem. (4) Cf. Deut. XIII, 13-18. (5) Cf. Num. XIX, 14. (6) The dead were buried the same day and not kept overnight.

were allowed to remain within it, except the tombs of the House of David and of the prophetess Huldah, which existed there since the days of the early prophets. And why, when they cleared the city of graves, did they not remove these tombs? It is said that there was an underground cave there through which the uncleanness passed out to the brook Kidron.[7] No plants were planted in it;[8] no gardens or orchards were laid out in it, except the rose-gardens which existed there from the days of the early prophets. No geese or fowl were reared in it,[9] and needless to say no pigs;[10] no dunghills were allowed to remain in it on account of uncleanness. No 'stubborn and rebellious son'[11] could be condemned in it, according to the view of R. Nathan, for it is stated, *Then shall his father and his mother lay hold on him, and bring him out unto the elders of his city, and unto the gate of his place,*[12] and Jerusalem is neither *his city* nor *his place.*[13] No houses could be sold there [together with the ground on which they stood], but only the structure above the ground; and no house sold in it became irredeemable after twelve months.[14] No payment was allowed to be taken there as rent, but a charge could be made for the hire of bed and bedding.[15] R. Judah said: It was not even allowed to make a charge for bed and bedding. What did they[16] do with the skins of the sacrifices?[17] They gave them to the proprietors of the guest-houses. Rabban Simeon b. Gamaliel said: Visitors were accommodated within the house while the owners lived outside; visitors therefore acted shrewdly and

(7) There was accordingly no danger of the defilement being spread. (8) The reason was the same as for the regulation forbidding all overhanging projections; here, too, the branches of the trees would form a 'tent' over a corpse and thereby spread the defilement. (9) These birds spread defilement by carrying reptiles in their beaks. (10) Cf. B.Ḳ. 79b (Sonc. ed., p. 453). (11) Cf. Deut. XXI, 18ff. (12) *ibid.* 19. (13) Because Jerusalem had not been divided among the tribes, but was in trust for all Israel collectively. There was therefore no ownership of land in the city. (14) As in the law with a dwelling-house in a walled city; cf. Lev. XXV, 29f. (15) The text is in disorder, and the translation follows the emendations of GRA. (16) i.e. the pilgrims who came to Jerusalem for the Festivals and lived in houses rent free. (17) The skins of private sacrifices belonged to the offerer.

used to bring as offerings Egyptian lambs[18] whose skins were worth four or five *selas* each which they gave to the owners of guest-houses in Jerusalem, and in this way the house-owners profited.

3. One verse of Scripture states, [*The place which the Lord shall choose*] *in one of thy tribes;*[19] and another verse states, [*The place which the Lord your God shall choose*] *out of all your tribes.*[20] *In one of thy tribes* refers to [a place in] the tribes of Judah and Benjamin;[21] *out of all your tribes* refers to Jerusalem, in which all Israel have a share. What was in the portion of Judah? The Temple mount, the priestly chambers and the courts. And what was in the portion of Benjamin? The Sanctuary, the porch and the Holy of Holies. A wedge[22] of land projected [from Judah's portion], entered [Benjamin's portion], and then fell back again [into Judah's portion], and on this the altar was built. Thus Benjamin was deemed worthy to become the host of the Almighty, as it is stated, *And He dwelleth between his shoulders.*[23]

4. Joshua[24] said, 'As soon as I know that the Temple will be situated in the region between Judah and Benjamin, I will go and set aside the fertile region around Jericho [as compensation]'.[25] And who enjoyed its produce all the intervening years? The children of the Kenite, Moses' father-in-law, as it is stated, *And the children of the Kenite, Moses' father-in-law, went up out of the city of palm-trees.*[26] They[27] said that when the Holy One, blessed be He, will again reveal His Presence, He will pay a goodly reward to Jethro and his sons. And whence did Jethro's

(18) According to another reading, 'multi-coloured'. (19) Deut. XII, 14. (20) *ibid.* 5. (21) i.e. the Temple, which was partly in Benjamin's lot and partly in Judah's. (22) lit. 'like the head of an ox'. (23) *ibid.* XXXIII, 12. Since the ark, symbolizing the Divine Presence, was in the Holy of Holies which was located in Benjamin's territory. (24) i.e. Joshua the son of Nun when he was about to apportion the land among the tribes. This is the reading of MS. E and the commentators. V reads 'R. Joshua b. Levi'. (25) The tribe which will give up part of its territory for the Temple will receive this fertile land in compensation. It is known that the tribe of Benjamin eventually claimed this land. (26) Judg. I, 16. *The city of palm-trees* is the fertile land at Jericho; cf. Deut. XXXIV, 3. Jethro's descendants enjoyed this region for four hundred and forty years, i.e. from the entry into Canaan until the building of the Temple. (27) i.e. the Sages.

descendants maintain themselves [in the meantime]?[28] From their pottery works,[29] as it is stated, *And the families of scribes that dwelt at Jabez;*[30] and it also states, *These were the potters, and those that dwelt among plantations,*[31] etc. For they were great men, possessed of houses, fields and vineyards, but for the sake of the work of the King of kings, the Holy One, blessed be He, they abandoned everything and departed, and *there they dwelt occupied in the king's work.*[32] Where did they go? To Jabez[33] to study Torah with him, and so they became the All-present's people. For Jabez was a good and worthy man, true and pious, who sat and expounded the Torah, as it is stated, *And Jabez called on the God of Israel, saying: Oh that Thou wouldest bless me indeed . . . And God granted him that which he requested.*[34]

5. TEN MIRACLES WERE WROUGHT FOR OUR FATHERS IN THE TEMPLE: NO FLY WAS EVER SEEN IN THE TEMPLE SLAUGHTER-HOUSE. NO UNCLEAN ACCIDENT EVER BEFELL THE HIGH PRIEST ON THE DAY OF ATONEMENT. There was an exception in the case of R. Ishmael b. Ḳimḥith who went out [on the Day of Atonement] to converse with a certain prince and some saliva dropped from the latter's mouth and fell upon his garments, [thereby rendering him unclean]; so his brother entered and officiated as High Priest in his stead. Their mother accordingly saw her two sons [officiating as] High Priests on that day. On seeing her the Sages asked her, 'What merit had you?' She replied, 'Never did the beams of my house see the hair of my head'.[35] No man[36] was ever injured in the Temple, and no man ever stumbled there. NO WOMAN EVER

(28) From the time they gave up possession of that region until the realization of their promised reward. (29) So according to the MSS. and the marginal reading. V has 'from charity'. (30) I Chron. II, 55. (31) *ibid.* IV, 23. (32) *ibid.* The word 'king' is understood of God. The translation of the passage follows a variant text. (33) According to Rabbinic tradition Jabez is identical with Othniel the son of Kenaz; cf. Tem. 16a (Sonc. ed., p. 111, n. 13). (34) *ibid.* 10. (35) It being improper, especially for a married woman, to expose her hair; cf. Yoma 47a (Sonc. ed., p. 223, n. 4). In the Talmudic version he conversed with an Arab, not with a prince. (36) V inserts 'No man was ever attacked in Jerusalem'. It is out of place in this paragraph which deals with the miracles in the Temple, and is omitted in the MSS.

MISCARRIED THROUGH THE SMELL OF THE HALLOWED FLESH. Never did the priests render a sacrifice disqualified. Whenever the priests ate too much of the hallowed flesh they used [31*b*] to drink the waters of Siloam, whereby the food was assimilated within them as in the normal process of digestion.

6. NO DISQUALIFYING DEFECT WAS EVER FOUND IN THE 'OMER,[37] OR IN THE TWO LOAVES,[38] OR IN THE SHEWBREAD.[39]

7. Whenever an earthenware vessel was broken, the fragments were swallowed up in the place [where they lay].[40] THE WIND NEVER PREVAILED OVER THE PILLAR OF SMOKE [which ascended from the altar]. When the pillar of smoke ascended from the altar of the burnt-offering it rose up straight as a stick until it reached the sky; and when the column of incense went forth from the golden altar, it proceeded in a direct line towards the Holy of Holies.

8. THE PEOPLE STOOD CLOSELY PRESSED TOGETHER YET FOUND AMPLE SPACE TO PROSTRATE THEMSELVES. When Israel went up to prostrate themselves before their Father in heaven, although they sat so closely pressed together that none could insert a finger between them, yet when they prostrated themselves they found ample space to do so. The greatest miracle of all was that even when a hundred people were bowing all at the same time, the superintendent of the assembly never found it necessary to call out, 'Make room for your brethren'. Miracles were wrought also in the Temple court; for even if all Israel entered there, the Temple court accommodated them all. The greatest miracle of all was that when Israel stood in prayer so closely pressed together that none could insert a finger between them, yet when they prostrated themselves there was the space of a man's height between them.[41]

9. Rabban Simeon b. Gamaliel said: Jerusalem is destined that all the nations and all the kingdoms will be gathered

(37) The measure of the new barley which was offered on the second day of Passover (Lev. XXIII, 10). (38) These were baked of the firstfruits of the wheat harvest and offered on Pentecost (*ibid.* 17). (39) Cf. *ibid.* XXIV, 5ff. (40) Cf. Yoma 21a (Sonc. ed., p. 92). (41) The several sentences in this passage are apparently different versions of the same tradition.

together in her midst, as it is stated, *And all the nations shall be gathered unto it, to the name of the Lord, [to Jerusalem]*,[42] and elsewhere it declares, *Let the waters be gathered together;*[43] as the 'gathering together' of the latter verse means that all the waters of creation are to be brought into one place, so the 'gathering together' of the former verse means that all the nations and kingdoms will be assembled in her midst, as it is stated, *And all the nations shall be gathered unto it.*

(42) Jer. III, 17. (43) Gen. I, 9.

CHAPTER XXXVI

1. The men of Sodom will neither come to life [in the hereafter] nor be brought to judgment,[1] for it is stated, *Now the men of Sodom were wicked and sinners against the Lord exceedingly:*[2] they were *wicked* towards one another, *sinners* by incest, *against the Lord* refers to the profanation of the Name, *exceedingly* implies that they deliberately set out to sin. This is the view of R. Eliezer; but R. Joshua said: They will be brought to judgment, as it is stated, *Therefore the wicked shall not stand in the judgment, nor sinners in the congregation of the righteous:*[3] they will not stand in the congregation of the righteous, but they will stand in the congregation of the wicked. R. Nehemiah said: They will not even enter into the congregation of the wicked [for judgment], as it is stated, *Let sinners cease out of the earth, and let the wicked be no more.*[4]

The children of the wicked[5] will neither come to life [in the hereafter] nor be brought to judgment, as it is stated, *For, behold, the day cometh, it burneth as a furnace;* [*and all the proud, and all that work wickedness shall be stubble; and the day that cometh shall set them ablaze, saith the Lord of hosts*], *that it shall leave them neither root nor branch.*[6] This is the view of R. Eliezer but R. Joshua said: They will enter [the world to come], and concerning them Scripture declares, *He cried aloud, and said this: Hew down the tree, and cut off*

(1) The eschatological doctrines assumed here are that some time in the future, after the Messianic era, the dead will come to life again. This will be followed by the Day of Judgment, and all who will be acquitted will then enjoy the world to come. It would seem that all, the wicked as well as the righteous, will be resurrected, with the exception only of the very wicked who, as enumerated here, will not come back to life and consequently will not stand in judgment. For a comprehensive study of this subject, cf. the chapters on 'The Hereafter' in G. F. Moore, *Judaism*, II, Part VII and A. Cohen, *Everyman's Talmud*, chap. XI. The Talmudic source is Sanh. 107b ff (Sonc. ed., pp. 737ff). (2) Gen. XIII, 13. (3) Ps. I, 5. (4) *ibid.* CIV, 35. (5) i.e. the young children of wicked parents in Israel who died in infancy and have not sinned; what will be their future? Cf. Sanh. 110b (Sonc. ed., p. 760). (6) Mal. III, 19.

its branches, shake off its leaves, and scatter its fruit;[7] but it also states, *Nevertheless leave the stump of its roots in the earth, even in a band of iron and brass.*[8] Now the word *root* is mentioned here and also in the former verse: as here[9] the word *root* refers to the stock of the tree,[10] so there[11] the word *root* refers to the stock of man.[12] How then am I to explain the words, *That it shall leave them neither root nor branch?* No merit will be found for them[13] upon which they can rely. Other Sages said: They will enter [the world to come], and concerning them Scripture states, *One shall say: I am the Lord's; and another shall call himself by the name of Jacob; and another shall subscribe with his hand unto the Lord, and surname himself by the name of Israel.*[14] *One shall say: I am the Lord's:* these are the perfectly righteous; *another shall call himself by the name of Jacob:* these are the children of the wicked;[15] *another shall subscribe with his hand unto the Lord;* these are the wicked who abandoned their ways, reformed and repented; *and surname himself by the name of Israel;* these are the proselytes from among the nations of the world.[16]

2. Korah and his company will neither come to life [in the hereafter] nor be brought to judgment, as it is stated, *And the earth closed upon them, and they perished from among the assembly.*[17] This is the view of R. Eliezer; but R. Joshua said: They will be brought to judgment, and concerning them Scripture declares, *The Lord killeth, and maketh alive; He bringeth down to the grave, and bringeth up.*[18] Now here [in connection with Korah] the word *grave* is mentioned, *So they, and all that appertained to them, went down alive into the grave,*[19] and there also the word *grave* is mentioned: as in the latter verse [Scripture speaks of] bringing down to the grave and also bringing up, so here too they went down but will come up in the hereafter. R. Eliezer

(7) Dan. IV, 11. (8) *ibid.* 12. (9) In Daniel. (10) i.e. it speaks of the preservation of the stock of the tree. (11) The passage in Malachi dealing with the destruction of the wicked. (12) i.e. the preservation of the stock which is man's posterity. Thus the wicked will be annihilated but their young children will be resurrected in the world to come. (13) viz. the wicked parents. (14) Is. XLIV, 5. Cf. Rashi *ad loc.* (15) Who, being entirely free from sin, have never forfeited the name of 'Jacob'. (16) Another reading is 'these are the true proselytes'. (17) Num. XVI, 33. (18) 1 Sam. II, 6. (19) Num. *ibid.* E.V. *pit.*

said to him, 'How then am I to explain the words, *And the earth closed upon them and they perished from among the assembly?*' He replied, 'They perished from among the assembly, but they did not perish from [entering into] the world to come'.

3. The generation of the wilderness will neither come to life [in the hereafter] nor be brought to judgment, as it is stated, *In the wilderness they shall be consumed, and there they shall die;*[20] and it also declares, *Wherefore I swore in My wrath, that they shall not enter into My rest.*[21] This is the view of R. Eliezer; but R. Joshua said: They will be brought to judgment, and concerning them Scripture states, *Gather My saints together unto Me; those that have made a covenant with Me by sacrifice.*[22] R. Eliezer said to him, 'How then am I to explain the words, *Wherefore I swore in My wrath?*' He replied, 'They refer to the spies and all the wicked of that generation'. R. Joshua said to him, 'And how am I to explain the words, *Gather My saints together unto Me?*' He replied, 'They refer to Moses, Aaron, the pious of that generation and the tribe of Levi'.[23] (They objected to his argument: Is it only of the wicked that the expression *there* is used and not of the righteous? Surely it is stated, There *they buried Abraham and Sarah his wife;*[24] and also, *In my grave which I have digged for me in the land of Canaan,* there *thou shalt bury me;*[25] and also, *And Miriam died* there *and was buried* there;[26] and it is also stated, *And Aaron the priest went up . . . and died* there;[27] and also, *So Moses the servant of the Lord died* there *in the land of Moab, according to the word of the Lord.*)[28] R. Jose the Galilean said: They will not be brought to judgment, as it is stated, *In this wilderness they shall be consumed, and* there *they shall die;*[29] and it is also stated, *And they shall break the heifer's neck* there *in the valley:*[30] as the word *there* used in con-

(20) *ibid.* XIV, 35. (21) Ps. XCV, 11. The psalmist speaks of the generation of the wilderness. (22) *ibid.* L, 5. The phrase *My saints* refers to the generation of the wilderness who made a covenant with God by sacrifices; cf. Ex. XXIV, 5-8. (23) This passage, enclosed in brackets, is undoubtedly out of place and should be inserted at the conclusion of the view of R. Jose the Galilean. It is against his argument that this objection is raised. (24) Gen. XLIX, 31. (25) *ibid.* L, 5. (26) Num. XX, 1. (27) *ibid.* XXXIII, 38. (28) Deut. XXXIV, 5. (29) Num. XIV, 35. (30) Deut. XXI, 4. The comparison is made on the strength of the common word *there,* mentioned in both verses.

nection with the heifer means that it will die and not be moved from its place,[31] so the word *there* used in this passage means that they will die and not be moved from their place.[32] Other Sages said: They will be brought to judgment, and concerning them Scripture declares, *Go, and cry in the ears of Jerusalem, saying: . . . I remember for thee the affection of thy youth.*[33]

4. The ten tribes will neither come to life [in the hereafter] nor be brought to judgment, as it is stated, *And the Lord rooted them out of their land . . . and cast them into another land, as it is this day.*[34] R. Simeon b. Yoḥai[35] said: As *this day* (in which they rebelled)[36] has passed never to return, so they will never return. R. 'Aḳiba said: As the day darkens and then becomes light, so their darkness will be followed by light in the hereafter.

Rabban Gamaliel said: It is stated, *That your days may be multiplied, and the days of your children,*[37] and it also declares, *The fathers shall not be put to death for the children:*[38] when the father prolongs his days the son also prolongs his days, and when the father does not prolong his days the son also does not prolong his days.[39]

R. Jose the Galilean supports the view of R. Eliezer, and Rabban Gamaliel supports that of R. Joshua.[40]

(31) The beheaded heifer had to be buried in the place where the ceremony took place. Cf. Sifrë *ad loc.* (32) Here follows logically the objection against the argument, viz. the bracketed passage above. Many verses are adduced which contain the word *there* and allude to the righteous. (33) Jer. II, 2. The generation of the wilderness are here praised for their loyalty to God, and the prophet declares that this act of faith will stand future generations in good stead so that they will be worthy of a place in the world to come. And if descendants will enter the world to come in their merit, surely they themselves will enter! Cf. Sanh. 110b (Sonc. ed., pp. 758f). (34) Deut. XXIX, 27. (35) In some texts: R. Simeon b. Judah. (36) The bracketed words are deleted by GRA and are missing in several MSS. (37) *ibid.* XI, 21. (38) *ibid.* XXIV, 16. (39) This statement of Rabban Gamaliel is, according to the commentators, out of place here. It would seem that he is expressing a favourable view with regard to the future of the generation of the wilderness. In the first verse he notes that the days of the parents and the days of the children are equated, and he argues therefrom that since the days of the children are prolonged, because they did not sin in the wilderness, and will merit life in the hereafter, so the parents' days will also be prolonged and they too will be deemed worthy of the hereafter on account of their children. The second verse adds force to his view that the children's virtue will stand in good stead for the parents.

5. Seven have no portion in the world to come,[41] viz. a scribe,[42] a writer,[43] the best [32a] of doctors,[44] a city judge,[45] a diviner,[46] a communal official[47] and a butcher.[48]

6. Three kings and four commoners have no portion in the

(40) Rabban Gamaliel and R. Joshua both hold a favourable view for the generation of the wilderness, while R. Eliezer is supported by R. Jose the Galilean in denying them life in the world to come. (41) If they do not conduct their affairs with the utmost caution and sincerity. (42) A writer of sacred texts such as Torah scrolls, and for *Tefillin* and *Mezuzoth*. Cf. 'Erub. 13a (Sonc. ed., p. 81) where the scribe is admonished to be meticulous in his work lest by the addition or omission of one letter he destroy the world by writing blasphemous matter. (43) A writer of deeds and documents who can do untold harm by careless writing, and even by forging documents. Some translate *sofer* as 'a teacher of young children', and refer to Mishnah Ḳid. 82a (Sonc. ed., pp. 421f). (44) A doctor who considers himself the 'best', and refuses in his conceit to consult others could be responsible for the patient's death; or one who is at the height of his profession and refuses to attend poor patients. Cf. Ḳid. *loc. cit.* (Sonc. ed., p. 423, n. 9). (45) One who sits alone as judge. This is strongly condemned by the Rabbis; cf. Aboth IV, 10 (Sonc. ed., IV, 8, p. 48). Such a man is too sure of himself and lacks the qualities essential in a judge: humility and responsibility. Some interpret the term as referring to judges in general; for their condemnation, cf. Shab. 139a (Sonc. ed., p. 700). (46) He misleads people by his prognostications. A variant, adopted by GRA, is 'a shopkeeper'. His trade is described in Ḳid. *loc. cit.* as the trade of robbers, because he frequently resorts to fraudulent practices. (47) Either the officer of the court who carries out its sentences and can inflict vindictive punishment upon the condemned, or the precentor of the Synagogue who renders the service not in a spirit of devotion but to display his vocal ability. (48) On account of monetary loss he is prepared to declare fit for consumption an animal about which there is a doubt. Cf. Ḳid. *loc. cit.* This passage [cf. Soferim XV, 10, below p. 287] has long been a perplexing problem to scholars, and much learning has been displayed to justify the severe condemnation of the seven types. Cf. the commentaries. An ingenious interpretation of the passage has been put forward by Rabbi Moses Kunitzer in his *Hammaẓref*, Part I, pp. 74f. He suggests that the seven occupations are merely a mnemonic for the seven names of persons listed in the following paragraph (and also in Sanh. 90a, Sonc. ed., pp. 602f) who have no portion in the world to come. Much ingenuity is exercised to find the link whereby the occupation is connected with the respective name. E.g. the 'writer' represents Ahab who, as reported in Sanh. 102b (Sonc. ed., p. 697), wrote on the gates of Samaria 'Ahab denies the God of Israel'; the 'diviner' represents Balaam who is described in Josh. XIII, 22 as *the soothsayer*.

world to come. [49]The three kings are: Jeroboam, Ahab and Manasseh. The four commoners are: Balaam, Doeg, Ahithophel and Gehazi. R. Judah said: Manasseh had since repented, as it is stated, *And he prayed unto Him; and He was entreated of him,* [*and heard his supplication, and brought him back to Jerusalem into his kingdom*].[50] The Sages said to him: Had the verse merely stated *And brought him back to Jerusalem* and no more, we should have agreed with your view; but since the verse adds *into his kingdom,* this signifies that He brought him back to his kingdom only, but not to life in the world to come.

R. Meir said: Absalom had no portion in the world to come.[51]

R. Simeon b. Eleazar said: Jeroboam, Ahab, Manasseh, Baasa, Ahaziah, and all the kings of Israel who acted wickedly, have no portion in the world to come.

R. Joḥanan b. Nuri said: Also he who pronounces the Name by its letters[52] has no portion in the world to come.

He used to say: He who renders the Song of Songs in a warbling manner,[53] and he who utters a charm over a wound, expectorating upon it,[54] and says, *I will put none of the diseases upon thee, which I have put upon the Egyptians; for I am the Lord that healeth thee,*[55] have no portion in the world to come.

The Sages said: Any scholar who once studied the Torah and abandoned it has no portion in the world to come, as it is stated, *Because he hath despised the word of the Lord,*[56] and it also declares, *What unrighteousness have your fathers found in Me, that they are gone far from Me?*[57]

R. Meir said: Whoever has a House of Study in his town and does not attend there has no portion in the world to come.

R. 'Aḳiba said: Also he who does not minister to the Sages has no portion in the world to come.

(49) Cf. Mishnah Sanh. 90a (Sonc. ed., pp. 602f). (50) 2 Chron. XXXIII, 13. (51) For this and the next paragraph, cf. Sanh. 103b (Sonc. ed., p. 702). (52) i.e. he pronounces the Tetragrammaton as it is spelt. Cf. Mishnah Sanh. 90a (Sonc. ed., p. 602). (53) lit. 'he trills with his voice'; cf. Tosiftha Sanh. XII, 5. According to Sanh. 101a (Sonc. ed., p. 684) the meaning is that he treats the verses of the Song of Songs as a secular poem. According to Rashi *ad loc.* he recites it not in agreement with the traditional cantillation. (54) Before uttering the charm; cf. Sanh. 90a (Sonc. ed., p. 602). (55) Ex. XV, 26. (56) Num. XV, 31. (57) Jer. II, 5.

CHAPTER XXXVII

1. There are seven creations [in the universe] in ascending degrees of importance. High above everything God created the firmament. Above[1] the firmament are[2] the stars which give light to the world. Above the stars are the trees, because trees yield fruit whereas the stars yield no fruit. Above the trees are the violent winds,[2a] because the violent winds go from place to place whereas the trees cannot move from their place. Above the violent winds are the beasts, because the beasts toil and eat whereas the violent winds neither toil nor eat. Above the beasts is man, because man is able to reason whereas the beasts cannot reason. Above man are the ministering angels, because the ministering angels wander from one end of the earth to the other whereas man cannot do so.

2. Six things are said of human beings, in three they resemble the animal and in three they resemble the ministering angels.[3] 'In three they resemble the animal'—they eat and drink like the animal, they multiply like the animal, and they excrete like the animal. 'In three they resemble the ministering angels'—they have understanding like the ministering angels, they walk erect like the ministering angels, and they converse in the holy tongue like the ministering angels.

3. Six things are said of demons, in three they resemble human beings and in three they resemble the ministering angels. 'In three they resemble human beings'—they eat and drink like human beings, they propagate like human beings, and they die like human beings. 'In three they resemble the ministering angels'—they have wings like the ministering angels, they know what will happen like the ministering angels, and they wander from one end of the earth to the

(1) i.e. of greater importance and usefulness. (2) lit. 'He created', and so throughout this passage. (2a) The phrase could also be translated 'evil spirits'. (3) For this and the next paragraph, cf. Ḥag. 16a (Sonc. ed., pp. 101f).

other like the ministering angels. Some say: They can also change their appearance into any form they wish, and they can see but are invisible.

4. There are eight types of Pharisees:[4] the 'Schechem' Pharisee,[5] the 'trembling' Pharisee,[6] the 'bruised' Pharisee,[7] the 'pestle' Pharisee,[8] the 'ever-busy' Pharisee,[9] the 'duty-seeking' Pharisee,[10] the Pharisee from love,[11] and the Pharisee from fear.[12]

5. There are eight things which are harmful in excess but beneficial in moderation:[13] wine, work, sleep, wealth, business affairs,[14] hot water,[15] cohabitation and blood-letting.

(4) The commentators without exception correct the number to 'seven' in conformity with the parallel passage in Soṭ. 22b (Sonc. ed., pp. 112f) and j.Ber. IX, 5, 14b, and therefore omit one of the types listed here. Cf. below, n. 9. This passage purports to denounce the types enumerated as being eccentric, sanctimonious and hypercritical. (5) Either the Pharisee who observes the Torah for what he can profit thereby, like Shechem (cf. Gen. XXXIV, 19) who submitted to the rite of circumcision only from an ulterior motive; or he who carries his good deeds upon his shoulder (שכם), i.e. ostentatiously. (6) He walks with exaggerated humility, scarcely lifting his feet from the ground, so that he strikes his feet against stones and stumbles. The reading here is נכפאי, in the parallel passages ניקפי; in either case the word must be derived from the root נקף, 'to strike'. (7) In order not to look at a woman he walks with closed eyes, so that he dashes his face against a wall and bruises himself and bleeds. The reading here, מקצואי, can only be explained by its parallel elsewhere, קיזאי, 'one who bleeds'. (8) He who walks with bowed head like a pestle in a mortar. It is a matter of doubt whether the word מכובאי (or its variant מדוכיא, as in the parallel passages) means the pestle or the mortar. The translation might well be 'the mortar Pharisee', i.e. he who wears a large cap on his head in the form of a mortar to cover his eyes. (9) lit. 'the Pharisee who has work (to do)'. This type is omitted in the parallel passages. (10) The text makes no sense and the reading adopted is that given in the margin מה חובתי ואעשנה, lit. '(who exclaims) what is my duty that I may perform it?' implying that he has already fulfilled every obligation. (11) The word in the text defies interpretation and is obviously a corruption. The reading adopted is that found in the parallel passages, מאהבה, 'from love', and even this is explained in a derogatory sense, viz. he performs the commandments for love of the reward or to win the love of his fellows, and not from disinterested motives. (12) i.e. fear of retribution. (13) Cf. Giṭ. 70a (Sonc. ed., p. 334). (14) Or, 'travel', omitting the second word *'ereẓ*. (15) Either for drinking or bathing.

6. With seven things did the Holy One, blessed be He, create the world, viz. knowledge, understanding, might, rebuke, justice, lovingkindness and mercy.[16]
7. And even as He created His world with seven so He created seven [ancestors]: the three Patriarchs and the four Matriarchs.[17]
8. The seven virtues which minister before the Throne of Glory are: wisdom,[18] righteousness, justice, lovingkindness, mercy, truth and peace, as it is stated, *And I will betroth thee unto Me for ever; yea, I will betroth thee unto Me in righteousness, and in justice, and in lovingkindness, and in mercy. And I will betroth thee unto Me in faithfulness; and thou shalt know the Lord.*[19] R. Meir said: Why does the verse add, *And thou shalt know the Lord?* It teaches that whoever possesses all these virtues knows the intention of the All-present.
9. There are seven [celestial] dwellings, viz. the highest abode, the lower abode, the world space, and the four upper regions.[20] R. Meir said: There are seven expanses, viz. the curtain, the firmament, the sky, the lofty height, the habitation, the dwelling and the clouds. Correspondingly the earth is described by seven names, viz. earth, land, ground, dry land, *terra firma, tebel* and world. Why is it called *tebel?*[21] Because it is seasoned [*metubbeleth*] with every thing. Another interpretation is: because its characteristic is to take in and not give out.[22]

(16) Cf. Ḥag. 12a (Sonc. ed., p. 65) where 'ten' things, i.e. powers, are listed; cf. Rashi *ad loc.* (17) The MSS. add: 'The three Patriarchs are Abraham, Isaac and Jacob; and the four Matriarchs are Sarah, Rebekah, Rachel and Leah'. (18) GRA substitutes 'faithfulness', since for 'wisdom' there is no proof-text adduced. (19) Hos. II, 21f. In these verses five virtues are enumerated (if 'faithfulness' is read in place of 'wisdom'). The remaining two virtues are inferred from Ps. LXXXV 11, *Mercy and truth are met together; righteousness and peace have kissed each other*. This verse is added to the text by GRA. (20) Cf. Ḥag. 12b (Sonc. ed., p. 69). (21) The Heb. noun means 'mixed, seasoned', from *tebalin,* 'spices'. (22) Deriving *tebel* from the root *yabal,* 'to lead, bring in'. Everything on earth returns to the earth; cf. Eccl. III, 20. Some restrict the term *tebel* in its application to the land of Israel which is seasoned with every thing, and has the power to attract all. In this connection reference is made to Mishnah Keth XIII, 11 (Sonc. ed., p. 709), where it is stated: 'All may be compelled to go up to the land of Israel to dwell there, but none may be compelled to leave it.' GRA suggests an entirely different reading, *shemmableh 'eth hakkol,* 'because it wears everything away'; but there is no MS. support for this reading.

In seven respects one righteous man is superior to his fellow: his wife is more comely[23] than his fellow's, his children are more handsome[24] than his fellow's, when the two eat from the same dish each enjoys the food according to his deserts, when the two dye material in the same vat for one the colour comes up beautiful and for the other it comes up dull. [Moreover, one is distinguished above the other] in wisdom, understanding, knowledge and stature,[25] as it is stated, *The righteous man is more excellent than his neighbour.*[26]

10. Hillel the Elder expounded seven exegetical rules[27] in the presence of the Sons of Bathyra,[28] viz.[29] the inference drawn from a minor premise to a major, the inference drawn from a similarity of words or phrases, [32*b*] a general principle established on the basis of a law contained in one verse or of laws contained in two verses, the rule when a generalization is followed in the text by a specification, and when a specification is followed in the text by a generalization, the inference drawn from an analogous passage elsewhere, the interpretation of a word or passage from its context. These are the seven rules which Hillel the Elder expounded in the presence of the Sons of Bathyra.[30]

11. SEVEN THINGS MARK THE CLOD AND SEVEN THE WISE MAN. [THE WISE MAN DOES NOT SPEAK BEFORE ONE WHO IS GREATER THAN HE IN WISDOM AND IN YEARS, AND DOES NOT BREAK IN UPON THE WORDS OF HIS FELLOW, AND IS NOT HASTY TO ANSWER; HE ASKS TO THE POINT AND ANSWERS ACCORDING TO THE ACCEPTED DECISION; HE SPEAKS ON THE FIRST POINT FIRST AND ON THE LAST POINT

(23) In virtue and righteous deeds. (24) Also in religious conduct and good deeds. (25) This last quality brings the number up to eight; it is omitted by GRA. (26) Prov. XII, 26. E.V., *The righteous is guided by his friend.* (27) Cf. Tosiftha Sanh. VII end. (28) A distinguished family, of Babylonian descent, at the head of the Sanhedrin in the reign of Herod, and noteworthy for their humility; cf. Pes. 66a (Sonc. ed., p. 333, n. 6) and B.M. 85a (Sonc. ed., p. 485). (29) Cf. with these rules the thirteen principles laid down by R. Ishmael; cf. Sifra, beginning, and P.B. pp. 13f. (30) This sentence is not found in the MSS. What follows is from Aboth V, 10 (Sonc. ed., V, 7, pp. 64f).

LAST;] AND OF WHAT HE HAS NOT HEARD A TRADITION HE SAYS, 'I HAVE NOT HEARD'; AND HE IS NOT ASHAMED TO ACKNOWLEDGE THE TRUTH. THE OPPOSITE OF THESE ARE SAID TO MARK THE CLOD.

12. 'The wise man does not speak before one who is greater than he in wisdom and in years':[31] such was Moses, as it is stated, *And Aaron spoke all the words which the Lord had spoken unto Moses, and did the signs in the sight of the people.*[32] Now who was the more competent to speak, Moses or Aaron? Surely Moses, since he had heard the words from the Almighty, whereas Aaron heard them from Moses. But Moses said, 'Is it proper for me to speak in the presence of my elder brother?' He therefore requested Aaron to speak, [which he did,] as it is stated, *And Aaron spoke all the words which the Lord had spoken unto Moses.*

'And he does not break in upon the words of his fellow': such was Aaron, as it is stated, *And Aaron spoke unto Moses: Behold, this day have they offered their sin-offering, and their burnt-offering,*[33] etc. Aaron accordingly held his peace until Moses had finished speaking and did not say to him, 'Be brief'. Only then did he reply to Moses, '*Behold, this day they have offered,* etc., and we are mourners!'[34] Some say that Aaron drew Moses away from the midst of the community and said to him, 'Moses, my brother, if it is forbidden a mourner to eat of the [second-] tithe, which is of lesser holiness, how much more is it forbidden a mourner to eat of the sin-offering, which is of greater holiness!'[35] At once Moses admitted [that he was right], as it is stated, *When Moses heard that, it was well-pleasing in his sight;*[36] and also in the sight of the Almighty.[37]

This[38] also may be derived from the passage, *And he* [Moses] *was angry with Eleazar and with Ithamar, the sons of Aaron that were left*[39] —hence it was said that when a man entertains[40] his disciples

(31) lit. 'and in number', i.e. either in number of years, or in the number of scholars who agree with the opposite view, they forming the majority. (32) Ex. IV, 30. (33) Lev. X, 19. (34) Because of the tragic death of Nadab and Abihu, Aaron's sons. *Ibid.* 2. (35) Cf. Zeb. 101a (Sonc. ed., p. 486). (36) *ibid.* 20. (37) i.e. Aaron's reply pleased the Almighty. (38) This and the following paragraph are clearly misplaced. (39) *ibid.* 16. (40) lit. 'makes a feast'. A variant is 'teaches'.

he only turns his face to the greatest, but when he is angry he only turns to the least of them, as it is stated, *And he was angry with Eleazar and with Ithamar,* although in fact Aaron was also included in the indignation.

Aaron was older than Moses, and the Holy One, blessed be He, is greater than Aaron; why then did He not speak direct with Aaron? Because he was not one to stand in the breach, for had he been one to stand in the breach, sin would not have caused the tragedy of Nadab and Abihu.[41]

Similarly in connection with our father Abraham.[42] When he was interceding on behalf of the men of Sodom, the Holy One, blessed be He, said to him, *If I find in Sodom fifty righteous within the city, then I will forgive all the place for their sake.*[43] Now it was revealed and known before Him Who spake and the world came into being that had there been three or five righteous men in Sodom, sin would not have brought upon them the calamity. Nevertheless the Holy One, blessed be He, waited until Abraham finished pleading and then answered him, as it is stated, *And the Lord went His way, as soon as He had left off speaking to Abraham*—if it is possible to say so, He said to him, 'I will now take My leave'—*and Abraham returned unto his place.*[44]

13. 'And he is not hasty to answer': such was Elihu the son of Barachel the Buzite, as it is stated, *I said: Days should speak.*[45] This teaches that they[46] sat in silence before Job; when he stood they stood; when he sat they sat; when he ate they ate; and when he drank they drank. Until finally he asked leave of them to speak, as it is stated, *After this opened Job his mouth and cursed his day . . . and said: Let the day perish wherein I was born, and the night wherein it was said: A man-child is brought forth.*[47] 'Perish the

(41) Adopting the reading as suggested by GRA. V has 'He had not sons able to stand in the breach; for had his sons, Eleazar and Ithamar, been able to stand in the breach, sin could not . . .' Because Aaron did not resist the people when they made the golden calf—it being Moses who stood in the breach to avert God's anger and not Aaron (Ps. CVI, 23)—he forfeited the privilege of God communicating directly with him. (42) God did not break in upon Abraham's words. (43) Gen. XVIII, 26. (44) *ibid.* 33. (45) Job XXXII, 7. Only after waiting some days did he venture to speak. (46) i.e. Job's friends. (47) *ibid.* III, 1-3.

day when my father drew near to my mother and she told him that she was with child!' And whence do we know that they did not speak confusedly together? Because it is stated, *And Job spoke and said;*[48] *Then answered Eliphaz the Temanite and said;*[49] *Then answered Bildad the Shuhite and said;*[50] *Then answered Zophar the Naamathite and said;*[51] *And Elihu the son of Barachel answered and said.*[52] Scripture places them in order, one following the other, to teach all who enter the world that a wise man does not speak before one who is greater than he in wisdom, and he does not break in upon the words of his fellow, and he is not hasty to answer.

'He asks to the point': such was Judah, as it is stated, *I will be surety for him.*[53] 'He asks not to the point': such was Reuben, as it is stated, *And Reuben spoke unto his father saying: Thou shalt slay my two sons.*[54]

'He speaks on the first point first': such was Jacob.[55] Others say: such was Sarah.[56] 'And on the last point last': such were the men of Haran.[57]

'And acknowledges the truth': such was Moses, as it is stated, *And when Moses heard that, it was well-pleasing in his sight.*[58] So also did the Holy One, blessed be He, acknowledge the truth, as it is stated, *And the Lord said unto me: They have well said that which they have spoken;*[59] and it is also stated, *The daughters of Zelophehad speak aright.*[60]

(48) *ibid.* 2. (49) *ibid.* IV, 1. (50) *ibid.* VIII, 1. (51) *ibid.* XI, 1. (52) *ibid.* XXXII, 6. (53) Gen. XLIII, 9. Judah's offer guaranteeing Benjamin's safe return was reasonable and impressed Jacob more than Reuben's wild offer. (54) *ibid.* XLII, 37. (55) Cf. *ibid.* XXXII, 18f, where Jacob instructs his servants in charge of the gift to Esau to reply on first things first and last things last. Cf. Rashi *ad loc.* (56) There is no verse to prove this of Sarah. The commentators substitute 'Rebekah' who, in conversation with Abraham's servant, answered the first question first and the last question last; *ibid.* XXIV, 24 and Rashi *ad loc.* Cf. II ARN XL end. (57) *ibid.* XXIX, 4f. Cf. II ARN *loc. cit.* where the men of Haran exemplify the virtue 'of what he has not heard, he says: I have not heard'. (58) Lev. X, 20. The text as emended by GRA is adopted. (59) Deut. XVIII, 17. (60) Num. XXVII, 7.

CHAPTER XXXVIII

1. SEVEN KINDS OF PUNISHMENT COME UPON THE WORLD FOR SEVEN CARDINAL TRANSGRESSIONS. IF SOME GIVE THEIR TITHES AND OTHERS DO NOT, THERE COMES A FAMINE THROUGH DROUGHT.[1] If some offer the heave-offering[2] and others do not, there comes a famine through tumult.[3] If some set apart the dough-offering[4] and others do not, there comes a famine of extermination. If all resolved not to give their tithes, they thereby caused the heavens to close from sending down dew or rain, and men toil but have no sufficiency. R. Josiah said: For the sin of [withholding] the dough-offering no blessing enters into the fruit; and men toil but have no sufficiency. For the sin of [withholding] the heave-offering and the tithes, the heavens are closed from sending down dew or rain; and the people are delivered into the hand of their enemies.

2. Pestilence comes upon the world for the sin of [withholding from the poor] the gleanings,[5] the forgotten sheaf,[6] the corner of the field, and the poor-tithe.[7] It is related that a widow lived in the vicinity of a landowner, and her two sons went into his field to glean, but he refused them permission. Their mother said, 'When will my sons return from the field? Perhaps they will bring home[8] something to eat'. The sons said, 'When can we return to our mother? Perhaps she will have with her something to eat'. She found nothing with them and they found nothing with her to eat. They put their heads between the knees of their mother and all three died in one day. The Holy One, blessed be He, said, 'You have taken

(1) Aboth V, 11 (Sonc. ed., V, 8, p. 65) adds: 'then some suffer hunger while others have plenty'; retribution on the principle 'measure for measure'. (2) Num. XVIII, 8ff. (3) Of war. (4) *Ibid.* XV, 20f. (5) Lev. XIX, 9f, XXIII, 22. (6) Deut. XXIV, 19-21. (7) *ibid.* XIV, 28f. The tithe of the poor took the place of the second tithe in the third and sixth years of the sabbatical cycle. (8) lit. 'I will find in their hand'.

their lives; as surely as you live, I will exact your lives from you'. For it is stated, *Rob not the weak, because he is weak, neither crush the poor in the gate; for the Lord will plead their cause, and despoil of life those that despoil them.*[9]

3. THE SWORD COMES UPON THE WORLD FOR THE DELAY OF JUSTICE,[10] AND FOR THE PERVERSION OF JUSTICE, AND BECAUSE OF THOSE WHO TEACH THE TORAH NOT ACCORDING TO THE TRADITIONAL MEANING.

When they seized Rabban Simeon b. Gamaliel and R. Ishmael [33*a*] [b. Elisha, the High Priest,] and led them to execution,[11] Rabban Simeon was perplexed in his mind[12] and said, 'Woe to us that we are to be put to death like desecrators of the Sabbath, or idolaters, or immoral persons, or murderers'. R. Ishmael b. Elisha said to him, 'May I say a word to you?' He said, 'Speak'; and R. Ishmael said,[13] 'Perhaps when you were sitting down to a meal, poor persons came and stood at your door, and you did not allow them to enter and eat with you'. Rabban Simeon replied, 'I swear by Heaven that I never did so; but I set watchers who sat at the door, and when poor persons came they brought them to me and they ate and drank with me, and blessed Heaven's name'. Then R. Ishmael said, 'Perhaps when you were sitting and expounding [the

(9) Prov. XXII, 22f. (10) This term includes *inter alia* the unnecessary delay caused by the Rabbi or judge in giving his decision on a question of religious law. This paragraph is from Aboth *loc. cit.* (11) These Rabbis were two of the 'Ten Royal Martyrs' who were executed by the Romans at various times for their insistence on teaching the Torah in spite of the interdict. [Bacher, *Ag. d. Tannaiten* I, p. 234, n. 3, holds that this martyr, Simon, was not Rabban Simeon b. Gamaliel.] (12) It was not the fear of death, but rather the mode of his impending execution, viz. decapitation, that troubled his mind. Cf. Büchler, *Studies in Sin and Atonement*, pp. 195ff. (13) There is an obvious gap here. In the parallel passages, Mekilta, *Mishpaṭim, Neziḳin* XVIII, Semaḥoth VIII, below p. 365, and II ARN XLI, R. Ishmael suggests that his sad fate might be attributed to his having delayed justice. It is on this score that the story finds its place here. The passage to be inserted reads: 'Did a woman ever come to you to ask about her monthly impurity, or a man about his vow, and they were kept waiting, because you were asleep or having a meal, or perhaps you had no free time, or perhaps the attendant would not allow them to enter?'

Torah] on the Temple mount, and all the multitudes of Israel were sitting before you, your mind was puffed up'. Rabban Simeon answered, 'Ishmael, my brother, a man must be prepared to accept his fate'.[14] They both pleaded with the executioner; one said, 'I am a priest, son of a High Priest; put me to death first so that I do not witness the death of my colleague'. The other said, 'I am a prince, the son of a prince; put me to death first so that I do not witness the death of my colleague'. The executioner said, 'Draw lots'. They did so, and the lot fell upon Rabban Simeon b. Gamaliel. The executioner took the sword and cut off his head. R. Ishmael b. Elisha took it up, held it to his bosom, wept and exclaimed, 'Holy mouth, faithful mouth! Holy mouth, faithful mouth! Mouth that gave forth beautiful gems, precious stones and pearls! Who has buried you in the dust and filled your tongue with dust and ashes? Concerning you was it stated, *Awake, O sword, against My shepherd, and against the man that is near unto Me*'.[15] He had not yet finished his words when they took the sword and cut off his head. Of them Scripture states, *My wrath shall wax hot, and I will kill you with the sword; and your wives shall be widows, and your children fatherless.*[16]

[17]From the simple meaning of the words, *And I will kill you with the sword,* do I not know that the wives will be widows and the children orphans? It signifies that they will be 'widows and not widows', as when there are no witnesses forthcoming [to testify to the death of their husbands] to permit them to remarry; as [happened at the destruction of] Bethar,[18] where not a single person escaped [to testify to the death of any individual] to permit the wives to remarry. Similarly, from

(14) The reason suggested—his elation and pride at the sight of men standing and listening to his teaching—apparently accounted for his fate, and Rabban Simeon acknowledged God's justice. (15) Zech. XIII, 7. (16) Ex. XXII, 23. This verse describes the punishment imposed for delaying the rights of widows and orphans. (17) This passage is only introduced here incidentally, quoting the full exposition of the verse cited from Ex. Cf. Mekilta *loc. cit.*, and B.M. 38b (Sonc. ed., p. 232), also Rashi on the verse. (18) The scene of the last stand of the Jews under Bar Kochba against the Romans in 135 C.E.

the simple meaning of the words, *And your wives shall be widows,* I know that the children will be orphans. It signifies that they will be 'orphans and not orphans'; for their property will remain in the presumed ownership of their fathers, and the children will not be permitted either to inherit the property or to transact any business with it.

4. EXILE COMES UPON THE WORLD BECAUSE OF IDOLATRY, IMMORALITY, AND THE SHEDDING OF BLOOD, AND BECAUSE OF NEGLECT OF THE YEAR OF RELEASE OF THE LAND.[19]

'Because of idolatry', as it is stated, *And I will destroy your high places.*[20] [And it is also stated, *And you will I scatter among the nations.*][21] The Holy One, blessed be He, said [to Israel], 'Since you take delight in idolatry, I will exile you to a place where idolatry is practised'. Therefore it is stated, *And I will destroy your high places,* etc.

'And because of neglect of the year of release of the land.' Whence do we know this? For it is stated, *Then shall the land be paid her sabbaths.*[22] The Holy One, blessed be He, said [to Israel], 'Since you do not give rest to the land, it will take its rest without you;[23] and according to the numbers of months that you failed to give it rest, it will rest of itself'. Therefore it is stated, *Then shall the land rest, and repay her sabbaths. As long as it lieth desolate it shall have rest.*[24]

'And because of immorality.' How is this to be understood? R. Ishmael b. R. Jose said: As long as Israel are dissolute in morals the Divine Presence departs from their midst, as it is stated, *That He see no unseemly thing in thee, and turn away from thee.*[25]

(19) Cf. Ex. XXIII, 10f; Lev. XXV, 2-5. Cited from Aboth *loc. cit.* (20) Lev. XXVI, 30. (21) *ibid.* 33. The verse is inserted by the commentators to prove the punishment of exile which will befall them. (22) *ibid.* 34. (23) Because you will be in exile and there will be nobody to till the land. Or, 'it will drive you out'. (24) *ibid.* 34f. (25) Deut. XXIII, 15.

CHAPTER XXXIX

1. Five persons are not granted forgiveness:[1] he who repents repeatedly, he who sins repeatedly, he who sins in a sinless generation, he who sins with the intention of repenting, and he who is guilty of profaning the Name.[2]

Because of his sinfulness[3] man has not the power to comprehend the Form on high;[4] otherwise he would have been entrusted with the keys [of the unknown] and discover how heaven and earth had been created.

He used to say: ALL IS FORESEEN and all is revealed, but everything is according to man's inclination.[5]

He used to say: EVERYTHING IS GIVEN ON PLEDGE, AND A NET IS SPREAD FOR ALL THE LIVING, etc.[6]

The repentance of the wicked delays [punishment], but their decree is sealed.[7] The well-being of the wicked ends in calamity. Power buries them who wield it.[8] [In some cases]

(1) The meaning is not that the doors of forgiveness are for ever shut against them, but that they are so hardened in sinning that they will not manifest any desire to repent. On this passage, cf. above XXIX, 5, p. 141f. (2) GRA alters the number at the opening to six, so bringing it into conformity with the other sayings of 'six' enumerated at the end of this chapter. He deletes 'he who sins with the intention of repenting', and in its place inserts the following two persons: 'he who sins with the intention of the Day of Atonement affording him atonement, and he who causes the many to sin'. (3) Some commentators attach בעונו, 'in his sin', to the preceding which would then read: 'he who has among his sins the guilt of profaning the Name'. (4) Probably the principles of theosophy and metaphysics. (5) i.e. freedom of choice is in man's hand. Cf. Aboth III, 19 (Sonc. ed., III, 15, p. 38) where an analogous maxim is ascribed to R. 'Aḳiba. The other anonymous statements given here belong most probably to him. (6) Cf. Aboth III, 20 (Sonc. ed., III, 16, p. 39) for the complete text. (7) Since for certain transgressions repentance is not sufficient and something more is required to annul the decree; cf. above XXIX, 5, p. 141f. In Yoma 86b (Sonc. ed., p. 432) the text reads: 'The repentance of confirmed sinners delays punishment even though the decree of punishment has already been sealed'. (8) Cf. Ber. 55a (Sonc. ed., p. 335).

repentance suspends [punishment] and the Day of Atonement effects atonement; [in others] repentance atones until the day of death, but the day of death together with repentance [cleanses completely].[9]

The wicked are paid outright, while the righteous are given credit. 'The wicked are paid outright': they are those who performed the precepts of the Torah with ill grace, and otherwise no good deed is found with them.[10] 'The righteous are given credit': these are they who fulfilled the precepts of the Torah with good grace and with whom no evil deed is found.[11] Both kinds are paid a little [here], but the remainder is held over for them [for the hereafter].

He used to say: All depart and leave [the world] naked [as they came into it]. Would that that man's exit were like his entrance![12]

R. Meir said: BELOVED IS MAN FOR HE WAS CREATED IN THE IMAGE OF GOD,[13] AS IT IS STATED, FOR IN THE IMAGE OF GOD MADE HE MAN.[14] BELOVED ARE ISRAEL FOR THEY WERE CALLED CHILDREN OF GOD, AS IT IS STATED, YE ARE THE CHILDREN OF THE LORD YOUR GOD.[15] BELOVED ARE ISRAEL FOR TO THEM WAS GIVEN THE PRECIOUS INSTRUMENT BY WHICH THE WORLD WAS CREATED, AS IT IS STATED, FOR I GIVE YOU GOOD DOCTRINE, FORSAKE YE NOT MY TEACHING.[16]

R. Eleazar b. Zadok said: To what are the righteous like in this world? To a tree which stands in a clean place, but one of its boughs overhangs an unclean place. What do people say? 'Lop off that bough from the tree, and then the whole of it

(9) Cf. above XXIX, 5, p. 141f. (10) These 'are paid outright', i.e. they will enjoy the reward of their grudging fulfilment of the precepts of the Torah on earth, while their punishment lies in store for them in the world to come. 'With ill grace' is lit. 'with an evil eye'. (11) These righteous men are punished during their lifetime for their few shortcomings and lapses, but a full reward for their good deeds is 'credited' to them to be enjoyed in the hereafter. (12) That man should leave this life as sinless as when he was born into it. (13) Cf. the fuller form of this saying in Aboth III, 18 (Sonc. ed., III, 14, pp. 37f), where it is ascribed to R. 'Aḳiba. (14) Gen. IX, 6. (15) Deut. XIV, 1. (16) Prov. IV, 2.

will stand according to its natural growth in a clean place.'[17] And to what are the wicked like in this world? To a tree which stands in an unclean place, but one of its boughs overhangs a clean place. What do people say? 'Lop off that bough from the tree, and then the whole of it will stand according to its natural growth in an unclean place.'[18]

2. The lion is designated by six words,[19] viz. *'aryeh,*[20] *kefir,*[21] *labi',*[22] *laish,* [23] *shaḥal*[24] and *shaḥaẓ.*[25]

3. The snake is designated by six words, viz. *naḥash,*[26] *saraf,*[27] *tannin,*[28] *ẓif 'oni,*[29] *'ef'eh*[30] and *'akshub.*[31]

4. Solomon is called by six names, viz. Solomon,[32] Jedidiah,[33] Ḳoheleth,[34] Bin Jaḳeh,[35] 'Agur[35] and Lemuel.[36] [33*b*]

(17) Cf. Ḳid. 40b (Sonc. ed., p. 201) where the exposition of the parable is given in the text. The single bough which overhangs an unclean place represents the few and minor failings of the righteous on earth, and the act of lopping off suggests the punishment they suffer in this world whereby they are purged of their sins. (18) Here the bough overhangs a clean place and represents the few good deeds of the wicked on earth, and the lopping off suggests the prosperity they enjoy in this world whereby they are paid off for the little good they did, so that in the hereafter they suffer for their misdeeds. (19) Cf. Sanh. 95a (Sonc. ed., p. 639). (20) This word, as well as its variant *'ari,* is the usual Heb. for 'lion', as in Gen. XLIX, 9; Prov. XXII, 13. (21) Strictly 'a young lion'; cf. Judg. XIV, 5; Amos III, 4. (22) Is. XXX, 6. (23) *ibid.* (24) Ps. XCI, 13. (25) lit. 'the proud one'; cf. Job XXVIII, 8. (26) e.g. Gen. III, 1. (27) Deut. VIII, 15. (28) Ex. VII, 9. (29) Is. XI, 8. (30) *ibid.* XXX, 6. (31) Ps. CXL, 4, but not found elsewhere. (32) Meaning 'the peaceful one'; cf. 2 Sam. XII, 24, 1 Chron. XXII, 9. (33) 'The beloved of the Lord', the name given to Solomon by God through the prophet Nathan; cf. 2 Sam. XII, 25. (34) 'The Preacher, or Convener' (Eccles. I, 1). According to Rabbinic tradition Solomon was also named Ḳoheleth because his words were spoken in 'the assembly' (*kahal*); cf. Midrash Rabbah, Ecclesiastes, I, 1, §2 (Sonc. ed., p. 3). (35) Cf. Prov. XXX, 1, where the superscription reads, *The words of Agur the son of Jakeh.* In view of the Rabbinic tradition that Solomon was the author of the Book of Proverbs, the names in this verse are interpreted as descriptive of him. 'He was called Agur because he stored up (הקיא) knowledge of the Torah, and the son of Jakeh because he spewed it out (*hiḳḳi'*) in that he ignored the warning against multiplying wives. Another interpretation: He was called Agur because he girded (*ḥagar*) his loins to acquire wisdom, and the son of Jakeh because he was free (*naḳi*) from sin' (Yalḳuṭ Prov. *ad loc.*). See also Midrash to Eccles. *loc. cit.* (36) Cf. Prov. XXXI, 1. The word Lemuel is explained as 'towards (למו) God (אל)', and is regarded as an epithet of Solomon who was dedicated to God; or 'against God' when he multiplied wives (Midrash to Eccles. *loc. cit.*).

CHAPTER XL

1. There are four acts that a man performs, the fruits of which he enjoys in this world, while the capital is laid up for him in the world to come. They are: honouring father and mother, deeds of lovingkindness, making peace between a man and his fellow, and the study of the Torah which is equal to them all.[1]

There are four things that a man performs, for which punishment is exacted from him in this world and also in the world to come. They are: idolatry, immorality, blood-shed, and slanderous talk which is the worst of them all.[2]

2. Merit has a capital value[3] and also bears fruit,[4] as it is stated, *Say ye of the righteous, that it shall be well with him, for they shall eat* the fruit *of their doings.*[5] Transgression has a capital value but bears no fruit,[6] as it is stated, *Woe unto the wicked! it shall be ill with him,* [*for* the work of his hands *shall be done to him*].[7] Some say that transgression also bears fruit,[8] as it is stated, *Therefore shall they eat of* the fruit *of their own way, and be filled with their own devices.*[9]

3. Whoever leads the many to righteousness will himself not fall into sin,[10] so that it may not be that his disciples will inherit the world to come while he goes down to the netherworld, as it is stated, *For Thou wilt not abandon my soul to the nether-*

(1) Cf. Pe'ah I, 1 (Sonc. ed., p. 5), Shab. 127a (Sonc. ed., pp. 632f) and P.B., p. 5. (2) Cf. Tosiftha Pe'ah I, 2. (3) Which will be enjoyed in the hereafter. (4) Which will be added to the capital, though a part of it may be enjoyed on earth. (5) Is. III, 10. (6) The transgressor therefore will be punished according to his act only and will not suffer for the consequences that may ensue. (7) *ibid.* 11. (8) Explained in Ḳid. 40a (Sonc. ed., p. 198) as when a great man sins, thereby setting a bad example which is copied by others. In such a case the consequences of the original transgression are added to the act and the punishment will be increased accordingly. (9) Prov. I, 31. Cf. Tosiftha Pe'ah I, 1, and Ḳid. *loc. cit.* (10) lit. 'they will not bring on sin to his hand', i.e. he himself will be safeguarded against sinning, for the righteousness of the many will act as a defence to him.

world.[11] And whoever leads the many to sin will not be afforded the means to repent,[12] so that it may not be that his disciples will go down to the nether-world while he inherits the world to come, as it is stated, *A man that is laden with the blood of any person shall hasten his steps unto the pit.*[13]

4. He who says, 'I will sin and repent later',[14] will be given no opportunity to repent. [He who says,] 'I will sin and the Day of Atonement will effect expiation',[15] the Day of Atonement does not effect expiation for him. [He who says,] 'I will commit a sin and the day of my death will completely cleanse it',[16] the day of his death will not completely cleanse it.

5. R. Eleazar b. R. Jose said: If a man sinned and repented and is sincere in his resolution,[17] he does not stir from his place before forgiveness is granted him. He who says, 'I will sin and repent later' is forgiven up to three times but no more.[18]

6. THERE ARE FOUR TYPES AMONG MEN: HE WHO SAYS, 'WHAT IS MINE IS YOURS AND WHAT IS YOURS IS MINE',[19] etc.

There are four types of disciple: he who desires to learn[20] and wishes that others should also learn is of a generous disposition; he who desires to learn but does not wish that

(11) Ps. XVI, 10. 'For God will prevent sin from bringing about his downfall' (Rashi to Yoma 87a). (12) Because the sins he caused others to commit are beyond the remedial action of his own repentance. (13) Prov. XXVIII, 17. (14) Cf. Mishnah Yoma VIII, 9 (Sonc. ed., p. 423). In the Mishnah the words 'I will sin and repent' are repeated, and according to the explanation in the Gemara (Yoma 87a, Sonc. ed., p. 433) it is only when a man said so on two occasions that he is precluded from repentance. Cf, however, Maimonides, *Hil. Teshubah,* IV, 1, where the words 'I will sin and repent' are only stated once. (15) According to the commentators, also if he said so on two occasions. (16) The Heb. *maraḳ* means primarily 'to scour, rub away', then 'to wipe away, cleanse completely'. (17) lit. 'and he walks in his integrity'. (18) This view contradicts the statement in the foregoing passage as well as Mishnah Yoma *loc. cit.* where it is taught that if a man says on two occasions 'I will sin and repent', the opportunity of repenting is denied him. It has been suggested that the text should read here, 'He who sins once and then a second time is granted pardon up to three times (inclusive), but no more'. Cf. Yoma 86b (Sonc. ed., p. 430). (19) Cf. Aboth V, 13 (Sonc. ed., V, 10, p. 67) for the full text. (20) GRA substitutes 'teach' for 'learn' throughout this passage.

others should also learn is of a grudging disposition; he who desires that others should learn but does not wish himself to learn is the average type[21]—though some say this is the type of Sodom;[22] he who will not learn and does not wish that others should learn is completely wicked.

7. There are four types among those who attend the House of Study: one sits near [the instructor] and receives a reward;[23] another sits near[24] and receives no reward; one sits at a distance and receives a reward; another sits at a distance and receives no reward. One asks questions[25] and receives a reward, another asks questions and receives no reward. One sits in silence and receives a reward, another sits in silence and receives no reward. He who sits near [the instructor] that he may hear and learn receives a reward, but he who sits near so that people may say, 'That man draws near and sits before the wise', receives no reward. He who sits at a distance to pay respect to a great scholar[26] receives a reward, but he who sits at a distance so that people may say, 'That man has no need of this master', receives no reward. He who asks questions so that he may understand and learn receives a reward, but he who asks questions so that people may say, 'That man asks questions before the Sages', receives no reward. He who sits in silence that he may listen and learn receives a reward, but he who sits in silence so that people may say, 'That man sits in silence before the Sages',[27] receives no reward.

8. THERE ARE FOUR TYPES AMONG THOSE THAT SIT BEFORE

(21) Who is pleased to see others study although he evinces no interest in learning for himself. (22) It is difficult to see how this type exhibits the characteristics of the men of Sodom, who were notoriously grudging and selfish. Perhaps it must be assumed that the type described is the man who has a special talent for teaching and grudgingly withholds it from the pupils. [It may be an erroneous insertion based on the analogous saying in Aboth V, 13, Sonc. ed., V, 10, p. 67.] (23) lit. 'has a portion', i.e. shares in the reward of the scholars. (24) So according to GRA and many commentators. In V a negative is inserted, reading 'and does not sit'. Similarly in the next phrase. (25) The text describing the third category is in disorder; it is reconstructed according to GRA and Schechter. (26) Allowing the great scholar to sit at the head while he sits at a distance. (27) Implying that he has nothing to learn from the Sages.

THE SAGES: ONE IS LIKE A SPONGE, ANOTHER LIKE A SIFTER, A THIRD LIKE A FUNNEL, AND A FOURTH LIKE A STRAINER.[28] 'Like a sponge'—what is meant by this? It describes the disciple who sits before the Sages and learns Scripture, Mishnah, Midrash, *halakoth* and *'aggadoth:* as a sponge absorbs everything so he absorbs everything.[29] 'Like a sifter'—what is meant by this? It describes the intelligent disciple who sits before the Sages and learns Scripture, Mishnah, Midrash, *halakoth* and *'aggadoth:* as a sifter lets out the bran and retains the fine flour, so he lets the worthless go and retains the good.[30] 'Like a funnel'—what is meant by this? It describes the stupid student who sits before the Sages and hears Scripture, Mishnah, [Midrash], *halakoth* and *'aggadoth:* as the funnel takes in at one end and lets out at the other, so is he: whatever is imparted to him goes in through one ear and out through the other, and what comes in first slips out first. 'Like a strainer'—what is meant by this? It describes the wicked student who sits before a Sage and hears Scripture, Mishnah, Midrash, *halakoth* and *'aggadoth:* as the strainer lets the wine out and retains the lees, so he lets the good out and retains the bad. R. Eliezer b. Jacob describes him as a horn, perforated and *ḳiṭṭu'ah.*[31] What is *ḳiṭṭu'ah?* It is like the conduct of a child who has been given a pearl; when offered some bread, he throws the pearl away and takes the bread; then when offered an earthenware vessel he

(28) Cf. Aboth V, 18 (Sonc. ed., V, 15, p. 69). (29) He has not the ability to discriminate between the weighty and the light, the important and the trivial. (30) The Heb. *ḳemaḥ* here denotes the superfine dust which is of useless quality (Maimonides). According to Taylor, quoted by J. H. Hertz in his P.B. with Commentary, p. 697, 'The sieve (or, sifter) spoken of is one which retains the fine flour in a receptacle attached to the machine, and is so constructed that the coarse grain passes out at the end of the sieve'. (31) The text as well as the meaning is dubious. To what does 'him' refer? Perhaps to the last type mentioned, the wicked student. According to R. Eliezer he is not so much wicked as deficient in discrimination. He describes him as a horn which is perforated at its sharp end, thereby allowing what enters to run out. Moreover, his mind is defective (קיטועה from the root קטע, 'to mutilate') and he can retain only what comes last, like the child who keeps only what he receives last and has not the sense to appraise relative values.

throws the bread away and takes the vessel, so that ultimately he has nothing but an earthenware vessel in his hand.

9. As regards disciples Rabban Gamaliel the Elder discerned four types: the unclean fish, the clean fish, the Jordan fish and the Great Sea fish. 'The unclean fish'—what is meant by this? [It describes] the son of poor parents[32] who, though he has learnt Scripture, Mishnah, *halakoth* and *'aggadoth*, remains without understanding.[33] 'The clean fish'—what is meant by this? [It describes] the son of wealthy parents[34] who, when he has learnt Scripture, Mishnah, *halakoth* and *'aggadoth*, has understanding.[35] 'The Jordan fish'—what is meant by this? [It describes] the student who has learnt Scripture, Mishnah, Midrash, *halakoth* and *'aggadoth*, but lacks the ability to discuss it.[36] 'The Great Sea fish'—what is meant by this? [It describes] the student who has learnt Scripture, Mishnah, Midrash, *halakoth* and *'aggadoth*, and has the ability to discuss it.[37]

10. There are four afflictions[38] [which can attack man]: that which sees and is visible, that which is visible but cannot see, that which sees and is invisible, and that which neither sees nor is visible. 'That which sees and is visible'; for example, a wolf, lion, tiger, bear, leopard, serpent, bandits and marauding troops; these see and are visible. 'That which is visible but cannot see': for example, a sword, bow, spear, knife, stick and rods;[39] these are visible but cannot see. 'That which sees and is invisible': such is an attack by an evil spirit.[40] 'That which neither sees nor is visible': such is an attack by an internal disease.

(32) Or, 'the student of poor intellect'; cf. Ned. 41a (Sonc. ed., p. 129): 'No one is poor save him who lacks knowledge'. (33) He is useless like the unclean and inedible fish. (34) Or, 'the student of rich intellect'. (35) His is a combination of wealth and learning, thus fulfilling the verse, *The crown of the wise is their riches* (Prov. XIV, 24). (36) The Jordan fish is small; and this student is narrow and restricted; he has limited knowledge but cannot develop it by argument. (37) Like the Great Sea fish which is large, so he is proficient and discerning, and by argumentation is able to interpret the Torah correctly in accordance with tradition. (38) So GRA. V reads 'qualities'. (39) A variant is 'a javelin'. (40) Evil spirits or demons were regarded as material beings, possessing human organs and exercising human functions; cf. above XXXVII, 3, p. 183.

11. There are four Sages [of significance in dreams].[41] If a man sees R. Joḥanan b. Nuri in a dream he may hope to be a sin-fearing man; if R. Eleazar b. 'Azariah, he may hope for eminence and wealth;[42] if R. Ishmael, he may hope for wisdom; but if R. 'Aḳiba,[43] let him be in fear of punishment.

12. There are three scholars[44] [of significance in dreams]. If a man sees Ben 'Azzai in a dream he may hope for piety; if Ben Zoma, he may hope for wisdom; but if Elisha b. 'Abuyah,[45] let him be in fear of punishment.

13. There are three Books of the Prophets [of significance in dreams]. If a man sees the Book of Kings in a dream he may hope for eminence and wealth; if Isaiah, he may hope for consolation; if Jeremiah, let him be in fear of punishment.

14. There are three books of the Hagiographa [of significance in dreams]. If a man sees the Book of Psalms in a dream he may hope for humility;[46] if the Book of Proverbs, he may hope for wisdom; if the Book of Job, let him be in fear of punishment. [34*a*]

15. The death of the wicked[47] is a benefit to them and a benefit to the world,[48] [but the death of] the righteous is a misfortune to them and a misfortune to the world.[49] [The sleep of the wicked is a benefit to them and a benefit to the world,[50] but the sleep of the righteous is a misfortune to them and a misfortune to the world.][51] The tranquillity of the wicked is a misfortune to them and a misfortune to the world, but the

(41) Cf. Ber. 57b (Sonc. ed., p. 356) where three Rabbis are named. (42) R. Eleazar was very wealthy; cf. Shab. 54b (Sonc. ed., p. 252). (43) He suffered martyrdom under the Romans. (44) They were leading authorities but never ordained as Rabbis. (45) He became a heretic and is referred to in the Talmud as *'Aḥer,* 'another'; cf. Ḥag. 15a (Sonc. ed., pp. 93ff). (46) Ber. *loc. cit.* has 'piety' in place of 'humility'. (47) Cf. Mishnah Sanh. VIII, 5 (Sonc. ed., p. 488). (48) Because they can no more sin and the world is more peaceful. (49) The righteous while alive add merit to themselves and stand as a protective shield for their generation. (50) While sleeping they can do no evil. (51) Because their time could be better spent in study and good deeds which would be an advantage to themselves and to others. This sentence is missing in V but is found in MS. E. and also in Mishnah Sanh. *loc. cit.* The insertion of this sentence brings the number of items up to three, which is the theme of this paragraph. Cf. GRA.

tranquillity of the righteous is a benefit to them and a benefit to the world.[52]

16. A man should not stand naked while opposite the Holy of Holies.[53] On entering a privy a man should not face east or west, but the other directions.[54] He should not uncover himself standing but sitting. He should not wipe himself with the right hand but with the left hand. And why did they say that a man should not wipe himself but with the left? R. Eliezer said: Because with it he points to the words of the Torah [when reading from the scroll]. R. Joshua said: Because with it he eats and drinks.[55]

17. ANY LOVE THAT DEPENDS ON SOME [TRANSIENT] THING, etc. WHICH LOVE IS THAT WHICH DEPENDED ON SOME [TRANSIENT] THING, etc.[56]

ANY CONTROVERSY THAT IS IN THE NAME OF HEAVEN, etc. WHICH CONTROVERSY WAS THAT WHICH WAS IN THE NAME OF HEAVEN, etc.[57]

EVERY ASSEMBLY CONVENED IN FULFILMENT OF A RELIGIOUS DUTY[58] will in the end be of lasting worth, etc. An assembly convened in fulfilment of a religious duty was that of the men of the Great Assembly;[59] and that not convened in fulfilment of a religious duty was the assembly of the generation of the Dispersion.[60]

(52) In quietude the wicked devise mischief but the righteous meditate on the Torah. (53) Cf. Mishnah Ber. IX, 5 (Sonc. ed., p. 328): 'A man should not act in an unseemly manner while opposite the Eastern Gate of the Temple since it faces the Holy of Holies'. (54) A variant reads 'but to north or south'. (55) Cf. Ber. 61b, 62a (Sonc. ed., pp. 387ff). (56) Cf. Aboth V, 19 (Sonc. ed., V, 16, p. 70) for the full text. (57) Cf. *ibid.* V, 20 (Sonc. ed., V, 17, p. 71) for the full text. (58) Cf. *ibid.* IV, 14 (Sonc. ed., IV, 11, p. 50) where the text reads: 'Every assembly which is in the name of Heaven', i.e. which is for a noble purpose. (59) Cf. above I, 3, n. 19. A variant reading is 'for example, the assembly of Israel before mount Sinai'. (60) Cf. Gen. XI, 1-9.

CHAPTER XLI

I. R. SIMEON SAID: THERE ARE THREE CROWNS: THE CROWN OF THE TORAH, THE CROWN OF THE PRIESTHOOD, AND THE CROWN OF ROYALTY; BUT THE CROWN OF A GOOD NAME EXCELS THEM ALL.[1] As to the crown of the priesthood, how is it? If a man were to offer all the silver and gold in the world, he would not be given the crown of the priesthood; for it is stated, *And it shall be unto him, and to his seed after him, the covenant of an everlasting priesthood.*[2] As to the crown of royalty, if a man were to offer all the silver and gold in the world he would not be given the crown of royalty, for it is stated, *And David My servant shall be their prince for ever.*[3] But with the crown of the Torah it is not so, for labour in the Torah [is open to all]; whoever is minded to take it up may do so, as it is stated, *Ho, every one that thirsteth, come ye for water.*[4]

Toil in the study of the Torah, and do not occupy yourself with idle matters. It is related that R. Simeon b. Yoḥai was visiting the sick, and met a man who was swollen and afflicted with intestinal disease, uttering blasphemies against the Holy One, blessed be He. R. Simeon addressed him, 'Worthless one![5] Pray rather for mercy for yourself; but instead you utter blasphemies!' The other said to him, 'May the Holy One, blessed be He, remove [these sufferings] from me and lay them on you!' Thereupon R. Simeon said, 'Justly has the Holy One, blessed be He, dealt with

(1) Aboth IV, 17 (Sonc. ed., IV, 13, p. 51). (2) Num. XXV, 13. The priesthood is strictly hereditary. (3) Ez. XXXVII, 25. (4) Is. LV, 1. Water is homiletically interpreted as the Torah; cf. B.Ḳ. 17a (Sonc. ed., p. 76). (5) *Reḳah*, 'empty one, good-for-nothing', the equivalent of 'Raca' in Matt. V, 22.

me, since I neglected the study of the Torah and occupied myself with idle matters'.[6]

It is related that R. Simeon b. Eleazar[7] was returning from his master's house in Migdal-eder[8] riding on an ass along the sea-shore when he met a man who was extremely ugly. He said to him, 'Worthless man! How ugly you are! Are all the men of your town as ugly as you?' The other replied, 'What can I do? Go to the Craftsman Who made me and say to Him, "How ugly is this vessel which Thou hast made!"' When R. Simeon realized that he had done wrong, he dismounted from the ass, prostrated himself before the man and said, 'I apologize to you, forgive me'. But the man answered, 'I will not forgive you until you say to the Craftsman Who made me, "How ugly is the vessel which Thou hast made!"' R. Simeon ran after him for three miles [until he reached his town]. When the people of the town came out to meet him, greeting him with the words, 'Peace be unto you, Master', the man asked them, 'Whom do you address as Master?' They replied, 'Him who follows you'. He said to them, 'If this man is a master, may there not be many like him in Israel!' 'Heaven forbid!' they exclaimed; 'what did he do to you?' He answered, 'This is how he behaved towards me'. They said to him, 'Nevertheless, forgive him'. The man replied, 'I will forgive him, but on condition that he will never again act in this manner'. That same day R. Simeon entered his great House of Study and lectured: At all times a man should be pliant as a reed and not hard like a cedar. Now what is the feature of the reed? Though all the winds come and blow upon it, it gives and bends with them; but when the winds are stilled it again

(6) R. Simeon censured himself for having wasted his time with this blasphemer. It is nevertheless strange to note that R. Simeon regarded the visiting of the sick as an 'idle thing' and a neglect of the Torah. In MS. E. the reading is: 'Justly has the Holy One, blessed be He, dealt with you since you neglected the study of the Torah and occupied yourself with idle things'. R. Simeon accordingly censured the sick person, whom he apparently knew to be a worthless person occupied with idle things. (7) Cf. Ta'an. 20a-20b (Sonc. ed., pp. 100). There the name is reversed, 'R. Eleazar b. R. Simeon'. (8) A village near Bethlehem; cf. Gen. XXXV, 21.

stands upright in its place. And what happens to the reed in the end?[9] It is privileged that of it a pen is made for writing a Torah scroll. The cedar, on the other hand, cannot stand in its place [against the winds], for when the south[10] wind blows upon it, it uproots and overturns it. And what happens to the cedar in the end? Lumbermen come and cut it up, and it is used for roofing houses while the residue is cast into the fire. Hence [the Sages] said: A man should be pliant as a reed and not hard like a cedar.

2. Three different tributes are paid to men [for their acts of charity]. He who gives alms, a blessing be upon him; he who lends is better than he; but he who provides [the poor man with money to do trade] sharing the profits with him[11] is the best of all.[12]

3. There are three types of disciple: he who asks questions and also makes answer is wise; he who asks but cannot answer is inferior to him; but he who can neither ask nor answer is lowest of all.

4. There are three kinds of sweat which are beneficial to the body: sweat caused by sickness, by a bath and by work. The sweat caused by sickness brings healing, and the sweat caused by a bath has no equal [as a cure].

5. There are six kinds of tears, three of them beneficial and three harmful. [Tears brought on] by weeping, by smoke, and in the privy are harmful; [tears brought on] by unguents, by laughter, and by [pungent] fruits are beneficial.[13]

6. There are three characteristics of an earthenware vessel: it absorbs, it does not exude, and it does not taint what is in it.

There are three characteristics of a glass vessel: It neither absorbs nor exudes, it exposes to view whatever is in it,[14] and in a hot place it is hot while in a cold place it is cold.

(9) So according to MS. E. and a variant reading. V has 'therefore the reed is privileged', etc. (10) A variant is 'north'. (11) lit. 'for half (profits) or more'. Cf. GRA. (12) For by his act he enables the poor man to retain his self-respect. (13) Cf. Shab. 151b (Sonc. ed., p. 774). A variant reading is: 'Tears produced by an unguent, and those brought about by taking mustard are good for the eyes, but tears caused by laughter are best of all'. (14) Being transparent.

7. At four times it is harmful to cohabit: on returning from a journey, on leaving a surgeon[15] [after blood-letting], on rising from an illness, and on being released from prison.[16]

8. Whoever undertakes to observe these four rules is accepted as an Associate:[17] he does not enter a graveyard,[18] he does not rear small cattle,[19] he does not give heave-offering[20] to a *kohen* who is an *'am ha-'areẓ,*[21] he does not handle clean things in the proximity of an *'am ha-'areẓ,*[22] and he eats his ordinary food in conditions of cleanness.[23]

9. [24][Three things returned to their original place: Israel, Egypt's wealth, and the heavenly writing. Israel returned to their original place,[25] as it is stated, *Your fathers dwelt of old time beyond the River,*[26] and it is also stated, *And carried the people away into Babylon.*[27]] Egypt's wealth returned to its original place,[28] as it is stated, *And they despoiled the Egyptians,*[29] and also *And Joseph gathered up all the money;*[30] and it is also stated, *And it came to pass in the fifth year of king Rehoboam, that Shishak king of Egypt came up against Jerusalem; and he took away the treasures of the house of the Lord.*[31] The

(15) lit. 'the barber'; he also functioned as a surgeon. GRA reads 'the cupper'. (16) Cf. Giṭ. 70a (Sonc. ed., p. 333). (17) Heb. *ḥaber,* the opposite of *'am ha-'areẓ;* one who is scrupulous in the observance of the Torah, particularly in relation to laws of ritual purity and the separation of the priestly and levitical dues. Cf. Demai II, 3 (Sonc. ed., pp. 57f) and Tosiftha Demai II, 1. (18) Lest he defile himself by the dead. (19) In Israel. Because small cattle like sheep and goats have the habit of straying into the fields of others and causing damage to the sown fields. Cf. B.Ḳ. VII, 7 (Sonc. ed., p. 453). (20) Heb. *terumah;* cf. Num. XVIII, 8f. (21) An illiterate or uncultured man, particularly one careless in the observance of the laws of ritual purity and priestly and levitical dues. (22) Lest they contract uncleanness. (23) So making a habit of it, and he has no difficulty in dealing with consecrated food. The list of requirements has obviously been extended since the passage enumerates five rules; and it is difficult to establish the four original requirements. Cf. Demai *loc. cit.* (24) The passage which follows is defective since it only deals with two items whereas the preceding paragraphs deal, for the most part, with subjects each comprising three items. The text here is restored from Mekilta, *Beshallaḥ* (ed. Lauterbach) II, pp. 139f, Pes. 87b (Sonc. ed., pp. 464f), II ARN XLVII and GRA. (25) To Babylon. (26) Josh. XXIV, 2. Israel's ancestry emanated from beyond the River, i.e. Babylon. (27) Ezra V, 12. GRA quotes instead Jer. XXVIII, 22, *They shall be carried to Babylon.* (28) To Egypt. (29) Ex. XII, 36. (30) Gen. XLVII, 14. (31) 1 Kings XIV, 25f.

heavenly writing[32] returned to its original place,[33] as it is stated, *Wilt thou set thine eyes upon it? It is gone; for it certainly takes to itself wings, like an eagle that flieth toward heaven.*[34]

10. R. JUDAH B. TEMA SAID: BE STRONG AS A LEOPARD, SWIFT AS AN EAGLE, [34*b*] FLEET AS A DEER AND BRAVE AS A LION TO DO THE WILL OF YOUR FATHER WHO IS IN HEAVEN.[35]

11. He used to say: Love God[36] and fear God, trembling and rejoicing at all the commandments.[37] If you have done a little wrong to your neighbour let it seem to you large; and if you have done him a big kindness let it seem to you small. If your neighbour has done you a little kindness let it seem to you large, and if he has done you a great wrong let it seem to you small.

A sponge and a glazed vessel describe the scholars;[38] a funnel and a hollow tube describe the wicked [disciples].[39]

Be like a skin bottle which has no opening to let the wind in.[40]

Learn to receive suffering and forgive an offence against you.

12. The things which were made and later hidden away are:[41] the Tent of Meeting and the vessels contained therein, the ark and the broken tablets, the jar of manna,[42] the staff [of Moses], the flask of anointing oil, Aaron's rod with its almonds and

(32) The divine writing (cf. Ex. XXXII, 16) upon the tablets which Moses broke (*ibid.* 19). (33) To heaven; cf. above II, 3, p. 21. (34) Prov. XXIII, 5. So lit., E.V., *for riches certainly make themselves wings.* Homiletically the verse is interpreted as referring to the heavenly script on the tablets which flew back to God. (35) From Aboth V, 23 (Sonc. ed., V, 20, p. 73). (36) lit. 'Heaven'. (37) The text of this sentence is corrupt and makes no sense as it stands. The reading adopted is that of MS. E. and as found in DEZ II (see below, p. 571). The meaningless words in the text, הדרוש של, are a misreading of חרד וששׂ על, 'trembling and rejoicing at'. (38) Who absorb everything and retain it in their minds. (39) Whatever they hear goes in one ear and out through the other. This sentence is apparently out of place here and belongs to XL, 8 above, p. 200. (40) Cf. DEZ I, below p. 567. The meaning may be: Be reserved, and give no ear to the idle talk and slanderous words of others. (41) Cf. Hor. 12a (Sonc. ed., p. 85), Ker. 5b (Sonc. ed., pp. 35f), and Yoma 52b (Sonc. ed., p. 245). (42) Cf. Ex. XVI, 33.

blossoms,[43] the robes of the priesthood,[44] the robes of the anointed [High] Priest; but the mortar of the House of Abṭinas,[45] the table,[46] the candelabrum, the veil[47] and the [High Priest's] head-plate are still located in Rome.

13. It is related[48] that R. Ṭarfon was sitting and teaching his disciples when a [poor] bride passed before him. He gave instructions for the bride to be taken to his house, and said to his mother and wife, 'Bathe her, anoint her, adorn her, and dance before her until she arrives at the house of her husband'.

14. [49]The following, so the Sages ordained, have no portion in the world to come: five kings and six [commoners] who sought power; [the latter being:] Cain, Korah, Balaam, Ahithophel, Doeg and Gehazi.[50]

15. R. Jose said: The thoroughly righteous will have no refining,[51] and the thoroughly wicked will also have no refining.[52] Who, then, will be refined? The intermediate ones,[53] [who cry:] *I beseech Thee, O Lord, deliver my soul:*[54] i.e. from the judgment of Gehinnom. Beth Shammai say:[55] They will go down to Gehinnom and be refined[56] there, then they will

(43) Cf. Num. XVII, 23, 25. (44) Probably the robes of the senior officials in the priesthood. It can hardly refer to the garments of the ordinary priests. (45) They were experts in compounding the incense for the Temple and used a mortar which had special properties; cf. Yoma III, 11 (Sonc. ed., p. 175). (46) On which lay the Shewbread; cf. Ex. XXV, 30. (47) The curtain which hung before the Holy of Holies. The sacrificial blood was sprinkled in its direction on special occasions; cf. Yoma 57a (Sonc. ed., p. 266). (48) This passage is out of place here and should be transferred to IV, 2, where it belongs. (49) This passage is also out of place and belongs to XXXVI, 5. (50) Cf. above XXXVI, 5, p. 182 and Sanh. X, 2 (Sonc. ed., p. 602) where the text reads: 'Three kings and four commoners'. The five kings would be Jeroboam, Ahab, Ahaz, Ahaziah and Amon; cf. Sanh. 103b (Sonc. ed., pp. 702f). (51) Reading מצרפין for מצטרפין throughout. The righteous need no refining process to purify them, but will be inscribed for everlasting life forthwith. Cf. R.H. 16b (Sonc. ed., p. 63). (52) The wholly wicked will at once go to their doom. (53) Those whose good and bad deeds are equal. For a short while they will be refined by the fires of Gehinnom and then become worthy of enjoying everlasting life. (54) Ps. CXVI, 4. (55) The words in the text, שמא אם, are a corruption of בית שמאי אומרים. (56) The word in the text is unknown in Heb. and is corrupt. The translation is based on the reading in MS. E., ונצרפין, 'and are refined'. A variant is ומצפצפין, 'and shriek in pain'; cf. R.H. 17a (Sonc. ed., p. 64).

burst forth and come up again, as it is stated, *And I will bring the third part through the fire, and will refine them as silver is refined, and will try them as gold is tried.*[57] But Beth Hillel say: They will not see it[58] at all, as it is stated, *For Thy lovingkindness is better than life; my lips shall praise Thee.*[59] And it further declares, *And spare them according to the greatness of Thy mercy:*[60] that they may be saved from the judgment of Gehinnom.

16. [61]WHATSOEVER THE HOLY ONE, BLESSED BE HE, CREATED IN HIS WORLD, HE CREATED ONLY FOR HIS GLORY, AS IT IS STATED, EVERYTHING THAT IS CALLED BY MY NAME, IT IS FOR MY GLORY I HAVE CREATED IT; I HAVE FORMED IT, YEA, I HAVE MADE IT.[62] AND IT DECLARES, THE LORD SHALL REIGN FOR EVER AND EVER.[63]

17. R. Ḥananiah b. 'Aḳashia said: The Holy One, blessed be He, was pleased to grant merit to Israel; therefore He multiplied for them Torah and precepts,[64] as it is stated, *The Lord was pleased for His righteousness' sake, to make the Torah great and glorious.*[65]

(57) Zech. XIII, 9. *The third part* alludes to the intermediate ones. (58) i.e. Gehinnom. (59) Ps. LXIII, 4. (60) Neh. XIII, 22. The verse reads *me* not 'them'. (61) Quoted from Aboth VI, 11 (Sonc. ed., p. 91), the concluding words of the Tractate. (62) Is. XLIII, 7. E.V., *Every one . . . and whom I created for My glory . . . formed him . . . made him.* (63) Ex. XV, 18. (64) God gave Israel the Torah as a mark of love so that through its numerous precepts Israel could the more readily acquire merit. Cf. the interpretation of Maimonides (at the end of his Commentary on Mishnah Makkoth): 'It is one of the fundamentals of our faith that if a man perform but one of the 613 commandments in the proper manner, with sincerity and devotion and from pure love of it, he thereby acquires life in the world to come'. (65) Is. XLII, 21, E.V., *the teaching great.* The words *for His righteousness' sake* are interpreted homiletically 'to make him (Israel) righteous'. This paragraph, found at the end of Makkoth, is recited after the reading of each chapter of Aboth.

MASSEKETH SOFERIM

TRACTATE FOR SCRIBES

TRANSLATED INTO ENGLISH
WITH INTRODUCTION
AND NOTES

BY

REV. DR. ISRAEL W. SLOTKI
M.A., Litt.D., F.R.S.L.

CONTENTS

INTRODUCTION

NAME OF TRACTATE

The tractate is known as *Masseketh Soferim* ('The Tractate for Scribes') or *Hilkoth Soferim* ('The Laws, or Regulations, for Scribes'). The scribes referred to were a class of pious and learned men who were partly or wholly engaged in copying scrolls of the Torah and other scripts used for religious purposes.

In consideration of the fact that the principal subject of the first nine chapters is the correct functioning of the scribes, their professional and religious duties, and guidance in the selection of the right materials for the sacred work, the entire tractate was given the title of 'Scribes'. Such a method of naming was not unusual in ancient Hebrew works, which were not, in their titles, always descriptive of their full contents.

DATE OF COMPILATION

From internal evidence it is clear that, in its present form, *Soferim* was compiled some time after the final redaction of the Babylonian Talmud. Most scholars hold that the date of its compilation was in the Gaonic period, about the middle of the eighth century (cf. J. E. and *Oẓar Yisrael, s.v.*, and the authorities there quoted).

PLACE IN RABBINIC LITERATURE

Soferim is one of the *Massektoth Ḳeṭannoth,* 'The Minor Tractates' of the Talmud, known also as *Sefarim Ḥiẓẓonim,* 'External Books'. This denotes the works outside the Talmudic Canon whose relation to the Talmud is somewhat analogous to that of the *Baraithoth* to the Mishnah. The number of these Minor Tractates is variously given as fifteen or thirteen, while earlier authorities mention only seven.

IMPORTANCE AND AUTHORITY

Soferim is regarded as the most authoritative in this category. The contents of the first five chapters, without the interpolations, are paralleled in a separate tractate in the *Massektoth Ḳeṭannoth* known as *Sefer Torah* ('Scroll of the Torah'). The latter also belongs to the Gaonic era.

The rulings in *Soferim* at times disagree with those of the Babylonian or Jerusalem Talmud, and in a number of instances, according to the Tosafists (cf., e.g., Ber. 18a, *s.v. Lemaḥar;* Pes. 40b, *s.v. 'Abal*), its guidance is to be followed. One example may be quoted where the ruling of a Mishnah is disregarded in favour of one in *Soferim:* In Meg. III, 6 (30b, 31a, Sonc. ed., p. 187) it is laid down that on fast days, other than the ninth of *Ab* and the fasts associated with supplications in times of drought, the Scriptural reading is the section of the Blessings and Curses (Lev. XXVI, 3-46); but nowadays the ruling of *Soferim* XVII, 7 is adopted to read the passage beginning *And Moses besought* (Ex. XXXII, 11-14 and XXXIV, 1-10). Much of the tractate has also been incorporated in the Synagogue liturgy, the *Masorah* and similar works.

SOLE AUTHORITY

Regarding the regulations for scribes, *Soferim* is in some respects the only source, no mention of them being found in the Mishnah. The explanation of this omission may possibly be that the regulations in question were so well known when the Mishnah was compiled (*c.* 200 C.E.) that there was no need to commit them to writing. A similar reason for other omissions, it may be added, is given by Maimonides in his *Commentary on the Mishnah,* Men. IV, 1.

NATURE OF THE MATERIAL

Legal *Baraithoth* and other Rabbinical teaching, mainly of Palestinian origin, constitute the bulk of the tractate, and to these were added customs which were in vogue in the Holy Land or Babylon. The *Baraithoth,* like the Mishnah and Gemara, were originally oral traditions and in outline, at least, must have taken shape before the redaction of the Talmud. In the last section of the tractate there is also embodied material from the Babylonian Talmud (cf. Rappaport, *Kerem Ḥemed,* VI, p. 247; Zunz, G.V., 2nd ed., p. 322).

IRREGULAR SEQUENCE

Originally that part of *Soferim* which is concise and systematic was prepared for the specific use of scribes. It has, however, undergone many changes, and the present text is not conspicuous for order and logical sequence. Rules for the preparation of scrolls, the statutory prayers, public readings and stories from the *'Aggada* all find their random places in the chapters of the tractate (cf. Zunz, *op. cit.,* p. 100).

A PRACTICAL MANUAL

Like the other *Massektoth Ḳeṭannoth, Soferim,* though containing considerable interpolations, is concerned in the main with the single theme of scribes and sacred documents. On account of their form, they are often regarded as the first manuals in Rabbinic literature which consist of systematic collections of concise and comprehensive rules for practical use. In older Rabbinic literature rules of this nature would be scattered over many tractates of the Talmud and embedded in complicated discussions.

MAIN DIVISIONS

In a rough classification the tractate may be divided into three sections:

(*i*) Rules concerning the preparation and proper writing and handling of sacred scrolls and the persons qualified for the work (chaps. I-V).

(*ii*) Continuation of the rules on the same subject (chaps. VI-IX).

(*iii*) Rules concerning the public reading of the Torah, the Prophets and Hagiographa, the statutory services on the New

Moon and Festivals, the fasts and other solemn days; liturgical rules in connection with one or other of these occasions (chaps. X-XV, XVII-XXI).

Chapter XVI discusses in the main the place of the *'Aggada* in Rabbinic literature, and about half of chapter XXI is devoted to it. In the edition of V the number of Rules is 226. M gives the number as 230 and J.E. as 225.

ANALYSIS OF THE CHAPTERS

I deals with the writing materials which must be used for the sacred scrolls, the permitted languages and translations, deviations in the Septuagint from the Masoretic Text, the sheets, columns, open and closed sections, and the persons qualified to do the writing.

II prescribes the spaces which must be left between letters, words, lines, columns and books of the Pentateuch; the number of columns in a sheet, lines in a column, the width and length of scrolls; the rollers, sewing, mending, and the final letters of the Hebrew alphabet.

III discusses which books may be written in one scroll, and which scrolls may be separated into smaller books; degrees of sanctity in the sacred writings, superscriptions, palimpsests, procedure in case of scribal errors, ornamentations, manner of rolling and unrolling the scrolls, their reverential handling, and the respectful use of foodstuffs.

IV enumerates the divine names which may not be erased, the names which are sacred and those of the same spelling which are secular; and prohibits the profane use of any of the sacred names.

V is concerned with errors in the writing of a divine name, the omission of lines; concentration and reverence when divine names are written by the scribe; procedure in cases where such names were written on a person's body, an article of furniture, the horn of an animal or any utensil; the storage of disused sacred writings, and the scrupulous treatment due to borrowed books.

VI indicates the sections of the Torah which must be marked

by blank spaces, the letters and words that are distinguished by dots above them in the text, places for the inverted *nun*, and quotes the textual variants in three scrolls in the Temple, and certain words whose orthography differs from their traditional form and reading.

VII contains a list of words whose pronunciation (*ḳerē*) is different from their written form (*kethib*).

VIII shows the variations in the parallel texts of Ps. XVIII and 2 Sam. XXII, and of Is. XXXVI-XXXIX and 2 Kings XVIII-XX.

IX prescribes which letters are to be ornamented, which are to be written larger than normal, words that are to be substituted in reading for those in the text, and sections which may not be translated in public readings.

X gives general rules for public readings from the Scriptures, the number of persons to be called to the Torah lection on different occasions, and the minimum number of adult males required for public religious functions.

XI regulates the length of the passages in public lections and translations, skipping from one part of Scripture to another, and the procedure in case of error in the sequence of the reading.

XII discusses the manner of reading the curses in Leviticus and Deuteronomy, songs and the Decalogue, the set readings for the New Moon and *Ḥanukkah*, the arrangement of the lines in the poems in Ex. XV, Deut. XXXII and Judg. V, and how Deut. XXXII is to be divided between six persons.

XIII tells how to write the Hagiographa in general and the scroll of Esther in particular, and gives the benedictions for reading from the Pentateuch and the *hafṭarah*.

XIV contains the benedictions for reading the Hagiographa and particularly the scroll of Esther, and the liturgical introductions to the readings; describes the persons qualified to act as readers of Scripture at the statutory services, the times for the reading of Esther, the Song of Songs and Ruth; and contrasts the degrees of sanctity of the Torah and other sacred scrolls.

XV discusses the use of the Assyrian script, Greek and other languages in religious books, the degrees of importance of the Rabbinical writings, and recommends to parents which occupations to choose for their children and which to shun.

XVI dwells on the importance of the Torah, the place of the *'Aggada,* the many-sided interpretations of Scripture, and the depth of the knowledge of the ancient Sages. It also indicates divisions in the Pentateuch, the number of Psalms, and under what conditions the *ḳedushshah* is to be recited.

XVII prescribes the readings with some relevant rules for the New Moon, the major and minor Festivals, and Mondays and Thursdays.

XVIII lays down the regulations for the daily and Festival Psalms, the order of service on the Ninth of *Ab,* and various customs appertaining to fast days.

XIX continues the regulations for the Psalms, and gives the forms of the statutory prayers for the solemn days and Festivals, the announcement of the New Moon, and the benedictions and some customs for weddings and funerals.

XX details the ceremony on seeing the new moon, rules for the *Ḥanukkah* lamp, the benedictions, Psalms, prayers and lections on that Festival.

XXI names *Nisan* as a month of joy, describes the fasts, feast and customs in connection with *Purim* and the benedictions for the Torah and the scroll of Esther on that Festival, concluding with aggadic passages relating to the Patriarchs.

I. W. SLOTKI.

SOFERIM

CHAPTER I

RULE 1. It is not permitted to write [the sacred] books,[1] *tefillin* and *mezuzoth*[2] on skins of ritually unclean cattle or on skins of ritually unclean wild animals. Nor may they[3] be sewn with their sinews, or [the parchment rolls of *tefillin*] be wound with their hair. It is an oral prescription delivered to Moses at Sinai that [all these] shall be written on the skins of ritually clean cattle or ritually clean wild animals, be sewn together with their sinews and [the *tefillin* rolls] wound with their hair. It is also an oral prescription delivered to Moses at Sinai that [the parchments] shall be ruled with a reed[4] and the writing on the skin be done with ink. [This latter requirement] has support in Scripture, *And I wrote them with ink in the book.*[5]

RULE 2. R. Joshua the grits-dealer was asked: 'Why is it permitted to write [sacred scrolls] on the skins of *nebeloth* and *ṭerefoth?*' 'I will give you an analogy,' R. Joshua replied. 'This is similar to the case of two men who were condemned to death by the State, one being executed by the king and the other by the executioner. Which of them is superior? He who was executed by the king.'[6] 'If so,' he retorted, 'they should be permitted to be eaten!' 'It is stated,' replied R. Joshua, '*Ye shall not eat any* nebelah.[7] Scripture has forbidden it, so what can I do for you?' (From here it is inferred that it is permitted to write on skins of *nebelah* and on skins of *ṭerefah* and there is no need to

(1) The scrolls of the Pentateuch used for the lections in public worship. (2) These two nouns are added by GRA and M. For Hebrew and other terms, see the Glossary. (3) The parchment sheets of which the scrolls are made up. (4) To guide the hand of the scribe, the letters being written under the ruled lines. (5) Jer. XXXVI, 18. (6) *Nebeloth* and *ṭerefoth* are the effect of an act of God. (7) Deut. XIV, 21. E.V. *of anything that dieth of itself.*

consider the possibility of their having been pierced at the animal's heart.)[8]

RULE 3. Skins[9] for the [sacred] books, *tefillin* and *mezuzoth* may be bought anywhere, and one need not consider the possibility that they might be skins which were pierced at the animal's heart.

RULE 4. The writing on *ḳelaf* must be on the side of the flesh, and on *gewil* it must be on the side of the hair, no deviation from this being permitted. It is an oral prescription delivered to Moses at Sinai that if one changed one for the other, [the scroll] may not be used for the lection [in the statutory services].

RULE 5. [The sacred texts][10] may not be written on *difthera* or erased paper;[11] nor with coal,[12] shoe-black, ink containing gum, vitriol or fruit-juice.[13] Vitriol may not be added to the ink.

RULE 6. [The sacred texts] may not be written in [obsolete] Hebrew characters,[14] or in the Aramaic, Median or Greek languages.[15] If they were written in any other language or in any other characters they may not be used for the lection [in the statutory services], since they must be written in the Assyrian [script].

RULE 7. It once happened that five elders wrote the Torah for King Ptolemy[16] in Greek, and that day was as ominous for

(8) This sentence is enclosed in brackets in some eds. It was a heathen practice to remove the heart from a live animal to be offered as a sacrifice; this, in Rabbinic law, rendered the entire animal, including its skin, forbidden as an idolatrous offering ('A.Z. 29b, Sonc. ed., p. 145). (9) Before they were dressed; but dressed skins may be bought only from trustworthy persons who can testify that the dressing had been done in accordance with the law. (10) Mentioned in Rule 1. (11) Others, 'palimpsest'. GRA omits 'erased'. (12) Or, 'black pigment'. (13) Others, 'rain-water', 'wine-lees'. (14) The script must be 'Assyrian' (the modern Hebrew square characters) and the language 'the holy tongue'. (15) According to Meg. 9a (Sonc. ed., p. 48) it is permitted to write the Torah in Greek although this is not allowed in the case of *tefillin* and *mezuzoth*. (16) Presumed to be Ptolemy Philadelphus who reigned over Egypt 285-247 B.C.E. He arranged for the Greek Version, the Septuagint, to be made, as narrated in the next paragraph. [The Tractate gives two accounts of the translation, the present one being the later which reflects the harmful effects which the Septuagint had in arresting the development of exegesis among the Hellenistic Jews (cf. Weiss, *Dor*, I, p. 90).]

Israel as the day on which the golden calf was made, since the Torah could not be accurately translated.

RULE 8. It also happened that King Ptolemy assembled seventy-two elders and placed them in seventy-two [separate] rooms without telling them the reason for which he had assembled them. He then went to each one of them and said to him,[17] 'Write for me [a translation of] the Torah of Moses your master'. The Omnipresent inspired them[18] and the mind of all of them was identical, so that each on his own[19] wrote the [same translation of the] Torah, introducing [the same] thirteen alterations[20] as follows: 'God created in the beginning'.[21] 'And God said I shall make a man in image and likeness.'[22] 'And He finished on the sixth [day] and rested on the seventh [day].'[23] 'Male and female He created him.'[24] 'Come let Me go down and there confound their language.'[25] 'And Sarah laughed among her relatives,[26] saying.' 'For in their anger they slew oxen[27] and in their self-will they digged up a stall.'[28] 'And Moses took his wife and his children and set them upon a carrier[29] of men.'[30] 'Now the time that the children of Israel

(17) lit. 'to them'. (18) lit. 'put counsel in the heart of each one of them'. (19) So GRA. (20) Deviations from the traditional text. In the extant Versions of the Septuagint only some of these are found. (21) Instead of *In the beginning God created* (Gen. I, 1) the Heb. of which might be misinterpreted to mean that a power named 'Bereshith' (in the beginning) created God. (22) The Heb. text reads: *Let us make man in our image, after our likeness* (Gen. I, 26). The plural *us* and *our* might erroneously suggest a plurality of deities. (23) For the Heb.: *And He finished on the seventh day* (Gen. II, 2) which could be understood to imply that God did some work on the seventh day. (24) Instead of *created them* (*ibid.* V, 2) from which it might be inferred that man and woman were, from the first, two separate beings, contrary to *ibid.* II, 21. (25) Instead of *let us go down* (*ibid.* XI, 7). (26) i.e. she laughed in the presence of people and therefore incurred censure (*ibid.* XVIII, 12). The Heb. means 'within herself' as Abraham had done when he *laughed . . . in his heart* (*ibid.* XVII, 17) and had not been rebuked. (27) So GRA, H and M. V incorrectly 'a man'. (28) Changing *men* (*ibid.* XLIX, 6) to 'oxen' and *oxen* to 'stall' in order to remove the stigma of murder from Jacob's sons. (29) So M. V and H read 'carriers of men'. (30) i.e. an animal conformable with the dignity of Moses, instead of *ass* (Ex. IV, 20).

dwelt in Egypt and in the land of Canaan and in other lands[31] was four hundred and thirty years.'[32] 'And he sent the elect of the children of Israel.'[33] 'And upon the elect of the children of Israel He laid not His hand.'[34] 'I have not taken one desirable thing[35] from them.' 'The [beast] with small legs.'[36] 'Which the Lord thy God hath allotted to give light unto all the peoples under the whole heaven.'[37] 'Which I commanded should not be served.'[38]

RULE 9. [The sacred scrolls] may not be written in gold. It is related that in an Alexandrian[39] scroll of the Torah all the divine names were written in gold, and when the matter came before the Sages they decided that it should be stored away.[40]

RULE 10. All the Torah is in Hebrew but it contains some Aramaic words.[41] What is in Hebrew may not be written in Aramaic and the Aramaic words may not be altered; for

(31) So M. V omits 'and in other lands'. [The reading of the Septuagint is 'in the land of Canaan and in the land of Egypt'.] (32) Instead of the Heb. which omits 'in the land of Canaan and in other lands' (Ex. XII, 40), and implies that all the 430 years were spent in Egypt when, in fact, they could not have dwelt there more than 210 years (cf. Rashi to Meg. 9a). (33) So GRA and Meg. 9a but omitted in V. 'Elect' is substituted for *young men* (*ibid*. XXIV, 5), the former being regarded as more suitable persons for the service. (34) Here also 'elect' was substituted for the Heb. for *nobles* (*ibid*. 11). The alteration was not essential, but 'elect' which was mentioned earlier was preferred. It should be noted that in the total of thirteen alterations, this and the preceding are counted as one. (35) A 'desirable thing' [which occurs in the Septuagint] for the Heb. *ass* (Num. XVI, 15) to avoid the suggestion that Moses did not take an ass but more precious objects. (36) Instead of the Heb. for *the hare* (Lev. XI, 6) which is *arnebeth*, so as not to give offence to Ptolemy the name of whose queen was Arnebeth. (37) The insertion 'to give light' (Deut. IV, 19) removes the possible misunderstanding that the heavenly bodies enumerated in the verse were intended by God to be objects of worship. (38) Deut. XVII, 3 reads *which I have commanded not*. This might be taken to mean that God did not desire their existence and their creation was consequently due to a power beyond His control. It should be noted that the last two alterations are regarded as one in the enumeration because both deal with heavenly bodies as objects of worship. (39) So M. V and H read 'a scroll of the Torah of Alexander' [i.e. Alexander Jannaeus (103-76 B.C.E.) according to Krauss, *Lehnwörter*, II, p. 55]. (40) lit. 'it shall be hidden'; not to be used for the lection. (41) lit. 'translation' (*Targum*).

example, *Jegar-sahadutha* and *Galeed.*[42] Others hold that the rule applies only to *Jegar-sahadutha* and *Galeed* because they are two specifically Aramaic and Hebrew expressions respectively.[43] If Hebrew words were written in Aramaic or Aramaic words in Hebrew, the scroll may not be used for the lection. The Aramaic [and Hebrew] words referred to are *Jegar-sahadutha, Galeed* and the like.

If *ha'azinu hashshamayim*[44] was arranged like the Song of Moses[45] or if the Song of Moses was arranged like *ha'azinu;* if continuous lines were written in broken ones or vice versa; [35*b*] or if the breaking up was not done according to the rule, the scroll may not be used for the lection.

RULE 11. If one finished [writing nearly] all the Torah and less than a column[46] remained of the text, one need not hesitate to make of this a small column on its own.[47]

RULE 12. A [parchment] sheet [of the Torah scroll] containing six

(42) Gen. XXXI, 47, 'the heap of witness' in Aramaic and Hebrew. (43) In the case of the other parts, however, although one language should not be changed for another, the scroll is not disqualified if a change was made (cf. N.Y. *ad loc.*). (44) *Give ear ye heavens,* the opening words of Deut. XXXII, 1-43, which is arranged in the scroll as follows:

(45) Ex. XV, 1-18 written as:

or, according to others:

(46) So GRA and H. V reads: 'If one finished all the column and left over less, one extends the wording so as to make', etc. A reading in M is 'if one finished all the book and left less than a column, one extends the writing so as to make', etc. (47) The extension of a short passage over a full column is done either by enlarging the characters or, according to others, by making each successive line shorter than the one preceding it.

columns may be divided into two sheets;[48] but one of five columns may not be divided, in order that it should not[49] be separated into one of two[50] and one of three columns. No one is allowed to write [a scroll of the Torah] unless one is able to read.[51]

RULE 13. A scroll of the Torah that was written by a Sadducee,[52] an informer,[53] a proselyte,[54] a slave, a woman,[55] a madman or a minor may not be used for the lection.[56] This is the rule: Whosoever cannot act in religious matters on behalf of the public is not permitted to write a scroll of the Torah.[57]

RULE 14. If an open section was written as closed or vice versa, the scroll must be stored away. What is an open section? One which does not begin at the beginning of a line. And what is a closed section? [One which is separated from what precedes by a vacant] space in the middle of the line. And how much space must be left at the beginning of a line so that a section may be called 'open'? A space in which a name of three letters may be written.[58] And how much space must be left in the middle of a line so that a section may be called 'closed'? A space in which a name of three letters may be written. If an entire section was completed at the end of a column, one vacant line must be left at the top [of the next column]; but if a vacant space in which a name of three letters may be written was left at the foot [of the column], one begins [the next column] from the top.

(48) Each containing three columns. (49) So GRA and N.Y. H and M read: 'perhaps one might'. (50) Not less than three columns may be contained in each sheet. (51) M inserts: 'one is not allowed to write unless [the parchment] was ruled; and if an unruled sheet was written on, it is disqualified'. (52) An adherent of a sect which was opposed to the teachings and traditions of the Pharisees. M adds *min,* a Jewish heretic or Jewish-Christian. (53) Against his fellow-Jews to the ruling Roman authorities. M adds משומד, an apostate. (54) This refers to a 'proselyte settler' (*ger toshab*), one who does not observe the commandments but, on account of domicile in the land of Israel, has renounced idolatry. (55) So GRA and M; not in V and H. (56) For the unsuitability of the persons enumerated, cf. Giṭ. 45b (Sonc. ed., p. 199). (57) So GRA. V reads: 'everyone who writes it [must be a person who] may act on behalf of the public [in discharging a religious obligation]'. (58) The view of Maimonides which has been adopted is that space must be left for three words, each of three letters (cf. Y.D. 275, §2).

CHAPTER II

RULE 1. Sufficient space must be left between words[1] so that they can be distinguished, and between letters so that they be not mixed. If the letters were mixed or a break was made in the middle of a word, the scroll must not be used for the lection in the statutory services.[2]

RULE 2. Between lines there must be left the space of a line, between words the space of a letter, between letters that of a hairbreadth, and between columns the space of the width of a thumb. If [a word at][3] the end of a column was copied[4] at the beginning [of the next column, the scroll] is disqualified. If the letters were mixed or if a break was made in the middle of a word, the lection may not be read from it.

RULE 3. It is permitted to insert[5] between columns [part of] a word of five[6] letters. One may not write two letters within[7] the column and three without;[8] but it is not so with a short word.[9] If the [part of a longer word, however, forms] a short word of two[10] letters on its own,[11] it is forbidden [to insert it between the columns].[12]

RULE 4. In a Torah scroll the space[13] of two finger-breadths must be left between columns, but in scrolls of the Prophets and ordinary Pentateuchs[14] a space of one thumb-breadth

(1) lit. 'between name and name'. (2) In V Rule 1 is enclosed within brackets, probably because it is included in the fuller version in the next Rule. (3) So according to GRA. (4) lit. 'made'. (5) lit. 'place'. (6) So N.Y. V, H and M read 'four'. (7) So N.Y. V and H have 'at the end'. (8) Because the greater part of the word must appear within the column. So N.Y. V, H and M read 'and two between the columns'. GRA emends to 'one at the end of the column and three between the lines'. (9) Of two letters (N.Y.). One letter may be written between columns (H). (10) So GRA. V, H and M, 'three letters'. (11) In a noun like שלחן (table), for instance, which consists of four letters, the last two can form the word חן (grace). (12) The reading of GRA and N.Y. (13) So M, H and N.Y. V repeats 'space' unnecessarily. (14) Intended for study only and not for public lections.

only. In the lower margin of a Torah scroll the space of a handbreadth is left, and in the upper margin three finger-breadths;[15] but in scrolls of the Prophets and ordinary Pentateuchs three finger-breadths in the lower margin and two finger-breadths in the upper. In all these cases,[16] if it is desired to extend [the margins] this may be done, provided they do not exceed [the space of] the written matter. Between the books[17] in a Torah scroll a vacant space of four lines must be left, and in a scroll of the Prophets three lines.[18]

RULE 5. If one finished [writing nearly] all the book[19] and one column of text remained, one need not hesitate to make a small sheet of it.[20] At the conclusion of the [last] column [sufficient parchment] must be left to wind [round the scroll]. It is proper[21] to attach a roller to the end of a scroll for winding, but there is no need to attach one at the beginning of a scroll. In a Torah scroll, however, rollers should be attached at both ends. A scroll[22] is therefore rolled up towards the beginning but a Torah scroll[23] towards its[24] centre. A Torah scroll may not be opened by [holding on to] a sheet;[25] and the height[26] of such a scroll must be six handbreadths.

RULE 6. A sheet of a Torah scroll must contain not less than three columns and not more than eight. As regards the lines [in a scroll] a reason was given [for four different numbers]: corresponding to the journeys,[27] forty-two; corresponding to

(15) So H in agreement with Men. 30a (Sonc. ed., p. 195). V and M read 'two parts of a handbreadth'. (16) lit. 'here and there'. (17) lit. 'between a book and a book'. The Torah scroll consists of five books. (18) Both in the case of the major and minor Prophets (N.Y.). (19) So N.Y. V, H and M read 'books'. The reference is either to one book of the Prophets or to several written in one scroll. (20) Cf. I, Rule 11. (21) lit. 'in the beginning', 'at the outset'. (22) Of the Prophets, having its cylinder at the end of the scroll. (23) Which has cylinders at both ends. (24) So H, M and GRA. V omits the pronoun. (25) Owing to its sanctity. It must be opened by manipulating the cylinders. Another reading for פורחין is פותחין (H, cf. N.Y.) which gives the clause the meaning that when a Torah scroll is used for reading the lection not less than a full sheet, which contains not fewer than three columns, must be kept unrolled throughout the reading. (26) lit. 'length from top to bottom'. (27) The reading of H and GRA. V and M have 'in the journeys'.

the myriads of Israel, sixty; corresponding to the elders of Israel, seventy-two; and corresponding to the reproofs in Deuteronomy, [36a] ninety-eight; all depending on [the size of] the script.[28]

'Corresponding to the journeys,' as it is said, *And Moses wrote their goings forth.*[29] 'Corresponding to the myriads of Israel,' as it is said, *Write thou these words . . . and with Israel;*[30] as Israel numbered sixty myriads so may the lines of the Torah be sixty [in a column]. 'Corresponding to the elders, seventy-two,' as it is said, *Gather unto Me seventy men*[31] *. . . there remained . . . in the camp . . . of them that were recorded.*[32] 'Corresponding to the reproofs, ninety-eight,' as it is said, *If thou wilt not observe to do all the words of this law that are written.*[33]

In the case of *ḳelaf* parchments no limit was prescribed, and one may add [as many lines][34] as desired, provided only there are not less than three columns [to the sheet].[35]

RULE 7. If a sheet [of a Torah scroll] is worn out, one may not remove two [columns only][36] and replace them by two new columns; but three columns should be removed and replaced by three new ones, and the new columns must be written in the same size as the original script.

RULE 8. The width of a column [in a Torah scroll] must be such as to be recognizable at one glance,[37] and in a small scroll not less than a handbreadth. R. Jose b. Judah says: It must not be less than the width of three fingers.

(28) The larger the characters the fewer the number of lines in a column. (29) Num. XXXIII, 2. As the expression of writing (*wrote*) occurs in the same context as the journeys (*goings forth*), the number of lines in a *written* column may be the same as the number of the journeys. (30) Ex. XXXIV, 27. *Write* and *Israel* (numbering sixty myriads) occur in the same context. (31) Num. XI, 16. (32) *ibid.* 26. The number of the elders is found in the same passage as the expression of writing (*recorded*, lit. 'written'). (33) Deut. XXVIII, 58, *the words of this law* refers to the reproofs numbering 98 and occurs with *written* in the same passage. (34) N.Y. explains, 'sheets'. (35) i.e. the lines in a column, or according to N.Y. the sheets, should not be so many as to leave less than three columns for the last sheet of the scroll. (36) So M. N.Y. (cf. Ṭur Y.D. 280) explains, 'sheets' instead of 'columns'. (37) i.e. not more than three Heb. words, each of ten letters, could be written in a line. If the column is wider, the reader experiences difficulty in passing from line to line.

RULE 9. Half the length [of a column][38] must not be greater than its width, nor its width greater than half its length, but they must be exactly alike,[39] and this is the most correct procedure.[40]

RULE 10. A Torah scroll may not consist of half *gewil* and half *ḳelaf*, but it may consist of half *gewil* and half *ḳelaf*[41] of deers, although[42] this is not the best procedure.

RULE 11. [A tear in a parchment sheet of a Torah scroll] may not be joined with glue, nor is it permitted to write on a patch, nor may [the sheets] be sewn together on the written side. R. Simeon b. Eleazar said in the name of R. Meir: [A torn sheet] may be joined with glue and it is permitted to write on a patch. It is forbidden, however, to do the sewing[43] on the written side within but [it must be done] on the outside.

A space should be left [unstitched] at the top and at the foot [of the sheets] in order that the scroll be not torn [in use].[44] This, however, was at once qualified by adding: from the foot towards the top and from the top towards the foot. It is an oral prescription delivered to Moses at Sinai that, if a Torah scroll was torn, a patch may be placed on its outside.

In the case of the double letters of the alphabet,[45] the first

(38) Of text. This is exclusive of the upper and lower margins. Others explain, 'sheet', instead of 'column'. (39) So GRA. The reading of V is: 'he takes the middle course and so does it in', etc. (40) Some versions omit 'half' twice in this paragraph which agrees with B.B. 14a (Sonc. ed., p. 67): 'A scroll of the Torah should be such that its length does not exceed its circumference nor its circumference its length [when rolled up]'. On this reading, the paragraph deals with the size of the scroll in its entirety. (41) So Asheri (cf. N.Y.). V and H have the plural of *ḳelaf*. (42) GRA and others. V reads 'because'. (43) GRA, H and M. According to V 'the writing'. (44) By leaving a part unstitched, the liability to tear when the scroll is rolled up would be reduced. GRA reads this paragraph as follows: 'It is an oral prescription delivered to Moses at Sinai that a space should be left [unstitched] at the top and at the foot [of the sheets]. This, however, was at once qualified [by the Sages who questioned whether this was such an oral prescription or merely a rule] so that the scroll should not be torn [cf. Meg. 19b, Sonc. ed., pp. 118f]. If a Torah scroll was torn a patch may be placed on its outside'. (45) The five letters כ׳, מ׳, נ׳, פ׳, צ׳ which have a different form as finals.

ones[46] are written at the beginning and in the middle of a word, and the second[47] at the end. If this is reversed,[48] the scroll is disqualified. If a scroll[49] is torn, a patch may be placed on the inside and[50] it is not [obligatory to attach it] on the outside.[51]

(46) i.e. the letters in the non-final form. (47) The final letters. (48) A final letter in the middle or at the beginning or vice versa. (49) Other than a Torah scroll. (50) So M. V reads 'but'. (51) The sentence is omitted in H, his reading being 'if a scroll was torn' instead of 'if a Torah scroll was torn'.

CHAPTER III

RULE 1. It is permissible to join the Torah and the Prophets in one scroll, so R. Judah; but the Sages say: The Torah and the Prophets must be written in separate scrolls.[1]

RULE 2. Between a book of the Prophets and another, one should not leave the same empty space as between two books of the Torah, but in each case the space must be that which has been prescribed for it.[2] Furthermore, [a book of the Prophets][3] must begin at the top.[4]

RULE 3. A Torah scroll[5] may not be made into the separate books of the Pentateuch, neither into single books nor into two or three joined together, because it is forbidden to reduce a major sanctity[6] to a minor sanctity.[7] From scrolls containing sections of the Pentateuch, however, it is permitted to make up a Torah scroll. When may this be done? When the measurements[8] and the numbers of the lines[9] are alike.

RULE 4. It is not permissible to join together two sections of the Pentateuch or one and a half of them to form a single scroll.[10] But if it was intended[11] that additional scrolls be attached to them,[12] it is permissible.

RULE 5. It is related that Boethus b. Zonin[13] had eight books

(1) So V, H, M. GRA adopts the reading of B.B. 13b (Sonc. ed., p. 66): 'It is permissible to fasten the Torah, the Prophets and the Hagiographa [in one scroll]'. (2) viz. four lines between books of the Torah, and three lines between books of the Prophets. (3) If the preceding book ended at the foot of a column. (4) Of the next column, the reason being that, if the books of the Prophets were separated one from the other, the beginning of each book would commence at the top of a column. This does not apply to Torah scrolls which may never be cut up into separate books. (5) Which contains the five books of Moses. (6) The Torah scroll in its entirety. (7) A section of the Pentateuch. (8) Of all the scrolls that are to be joined together. (9) In each column. (10) Because it might be mistaken for a proper Torah scroll. (11) When these were written. (12) To complete a Torah scroll. (13) [A pious Jew at the end of the first cent. C.E., not to be identified with the Boethus named in ARN V.]

of the Prophets[14] joined together in one scroll in accordance with a ruling of R. Eleazar b. 'Azariah. Others maintain that he had them all in separate scrolls. It is also related that a certain person brought before the Sages a single scroll containing the Torah, the Prophets and the Hagiographa.[15]

RULE 6. This[16] applies only to a codex,[17] but in the case of a scroll[18] the Torah and the Prophets must each consist of a separate parchment.

RULE 7. If a Torah scroll has spaces or stops [to mark] the beginning of verses, it may not be used for the lections.[19] So also if a letter has been engraved or joined to another, the scroll may not be used for the lections.

RULE 8. A scroll [some of whose letters] are faded may not be used for the lections.[20] R. Simeon b. Eleazar says: If the outline [of the effaced letters] is distinguishable, it is permitted [to rewrite them].

RULE 9. A scroll of the Torah in which a whole line is faded may not be used for the lections. If the greater part of a line is faded and the smaller part intact, the use of the scroll is permitted. If a Torah scroll contains an error, it may not be used for the lections. How many [errors disqualify it]? One in a column, is the view of R. Judah. R. Simeon b. Gamaliel says: Even if there be one error in three columns[21] the scroll may not be used for the lections.

RULE 10. Not less than three columns of the Torah scroll [may be unrolled at one time during the reading], but there is no objection to the reading of ten [columns] in one [lection]. It

(14) Joshua, Judges, Samuel, Kings, Isaiah, Jeremiah, Ezekiel and the Twelve Prophets reckoned as one book. (15) And, as recorded in B.B. 13b (Sonc. ed., p. 66), the Sages ruled that it was a proper scroll. (16) That the Torah, Prophets and Hagiographa may be included in one scroll. (17) Since, as a book for study, no one could attribute to it the sanctity of a Torah scroll. (18) In that form only the contents could show whether it was a Torah scroll only. (19) Because the Torah scroll must conform to the original form without any alterations. (20) So H and GRA. V reads 'one should not rewrite them'. (21) The reading of GRA. In V and M, 'even three errors in a column'. The reading of H is: 'Three in a column is the view of R. Judah. Rabban Simeon b. Gamaliel says: Even if there be one error in one column'.

is a religious precept that the most important member[22] shall roll up the scroll.[23] When one rolls up a Torah scroll he should roll it [so that it closes] at the seam[24] and not at [the middle of] a sheet.[25] A Torah scroll should [36b] be rolled up[26] from without,[27] but the [band][28] should be tied from within.[29]

When one hands a Torah scroll to another person it must be done with the right hand only, and he who receives it must also do so with the right hand only, because the Torah was delivered at Mount Sinai in this manner, as it is stated, *At His right hand was a fiery law unto them.*[30]

R. Shefaṭai[31] said in the name of R. Joḥanan: If one reads the Scripture without a melody[32] or learns the Mishnah without a tune,[33] of him Scripture says, *Wherefore I gave them also statutes that were not good.*[34]

RULE II. A scribe may not put upon the written part [of a Torah scroll] a reed-pen with ink on it; nor may he take hold of the sheets of parchment[35] and thereby unroll [the scroll]; nor may he grasp them to extract the written sheets; [36] nor may he remove a scroll from its [case] by shaking it out. All these [restrictions] are relaxed with the official revisers of Scripture scrolls. A Torah scroll may not be released from its case while it is lying on one's lap[37] because this is disrespectful treatment. It is not permissible to place a Torah scroll on one's

(22) Of the congregation, or of those who have taken part in the reading. (23) Thus showing honour to the Torah. (24) So that if the scroll is pulled, only the seam will be affected. (25) Which might be torn by the pull. (26) So GRA. V and M: 'it shall not be fastened from within, but it must be fastened from without'. (27) i.e. the back of the written side, while the scroll is being held up by another person who is faced by the written side. (28) Which is wound around the scroll to prevent it from unrolling. (29) The knot facing the written side. In this way, when the next lection is to be read, the knot can be easily undone without having to turn the scroll over. (30) Deut. XXXIII, 2. (31) In Meg. 32a (Sonc. ed., p. 194) the name is Shefaṭiah. (32) Indicated in the printed Pentateuch by the traditional cantillation. (33) Which aids the memory. (34) Ezek. XX, 25. An accompanying melody enlivens one's studies, and endears the *statutes* which one learns. If such are described as *not good* it is because the melody is lacking. (35) So H. V, 'folds'. (36) Which are rolled up; lit. 'and bring forth the writing without'. (37) lit. 'one shall not slip a Torah scroll from one's lap and release it'.

knees or lean on it with one's elbows while reading; so according to the ruling of R. Nehemiah.

RULE 12. A Torah scroll may not be placed over a chair [with its sheets] hanging down while it is being read, in the manner of ordinary documents, because [sacred] books must not be treated with disrespect. The proper procedure is[38] to hold it in the hands[39] with reverence and so read it. [Sacred] books[40] may not be thrown about[41] nor may they be treated in [any other] disrespectful manner.

RULE 13. A scroll of the Torah may not be placed on a bed and [certainly][42] not at its foot or under it; nor may one sit on a bed on which a [Torah] scroll [happens to] rest. It is related that R. Eleazar once sat [unwittingly] on a bed on which lay a [Torah] scroll and [when he realized it] he jumped up as if a snake had bitten him. [Respect is shown for the Torah] because Scripture states, *Ye shall keep My sabbaths, and reverence My sanctuary*[43]—it is not the sabbaths that one reverences but Him who commanded [to keep them], nor is one to reverence the sanctuary but Him who commanded [to make] it.

It is obligatory to make beautiful *ẓiẓith*, beautiful *mezuzoth*, to write a beautiful scroll of the Torah with choice ink, with a fine reed-pen [written] by an expert penman[44] on well-finished parchments, on deer skins,[45] and to wrap it in precious silks; for Scripture states, *This is my God, and I will glorify Him*,[46] which means, perform the commandments in a beautiful manner to His glory.[47] Such is the interpretation of R. Ishmael. R. 'Aḳiba expounds the text as meaning that one should expatiate on His excellencies. Abba Saul explains: Be like Him;[48] as He is merciful and gracious so be thou merciful and gracious.

(38) lit. 'but'. (39) By means of a cloth since, according to Rule 16 below, it is forbidden to touch a Torah scroll with the bare hands. (40) Not only Torah scrolls (Maimonides). (41) lit. 'from place to place'. (42) Cf. N.Y. The addition of 'certainly' avoids an anticlimax. (43) Lev. XIX, 30. (44) [Reading with Bacher, *Ag. d. Tannaiten*, I, p. 254n לבלר אומן for לבלרין נאים (fine penmen).] (45) So GRA. V and H, 'dyed skins'. (46) Ex. XV, 2, *I will glorify Him* (ואנוהו) is connected homiletically with נאה, 'beautiful', and understood as 'I will serve Him in a beautiful manner'. (47) lit. 'before Him'. (48) He explains ואנוהו as the equivalent of אני והוא, 'I and He'.

RULE 14. Foodstuffs may not be treated with disrespect, nor may they be thrown about. One may not sit on a basket containing dates or dried figs;[49] but he may sit on a basket which contains pulse or on a cake of pressed figs, because it is customary to do so.[50] Foodstuffs may not be used as a support[51] or as a covering, nor may foodstuffs be eaten with the aid of foodstuffs,[52] unless [the latter] are fit to be eaten.[53] R. Eliezer b. Jacob says: Any fruit which has a stem or stalk[54] may be used as a covering.[55] R. Simeon b. Gamaliel says: Any foodstuff which requires processing may be used as a covering.[56] R. Simeon b. Gamaliel also says: Any foodstuff which has a protection[57] may be used as a covering. One who writes [Torah] scrolls may not turn over a sheet on its face[58] because this is disrespectful treatment.

RULE 15. If one finished [writing nearly] all the [Torah] scroll and left over one column, there is no objection to his arranging it on a small sheet [on its own].[59]

Foodstuffs may not be used as a covering.[60] R. Meir says: Any fruit which has a husk may be used as a covering. R. Judah says: Any fruit which has a stem or a stalk may be used as a covering.

RULE 16. Foodstuffs may not be eaten with the aid of foodstuffs unless they are consumed simultaneously. If a scroll cannot be covered with a cloth,[61] it may be turned over on its writing.[62] R. Joḥanan said: Whoever holds a Torah scroll without a covering[63] will be buried without a covering.[64] Buried without a covering! Is this thinkable? It means, Without the covering protection of that religious performance.[65]

(49) Because they might be crushed and spoilt. (50) Pulse or dried figs are not spoilt by sitting on them. (51) For any object. (52) Using them, e.g., in place of a spoon. (53) Immediately after use and would not be thrown away. (54) Whereby it can be lifted if it should happen to fall into the contents of the vessel which it covered. (55) Since it would not be necessary to throw it away after use. (56) In its raw state, since its use causes no deterioration. (57) e.g. a shell. (58) lit. 'scroll', with the writing downwards to protect it from falling dust while it is drying. (59) Cf. I Rule 11 and II Rule 5. (60) This and the following are repeated from Rule 14. (61) lit. 'on which there is no'. To protect the wet ink from dust while it is drying. (62) This qualifies what was stated in Rule 14 in accordance with 'Erub. 98a. (63) lit. 'naked'; this is regarded as disrespectful. (64) i.e. a shroud. (65). The reverential treatment of the Torah scroll is accounted an act of piety.

CHAPTER IV

RULE 1. The following divine names may not be erased,[1] viz. *Alef-lamed,*[2] *Alef-daleth,*[3] *Yod-he,*[4] *Shaddai,*[5] *Ẓeba'oth,*[6] *'Eheyeh 'asher 'Eheyeh.*[7] R. Jose says: *Ẓeba'oth* is a secular noun.[8] R. Simeon b. Eleazar said: The Aguddah[9] family, who were scribes in Jerusalem, used to erase *Ẓeba'oth,* because they treated it as a secular noun, as it is stated, *Captains of* hosts *shall be appointed at the head of the people.*[10]

RULE 2. If one writes *Alef-lamed* of the four letters [of *Alef-lamed-waw-he*][11] or *Yod-he* of the four letters [of *Yod-he-waw-he*][12] they may not be erased, because there are divine names corresponding to them.[13] *Shin-daleth* of *Shin-daleth-yod* (*Shaddai*) or *Ẓadi-beth-alef* of *Ẓadi-beth-alef-waw-taw* (*Ẓeba'oth*) or *Alef-he* of *Alef-he-yod-he* (*'Eheyeh*) may be erased, because there are no divine names corresponding to them.

RULE 3. All prefixes and suffixes connected with a divine name may be erased. [Prefixes such as] *in* the Lord, *like* the Lord, *to* the Lord, *and* the Lord [represented respectively by the letters] *beth, kaf, lamed, waw* and suffixes such as *our* God, *your* God, *their* God [represented respectively by the letters] *nun-waw, kaf-mem, he-mem* and others of the same kind, may be erased. Some Sages say: The *kaf-mem* of 'your [God]'[14] must not be erased.

RULE 4. All ordinary nouns the letters of which are the same as those of a divine name may be erased.[15] [For instance in] *For God doth know that in the day ye eat thereof, your eyes shall be opened,*

(1) lit. 'he who writes'. (2) Pronounced *'El* (God). (3) The first two letters of the divine name *Alef-daleth-nun-yod* (Lord). (4) The first half of the Tetragrammaton and also constituting a name of God, *Yah.* (5) Almighty. (6) [Lord of] hosts. (7) 'I am that I am' (cf. Ex. III, 14). (8) And may be erased. (9) [H reads הגירה in agreement with j. Meg. 71d.] (10) Deut. XX, 9. Here צבאות refers to the army of Israel. (11) Meaning 'God of'. (12) The Tetragrammaton. (13) אל and יה. (14) And so also all other suffixes (cf. Y.D. 276, §9), because the divine name which precedes the suffix imparts sanctity to it (N.Y.). (15) Since they possess no sanctity

and ye shall be as God,[16] the first [divine name] is sacred and the second[17] is secular; in *For the Lord your God, He is God of gods,*[18] the first[19] is sacred and the second[20] is secular.

RULE 5. In *Lord of lords,*[21] the first is sacred and the second is secular; in *the God of Abraham*[22] it is sacred; in *the God of Nahor*[23] it is secular; in *the God of their father*[24] it is secular. In *Thou shalt not revile God*[25] [the noun may bear] a sacred or secular meaning.[26] R. Simeon maintains that the noun is sacred.[27] In *Forasmuch as I have seen thy face, as one seeth the face of God*[28] the noun is secular;[29] in *God's camp*[30] the noun is sacred.

RULE 6. All the names [signifying God] mentioned in connection with Abraham are sacred, except one which is secular, viz. where it is stated, *And he said: My lord, if now I have found favour in thy sight.*[30a] Others say that it is sacred.[31] In *And it came to pass, when God caused me to wander*[32] the name is secular.[33] R. Ḥanina the brother[34] of R. Joshua maintains that it is sacred [since the verse means] that, had it not been for God,[35] they[36] would long ago have *caused me to wander.*[37]

RULE 7. All [divine] names mentioned in connection with Lot are secular[38] except the last, viz. *And Lot said unto them: Oh, not so*

(16) Gen. III, 5. (17) *as God;* according to the Targum it means 'as angels'. (18) Deut. X, 17. (19) i.e. the first two, *your God, He is God.* (20) *of gods,* signifying judges or princes. (21) Deut. X, 17. (22) Gen. XXXI, 53. (23) *ibid.;* Nahor did not worship the true God. (24) *ibid.;* Terah (their father) was an idolater. (25) Ex. XXII, 27. (26) It may denote God or judges. (27) V inserts 'as it says' within brackets, the words being redundant. [H omits and reads 'Ishmael' instead of 'Simeon'.] (28) Gen. XXXIII, 10. (29) Because it refers to an angel or prince. (30) *ibid.* XXXII, 3. (30a) *ibid.* XVIII, 3. *My lord* was addressed to the leader of the three angels. (31) *My Lord* was addressed to God. (32) *ibid.* XX, 13. (33) So GRA. By 'God' is meant princes or rulers who were the cause of Abraham's wanderings. (34) [H reads 'nephew' in agreement with Shebu. 33b (Sonc. ed., p. 205). The correct form of the name is Ḥananiah, Bacher, *Ag. d. Tannaiten,* I, p. 385.] (35) Who protected him. (36) The wicked rulers. (37) The verse will accordingly bear the following interpretation: *And it came to pass, when they* (the wicked men) *caused me to wander, God of my father's house was with me* (to help me). [For various interpretations of the verse, cf. Midrash Rabbah, Genesis, LII, §11 (Sonc. ed., I, p. 457).] (38) There is only one secular name in the Lot passages. The Tetragrammaton, which is of course sacred, occurs twice. The word 'all' is not intended to be taken literally (cf. N.Y.).

my Lord.[39] All [divine] names mentioned in the story of Micah[40] are secular. R. Jose says: When they begin with *Yod-he*[41] they are sacred, but when with *Alef-lamed*[42] they are secular except in the phrase *the house of God was in Shiloh.*[43] All the [divine] names which occur in the story of Naboth are sacred except in the sentence *Naboth did curse god*[44] *and king.*[45] All the [divine] names which occur in the narrative of Gibeah of Benjamin[46] are secular according to R. Eliezer, but R. Joshua says: They are sacred. R. Eliezer said to him, 'Is it possible that the Omnipresent would promise [victory][47] and not fulfil?'[48] R. Joshua replied, 'The Omnipresent promises and fulfils'.[49] [37a]

RULE 8. In *I will tell* ['*El*] *of the decree*[50] the word '*El*[51] is sacred;[52] but the Sages maintain that it is secular.[53] In '*el God in Ẓion*[54] the first is secular[55] and the second is sacred. In *When he should go 'el God in judgment*[56] the first is secular and the second ['*Elohim*] is sacred. In the case of *Immanuel*[57] and *Immanu'el*[58] the first is secular[59] and the second[60] is sacred. The first must not be divided[61] but the second is divided.[62]

RULE 9. [In the verses] *And it came to pass when they*[63] *caused me to*

(39) Gen. XIX, 18. Lot's address to the angels is taken to end at *not so,* and then his petition to God begins, *My Lord, behold,* etc. [So the Targum and Shebu. 35b (Sonc. ed., pp. 205f).] (40) Judg. XVIIIf. (41) The Tetragrammaton. (42) The word for 'God'. (43) *ibid.* XVIII, 31. (44) Referring to one of the strange gods introduced by Jezebel. E.V. *God.* (45) I Kings XXI, 13. (46) Judg. XXf. (47) According to Judg. XX, 18, 23 God told Israel to wage war against Benjamin, which implied that they would be victorious. (48) Israel was defeated on both occasions (*ibid.* 21, 25). (49) The Israelites did not appreciate that on the first two occasions God only told them that they may go to war but promised no victory. Only on the third occasion were they assured that Benjamin would be delivered into their hands (*ibid.* XX, 28). (50) Ps. II, 7. (51) Heb. אל with a difference of vowels may mean 'God' or 'to'. (52) The sense of the text being 'I will tell God of the decree'. (53) The text means, as in E.V., *I will tell of the decree.* (54) Ps. LXXXIV, 8. (55) '*El* meaning *before* (E.V.). (56) Job XXXIV, 23. (57) Isa. VII, 14. (58) *ibid.* VIII, 8. (59) Being the name of a child. (60) Meaning 'God is with us'. (61) Into two words, since it forms a single name. (62) Because it consists of two separate words, עמנו (with us) אל (God). The reading adopted here is that of H and N.Y. (63) Foreign princes or rulers. E.V. *God.*

wander, God, etc.,[64] and *Which god*[65] *is like unto Thee*[66] the first[67] are sacred and the second[68] are secular. [The divine name in] *Samaria shall bear her guilt, for she hath rebelled against her God*[69] is sacred. R. Nathan says: [In the phrase] *in the house of his God*[70] it is sacred. In *therefore turn thou to thy God*[71] it is sacred. In *God standeth in the congregation of God; in the midst of the judges*[72] *He judgeth*[73] it is used as sacred[74] and secular.[75] In *God delivereth me to*[76] *the ungodly*[77] the first is sacred and the second[78] is secular. In *For hath any said unto God: I have borne*[79] the first ['*el*] is secular and the second sacred.

R. Eleazar the son of R. Jose the Galilean said:[80] [In the verses] *And let my cry have no*[81] *resting-place;*[82] *It is in the power*[83] *of my hand; And there shall be nought in the power of thy hand;*[84] *When it is in the power of thy hand;*[85] *Unto death,*[86] all [the words whose consonants are the same as those for God] are secular. In *God hath given command to speed me*[87] it is sacred. In *Forbear thee from meddling with God, who is with me*[88] it is sacred according to R. Jose b. Judah. In *O God, the proud are risen up against me*[89] it is sacred but the reader must pause in reading [after *God*]:[90] *God, the proud are risen up against me.*

[The terms] merciful and gracious, long-suffering and abounding in lovingkindness, king, kings, exalted, great, Most High, righteous and upright, pious, perfect, mighty, may be erased.[91] He who curses himself or his neighbour by [any

(64) Gen. XX, 13. Cf. Rule 6 above. (65) E.V. *who is a God.* (66) Micah VII, 18. (67) The pronoun 'they' in Gen. XX, 13 and *god* in Micah VII, 18. (68) *God* in Gen. and *Thee* in Micah. (69) Hos. XIV, 1. (70) *ibid.* IX, 8. (71) *ibid.* XII, 7. (72) The Heb. has the divine name. (73) Ps. LXXXII, 1. (74) In *God standeth.* (75) In the sense of 'judges'. (76) Heb. אל (to) which has the same consonants as the word for 'God'. (77) Job XVI, 11. (78) '*el* in the sense of 'to'. (79) *ibid.* XXXIV, 31. (80) So M. V and H read 'and R. Eleazar . . . said'. (81) Heb. '*al*, the same consonants as for the name of God. (82) Job XVI, 18. (83) Gen. XXXI, 29. The Heb. for *power* ('*el*) equals the divine name. (84) Deut. XXVIII, 32. (85) Prov. III, 27. (86) *ibid.* II, 18; *unto* is '*el* in Heb. (87) 2 Chron. XXXV, 21. (88) *ibid.* (89) Ps. LXXXVI, 14. (90) In the absence of the pause, the adjective *proud* might erroneously be taken as qualifying God. (91) Although attributed to God, they do not possess the sanctity of the divine name.

of] these[92] incurs guilt. [If he curses] heathens or the dead no guilt[93] is incurred. [If he curses] a judge or a prince he incurs twofold guilt;[94] according to others he incurs threefold guilt for cursing a prince.[95] If a person curses his father or mother with the Tetragrammaton[96] he is liable to the penalty of stoning,[97] but if only with the attributes he is liable to a warning.[98]

(92) Using any of these attributes instead of the divine name. (93) So M and N.Y. V and H read 'guilty of one [offence]'. (94) Since a judge or prince must not be cursed as any other person, and as men holding offices of responsibility. (95) The two mentioned in the preceding note, and a third because the Heb. word for 'judge' in the text is identical with the divine name. (96) lit. 'the distinguished name'. (97) Cf. Lev. XXIV, 14. Stoning is one of the major penalties imposed by a court. (98) i.e. he is guilty of transgressing a negative commandment, the penalty of which is scourging with thirty-nine stripes.

CHAPTER V

RULE 1. If one wrote a sacred name twice,[1] he retains the first and erases the latter.[2] R. Judah says: If the first occurs at the end of a column, he erases the first and retains the second.[3] [If he wrote] a secular noun twice,[4] he retains the first and wipes away the latter.[5] R. Judah says: If the first was at the end[6] of a column, he wipes away the first and retains the latter.

RULE 2. If one writes *Yehudah* and omits the *daleth*, he inserts[7] it above the line. If he intended to write the Tetragrammaton[8] and wrote *Yehudah*[9] instead,[10] he alters the *daleth* into a *he*[11] and wipes away the final letter *he*. If it was required to write *Yehudah* and he intended to write the Tetragrammaton, although he [inadvertently] inserted the *daleth*,[12] he erases it[13] and writes another *Yehudah*.

RULE 3. If it was required to write the Tetragrammaton but he intended to write *Yehudah*, although he did not insert the *daleth*[14] he must wipe away [the entire word] and re-write the Tetragrammaton. R. Judah says: He should go over it with the reed-pen and so sanctify it. [The Sages] said to him: This is not the best procedure.

RULE 4. He who writes the divine name and made an error [by omitting] one letter should suspend it above [the line].[15] R. Simeon of Shezur says: All the name may be suspended [if

(1) lit. 'he who writes a name of two sacred names'. H omits 'a name of'. (2) The first is retained because it was properly written; the second is erased because it was written in error. (3) It spoils the appearance to leave a blank at the beginning of the top line of a column. (4) lit. 'two secular nouns'. (5) While the ink is still wet. (6) So GRA. V and H, 'at the top'. (7) lit. 'suspends' between the *waw* and the *he*. (8) The four letters *Yod-he-waw-he*, lit. 'the name'. (9) יהודה. (10) This is the reading of GRA and H. V omits 'if he intended to write'. (11) This is done by adding a short vertical line to the *daleth*. (12) So H. V reads: 'he did not write in it'. (13) Following GRA. V and H 'detains it'. (14) So that the Tetragrammaton was written correctly but unintentionally so. (15) Neither erasure nor wiping away of the written words is necessary.

omitted] but a single letter of it may not be suspended. If one erred [by omitting] all the name, he should suspend it between the lines, according to the view of R. Judah. R. Meir says: He wipes away the writing that precedes and writes the name on the part which he wiped away. R. Simeon b. Eleazar said in the name of R. Meir: The name only may be suspended but the Tetragrammaton must not be written on an erasure. R. Ḥanina b. 'Aḳabia says: The whole sheet[16] must be stored away.[17]

RULE 5. If one wrote three[18] times *Alef-lamed* by mistake in the phrase *God delivereth me to the ungodly,*[19] he retains the first and erases the second.[20]

RULE 6. When one is writing the Tetragrammaton he may not respond even if the king greets him.[21] If he was about to write two or three divine names successively,[22] he may pause between them and respond. After dipping the reed-pen in ink, he may not start with the letters of a divine name[23] but with

(16) In which the omission of the Tetragrammaton had occurred. (17) As with all sacred objects that are worn out or decaying, or are for any other reason unfit for further use. GRA revised the wording of this Rule to conform in the main with the text in Men. 30b (Sonc. ed., p. 196): 'If the Tetragrammaton was omitted in error [and a number of the words following it already written], what had been written is erased, the erased words are suspended [above the line] and the Tetragrammaton is inserted in the space of the erasure; so R. Judah. R. Meir said: He wipes the writing away and writes [the Tetragrammaton] in the space. R. Jose said: Even the Tetragrammaton may be suspended [above the line]. R. Simeon of Shezur said: It is permissible to suspend all the Tetragrammaton [above the line] but not a part of it. R. Simeon b. Eleazar said in the name of R. Meir: The Tetragrammaton may not be written in a space which has been erased or wiped away, nor may it be suspended [above the line]; but the entire sheet is removed and stored away'. (18) So GRA. V 'twice'. (19) Job XVI, 11. The text has the word twice, the first being the divine name and the second the preposition; inadvertently he wrote it three times, intending the first two to stand for 'God' (thus sanctifying both) and the third for 'to'. (20) So GRA and H. The first occurrences of *'el* were meant to be the divine name and Rule 1 above applies. By quoting an illustration from Job, the inference to be drawn is that the regulation with respect to a Torah scroll holds good also of the Prophets and Hagiographa. (21) All his attention must be concentrated on the sanctity of the divine name. (22) E.g. *The Lord, the Lord, God* in Ex. XXXIV, 6. (23) Because a pen full of ink may cause a blot.

the preceding letter.[24] One who erases a single letter of a divine name transgresses a negative commandment. R. Simeon said:[25] On account of this it is stated, *Ye shall destroy their name out of that place. Ye shall not do so unto the Lord your God.*[26]

RULE 7. It is permissible, however, to wipe away ink that dropped upon the writing,[27] since one's intention is only to rectify it.

RULE 8. If one omits a line in error, he may not suspend it between the lines, but inserts it in close proximity[28] to the place[29] of the error by erasing one [adjacent line] and inserting two[30] in its place, or [by erasing] two lines and writing three;[31] provided only that he does not erase three lines.[32]

RULE 9. It is not permissible to make a scroll of the *Shema*ʻ or of the *Hallel* for children,[33] but if the scribe intends to add to it, it is permissible.[34] R. Judah permits the writing of a scroll from *In the beginning*[35] to the story of the flood,[36] and from the beginning of Leviticus to *And it came to pass on the eighth day;*[37] but in the case of all the other books [of Scripture the writing of extracts is] forbidden.[38]

RULE 10. The following names are to be divided:[39] Beth-el,[40] Beth-'awen,[41] Beer-sheba,[42] Ẓofenath-paʻneaḥ, [37b] Poṭi-fera,[43]

(24) Which, if blotted, can be erased or wiped away. (25) Citing the Scriptural basis of the regulation. (26) Deut. XII, 3f, i.e. the name of God must not be erased. (27) Even of a divine name. (28) lit. 'opposite'. (29) So GRA. V and H omit 'inserts in . . . place of'. (30) The one omitted and the one erased. (31) The two erased and the one omitted. (32) In order to insert more than one missing line. The erasure of one or two lines is sufficient for the insertion of the omitted line without undue pressure on the space between the lines; but the treatment of more than one line in this manner would disfigure the entire column (N.Y.). (33) Extracts from Scripture may not be made for study by children. (34) From 'but if' to 'permissible' is an addition by GRA. (35) Gen. I, 1. (36) i.e. to Gen. VI, 8. In each instance the extract is a connected theme. (37) Lev. IX, 1. (38) Only in the case of the Pentateuch were the two extracts mentioned allowed to be written for the instruction of children. V adds here, 'if he intends to add to it, it is permitted'. (39) Although each represents one name, it is to be written as two words. (40) e.g. Gen. XII, 8. (41) Hos. IV, 15, X, 15. (42) E.g. Gen. XXI, 31. (43) *ibid.* XLI, 45. E.V. *Zaphenath-paneah* and *Poti-phera.*

Ben-'oni,[44] Yedid-yah,[45] Halelu-yah.[46] R. Jose says: These must not be divided.[47] All, however, agree that there must be no breaking up of 'Ammi'el,[48] 'Amminadab,[49] Ẓuri'el,[50] Ẓurishaddai.[51]

RULE 11. The following names may not be broken up: Yisra'el, Ga'tham,[52] Poṭifar, Nebukadneẓẓar.[53]

RULE 12. If a person writes a divine name on his body, he must neither bathe nor anoint himself[54] (nor stand in an unclean place.[55] If he must perform an obligatory immersion,[56] he should wind a reed about it,[57] descend and perform an immersion. R. Jose said: He may at all times descend and perform an immersion in the ordinary way)[58] provided he does not rub **it** off.

RULE 13. [If one wrote a divine name] on the horn of a cow or on the legs of a bed,[59] he scrapes it off[60] and stores it away. [If he wrote it] on a stone, he detaches it and stores it away.[61]

RULE 14. If the seam of a sacred scroll was broken for the first time,[62] it may be sewn up again;[63] if a second time, it may be sewn up again; if a third time, it must not be sewn up again.[64] If one cuts off a strip of a new scroll,[65] it may [be used for

(44) *ibid.* XXXV, 18. (45) 2 Sam. XII, 25. E.V. *Jedidiah.* (46) E.g. Ps. CXI, 1, 'praise ye the Lord'. E.V. prints it as one word. V and H add: וחרה אף, וחרה אפי, *and the anger [of the Lord] was kindled, My wrath shall wax hot* (Ex. XXII, 23; Num. XI, 10). (47) But written as one word. (48) A name meaning 'God is with me' (e.g. Num. XIII, 12). Another reading is עזיאל, 'God is my strength' (e.g. Ex. VI, 18). (49) A name meaning 'my kinsman is noble' (e.g. *ibid.* 23). (50) A name meaning 'my Rock is God' (Num. III, 35). (51) A name meaning 'my Rock is Shaddai' (cf. Num. I, 6). (52) A name occurring in Gen. XXXVI, 11, 16, 1 Chron. I, 36. E.V. *Gatam.* (53) V and H unnecessarily repeat צמיאל, עוריאל, צורישדי. (54) So that the name be not washed away. (55) Out of respect. (56) As, e.g., after a period of ritual impurity. (57) To prevent the name from coming into contact with the water which might wash it away. (58) The words in brackets are inserted by GRA who follows Shab. 120b (Sonc. ed., p. 597). V and H read: R. Jose permits, provided, etc. (59) For magical purposes. (60) [The correct reading is perhaps גודדד for גוררד, 'he chops off (the horn or leg)'.] (61) From respect for the divine name. (62) lit. 'one'. (63) On the undamaged part of the sheet, near the writing, although the margins between the columns are thereby reduced. (64) Because the margins would become too small. (65) lit. 'scrolls'.

ordinary purposes],[66] but if it is cut off an old scroll,[67] [its use is] forbidden. Worn-out scrolls, phylacteries and wraps of scrolls must be stored away.[68]

RULE 15. It is related of R. Ḥalafta that, when he visited Rabban Gamaliel, he found him sitting at his table with the Targum of Job[69] in his hand and reading it. He said to him, 'Master, will you permit me to tell you what my eyes saw?' 'Tell me,' he replied. 'I was watching Rabban Gamaliel the Elder, your father's[70] father, while he was sitting at the side of a building [in course of construction] on the Temple Mount, when a Targum of Job was brought to him. "Remove a course of stones," he ordered the builder,[71] "and bury this under it." ' R. Jose b. R. Judah said: They overturned a tub of mortar upon it.[72] Rabbi said: There are two objections to the statement —firstly, how could mortar[73] be available on the Temple Mount?[74] Further, it is not permissible to destroy such writings[75] with one's own hands! [They should not be deposited in an unclean place] but in a deserted spot where they decay of their own accord.[76]

RULE 16. If one lends a Torah scroll to his friend, the latter may not lend it to another person. If one deposits a Torah scroll with his friend, the latter must unroll it once in twelve months.[77] If he is capable of reading it, he may do so,[78] but if he unrolled it for his own benefit,[79] reading it is forbidden. Symmachos said: He unrolls a new scroll once in thirty days

(66) Being new, the scroll had not yet been consecrated. (67) Which has been consecrated by the script. (68) Having once been consecrated, they may no longer be used for ordinary purposes. (69) This must have been an earlier work than the extant Targum. [The anecdote is related in Shab. 115a (Sonc. ed., p. 565) with some variants.] (70) V rightly corrects 'mother's' to 'father's'. (71) V incorrectly 'his children'. (72) This sentence is added by GRA from Shab. 115a. (73) Which is composed of earth and water. (74) Where only a mixture of sand and lime was used. (75) Books like the Targum of Job whose use was forbidden on account of their exclusion from the Canon. (76) The objection to a written, as against an oral, Targum at the time was the fear that the same sanctity might be attached to it as to the Hebrew text. (77) This sentence is inserted by GRA following B.M. 29b (Sonc. ed., p. 182). (78) While the scroll is being unrolled in accordance with this Rule. (79) So corrected by GRA.

and an old one once in twelve months. R. Eliezer b. Jacob says:[80] Both a new and an old scroll [should be unrolled] once in twelve months.[81]

RULE 17. All occurrences of the name Solomon in the Song of Songs are sacred[82] except one which is secular. Which one is it? *Behold, it is the litter of Solomon.*[83] Others say: *Thou, O Solomon, shalt have the thousand.*[84]

RULE 18. All references to 'kings' in Daniel are secular except one which is sacred. Which one is it? *O king unto whom the King*[85] *of kings, the God of heaven, hath given the kingdom, the power, and the strength, and the glory.*[86] Others say: *My Lord,*[87] *the dream be to them that hate thee, and the interpretation thereof to thine adversaries.*[88]

(80) From 'and an old' to 'says' is added by GRA from B.M. 29b. (81) In the course of the discussion in B.M. 29b this is amended to 'thirty days' to differentiate the opinion of R. Eliezer from that of the first authority who is quoted above. (82) Referring to God in the Rabbinical interpretation of the Book. (83) Cant. III, 7. (84) *ibid.* VIII, 12. (85) Understood as referring to God. (86) Dan. II, 37. E.V. *O king, king of kings, unto whom,* etc. (87) Interpreted as an invocation to God in Shebu. 35b (Sonc. ed., p. 207). (88) *ibid.* IV, 16.

CHAPTER VI

RULE 1. A scribe must provide a distinguishing mark[1] for the section[2] beginning *And it came to pass when the ark set forward,*[3] both at its beginning and at its end, because it is a book on its own. Others maintain that its proper place is in the section of the setting forward of the standards.[4]

RULE 2.[5] The scribe must leave a prescribed space at the opening of the section which begins *And the people were as murmurers;*[6] [and not only] at its beginning [but also] at its end, because it is a book on its own. Others hold that its proper place is in the section of the setting forward of the standards.

RULE 3. Ten [letters or groups of letters] in the Torah are marked by dots:[7] In *the Lord judge between me and thee*[8] there is a dot on the *beth*[9] of *ubeneka* (and between thee). In *and they said unto him,*[10] there are dots on *alef-yod-waw* of *'elaw* (unto him). In *and he knew not when she lay down, nor when she arose,*[11] the [second] *waw* in *ubekumah* (nor when she arose) is marked with a dot. In *and kissed him,*[12] the entire word *wayyishshaḳehu* is marked by dots. In *and his brethren went to feed their father's flock,*[13] the letters of *'eth* (the mark of the defined accusative) are dotted. In *whom Moses and Aaron numbered*[14] the word *Aaron* is marked with dots. In *or be in a journey afar off,*[15] the *he* in *reḥoḳah* (afar off) has a dot. In *and we have laid waste even unto Nopha, which*[16] the *resh* in *'asher* (which) has a dot. In *and a several tenth part,*[17] in the section dealing with

(1) The traditional mark is an inverted *nun*. (2) So GRA. V reads 'a prescribed space at the opening'. (3) Num. X, 35. The section consists of the two verses, *ibid.* 35f. (4) Num. II. (5) This Rule is partly a repetition of the preceding, since the end of the section, *ibid.* X, 35f, is followed by the beginning of *And the people were as murmurers* (*ibid.* XI, 1); and partly incorrect since no mark is inserted at the end of the latter section. The entire Rule is to be deleted according to GRA. (6) *ibid.* XI, 1. (7) The dots are placed above the letters. Cf. above, ARN XXXIV, p. 165 where the Rabbinical explanations are given. (8) Gen. XVI, 5. (9) So GRA. V and H 'the *yod*'. (10) *ibid.* XVIII, 9. (11) *ibid.* XIX, 33. (12) *ibid.* XXXIII, 4. (13) *ibid.* XXXVII, 12. (14) Num. III, 39. (15) *ibid.* IX, 10. (16) *ibid.* XXI, 30. (17) *ibid.* XXIX, 15.

the first day of the festival of Tabernacles, the second *waw* in *we'issaron* (and a tenth part) has a dot. In *the secret things belong unto the Lord our God; but the things that are revealed belong unto us and to our children for ever,*[18] the '*ayin* in '*ad* (for) has a dot.

RULE 4. R. Simeon b. Laḳish said: Three scrolls of the Torah were found in the Temple court:[19] the *Ma'on*[20] scroll, the *Za'aṭuṭë* scroll, and the *Hu'* scroll. In one of these they found the expression of *ma'on,*[21] and in the other two it was written, *The eternal God is me'onah*[22] (a dwelling place), so they adopted the reading of the two scrolls and discarded that of the one scroll. In another of the scrolls they found it written, *And he sent the za'aṭuṭë* (nobles) *of the children of Israel,*[23] and in the other two they found written *And he sent na'arë* (the young men of) *the children of Israel,* so they retained the reading of the two and abandoned that of the one. In one of the scrolls *hu'*[24] was written eleven times, but in the other two *hi'*[25] was written eleven times, so they adopted the reading of the two and discarded that of the one.

RULE 5. Three expressions of *lo'* are written *lamed-alef*[26] but read as *lamed-waw.*[27] They are: *'asher lo'*[28] *jointed legs above their feet;*[29] *'asher lo' ḥomah;*[30] and *'asher lo' ye'adah.*[31]

RULE 6. The following [occurrences of *lamed-alef* (not)] which have to be read as *lamed-waw* (to, by, has) are found in the Pro-

(18) Deut. XXIX, 28. [H more correctly, 'unto us and to our children and the '*ayin* in עד'. Cf. Sanh. 43b (Sonc. ed., p. 285, n. 4) and ARN above, p. 166.] (19) Presumably when the text of Scripture was about to be fixed. (20) So GRA. V has מעונה. This and the following two names were derived from the peculiar word which distinguished each scroll. (21) Meaning 'dwelling place', the noun being in the masculine form. (22) Deut. XXXIII, 27, the same noun in the feminine. (23) Ex. XXIV, 5. (24) The third person sing. masc. which is used in the Pentateuch for *hi'*, third person fem. sing. pronoun. (25) The correct feminine form, being exceptions to the usual written form. A list of these is given in ARN XXXIV, above p. 167. (26) Meaning 'not'. (27) Which means 'to him, has'. (28) לא, lit. 'which not' but read לו 'which has'. (29) Lev. XI, 21. (30) *ibid.* XXV, 30, *lamed-alef,* meaning 'which has no wall' but read as *lamed-waw* 'which has a wall'. E.V. *in a walled city*. (31) Ex. XXI, 8. The written form with *lamed-alef* means 'who hath not espoused her', but the reading with *lamed-waw* means, as E.V., *who hath espoused her to himself.*

phets and Hagiographa: *multiply;*[32] *Hushai;*[33] *said;*[34] *thou hast multiplied;*[35] *their affliction;*[36] *He slay me;*[37] *I keep silence;*[38] *as the (wandering) sparrow;*[39] *his friends;*[40] *Zerubbabel;*[41] *were fashioned;*[42] *know ye;*[43] *be gathered;*[44] *name,*[45] [this last also] in the corresponding passage.[46] [38*a*]

RULE 7.[47] Four [occurrences of the name] Jeuel are to be read Jeiel; viz. *and in Gibeon,*[48] *the Ashterathite,*[49] *the scribe,*[50] *[and of the sons of] Elizaphon.*[51]

RULE 8. The following words are to be read but are not written [in the text]: *the children of;*[52] *Euphrates;*[53] *man;*[54] *as;*[55] *his sons;*[56] *of hosts;*[57] *come;*[58] *thereof;*[59] *unto me;*[60] *to me.*[61]

(32) The introductory word of 1 Sam. II, 3 in which occurs the phrase *and by Him are actions weighed* according to the *ķerë*, but the *kethib* reads 'and actions are not weighed'. (33) i.e. 2 Sam. XVI, 18, where the *ķerë* is *his will I be* and the *kethib* 'I will not be'. (34) i.e. 2 Kings VIII, 10. Here the *ķerë* is *say unto him, thou shalt surely recover,* and the *kethib* 'say, thou shalt not surely recover'. (35) i.e. Isa. IX, 2.The *ķerë* is *Thou hast increased their joy,* and the *kethib* 'Thou hast not increased joy'. (36) i.e. Isa. LXIII, 9. The *ķerë* is *In all their affliction He was afflicted* (lit. there was affliction to Him) and the *kethib* 'in all their affliction He was not an adversary'. (37) i.e. Job XIII, 15. The *ķerë* is *yet will I trust Him,* the *kethib* 'I have nothing to hope for'. (38) i.e. Job XLI, 4. The *ķerë* is *would I keep silence* (to him), the *kethib* 'I would not keep silence'. (39) i.e. Prov. XXVI, 2. The *ķerë* is *shall come home* (to him), the *kethib* 'shall not come home'. (40) i.e. Prov. XIX, 7. The *ķerë is they turn against him,* the *kethib* 'they do not turn'. (41) i.e. Ezra IV, 2, The *ķerë* is *we do sacrifice unto Him,* the *kethib* 'we do not sacrifice'. (42) i.e. Ps. CXXXIX, 16. The *ķerë* is 'and for it there was one among them', the *kethib when as yet there was none of them.* In this instance E.V. follows the *kethib.* (43) i.e. Ps. C, 3. The *ķerë* is *we are His,* the *kethib* 'and not we (have made) ourselves'. (44) i.e. Isa. XLIX, 5. The *ķerë* is *be gathered unto Him,* the *kethib* 'be not gathered'. (45) i.e. 1 Chron. XI, 20. The *ķerë* is *and had a name among the three,* the *kethib* 'and not a name among the three'. (46) viz. in 2 Sam. XXIII, 18. This reading is suggested by N.Y. to replace that of V 'and his word' which is meaningless. In this verse, however, *lamed-waw* is both written and read. [More probably ודבר in V is a misreading of *daleth* signifying 'four' which should be attached to the beginning of the next Rule.] (47) [V is unintelligible and the reading of H has been adopted.] (48) i.e. in 1 Chron. IX, 35. (49) *ibid.* XI, 44. (50) 2 Chron. XXVI, 11. (51) *ibid.* XXIX, 13. (52) In Judg. XX, 13. (53) In 2 Sam. VIII, 3. (54) In 2 Sam. XVI, 23. (55) *ibid.* XVIII, 20. V incorrectly בן for כן. (56) 2 Kings XIX, 37. (57) *ibid.* 31. (58) In Jer. XXXI, 38 (some edd. 37). (59) In Jer. L, 29. V incorrectly *lo'* for *lah.* (60) In Ruth III, 5. (61) *ibid.* 17.

RULE 9. [With the following] it is the reverse;[62] they are written [in the text] but are not to be read: *Amnon;*[63] *as he shall say;*[64] *in (what) place;*[65] *kinsman;*[66] *let . . . bend;*[67] *five.*[68]

(62) Of those mentioned in the preceding Rule. The former are to be read but are not written; the latter are written but are not to be read. (63) In 2 Sam. XIII, 33 the word *'im* is written but not to be read. (64) In Jer. XXXIX, 12 where similarly, *'im* is written but not read. V incorrectly indicates the verse with *ba'asher* for *ka'asher*. (65) In 2 Sam. XV, 21 the word אם is written but not read. (66) In Ruth III, 12, the word *'im* is written but not read. (67) In Jer. LI, 3 the verb is repeated in the text. (68) In Ezek. XLVIII, 16 *the south side . . . five hundred* the number *five* is written twice but read only once. [H adds two further instances: נא in 2 Kings V, 18 and *'eth* in Jer. XXXVIII, 16.]

CHAPTER VII

RULE 1. The following words are written without a *waw*,[1] but are to be read with the *waw*: *and offered it*;[2] *said*;[3] *and [they] said*;[4] *and they spoke*;[5] *shall they take away*;[6] *and let them deliver*;[7] *and eat*;[8] *together*;[9] *and they shall profane it*;[10] *and they offered*;[11] *was made*;[12] *and took upon them*;[13] *Hananiah*;[14] *Malchijah*.[15] The reverse of this [occurs in the following words]:[16] *my feet*;[17] *throw her down*;[18] *and . . . commanded*;[19] *straight before him*;[20] *the fountain gate*;[21] *and called him*;[22] *and he assembled*;[23] *took*.[24]

RULE 2. The following are written with a *he* which is not pronounced: *when I saw*;[25] *and I brought*;[26] *the lion*[27] in the Book of Samuel;[28] *was he found*;[29] *and . . . saw*;[30] *this [city]*;[31] *evil*;[32] *[the]*

(1) At the end of the word. (2) 1 Sam. VII, 9. (3) *ibid.* 19. Here and in the other verses which are cited the *kethib* is the singular and the *ķerë* the plural. (4) *ibid.* XII, 10. (5) 1 Kings XII, 7. (6) 2 Kings XX, 18. (7) *ibid.* XXII, 5. (8) Isa. XXXVII, 30. (9) Jer. XLVIII, 7, *yaḥdaw* to be read for *yaḥad*. (10) Ezek. VII, 21. (11) Ezra III, 3. (12) Dan. V, 21. (13) Esth. IX, 27. (14) Added by GRA and H. The name *Hananiah* indicates Neh. III, 30 where the text omits the *waw* at the end of *'aḥaraw* (*after him*). (15) Indicating *ibid.* 31 where the *waw* at the end of *'aḥaraw* is also omitted. (16) A superfluous *waw* is written but not read. (17) 2 Sam. XXII, 34; the *kethib* is 'his feet'. [Although not included here, in the preceding verse *my way* is 'his way' in the *kethib*.] (18) 2 Kings IX, 33. [The added *waw* is due to dittography and superfluous.] (19) *ibid.* XVI, 15. The *kethib* means 'commanded him'. (20) In Ezek. XLVI, 9 where the verb *shall go forth* is written as plural but to be read as singular. (21) In Neh. III, 15 where the *kethib* is 'they set up' and the *ķerë* (he) *set up*. (22) In 1 Kings XII, 3. The reference is to the word which follows which is plural in the *kethib* and singular in the *ķerë*. (23) *ibid.* 21. Here the reference is to the first verb *was come* which is written as plural but to be read as singular. (24) In 2 Kings XIV, 13. The reference is again to the verb *came* with the singular to be read for the plural in the text. (25) Josh. VII, 21, written *wa'er'eh* and read *wa'erë'*. (26) *ibid.* XXIV, 8, written *wa'abih* and read *wa'abi*. (27) 2 Sam. XXIII, 20, written *ha'aryeh* and read *ha'ari*. (28) This excludes the parallel passage in 1 Chron. XI, 22 where *ha'ari* is both written and read. (29) Jer. XLVIII, 27, written *nimẓa'ah* but the reading is *nimẓa'*. (30) *ibid.* III, 7, written *wattir'eh* and read *watter'ë'*. (31) *ibid.* XXVI, 6, written *hazzothah* and read *hazzoth*. (32) Micah III, 2, written *ra'ah* and read *ra'*.

evil;[33] *gone down;*[34] *and he shall come;*[35] *and a line;*[36] *and a line;*[37] *thoroughly;*[38] *them that love me;*[39] *and . . . friend;*[40] *deal;*[41] *open;*[42] *a lion;*[43] *these;*[44] *venison.*[45]

The reverse is the case with the following:[46] *and multiplied;*[47] *on the housetop;*[48] *and they;*[49] *be he;*[50] *and . . . shall be;*[51] *and behold;*[52] *behold;*[53] *planted;*[54] *Gedaliah;*[55] *and . . . she doted;*[56] *the measure;*[57] *and I shall be glorified;*[58] *three;*[59] *she considereth;*[60] *she perceiveth;*[61] *arise;*[62] *remember;*[63] *turn Thou us;*[64] *thou hast declared;*[65] *thou . . . hast cursed;*[66] *Thou hast set;*[67] *Thou hast made;*[68] *is sore affrighted;*[69] *the carved work thereof;*[70]

(33) Jer. XVIII, 10, written *hara'ah* and read *hara'*. (34) *ibid.* XV, 9, written *ba'ah* and read *ba'*. (35) *ibid.* XLIII, 11, written *uba'ah* and read *uba'*. (36) 1 Kings VII, 23, written *weḳaweh* and read *weḳaw*. (37) Zech. I, 16, as in the preceding note. (38) V incorrectly gives the keyword as *wera'*. Ps. LI, 4, written *harbeh* and read *hereb*. (39) Prov. VIII, 17, written *'ohabehah* and read *'ohabai*. (40) *ibid.* XXVII, 10, written *were'eh* and read *were'a*. (41) Ruth I, 8, written *ya'aseh* and read *ya'as*. (42) Dan. IX, 18, written *piḳḥah* and read *peḳaḥ*. (43) Lam. III, 10, written *'aryeh* and read *'ari*. V incorrectly connects this with the next word joining them together as one. (44) Ezra V, 15, written *'elleh* and read *'el*. (45) V incorrectly reads *ẓur*. Gen. XXVII, 3, written *ẓedah* and read *ẓayid*. (46) In the preceding a written *he* is not pronounced, but the following are spelt without a *he* which is to be pronounced. (47) Josh. XXIV, 3, written *wa'ereb* and read *wa'arbeh*. (48) 1 Sam. IX, 26, written *haggag* and read *haggagah*. (49) 2 Sam. XXI, 9, written *wehem* and read *wehemmah*. (50) 1 Kings I, 37, written *yehi* and read *yihyeh*. (51) 2 Kings IX, 37, written *wehayath* and read *wehayethah*. (52) Isa. XLI, 23, written *wenerë* and read *wenireh*. (53) *ibid.* LIV, 16, written *hen* and read *hinneh*. (54) In Jer. XVII, 8, referring to *yireh* (*shall . . . see*) which is spelt without the final *he*. (55) *ibid.* XL, 16, referring to *ta'aseh* (*do*) which is without the final *he*. (56) Ezek. XXIII, 16, written *watta'gob* and read *watta'gebah*. (57) *ibid.* XLV, 3, where *ḥamesh* (*five*) is written and *ḥamishshah* read. (58) Hag. I, 8, written *we'ekkabed* and read *we'ekkabedah*. (59) In Prov. XXX, 18, *we'arba'* (*yea, four*) is written and *we'arba'ah* read. (60) *ibid.* XXXI, 16, *naṭa'* (*planteth*) is written and *naṭ'ah* read. (61) *ibid.* 18, *ballayil* (*by night*) is written and *ballayelah* read. (62) In Lam. II, 19, the same variant occurs as in the preceding. (63) *ibid.* V, 1, *habbeṭ* (*behold*) is written and *habbiṭah* read. (64) *ibid.* 21, *wenashub* (*and we shall be turned*) is written and *wenashubah* read. (65) 1 Sam XXIV, 19, *we'at* is written and *we'attah* read. (66) Eccles. VII, 22, where the same variant occurs as in the preceding. (67) Ps. XC, 8, written *shatta* and read *shattah*. (68) Neh. IX, 6, written *'at* and read *'attah*. (69) In Ps. VI, 4 the same variant occurs as in the preceding. (70) *ibid.* LXXIV, 6, written *we'at* and read *we'attah*.

***with her harlotries*;[71] *turn back*;[72] *disclose*;[73] *Thou [hast] made an hedge*;[74] *and [he] saw*.[75]

RULE 3. The following are written as one word and read as two words: *fortune is come*;[76] *a fiery law*;[77] *consumed of the fire*;[78] *what mean ye*;[79] *and, behold, he*;[80] *what they*;[81] *Bani, of*;[82] *of the Benjamites*;[83] *the helpless*;[84] *may He incite death*;[85] *of the proud oppressors*;[86] *out of the whirlwind*;[87] *out of a whirlwind*;[88] *were broken down*.[89]

The reverse of the above are the following:[90] *when . . . were merry*;[91] *of Benjamin*;[92] *that . . . may be increased*;[93] *out of the cave*;[94] *by Myself*;[95] *with their axes*;[96] *from the daughter*;[97] *like the ostriches*.[98]

RULE 4. The following are spelt with a *waw* but read with a *yod*: *prisoners*;[99] *Abigail*;[100] *I make thee . . . go up and down*;[101] *chief men*;[102] *I will . . . make . . . straight*;[103] *I will . . . make them run away*;[104]

(71) In Ezek. XXIII, 43, written *'at* and read *'attah*. (72) In Ruth I, 12, *lekna* (*go your way*) omits the final *he*. (73) *ibid*. IV, 4, where *we'eda'* (*that I may know*) is written and read *we'ede'ah*. (74) In Job I, 10, *'at* (*Thou*) is written and *'attah* read. (75) *ibid*. XLII, 16, written *wayyar* and read *wayyireh*. (76) Gen. XXX, 11, written *baggad* and read *ba'gad*. (77) Deut. XXXIII, 2, written *'eshdath* and read *'esh dath*. (78) Jer. VI, 29, written *me'eshtam* and read *me'esh tam*. (79) Isa. III, 15, written *mallakem* and read *mah lakem*. (80) Jer. XVIII, 3, written *wehinnehu* and read *wehinneh hu'*. (81) Ezek. VIII, 6, written *mahem* and read *mah hem*. (82) 1 Chron. IX, 4, written *Binyamin* and read *Bani min*. (83) *ibid*. XXVII, 12, written *lebenyemini* and read *labben yemini*. (84) Ps. X, 10, written *ḥelka'im* and read *ḥel ka'im*. (85) *ibid*. LV, 16, written *yashshimaweth* and read *yashshi maweth*. (86) *ibid*. CXXIII, 4, written *lig'eyonim* and read *lig'ë yonim*. (87) Job XXXVIII, 1, written *minhasse'arah* and read *min hasse'arah*. (88) *ibid*. XL, 6, written *minse'arah* and read *min se'arah*. (89) Neh. II, 13, written *hammeperuẓim* and read *hem peruẓim*. (90) Which are written as two words and read as one. (91) Judg. XVI, 25, written *ki ṭob* and read *ḳetob*. (92) 1 Sam. IX, 1, written *mibben yamin* and read *mibbinyamin*. (93) Isa. IX, 6, written *lamed-mem resh-beth-he* and read *lemarbeh*. (94) 1 Sam. XXIV. 8, written *min hamme'arah* and read *mehamme'arah*. (95) Isa. XLIV, 24, written *mi'itti* and read *me'itti*. (96) 2 Chron. XXXIV, 6, written *beḥar bothehem* and read *beḥarbothehem*. (97) Lam. I, 6, written *min bath* and read *mibbath*. (98) *ibid*. IV, 3, written *kaye 'enim* and read *kayye'enim*. (99) Gen. XXXIX, 20, written *'asurë* and read *'asirë*. (100) 1 Sam. XXV, 18, written *Abugail* and read *Abigail*. (101) 2 Sam. XV, 20, written *anu'aka* and read *ani'aka*. (102) 2 Kings XXIV, 15, written *'ulë* and read *'elë*. (103) Isa. XLV, 2, written *'aushir* and read *'ayashsher*. (104) Jer. L, 44, written *'aruẓem* and read *'ariẓem*.

on mine eye;[105] *cistern;*[106] *in their march;*[107] *set apart;*[108] *wilt thou set;*[109] *ye might provoke Me;*[110] *make straight;*[111] *who were set;*[112] *that taught;*[113] *Birzaith;*[114] *will greatly rejoice;*[115] *Dehites;*[116] *bring forth;*[117] *Harsith;*[118] *Luhith;*[119] *the entry;*[120] *the strong;*[121] *made to murmur;*[122] *and Shahazim;*[123] *and a royal diadem;*[124] *and a thing of nought and the deceit;*[125] *and the swallow;*[126] *and the galleries thereof;*[127] *and Tilon;*[128] *Jehiel;*[129] *and prepare ye;*[130] *thy bosom;*[131] *a side-structure;*[132] *Jair;*[133] *alienate;*[134] *Jeiel;*[135] *they wander up and down;*[136] *let . . . cover them;*[137] *they cause . . . to fall;*[138] *to strive;*[139] *singing;*[140] *Laish;*[141] *for fishers;*[142] *dross;*[143] *for a spoil;*[144] *their*

(105) 2 Sam. XVI, 12, written *ba'awoni* and read *be'eni*. (106) Jer. VI, 7, written *bor* and read *bayir*. (107) Nahum II, 6, written *bahalokotham* and read *bahalikotham*. (108) 2 Chron. XXVI, 21, written *haḥofshuth* and read *haḥofshith*. V inserts here another example, viz. 'my way', but N.Y. declares it to be incorrect and H omits it. (109) Prov. XXIII, 5, written *hata'uf* and read *hata'if*. (110) Jer. XXV, 7, written *hik'oseni* and read *hak'iseni*. (111) Ps. V, 9, written *haushar* and read *hayeshar*. (112) Ezra VIII, 17, written *hannethunim* and read *hannethinim*. (113) 2 Chron. XXXV, 3, written *hammebonim* and read *hammebinim*. (114) 1 Chron. VII, 31, written *Birzoth* and read *Birzaith*. (115) Prov. XXIII, 24, written *gol yagul* and read *gil yagil*. (116) Ezra IV, 9, written *Dehawë* and read *Dehayë*. (117) Gen. VIII, 17, written *hawẓë'* and read *hayẓë'*. (118) Jer. XIX, 2, written *haḥarsoth* and read *haḥarsith*. (119) *ibid.* XLVIII, 5, written *halluḥoth* and read *halluḥith*. (120) Ezek. XLII, 9, written *hammebo'* and read *hammebi'*. (121) Zech. XI, 2, written *habbaẓur* and read *habbaẓir*. (122) Numb. XIV, 36, written *wayyillonu* and read *wayyalinu*. (123) Josh. XIX, 22, written *weshaḥaẓumah* and read *weshaḥaẓimah*. (124) Isa. LXII, 3, written *uẓenuf* and read *uẓenif*. (125) Jer. XIV, 14, written *we'elul wetarmuth* and read *we'elil wetarmith*. (126) *ibid.* VIII, 7, written *wesus* and read *wesis*. (127) Ezek. XLI, 15, written *we'attoḳeha* and read *we'attiḳeha*. (128) 1 Chron. IV, 20, written *wetolon* and read *wetilon*. (129) 2 Chron. XXIX, 14, written *Jeḥu'el* and read *Jeḥi'el*. (130) *ibid.* XXXV, 4, written *wehikkonu* and read *wehakkinu*. (131) Ps. LXXIV, 11, written *ḥoḳeka* and read *ḥeḳeka*. (132) 1 Kings VI, 5, written *yaẓu'a* and read *yaẓi'a*. (133) 1 Chron. XX, 5, written *Ya'or* and read *Ya'ir*. (134) Ezek. XLVIII, 14, written *ya'abor* and read *ya'abir*. (135) 1 Chron. IX, 35, written *Je'u'el* and read *Je'i'el*. (136) Ps. LIX, 16, written *yenu'un* and read *yeni'un*. (137) *ibid.* CXL, 10, written *yekassumo* and read *yekassemo*. (138) Prov. IV, 16, written *yiksholu* and read *yakshilu*. (139) Judg. XXI, 22, written *larub* and read *larib*. (140) 1 Sam. XVIII, 6, written *lashur* and read *lashir*. (141) 2 Sam. III, 15, written *Lush* and read *Layish*. (142) Jer. XVI, 16, written *ledogim* and read *ledayyagim*. (143) Ezek. XXII, 18, written *lesog* and read *lesig*. (144) Isa. XLII, 24, written *limshoseh* and read *limshissah*.

furrows;[145] *Mephaath;*[146] *from Naioth;*[147] *stretched-forth;*[148] *fruit;*[149] *Nebai;*[150] *Nephishesim;*[151] *leave;*[152] *ready dressed;*[153] *Ephai;*[154] *Ephrain;*[155] the second[156] *ready;*[157] *their lads;*[158] *her little ones;*[159] *dung.*[160] [38b]

(145) Ps. CXXIX, 3, written *lema'anotham* and read *lema'anitham.* (146) Jer. XLVIII, 21, written *mopha'ath* and read *mepa'ath.* (147) 1 Sam. XX, 1, written *minnawoth* and read *minnayoth.* (148) Isa. III, 17, written *neṭuwothn* and read *neṭioth.* (149) *ibid.* LVII, 19, written *nob* and read *nib.* (150) Neh. X, 20, written *Nubai* and read *Nebai.* (151) *ibid.* VII, 52, written *Nefushesim* and read *Nefishesim.* (152) 2 Sam. XIV, 7, written *sum* and read *sim.* (153) 1 Sam. XXV, 18, written *'asuwoth* and read *'asiyoth.* (154) Jer. XL, 8, written *'ufai* and read *'ephai.* (155) 2 Chron. XIII, 19, written *'Efron* and read *'Efrain.* V incorrectly reads *'Abarim.* (156) This excludes the first *ready* in Esth. III, 14. (157) Esth. VIII, 13, written *'athudim* and read *'athidim.* (158) Jer. XIV, 3, written *ẓe'orehem* and read *ẓe'irehem.* (159) *ibid.* XLVIII, 4, written *ẓe'oreha* and read *ze'ireha.* (160) Ezek. IV, 15, written *ẓefu'ë* and read *ẓefi'ë.*

CHAPTER VIII

RULE I. Variants[1] between the poem[2] of Psalm [XVIII] and Samuel[3] are the following: *and . . . spoke;*[4] *and my deliverer;*[5] *my God, my rock;*[6] *my high tower, and my refuge;*[7] *from mine enemies;*[8] *for . . . compassed me;*[9] *the waves of;*[10] *the floods of;*[11] *compassed me;*[12] *I called;*[13] *and . . . He heard;*[14] *then . . . did shake;*[15] *the foundations of heaven;*[16] *yea, He was seen;*[17] *and He made;*[18] *pavilions;*[19] *gathering of;*[20] *coals of fire flamed forth;*[21] *thundered from heaven;*[22] *arrows;*[23] *and discomfited them;*[24] *the channels of waters;*[25] *and . . . were laid bare;*[26] *by the rebuke of the Lord;*[27] *His nostrils;*[28] *from them that hated me;*[29] *a stay;*[30] *He brought me forth also;*[31] *according*[32] *to my righteousness;*[33] *I did not depart from them;*[34] *and I was;*[35] *toward Him;*[36] *and I kept myself;*[37] *according to*

(1) In words, letters or vowels. (2) So H. V has the plural. (3) 2 Sam. XXII. (4) Sam. 1; in Ps. 1 this is replaced by *For the Leader*, etc. (5) Sam. 2 represents *my* by a suffix and pronoun; Ps. 3 omits the pronoun. (6) Ps. 3; Sam. 3, *the God who is my rock.* (7) Sam. 3; Ps. 3 omits *and my refuge.* (8) In Sam. 4 the Heb. for *from* is the prefix *mem*, in Ps. 4 the preposition *min.* (9) Sam. 5; in Ps. 5 *for* is wanting. (10) Sam. 5; Ps. 5 *the cords of.* (11) Sam. 5; Ps. 5 *and the floods of.* (12) In Sam. 6 the Heb. is *sabbuni*, in Ps. 6 *sebabuni*. The meaning is the same. (13) Sam. 7; Ps. 7 *I cried.* (14) Sam. 7; Ps. 7 omits *and.* (15) The Heb. in Sam. 8 is *wayyithga'ash*, in Ps. 8 *wattig'ash*. The meaning is practically the same. (16) Sam. 8; Ps. 8 *the foundations of the mountains.* (17) Sam. 11; Ps. 11 *yea, He did swoop.* (18) Sam. 12; Ps. 12 omits *and.* (19) Sam. 12; Ps. 12 *His pavilion.* (20) Sam. 12; Ps. 12 *darkness of.* (21) Sam. 13; Ps. 13 *hailstones and coals of fire.* (22) Sam. 14; Ps. 14 *thundered in the heavens.* (23) Sam. 15; Ps. 15 *His arrows.* (24) In Sam. 15 the Heb. is *wayyahom* (*ḳerē*), but the *kethib* is the same as in Ps. 15 *wayyehummem.* (25) Ps. 16; Sam. 16 *the channels of the sea.* (26) Ps. 16; in Sam. 16 *and* is wanting. (27) Sam. 16; Ps. 16 *at Thy rebuke, O Lord.* (28) Sam. 16; Ps. 16 *Thy nostrils.* (29) Sam. 18; Ps. 18 adds *and.* (30) In Sam. 19 *mish'an;* in Ps. 19 *lemish'an*. The sense is the same. (31) The Heb. in Sam. 20 has a verb and pronoun; in Ps. 20 a verb with a pronominal suffix. There is no difference in meaning. (32) V prints 'in' for 'according' in error. (33) In Sam. 21 the Heb. is *keẓidḳathi*, in Ps. 21 *keẓidḳi*. The nouns are practically synonymous. (34) Sam. 23; Ps. 23 *I put not away . . . from me.* (35) In Sam. 24 the Heb. is *wa'ehyeh;* Ps. 24 *wa'ehi* is a shortened form of the same verb. (36) Sam. 24; Ps. 24 *with Him.* (37) Both Sam. 24 and Ps. 24 have the same verb, but the former adds a *he* at the end.

my righteousness;[38] *according to my cleanness;*[39] *man;*[40] *Thou dost show Thyself pure;*[41] *Thou dost show Thyself subtle;*[42] *and . . . Thou dost save;*[43] *but Thine eyes are upon the haughty, that Thou mayest humble them;*[44] *and the Lord;*[45] *by my God;*[46] *who is God;*[47] *save;*[48] *my . . . fortress;*[49] *who letteth . . . go forth;*[50] *do bend;*[51] *and Thy condescension;*[52] *under me;*[53] *I have pursued;*[54] *and destroyed them;*[55] *and I have consumed them;*[56] *and smitten them;*[57] *that they cannot arise;*[58] *yea, they are fallen;*[59] *for Thou hast girded me;*[60] *under me;*[61] *yea, them that hate me, that I might cut them off;*[62] *they looked;*[63] *even unto the Lord;*[64] *as the dust of the earth;*[65] *I did stamp them . . . I did tread them down;*[66] *Thou also hast delivered me . . . my people. Thou hast kept me;*[67] *dwindle away . . . as soon as they hear of me;*[68] *and come halting out of their close places;*[69] *my Rock of salvation;*[70] *and bringeth down . . . under me;*[71] *and that bringeth me*

(38) Sam. 25 *kezidkathi;* Ps. 25 *kezidki.* (39) Sam. 25; Ps. 25 *according to the cleanness of my hands.* (40) In Sam. 26 the noun is *gibbor* (lit. mighty man), in Ps. 26 *gebar (man).* (41) There is a difference in the form of the verb; in Sam. 27 *tittabar,* in Ps. 27 *tithbarar.* (42) Another difference in the form of the verb; in Sam. 27 *tittappal,* in Ps. 27 *tithpattal.* (43) Sam. 28; Ps. 28 *for Thou dost save.* (44) Sam. 28; Ps. 28 *but the haughty eyes Thou dost humble.* (45) Sam. 29; Ps. 29 *the Lord my God.* (46) Sam. 30; Ps. 30 *and by my God.* (47) Sam. 32 reads *'el,* Ps. 32 *'elo'ah.* (48) Sam. 32; Ps. 32 *except.* A different preposition is used. V *ba'adi* is an error for *mibbal'adë.* (49) Sam. 33; Ps. 33 *that girdeth me.* (50) Sam. 33; Ps. 33 *and maketh.* The former reads *wayyater,* the latter *wayyitten.* (51) Sam. 35 *weniḥath,* Ps. 35 *weniḥathah,* with the same sense. (52) Sam. 36 *wa'anotheka,* Ps. 36 *we'anwatheka.* (53) Sam. 37 *taḥteni,* Ps. 37 *taḥtai.* (54) Sam. 38 *'erdefah,* Ps. 38 *'erdof.* (55) Sam. 38; Ps. 38 *and overtaken them.* (56) Sam. 39; wanting in Ps. 39. (57) Sam. 39; Ps. 39 omits *and.* (58) Sam. 39, lit. 'that they will not arise'; Ps. 39 *that they are not able to rise.* (59) Sam. 39; Ps. 39 *they are fallen.* (60) Sam. 40 omits the *alef* from the verb. (61) Sam. 40 *taḥteni,* Ps. 40 *taḥtai.* (62) Sam. 41; Ps. 41 *and I did cut off them that hate me.* (63) Sam. 42; Ps. 42 *they cried.* (64) In Sam. 42 the Heb. for *unto* is *'el,* in Ps. 42 *'al.* (65) Sam. 43; Ps. 43 *as the dust before the wind.* (66) Sam. 43; Ps. 43 *I did cast them out.* (67) Sam. 44; Ps. 44 *Thou hast delivered me . . . the people; Thou hast made me.* (68) Sam. 45; Ps. 45 *as soon as they hear of me . . . dwindle away.* In Sam. the Heb. for *hear* and *dwindle away* is *lishmoa'* and *yithkaḥashu,* in Ps. *leshema'* and *yekaḥashu.* (69) Sam. 46; Ps. 46 *and come trembling out of their close places.* The Heb. for *out of their close places* is *mimmisgerotham* in Sam. and *mimmisgerothehem* in Ps. There is no difference in the Heb. verb despite the different translation. (70) Sam. 47; Ps. 47 lacks *my rock* in the second part of the verse. (71) Sam. 48; Ps. 48 *and subdueth . . . under me.* There is also a difference in the Heb. for *under me* as in verses 37, 40.

forth . . . yea . . . above them that rise up against me . . . violent;[72] the Tetragrammaton is placed first;[73] *I will sing praises;*[74] *a tower of salvation.*[75]

RULE 2. The following are variants between Isaiah[76] and the text of Kings:[77] *Now in the four[teenth];*[78] *Hezekiah;*[79] *Rab-saris . . . to king Hezekiah . . . unto Jerusalem. And they went up and came to Jerusalem. And when they were come up, they came and stood by.*[80] *And when they had called to the king . . . unto them.*[81] *Sayest thou*[82] *now . . . thou trustest;*[83] *ye say . . . in Jerusalem;*[84] *with . . . king;*[85] *now . . . against this place . . . against this land and destroy it;*[86] *the son of Hilkiah . . . with us;*[87] *unto them . . . hath . . . to;*[88] *and spoke . . . the word of;*[89] *and hearken not . . . when he persuadeth;*[90] *hath . . . ever delivered;*[91] *Hena, and Ivvah have they delivered;*[92] *the countries;*[93] *but the people held their peace;*[94] *the words of Rab-shakeh.*[95]

(72) Sam. 49; Ps. 49 *he delivereth me . . . yea . . . above them that rise up against me . . . violent.* The Heb. for *above me* and *violent* in Sam. is *umiḳḳamai* and *ḥamasim;* in Ps. *min ḳammai* and *ḥamas.* (73) In Sam. 50 it precedes *among the nations,* in Ps. 50 it follows it. (74) The Heb. in Sam. 50 is *'azammer,* in Ps. 50 *'azammerah.* 'Omer' in V is a printer's error. (75) Sam. 51; Ps. 51 *great salvation giveth He.* The Heb. in the former is *migdol,* in the latter *magdil.* (76) Chapters XXXVI-XXXIX. (77) 2 Kings XVIII-XX. (78) Kings XVIII, 13; Isa. XXXVI, 1 *now it came to pass in the four[teenth].* (79) In Kings *ibid.* 14-16 the name is spelt *Ḥizḳiyyah* instead of *Ḥizḳiyyahu.* (80) Kings 17. In Isa. XXXVI, 2 *Rab-saris* is lacking, the order of the words is *to Jerusalem unto the king.* The clause *and they went up . . . they came* is lacking, and *stood* is in the singular but the plural in Kings. (81) Kings 18; *and when they . . . king* is lacking in Isa. 3 which has *unto them* for *unto him.* (82) Kings 20; Isa. 5 *I said.* (83) In Isa. 6 *now* is lacking, as is also *leka* (lit. thou trusteth for thyself), compared with Kings 21. (84) For *ye say* in Kings 22, Isa. 7 has *thou say* and omits *in Jerusalem.* (85) Kings 23, the Heb. for *with . . . king* is *'eth melek;* in Isa. 8 it is *'eth hammelek.* (86) For *now* in Kings 25, Isa. 10 reads *and . . . now.* In *against this land* the preposition is *'al* for *'el.* (87) Kings 26; in Isa. 11 *the son of Hilkiah* is lacking, and *to us* occurs instead of *with us.* (88) Kings 27; in Isa. 12 *unto them* is omitted, and *hath . . . to* is *ha'al* for *ha'el.* (89) Kings 28; in Isa. 13 *and spoke* is omitted and *word* is in the plural. (90) Kings 32; in Isa. 18 *and hearken not* is lacking, and *when* is replaced by *beware lest.* (91) Kings 33; Isa. 18 *hath . . . delivered.* (92) Kings 34; in Isa. 19 *Hena and Ivva* is lacking, and before *have* the conjunction *and* is inserted. (93) Kings 35; Isa. 20 *these countries.* (94) Kings 36; in Isa. 21 *the people* is lacking and *wayyaḥarishu* is read for *weheḥerishu.* (95) Kings 27 and Isa. 22 are identical in the Heb. The reference is probably to 2 Kings XIX, 4 and Isa. XXXVII, 4 where the former reads *all the words of Rab-shakeh* while the latter omits *all.*

And Shebna;[96] *the prophet* precedes *the son of Amoz;*[97] *all the words of;*[98] *unto them;*[99] *to his own land;*[100] *of Tirhakah;*[101] *behold he is come out . . . again;*[102] *what;*[103] *O Lord, the God of;*[104] *I have heard thee;*[105] *against the Holy One;*[106] *thy messengers;*[107] *the choice;*[108] *and I have entered into his farthest lodge;*[109] *strange;*[110] *in . . . times*[111] *. . . should be laid waste;*[112] *and confounded;*[113] *and as corn blasted;*[114] *that which springeth of the same;*[115] *he came;*[116] *will defend this city;*[117] *and it came to pass that night;*[118] *and smote;*[119] *fourscore.*[120]

His face;[121] *saying;*[122] *I beseech Thee;*[123] *heart;*[124] *return . . . the princes of My people . . . I will heal thee;*[125] *and I will add;*[126] *for Mine own sake and for My servant David's sake;*[127] *take . . . and he recovered;*[128] *and Hezekiah said unto Isaiah . . . the third day;*[129] *this;*[130] *that the Lord;*[131] *will do the thing;*[132] *go forward.*[133] *Berodach*[134] *. . . for he had heard;*[135] *Hezekiah had been sick;*[136] *hearkened unto them;*[137] *all his treasure house;*[138] *oil*[139] *. . . the*

(96) 2 Kings XIX, 2; in Isa. XXXVII, 2 *we'eth* precedes the name. (97) *ibid.;* in Isa. *ibid. the prophet* follows. The order in E.V. is the same in both. (98) Kings 4; in Isa. 4 *all* is omitted. (99) Kings 6 *lahem;* Isa. 6 *'alehem.* (100) Kings 7 has the preposition *l*, Isa. 7 *'el.* (101) Kings 9 has the preposition *'el*, Isa. 9 *'al.* (102) *ibid.;* Isa. 9 omits *behold* and for *again* (*wayyashab*) reads *and when he heard* (*wayyishma'*). (103) Kings 11 has *'eth 'asher*, Isa. 11 *'asher.* (104) Kings 15. Isa. 16 inserts *of hosts* after *Lord.* (105) Kings 20, wanting in Isa. 21. (106) Kings 22 reads *'al*, Isa. 23 *'el.* (107) Kings 23; Isa. 24 *thy servants.* (108) Kings 23 reads *mibḥor;* Isa. 24 *mibḥar.* (109) *ibid.;* in Isa 24 *and I come up to the height of the mountains.* (110) Kings 24; lacking in Isa. 25. (111) Kings 25 reads *lemimë*, Isa. 26 *mimë.* (112) In Kings 25 the reading is *lahshoth*, in Isa. 26 *lehash'oth.* (113) Kings 26 has *wayyeboshu*, Isa. 27 *waboshu.* (114) *ibid.;* Isa. 27 *and as a field of corn.* (115) Kings 29 reads *saḥish*, Isa. 30 *shaḥis.* (116) Kings 33 reads *yabo'*, Isa. 34 *ba'.* (117) Kings 34 has the preposition *'el*, Isa. 35 *'al.* (118) Kings 35; lacking in Isa. 36. (119) *ibid.* the reading is *wayyak*, in Isa. 36 *wayyakeh.* (120) Kings 35; Isa. 36 *and fourscore.* (121) 2 Kings XX, 2 reads *'eth panaw;* Isa. XXXVIII, 2 omits *'eth.* (122) *ibid.;* lacking in Isa. 2. (123) Kings 3; in Isa. 3 *and said* is inserted before *I.* (124) *ibid. ubelebab*; Isa. *ubeleb.* (125) Kings 5; lacking in Isa. 5. (126) Kings 6 *wehosafti*; Isa. 5 *behold, I will add (hinneni yosif).* (127) *ibid.*; lacking in Isa. 6. (128) Kings 7. The whole sentence is lacking in Isa. (129) Kings 8. The whole sentence is lacking in Isa. (130) Kings 9; Isa. 7 *and this.* (131) *ibid.* the Heb. particle is *ki*, in Isa. 7 *'asher.* (132) *ibid.;* Isa. 7 *this thing.* (133) *ibid.;* Isa. 8 *behold, I will cause . . . to return.* (134) Kings 12; Isa. XXXIX, 1 *Merodach.* (135) *ibid.* the reading is *ki shama';* Isa. *ibid. wayyishma'.* (136) *ibid.;* Isa. *ibid. that he had been sick, and was recovered.* (137) Kings 13; Isa. 2 *was glad of them.* (138) *ibid.;* Isa. *ibid.* omits *all.* (139) *ibid.* Isa. *ibid. the . . . oil.*

house of his armour[140] . . . *they are come;*[141] *the word of the Lord;*[142] *to Babylon;*[143] *is it not so, if.*[144]

(140) *ibid.; Isa. ibid.* inserts *all* before *the house.* (141) Kings 14; Isa. 3 adds *unto me.* (142) Kings 16; in Isa. 5 *of hosts* follows *Lord.* (143) Kings 17 the reading is *Babelah,* in Isa. 6 *Babel.* (144) Kings 19 reads *halo 'im,* Isa. 8 *if but* (*ki*). The variants here listed are not complete and there are others which are not included (cf. GRA).

CHAPTER IX

RULE 1. On the *beth* of *bereshith*[1] there must be four crownlets,[2] and the letters[3] of the word must be extended above all the other letters, because by its means[4] the world came into existence.[5]

RULE 2. The *waw* of *gaḥon*[6] must be enlarged,[7] because it is the middle of the letters of the Torah;[8] *darosh darash*[9] is the middle of the words of the Torah. *Darosh* is written at the end of the line[10] and *darash* at the beginning of the next line.[11]

RULE 3. *Wayyishḥaṭ*[12] must be enlarged,[13] because it is half of the verses of the Torah.[14]

RULE 4. *Shema' Yisra'el*[15] must be written at the beginning of a line, and all its letters are to be enlarged,[16] while *'eḥad*[17] must come at the end of [the same] line.[18]

(1) Gen. I, 1 the first word of the Pentateuch. (2) Short upward strokes on the top of the letter. (3) Some eds. read 'letter' in the singular, and the general practice is to enlarge only the *beth*. (4) This idea is also expressed in *'Othioth deRabbi 'Aḳiba*, quoted by M (p. 131): The world was created by means of the letter *beth*. (5) So M. V reads, 'for it (the world) will exist for ever', the *beth* representing *berakah* (blessing). [Cf. Midrash Rabbah, Genesis, I, §9 (Sonc. ed., p. 9).] (6) Lev. XI, 42, *belly*. (7) lit. 'upright, erect'. (8) The number of letters from the beginning of the Pentateuch to the *waw* of *gaḥon* equals the number from the *waw* to the end. (9) *ibid.* X, 16, *diligently inquired*. (10) Indicating the end of the first half of the number of words. (11) Marking the beginning of the second half of the number of words. (12) *And when it was slain;* it is uncertain whether this refers to Lev. VIII, 15 (N.Y.) or *ibid.* 23 (M) both of which begin with the same word. (13) According to M and H only the *ḥeth* of the word, it being also the initial of *ḥaẓi* (half), is to be enlarged. (14) In Ḳid. 30a (Sonc. ed., p. 144) *wehithgallaḥ* (Lev. XIII, 33, *then he shall be shaven*) is given as the middle of the verses and, according to the Masorah, its *gimel* is to be enlarged. On the number of verses opinions differ. It is variously computed as 5,844, 5,845, 5,885 and 5,888. (15) Deut. VI, 4, *Hear, O Israel*. (16) According to the Masorah only the *'ayin* of *Shema'* is enlarged. (17) *ibid., one*. (18) The final letter of the word is also enlarged according to the Masorah.

RULE 5. The *lamed* of *wayyashlikem*[19] must be long.[20]
RULE 6. The *he* of *haladonai*[21] must be longer than any other *he*, because it is[22] a word on its own.
RULE 7. The *yod* of *teshi*[23] must be smaller than any *yod* in the Scriptures. The *yod* of *yigdal*[24] must be bigger than any *yod* in the Torah.[25] *Yisra'el* at the end of the Torah[26] must be enlarged, while the *lamed* in it must be higher than any other *lamed*.
RULE 8. The following words[27] are written but not read [in their written form]:[28] It is written *ba'folim*[29] but we read *batteḥorim*;[30] it is written *yishgalennah*[31] but we read *yishkabennah*;[32] it is written *weroba' hakkab ḥiryonim*[33] but we read *weroba' hakkab dibyonim*;[34] it is written *memë shinehem*[35] but we read *memë raglehem*;[36] it is written *ḥorehem*[37] but we read *ẓo'atham*;[38] it is written *wayyesimehu lemaḥara'oth*[39] but we read *lemoẓa'oth*.[40]

If a person uses euphemisms in the section of forbidden marriages[41] he is silenced.[42] R. Jonah explained:[43] [39*a*] [When one says][44] 'the nakedness of his father' or 'the nakedness of his[45]

(19) Deut. XXIX, 27, *and cast them*. (20) i.e. longer than the other letters. By its elongation, the *lamed* is treated as the beginning of a word consisting of it and the following two letters, *LaKem* which means 'to you', implying homiletically God's promise, 'I will be a God *to you* even after you have been *cast into another land*'. (21) *ibid*. XXXII, 6, *do . . . the Lord*. (22) So GRA. V reads, 'so that it shall form'. [N.Y. gives the meaning, 'as though it were', viz. the initial of הוי, 'alas'; cf. Midrash Rabbah, Exodus, Sonc. ed., p. 294, n. 1.] (23) Deut. XXXII, 18, *thou wast unmindful*. (24) Num. XIV, 17, *let . . . be great*. (25) So GRA and N.Y. V erroneously 'big, because they are letters which are in Scripture'. H lacks the sentence. (26) Deut. XXXIV, 12, *Israel*. (27) Which have an indelicate nuance. (28) A more polite word is substituted. (29) Meaning 'posteriors'. (30) 1 Sam. V, 5, *emerods*. (31) Meaning 'rape'. This is the reading of N.Y. and M. V has *thishgalennah*. (32) Deut. XXVIII, 30, *shall lie with her*. (33) 2 Kings VI, 25, *and the fourth part of a kab of dove's dung*. (34) Meaning 'and the fourth . . . of decayed leaves'. (35) *ibid*. XVIII, 27, *their own water*. (36) lit. 'the water of their feet'. (37) *ibid*. *their own dung*. (38) lit. 'their evacuation'. (39) *ibid*. X, 27, *and made it a draught-house*. (40) lit. 'retreats'. (41) Lev. XVIII, 6–20. (42) [The text in V is corrupt and emended in agreement with the Mishnah in Meg. 25a (Sonc. ed., p. 149).] (43) What is meant here by 'euphemisms'. (44) By trying to be more considerate than Scripture. (45) Instead of *thy father* and *thy mother* (Lev. XVIII, 7). R. Joseph (Meg. *loc. cit.*) gives a different interpretation, viz. the alteration of *nakedness* to 'shame' (cf. Sonc. ed., p. 151, n. 2).

mother'. If a person says[46] 'and thou shalt not cause any of thy seed to be conceived by a Gentile woman',[47] he is silenced with a rebuke.

RULE 9. The incident of Reuben[48] is read[49] but not translated.[50] The story of Tamar[51] is both read and translated.[52] The first [account of] the golden calf[53] is read and translated,[54] the second[55] is read but not translated.[56]

RULE 10. Where [does the translator] begin? At *Oh this people have sinned.*[57] The blessing of the priests[58] and the stories of David[59] and Amnon[60] are neither read nor translated.[61]

RULE 11. The section dealing with the heavenly chariot[62] must not be read as a *hafṭarah*. R. Judah permits it.[63] R. Eleazar says: The section beginning *Cause Jerusalem to know*[64] must not be read as a *hafṭarah*.[65] It once happened that a person read the section beginning *Cause Jerusalem to know* [*her abominations*] as a *hafṭarah* and R. Eleazar exclaimed, 'Let that man go and investigate the

(46) [Or, according to J. Rabbinowitz, *Mishnah Megillah*, p. 133. 'And thou shalt not give any of thy seed (to a heathen woman) to become with child in idolatry,] instead of *and thou shalt not give of thy seed to set them apart to Molech* (Lev. XVIII, 21). (47) So altering the true meaning of the text which deals with the worship of Molech (cf. Sonc. ed., Meg. p. 149, n. 3). (48) Gen. XXXV, 22. (49) In the public lection of the Scriptures. (50) Out of respect for the memory of Reuben. In the ancient Synagogues, the readings from the Scriptures were rendered into Aramaic by an official for the benefit of those who were unable to follow the Hebrew. (51) Gen. XXXVIII. (52) So GRA and H in agreement with Meg. 25a (Sonc. ed., p. 151). V inserts the negative before both verbs. The reflection on Judah's behaviour is mitigated by his frank confession. (53) Ex. XXXIII, 1-20. (54) Since the sin was forgiven (Meg. 25b, Sonc. ed., p. 152). (55) *ibid.* 21-25 according to Meg. *loc. cit.* (Sonc. ed., p. 153). (56) Because of the statement *and there came out this calf* (*ibid.* 24) which seems to indicate that the calf had abnormal powers. (57) *ibid.* 31-35. This disagrees with Meg. quoted above. (58) Num. VI, 24-27 which includes the phrase *lift up . . . countenance* which in the Heb. could be misunderstood in its lit. meaning of 'favouritism'. (59) 2 Sam. XI, 2-17 which is discreditable to David. (60) *ibid.* XIII, 1-14 which records Amnon's disgrace. (61) So V and H in agreement with Meg. *loc. cit.*; but GRA and others omit the negative before 'read'. (62) Ezek. I and X which are too abstruse for the ordinary layman. (63) The custom is for Ezek. I to be read as the *hafṭarah* on the first day of Pentecost. This is in accordance with R. Judah's view. (64) Ezek. XVI. (65) Because of the denunciation of Jerusalem.

abominations of his mother'.[66] Enquiries were made about him and he was found to be illegitimate.

(66) In. Meg. 25b (Sonc. ed., p. 153) the reading is: R. Eleazar said to him, 'While you are investigating the abominations of Jerusalem, go and investigate the abominations of your mother'.

CHAPTER X

RULE 1. Moses[1] warned[2] Israel that they should read out of the Torah[3] on Sabbaths, Festivals, New Moons and the intermediate days of the Festivals;[4] as it is stated, *And Moses declared unto the children of Israel the appointed seasons of the Lord.*[5]

RULE 2. Ezra ordained for Israel that they should read in the Torah on Mondays and Thursdays and in the afternoon service on the Sabbath.[6]

RULE 3. There is no difference between a Festival and the Sabbath[7] save only in the matter of preparing food.[8] There is no difference between the Sabbath and the Day of Atonement save only that a wilful violation of the former [is punishable] by men[9] while a wilful violation of the latter [is punished] by *kareth*.

(1) In V and H a passage has been interpolated after 'Moses' which has no relation to the subject-matter. It seems to have been originally a marginal note explanatory of the meaning of *hiḳni'*, an unusual verb to be employed in the sense of 'warn'. It reads as follows: *Hiḳni'*, i.e. 'he warned', as we have learned in a Mishnah (Soṭ. I, 1), *hammeḳannē'* (of the same root as *hiḳni'* which means), If [a husband] 'warns' his wife [not to associate with a certain man], R. Eliezer said: His warning is valid if it was given in the presence of two witnesses, though he makes her drink [the water of bitterness] on the evidence of one witness [who saw that she had secluded herself with the man after she had been given due warning], because a warning is not valid if given in the presence of less than two witnesses; for [only where there are two witnesses] would she be able to plead, 'I was not warned', but when [there was only] one witness she might dare to plead, 'I was not warned'. (2) For *hiḳni'* some eds. read the normal verb *hithḳin*, 'he established a custom, ordained'. (3) In the service of the Synagogue. (4) lit. 'the secular [part] of the Festival', the days intervening between the holy days which begin and end the Festivals of Passover and Tabernacles. (5) Lev. XXIII, 44. (6) [For this and other ordinances of Ezra, cf. B.Ḳ. 82a (Sonc. ed., p. 466) where the reason is given for these additional lections.] (7) In regard to forbidden work. (8) lit. 'food of a person'. On a Festival, but not when it falls on the Sabbath, the preparation of food for the day by cooking is permitted. (9) i.e. a court of law.

RULE 4. R. Judah said: At the place [in the Torah] where we leave off on the Sabbath morning we begin to read at the afternoon service, and on the following Monday, Thursday and Sabbath.

RULE 5. On Mondays and Thursdays[10] and at the Sabbath afternoon service three men read [from the Torah].[11] Their number must be neither reduced nor increased; nor is a *hafṭarah* read from [a book of] a Prophet. He who begins as well as he who concludes [the reading of the prescribed section of] the Torah recites the appropriate benedictions before and after his reading.[12]

On the New Moon and during the intermediate days of a Festival, four [persons read from the Torah]. Their number must be neither reduced nor increased. This is the general rule: On any day which has a *musaf* and is not a Festival, four persons read [from the Torah].

RULE 6. On a Festival five [persons read from the prescribed portion of the Torah]; on the Day of Atonement, six; and on the Sabbath, seven. The number must not be reduced but may be increased. On a Festival, for the violation of which only a negative precept is infringed, five persons [read in the Torah]; on the Day of Atonement, for the violation of which *kareth* is incurred, six; on the Sabbath, the violation of which is punishable by stoning, seven; and one concludes with [a reading from a book of] a Prophet.

The one who begins as well as the one who concludes [the lection] recites the benediction before and after his reading.

RULE 7. The accompanying benedictions of the *Shema'*[13] may

(10) During the morning service. (11) The first of the seven portions into which the weekly *sidra'* or section is divided for the Sabbath lection. On the specified occasions it is subdivided between three worshippers. (12) For the benedictions, cf. P.B., p. 68. (13) These are the *ḳaddish, bareku* and *yoẓer 'or* (P.B., pp. 37ff) which precede the *Shema'*, and the three benedictions of the *'Amidah* which follow it (P.B., pp. 44ff) including the *ḳedushshah*.

not be repeated[14] in congregational prayer, irrespective of whether they are said standing[15] or sitting;[16] nor may one act as reader in public worship;[17] nor may [the *kohanim*] lift their hands;[18] nor may the *hafṭarah* be read from the Prophet;[19] nor may halts[20] be made [at funerals][21] for men, how much less for women since no halts are made for women; nor may *ḳaddish*[22] and *bareku* be said[23]—if less than ten adult males[24] are present.

Our teachers in the West[25] rule that seven [adult males[26] are sufficient][27] and, as a reason for their ruling, they quote, *When men let grow their hair in Israel, when the people offer themselves willingly, bless ye the Lord,*[28] [which implies that the number present must be the same] as that of the [Hebrew] words.[29] Others hold that even six [adult males are sufficient for the purpose, since up to] *bareku* [the number of words] is six.

Furthermore, where there are nine or ten persons who have heard either *bareku* or *ḳaddish* and, after the service, one of them [who missed one of the benedictions] said *bareku* or *ḳaddish*, he has thereby performed [the duty of public worship].[30]

(14) lit. 'they must not break off in connection with the *Shema*''. The ruling applies to persons who had read the morning prayers in private and now wish to join in congregational worship. They do not repeat all the statutory morning prayers, but may repeat 'broken off' parts, viz. those specified in the preceding note (cf. N.Y. and Rashi to Meg. 23b). For other interpretations, cf. Meg. (Sonc. ed., p. 141, n. 1) [and J. Rabbinowitz, *Mishnah Megillah*, pp. 114ff]. (15) i.e. the benedictions which follow the *Shema*' said while the worshippers are standing. (16) The benedictions which precede the *Shema*' said while the worshippers are sitting. (17) In connection with any part of the prayers. Lit. 'they do not pass before the [reading] chest', to lead the congregation in the conduct of the service. (18) To bless the people during the service; cf. P.B., p. 238a. (19) As is the law in regard to the Torah itself; cf. Meg. 23b (Sonc. ed., p. 141). (20) lit. 'a standing and a sitting'. (21) It was customary, when returning from a burial, to halt and sit seven times to praise and lament the dead. (22) P.B., p. 37. (23) Even without the other statutory prayers. (24) Who have attained their thirteenth birthday. (25) The land of Israel which was west of Babylon. (26) Who have not heard one of the benedictions indicated above. (27) For the purpose of repeating the benedictions. (28) Judg. V, 2. (29) Because the verse contains the word *bareku (bless ye)*. (30) Contrary to the ruling of the Rabbis of the West and the others who hold that seven or even six are enough.

The Sages long ago issued an ordinance to Synagogue precentors to say after the prayer for redemption,[31] *Blessed be the name of the Lord from this time forth and for ever,*[32] and after that, 'Bless ye the Lord Who is to be blessed',[33] so as to enable those who had not heard the benedictions[34] to perform the duty of public worship; for R. Joḥanan said: Would that a man read his prayers all the day long.[35]

The congregations of the West and the congregations of the East[36] have a custom to say it[37] after 'He Who maketh peace'[38] in the three statutory prayers[39] of the Eighteen Benedictions,[40] as a provision for the benefit of those who arrived late and for those who leave early.[41] [The verse from Psalms with the benedictions is also said] even after the public reading from the Torah.[42]

As regards the redemption of land,[43] however, [the presence is required of] nine male adults and a *kohen*; and the same law applies to the redemption of a human being.[44]

(31) 'O Rock of Israel,' etc. (P.B., p. 44). (32) Ps. CXIII, 2. (33) *Bareku*, etc. (P.B., p. 37). (34) Owing to their late arrival. (35) Therefore it is permissible for the precentor to repeat the benedictions under discussion more than once for the benefit of those who did not hear him when he first read them. (36) The land of Israel and Babylon respectively. (37) The verse from Psalms followed by the benedictions mentioned. (38) P.B., p. 54, forming the conclusion of the *'Amidah*. (39) For the evening, morning and afternoon. This custom is contrary to the previous opinion which permits an interruption between the prayer for redemption and the *'Amidah* which immediately follows it. The originators of the custom forbid such an interruption. (40) The actual number is nineteen, but it was eighteen when originally instituted. (41) It is for their benefit that the repetition is not made at the end of the entire service. (42) If persons came in as late as that. (43) Which had been dedicated to the Temple. (44) Cf. Lev. XXVII, 2ff, 16ff.

CHAPTER XI

RULE 1. One who reads the Torah [in public worship] should read not less than three verses,[1] and he should not read for the interpreter[2] more than one verse [at a time].[3] In the case of [the lection from] a Prophet, however, three [verses at a time may be read];[4] but if the three verses constituted three different paragraphs, he may read one verse at a time[5]—for instance, *For thus saith the Lord; Ye were sold for nought*[6] . . . [39b] *For thus saith the Lord God: My people went down aforetime into Egypt*[7] . . . *Now, therefore, what do I here, saith the Lord.*[8]

In a city where only one person is able to read [from the Torah scroll] he reads all[9] the prescribed sections, provided he sits down between the reading of one section and the next.[10]

RULE 2. It is permitted to skip from place to place in [a scroll of] a Prophet,[11] but not in a Torah scroll, because [the scroll of] a Prophet may be unrolled in public but not of the Torah.[12] Similarly ruled R. Jeremiah in the name of R. Simeon b. Laḳish: A Torah scroll may not be unrolled in public.

(1) The number corresponds to the three main divisions of the Bible: the Pentateuch, Prophets and Hagiographa; Meg. 24a (Sonc. ed., p. 143). (2) Who translated and expounded the Heb. text into Aramaic for the congregation. (3) So that the interpreter, who had no book before him, should not become confused. (4) If desired. Since no instruction in law is involved in the lection from the Prophets as in the Torah, a mistake would not be serious. (5) For the interpreter. (6) Isa. LII, 3. (7) *ibid.* 4. (8) *ibid.* 5. (9) 'All' is added by GRA, M and H. (10) lit. 'between reading and reading'. The number of times he sits down corresponds to the number of persons who are to be called up for the reading. This ruling applies to the time when only the first and last who were called up recited the benedictions before and after the reading. At the present time, when each person called up recites the benedictions before and after his portion, there is no need for the sitting down. (11) Omitting the intermediate portions. (12) The unrolling of which might disturb the congregation.

R. Jose enquired: Suppose[13] there was only a small section [which one wished to skip]![14] The real reason[15] is that Israel shall hear the Torah in its proper order. But have we not learned: [The High Priest] reads [in public] *aḥarē moth*[16] and *'ak be'asor?*[17] [With these two sections] it is different,[18] because they deal with the statutory order [of the reading] of the day.[19] You can see the reason[20] for yourself, because R. Simeon b. Laḳish ruled, 'No part of the Torah may be[21] read by heart', and yet here[22] [the High Priest] reads by heart.[23]

RULE 3. R. Jose gave the following instruction to Bar[24] 'Ula, the precentor of the Babylonian Synagogue [in Sepphoris]:[25] When only one Torah scroll is available the unrolling[26] should be done in front of the ark curtain,[27] but when two scrolls are available you should carry the first [back to the ark] and then take out the other.[28] To what extent [is skipping in the Torah permitted]? R. Jose said: As, for instance, the sections[29] [read on the Day of Atonement] by the High Priest.[30]

(13) GRA in agreement with j.Meg. IV, 5, 75b. V and H read 'interpreted it, as for instance'. (14) And consequently no unrolling is required. Why, then, should skipping in such a case be forbidden? (15) lit. 'but' added by GRA. V and H omit. (16) lit. *after the death,* designating the section Lev. XVI. (17) lit. *howbeit on the tenth,* designating the section beginning Lev. XXIII, 27. These sections are far removed from one another and the Torah scroll must consequently be unrolled in public. Why is this permitted? (18) Therefore unrolling in public is permitted. (19) i.e. the Day of Atonement. As they form one subject, skipping from place to place is allowed. (20) lit. 'and you may know'. (21) lit. 'in every place one may not'. (22) The section beginning *And on the tenth day* (Num. XXIX, 7). (23) For the reason stated above. (24) So j.Meg. IV, 5, 75b, the text of which is followed here. V has 'Mar'. (25) In Upper Galilee. (26) When skipping is necessary from one passage to another. (27) There is no need to return the scroll to the ark after the first reading had concluded and then take it out again for the second section. (28) The present custom is to take both scrolls from the ark at the same time and to keep the second rolled and wrapped until the completion of the reading from the first. (29) Which are not so far from one another as to cause the interpreter to stop and keep the congregation waiting while the scroll is being unrolled to the second section, and deal with the same subject, thus causing no confusion to the hearers. (30) So GRA and H in agreement with j.Meg. *loc. cit.* The reading of V is 'Jehoiada the priest'.

RULE 4. If the precentor read in the Torah on a Sabbath for less than seven persons,[31] having forgotten and thought that he had already read for[32] seven persons, he should read again completing the number of seven, and call up an eighth as *maftir;* provided always that the lection[33] consists of [a minimum of] twenty-one verses and allows three verses for each of the seven persons who are called up. And if a section consists of less [than three verses for each of the seven persons][34] an addition should be made to the section from the one following it.[35]

RULE 5. If a section consisted of four or five verses, he reads the whole of it, but with a section of six verses he may read and make a break[36] because it has the [minimum] length for two readings. If on a Monday or Thursday, or the Sabbath afternoon service or the afternoon service of Festivals[37] less than ten verses[38] were read, he should repeat the reading to complete ten verses. From where [in the Torah] does one read in the afternoon service of a Festival [when it occurs on a Sabbath]?[39] In the regular order where [the Torah reading] was interrupted before the Festival.[40]

RULE 6. If in the course of public reading he skipped a verse and omitted to read it, should he have read ten verses exclusive[41] of the verse skipped, he need not go back; but if less than[42] ten, he must go back and read ten verses in correct

(31) lit. 'readings or callings', i.e. the lection was allocated to less than the minimum number. (32) Or, 'had called up'. (33) lit. 'the order', the prescribed section for the reading of the day. (34) This apparently refers to ancient Synagogues where only short portions of the Torah were read or where it was completed once in three years, not annually as is the present custom. Then the section for a Sabbath may sometimes have been very short. (35) lit. 'from another portion'. (36) At the end of the third verse. (37) On which occasion three persons are called to the reading of the Torah. (38) According to some authorities, if nine verses were read no repetition of the reading is necessary (cf. *'Oraḥ Ḥayyim* CXXXVII, §1 and commentaries *ad loc.*). Others maintain that in general ten is the minimum number. (39) On a Festival which occurs on a weekday there is no reading from the Torah in the afternoon service. (40) i.e. from the beginning of the lection of the next Sabbath. (41) So GRA and H. V has 'from'. (42) lit. 'within'.

order so that none is left out. This is the case with [the reading of] a week-day,[43] Sabbath afternoon and Festival afternoon;[44] but on a Sabbath [morning] if he forgot and passed over a verse and then realized [his mistake], he must stop[45] and re-read [the passage in full]. Even after one had read the *hafṭarah* in [a Book of] a Prophet and recited the *musaf*, he must stop forthwith and read [the Scriptural passage]. The *musaf*, however,[46] need not be repeated.

(43) i.e. Monday and Thursday. (44) Since the omitted verses will be read on the following Sabbath morning in the course of the lection. (45) Added by GRA. (46) So GRA. V inserts 'because' which cannot be justified.

CHAPTER XII

RULE 1. It is permitted to make a break[1] in the blessings[2] but not in the curses.[3] R. Ḥiyya b. Gamda said: What is the reason?[4] Because it is written [*My son, despise not the chastening of the Lord,*][5] *neither cut thou up His correction*[6]—do not cut them[7] up into pieces.[8]
RULE 2. R. Levi said:[9] The Holy One, blessed be He, said: It is not proper that My children shall be cursed while I am being blessed.[10] R. Jose b. Abin said: It is not for this reason, but because one who stands up to read in the Torah must begin and conclude with something auspicious.[11]
RULE 3. Levi b. Paṭi enquired of R. Ḥanina, 'What is the law in regard to the curses each of which begins with *'arur?*[12] Must they be read by one person only,[13] and must a benediction be recited before and after them?' He replied, 'There is no [passage] that requires a benediction before and after its reading but the curses of Leviticus[14] and Deuteronomy'.[15]

(1) i.e. the passage may be divided and two persons called up to the reading. (2) e.g. Lev. XXVI, 3-13. (3) *ibid.* 14-46. (4) Why may not more than one person be called to the section of the curses? (5) This is the first part of the verse which is not quoted in the text of the Tractate. (6) Prov. III, 11, E.V. *neither spurn.* (7) lit. 'make it', a section in the Torah which deals with God's chastening of Israel. (8) The Heb. root may bear both meanings: 'spurn' and 'cut up'. (9) Explaining the reason that no more than one person may be called to the reading of the curses in Lev. XXVI, 14ff. (10) By the recital of the benedictions in the middle of reading the curses. (11) If two persons were to be called to the reading, the first would finish and the second begin with a verse which threatens a curse. (12) Deut. XXVII, 15-26, each verse commencing *Cursed be.* (13) As with the curses of Lev. XXVI, 14ff which must not be read by more than one person. (14) *Torath Kohanim,* lit. 'the law of the priests', the name of the Book of Leviticus. The passage is XXVI, 14-46. (15) *Mishneh Torah,* lit. 'the repetition of the law', the name of the Book of Deuteronomy. The passage is XXVIII, 15-68. Only with these passages, which are not restricted to a particular time, are the benedictions recited before and after they have been read; but with the *'arur* curses, which were spoken by the Levites only (cf. Deut. XXVII, 14) and at the time when the Jordan was crossed (*ibid.* 2), no benedictions are to be recited.

RULE 4. When Jonathan, a children's teacher from Gufta,[16] came down here,[17] he saw a children's teacher, R. Abuna, reading the Song of the Well[18] and reciting the benedictions before and after it. 'Is it proper,' he asked him, 'to act in this manner?'[19] 'Do you,' the other retorted, 'still require [a ruling] on this subject? All poems[20] must be preceded and followed by benedictions.'

RULE 5. A question[21] was asked of[22] R. Simon. 'There is no section',[23] he told them in the name of R. Joshua b. Levi, 'which requires a benediction before and after its reading other than the Song at the Sea, the Ten Words,[24] and the curses in Deuteronomy'.[25]

RULE 6. R. Abahu[26] said: I have not heard [such a ruling],[27] but it is feasible to apply it to the Ten Words. R. Jose b. Abin said in the name of Rabbi:[28] The last ten verses in Deuteronomy[29] require a benediction before and after they have been read.[30]

RULE 7. R. Isaac Seḥorah asked R. Isaac Nappaḥa, 'What do we read [first][31] when the New Moon of *Ṭebeth*[32] falls on a Sabbath?'[33] [He replied,] 'In the section of

(16) In Galilee. V incorrectly 'Gufthera'. (17) Tiberias where R. Abuna resided. The city is a on lower level, hence the verb 'came down'. (18) Num. XXI, 17-20. (19) The rule is that the benedictions are recited only at the beginning and end of the entire section to be read. The Song of the Well, appearing in the middle of a section, should consequently require no benedictions before and after its reading. (20) Such as the Song of the Sea (Ex. XV, 1-19), the Song of the Well and probably also Deut. XXXII, 1-43. (21) In connection with the preceding Rule. (22) Another reading is 'he came and asked'. (23) lit. 'you have not'. (24) The Decalogue (Ex. XX, 2-17). (25) Deut. XXVIII, 15-68. Others add 'the curses in Leviticus'. (26) So GRA and H. V reads 'Abi'. (27) That in the case of the passages specified benedictions are to be recited before and after the reading. (28) [The reading should be 'R. Berekiah' or 'R. Simon'; cf. Bacher, *Ag. d. pal. Amoräer*, III, p. 727, n. 7.] (29) So GRA and N.Y. The text in V is difficult. (30) These verses, which describe the death of Moses, form a section of their own, because they were written by Joshua (according to R. Judah or R. Nehemiah) or, if written by Moses, they were dictated to him by God while he 'wrote them down with tears' (B.B. 15a, Sonc. ed., p. 72). (31) In the second and third scrolls. (32) Which always occurs in the week of *Ḥanukkah*. (33) Three scrolls are then taken from the ark. The usual weekly portion is read in the first, and the passages for New Moon and *Ḥanukkah* in the second and third.

kalloth,[34] while the *maftir* reads[35] the passages relating to the Sabbath and the New Moon.[36] If it falls on a week-day we call up on the first day[37] three persons for the reading of the New Moon, the fourth reading that of *Ḥanukkah*, because that which is more frequent takes precedence.[38] But since the reading of the New Moon was read first,[39] [40*a*] three persons are to be called up on the second day for the reading of the *Ḥanukkah* passage,[40] while the fourth reads[41] the section of the New Moon, viz. *uberashë ḥodshekem*[42] to the end of the passage.[43] Why is this so?[44] Because it was only on account of the New Moon *musaf* that a fourth person is added'.[45]

RULE 8. R. Jose b. Abin said: For the Song of *Ha'azinu*[46] not less than six persons[47] are to be called up, and your mnemonic sign[48] is *h z y w l k*,[49] which stands for *ha'azinu*,[50] *zekor*,[51] *yarkibehu*,[52] *wayyishman*,[53] *lu*,[54] *ki yadin . . . 'ammo*.[55] It must also be provided

(34) E.V. *made an end* (Num. VII, 1). This designates the entire section, descriptive of the dedication offerings brought by the princes of Israel, which is prescribed for the reading of the day. (35) In the third scroll. (36) Num. XXVIII, 9-15. The present custom is always to read the section for the Sabbath and New Moon first, and then the passage for *Ḥanukkah*. (37) Of the two days of the New Moon. (38) The New Moon occurs monthly, *Ḥanukkah* once a year. (39) On the first day of the New Moon. (40) In the first scroll. Only two scrolls are taken out on a week-day during *Ḥanukkah*. (41) In the second scroll. (42) E.V. *and in your new moons* (Num. XXVIII, 11). (43) *ibid.* 15. (44) i.e. why is the fourth person called to the reading of the New Moon passage and not, as on the first day, to the *Ḥanukkah* passage? (45) On the other week-days of *Ḥanukkah* there is no *musaf*. This argument cannot be applied to the first day of the New Moon because it is the second day which begins the month. The first of the two days of the New Moon is the last day of the preceding month. V and H insert here a ruling which has no connection with this chapter and is practically identical with XIV, 2 below. (46) E.V. *give ear*, designating the section Deut. XXXII, 1-43. For *Ha'azinu* (the reading of GRA) V and H read 'the Levites', because the poem was sung by the Levites in the Temple during the Sabbath *musaf* in six parts on successive Sabbaths. (47) Because the Levites concluded it in cycles of six Sabbath divisions. (48) For the words beginning each of the six parts. The divisions, according to Maimonides, emphasize the exhortations and arouse the people to repentance. (49) pronounced הזי״ו ל״ך. (50) E.V. *give ear* (Deut. XXXII, 1). (51) E.V. *remember* (*ibid.* 7). (52) E.V. *He made him ride* (*ibid.* 13). (53) E.V. *but . . . waxed fat* (*ibid.* 15). (54) E.V. *if* (*ibid.* 29). (55) E.V. *for the Lord will judge His people* (*ibid.* 36).

with[56] the space of a full line above it and of a full line below it. Corresponding to it the custom has been adopted to write in the Torah its number of lines.[57]

RULE 9. A mnemonic sign for the beginnings of the lines[58] is the following: *ha'azinu*,[59] *ya'arof*,[60] *kise'irim*,[61] *ki*,[62] *hazzur*,[63] *'el*,[64] *shiheth*,[65] *halaH*,[66] *halo'*,[67] *zekor*,[68] *she'al*,[69] *behanhel*,[70] *yazzeb*,[71] *ki*,[72] *yimza'ehu*,[73] *yesobebenhu*,[74] *kannesher*,[75] *yifros*,[76] the Tetragrammaton,[77] *yarkibehu*,[78] *wayyenikehu*,[79] *hem'ath*,[80] *we'elim*,[81] *wedam*,[82] *shamanta*,[83] *wayyenabbel*,[84] *betho'eboth*,[85] *'Elohim*,[86] *lo'*,[87] *wattishkah*,[88] *mikka'as*,[89] *'er'eh*,[90] *banim*,[91] *ki'asuni*,[92] *begoi*,[93] *wattikad*,[94] *wattelahet*,[95] *hizzai*,[96] *weketeb*,[97] *'im*,[98] *umehadarim*,[99] *yonek*,[100] *'ashbithah*,[101] *pen*,[102] *welo'*,[103] *we'ain*,[104] *yabinu*,[105] *ushenayim*,[106] *waH*,[107] *w'oyebenu*,[108] *umishshadmoth*,[109] *'ashkeloth*,[110] *werosh*,[111] *hathum*,[112] *le'eth*,[113] *wehash*,[114] *we'al*,[115] *we'efes*,[116] *zur*,[117] *yishtu*,[118] *yehi*,[119] *we'ain*,[120] *mahazti*,[121], *ki*,[122] *'im*,[123] *'ashib*,[124] *'ashkir*,[125] *middam*,[126] *harninu*,[127] *wenakam*.[128]

(56) lit. 'and it has'. (57) The number is 72 according to GRA who apparently includes the two blank lines. Maimonides and others give the number as 70. (58) Of the song *Ha'azinu*. The following renderings are from E.V. While the Heb. words stand at the beginning of the respective lines, the translations, owing to English idiom, do not always occupy the same position in the sentence. (59) *Give ear* (Deut. XXXII, 1). (60) *Shall drop* (*ibid.* 2). (61) *As the small rain* (*ibid.*). (62) *For* (3). (63) *The Rock* (4). (64) *A God* (*ibid.*). (65) *Is corruption* (5). (66) *The Lord* (6). (67) *Is not* (*ibid.*). (68) *Remember* (7). (69) *Ask* (*ibid.*). (70) *When . . . gave . . . inheritance* (8). (71) *He set* (*ibid.*). (72) *For* (9). (73) *He found him* (10). (74) *He compassed him* (*ibid.*). (75) *As an eagle* (11). (76) *Spreadeth abroad* (*ibid.*). (77) *The Lord* (12). (78) *He made him ride* (13). (79) *And He made him to suck* (*ibid.*). (80) *Curd of* (14). (81) *And rams* (*ibid.*). (82) *And of the blood of* (*ibid.*). (83) *Thou didst wax fat* (15). (84) *And contemned* (*ibid.*). (85) *With abominations* (16). (86) *Gods* (17). (87) *Not* (*ibid.*). (88) *And didst forget* (18). (89) *Because of the provoking* (19). (90) *I will see* (20). (91) *Children* (*ibid.*). (92) *They have provoked Me* (21). (93) *With a . . . nation* (*ibid.*). (94) *And burneth* (22). (95) *And setteth ablaze* (*ibid.*). (96) *Mine arrows* (23). (97) *And bitter destruction* (24). (98) *With* (*ibid.*). (99) *And in the chambers* (25). (100) *The suckling* (*ibid.*). (101) *I would make . . . cease* (26). (102) *Lest* (27). (103) *And not* (*ibid.*). (104) *And there is no* (28). (105) *They would understand* (29). (106) *And two* (30). (107) *And the Lord* (*ibid.*). (108) *Even our enemies* (31). (109) *And of the fields* (32). (110) *Clusters* (*ibid.*). (111) *And . . . poison* (33). (112) *Sealed up* (34). (113) *Against the time* (35). (114) *And . . . shall make haste* (*ibid.*). (115) *And . . . for* (36). (116) *And there is none* (*ibid.*). (117) *The rock* (37). (118) *And drank* (38). (119) *Let him be* (*ibid.*). (120) *And there is no* (39). (121) *I have wounded* (*ibid.*). (122) *For* (40). (123) *If* (41). (124) *I will render* (*ibid.*). (125) *I will make drunk* (42). (126) *With the blood of* (*ibid.*). (127) *Sing aloud* (43). (128) *And . . . vengeance* (*ibid.*).

RULE 10. R. Ze'ira, quoting R. Jeremiah, in the name of Rab, said; The Song at the Sea[129] and the Song of Deborah[130] are written in the form of a half-brick over a whole brick,[131] and a whole brick over a half-brick.[132]

RULE 11. The Song at the Sea consists of thirty lines [beginning with the words:] *'az,*[133] *le'mor,*[134] *werokebo,*[135] *lishu'ah,*[136] *'abi,*[137] *shemo,*[138] *shalishaw,*[139] *'aben,*[140] the Tetragrammaton,[141] *kameka,*[142] *'appeka,*[143] *nozelim,*[144] *'oyeb,*[145] *nafshi,*[146] *beruḥaka,*[147] *'addirim,*[148] *kamokah,*[149] *pele',*[150] *beḥasdeka,*[151] *kodsheka,*[152] *'aḥaz,*[153] *'Edom,*[154] *kol,*[155] *wafaḥad,*[156] *ya'abor,*[157] *ḳanitha,*[158] *leshibteka,*[159] *yadeka,*[160] *ba',*[161] *më.*[162]

RULE 12. The mark for the Song of Deborah is 'sixty-four lines'[163] [beginning with the words:] *wattashar,*[164] *le'mor,*[165] *'am,*[166] *rozenim,*[167] *laH,*[168] *misse'ir,*[169] *ra'ashah,*[170] *mayyim,*[171] *Sinai,*[172] *'Anath,*[173] *nethiboth,*[174] *ḥadelu,*[175] *'em,*[176] *ḥadashim,*[177] *'im,*[178] *beYisra'el,*[179] *ba'am,*[180] *ẓeḥoroth,*[181] *'al,*[182] *mash'abim,*[183] *pirzono,*[184] the Tetragrammaton,[185] *'uri,*[186] *'Abino'am,*[187] *yerad,*[188] *ba'Amaleḳ,*[189] *Makir,*[190] *sofer,*[191] *ken,*[192]

(129) Ex. XV, 1-18. (130) Judg. V, 1-31. (131) Or 'blank space'; the Heb. לבינה may bear both meanings. (132) Cf. above. p. 215, n. 45. (133) *Then* (Ex. XV, 1). (134) *Saying (ibid.).* (135) *And his rider (ibid.).* (136) *Salvation* (2). (137) *My father's (ibid.).* (138) *His name* (3). (139) *His . . . captains* (4). (140) *A stone* (5). (141) *O Lord* (6, the second occurrence). (142) *Them that rise up against Thee* (7). (143) *Thy nostrils* (8). (144) *The floods (ibid.).* (145) *The enemy* (9). (146) *My lust (ibid.).* (147) *With Thy wind* (10). (148) *Mighty (ibid.).* (149) *Like unto Thee* (11). (150) *Wonders (ibid.).* (151) *In Thy love* (13). (152) *Thy holy (ibid.).* (153) *Have taken hold* (14). (154) *Edom* (15). (155) *All (ibid.).* (156) *And dread* (16). (157) *Pass over (ibid.*, the first occurrence). (158) *Thou hast gotten (ibid.).* (159) *For Thee to dwell in* (17). (160) *Thy hands (ibid.).* (161) *Went in* (19). (162) *The waters of (ibid.).* Others read הים (*the sea*) which follows מי; while GRA, quoting Maimonides, reads את (the sign of the defined accusative) which precedes מי. (163) So GRA. V and H 'sixty-five'. (164) *Then sang* (Judg. V, 1). (165) *Saying (ibid.).* (166) *People* (2). This is the reading of GRA. V has *Bless ye (ibid.).* (167) *O ye princes* (3). (168) *To the Lord (ibid.).* (169) *Out of Seir* (4). (170) *Trembled (ibid.).* (171) *Water (ibid.).* (172) *Sinai* (5). (173) *Anath* (6). (174) *Paths (ibid.).* E.V. renders this word together with the preceding as *travellers.* (175) *They ceased* (7). (176) *A mother (ibid.).* (177) *New* (8). (178) *Was there (ibid.).* (179) *In Israel (ibid.).* (180) *Among the people* (9). (181) *White* (10). (182) *By (ibid.).* (183) *Watering-troughs* (11). (184) *Of His rulers (ibid.).* (185) *The Lord (ibid.).* (186) *Awake [utter a song]* (12). (187) *Abinoam (ibid.).* (188) *Made me have dominion* (13). (189) *In Amalek* (14). (190) *Machir (ibid.).* (191) *Marshal's (ibid.).* (192) *So* (15).

beraglaw,[193] *ḥikeḳe leb,*[194] *hammishpethayim,*[195] *Re'uben,*[196] *shaken,*[197] *yashab,*[198] *yishkon,*[199] *'al,*[200] *nilḥamu,*[201] *'al,*[202] *laḳaḥu,*[203] *mimmesilotham,*[204] *gerafam,*[205] *nafshi,*[206] *sus,*[207] *Meroz,*[208] *yoshebeha,*[209] the Tetragrammaton,[210] *Ya'el,*[211] *ba'ohel,*[212] *nathanah,*[213] *layyathed,*[214] *'amelim,*[215] *weḥalefah,*[216] *shakab,*[217] *kara',*[218] *watteyabbeb,*[219] *boshesh,*[220] *markebothaw,*[221] *hi,'*[222] *shalal,*[223] *ẓeba'im,*[224] *riḳmah,*[225] *yobedu,*[226] *bigburatho.*[227]

(193) *At his feet (ibid.).* (194) *Resolves of heart (ibid.).* (195) *Among the sheepfolds* (16). (196) *Reuben (ibid.).* (197) *Abode* (17). (198) *Dwelt (ibid.).* (199) *Abideth (ibid.).* (200) *Upon* (18). (201) *They fought* (19). (202) *By (ibid.).* (203) *They took (ibid.).* (204) *In their courses* (20). (205) *Swept them away* (21). (206) *O my soul (ibid.).* (207) *Horse [hoofs]* (22). (208) *Meroz* (23). (209) *The inhabitants thereof (ibid.).* (210) *The Lord [against the mighty] (ibid.).* (211) *Jael* (24). (212) *In the tent (ibid.).* (213) *She gave* (25). (214) *To the tent-pin* (26). (215) *Workmen (ibid.).* (216) *And struck through (ibid.).* (217) *He lay* (27). (218) *He sunk (ibid.).* (219) *And peered* (28). (220) *So long (ibid.).* (221) *His chariots (ibid.).* (222) *She* (29). (223) *Spoil* (30). (224) *Dyed garments (ibid.).* (225) *Embroidery (ibid.).* (226) *So perish* (31). (227) *In his might (ibid.).* The last twelve words are according to the reading of GRA. V has instead only ten, which do not present a likely division of the lines and are not followed in current editions of the Hebrew Bible.

CHAPTER XIII

RULE 1. In regard, however,[1] to the Song of David in Samuel[2] and in the Psalms,[3] the Sages have not prescribed a limit;[4] but a skilled scribe spaces them out symmetrically[5] according to the beginnings, the middle pauses, and the endings of the verses.[6] A similar arrangement is also followed throughout the Psalms and in Job and Proverbs.

RULE 2. The scroll of Esther[7] requires ruled lines[8] as does the real[9] Torah,[10] because it is called 'a scroll'.[11]

RULE 3. The ten sons of Haman[12] and the kings of Canaan[13] are written in the form of a half-brick over a half-brick and a brick over a brick.[14] Such a structure[15] does not endure.[16] What is implied by 'such'?[17] Does it indicate a recommendation[18] or an indispensable condition?[19]

RULE 4. R. Jose[20] said to R. Ḥanina, the nephew of R. Hoshaiah, 'Surely you remember that when we were standing in front of the shop of your uncle, R. Hoshaiah, R. Ba' b. Zabda passed

(1) In contrast to the poems dealt with in the previous Rule. (2) 2 Sam. XXII. (3) Ps. XVIII. (4) For the number of lines in a column. (5) In the form of stichoi. (6) This rendering follows the text in M and H. (7) Which is read on *Purim*. (8) To guide the scribe in writing the letters which are suspended from them. (9) lit. 'its truth of'. (10) Here denotes the Pentateuch. (11) The text corrected by GRA. V has 'scroll called'. 'Scroll' is lit. 'book', the word used in Esth. IX, 32. For another reason, cf. Meg. 16b (Sonc. ed., p. 100). (12) Esth. IX, 7-9. (13) Josh. XII, 9-24. (14) Like the song of *Ha'azinu* (cf. above XII, 8). (15) In which bricks and half-bricks rest one above the other and do not overlap. (16) And so is symbolic of the fate of Haman's sons. (17) The statement 'such a structure does not last'. (18) As the arrangement is only a symbol, a deviation from it would not disqualify the scroll. (19) A deviation would then lead to disqualification. The answer follows in the next Rule. (20) The translation follows GRA and H in agreement with j.Meg. III, 7, 74b. V reads: 'R. Jose b. Ḥanina, the brother of R. Hoshaiah, R. Abba b. Zabda surrounded thee, and we asked him this, and he said in the name of Rab that the condition was indispensable'.

by and we put the question to him, and he replied that the condition was indispensable'.

RULE 5. R. Ḥiyya b. R. Adda of Jaffa, quoting R. Jeremiah in the name of R. Ze'ira, said: The names of the ten sons of Haman and the word *ten*[21] must be recited in one breath.

RULE 6. R. Jose b. Abin said: When they[22] are written down, the word *'ish*[23] must be at the top of the column[24] and each *we'eth*[25] at the end [of the lines, a total] of eleven lines,[26] and *'asereth* at the end of the column. Thus, in reading transversely, the columns[27] appear laced and closely corded like transverse lacing [of a web].[28] It symbolizes that when [the ten sons] fall there will be no rising for them.

The phrase *'aḥar haddebarim . . . Hammedatha*[29] was translated by R. Joseph as follows:[30] 'After these things did king Ahasuerus promote Haman the son of Hammedatha the Aggagite, son of Seraḥ,[31] son of Buza, son of Aflutos,[32] son of Deosis,[33] son of Padom,[34] son of Ma'adi,[35] son of Be'alkon,[36] son of Antamarus,[37] son of Ḥarum,[38] son of Hadoram,[39] son of Shazar,[40] son of Nagar,[41] son of Parshandatha,[42] son of Waye-

(21) Esth. IX, 10. (22) The names of Haman's sons. (23) *Man*, the last word of Esth. IX, 6. (24) And at the beginning of the first line. (25) Sign of the defined accusative which occurs ten times, each preceding the names of the ten sons. (26) The first line consisting of *'ish* on the right and *we'eth* on the left, the next nine lines having the name on the right and *we'eth* on the left, while the eleventh line has the name *Wayezatha* on the right and *'asereth* (*ten*) on the left. (27) On the right (consisting of *'ish* and the ten names), and the left (ten times *we'eth* and *'asereth*). (28) The reading of V is corrupt and the translation follows GRA, N.Y. and Jastrow. (29) Esth. III, 1, E.V. *After these things did king Ahasuerus promote Haman the son of Hammedatha.* (30) R. Joseph is the reputed author of a later Aramaic translation of the Prophets and Hagiographa. (31) A name derived from a root 'to stink'. The object of the genealogy is to trace Haman, the symbol of the enemies of Jews throughout their history, through a chain of despicable men to Esau, the brother but enemy of the patriarch Jacob. (32) Buza means 'contempt', and Aflutos is probably Plutos, a heathen god. (33) Dionysus (?). (34) Or, Pados (putrid?). (35) Meaning 'sickness'. (36) The meaning is 'cunning'. (37) Signifying 'crushed stones'. (38) Or, Ḥuram, possibly the heathen god Ares. (39) Or, Heridos, i.e. Herod who is known in history as a tyrant. (40) Meaning 'hip disease'. (41) Or, possibly, Negad (a whip). (42) This and the following were also names of two of Haman's sons.

zatha, son of 'Amaleḳ,[43] son of the concubine of Eliphaz the firstborn of Esau; he advanced him and set his seat above all his princes and his servants, because pride goeth before destruction'.[44]

RULE 7. R. Ze'ira said: The *waw* of *Wayezatha*[45] must project like a boat-pole on the river Libruth.[46]

RULE 8. If a person holds a scroll of the Torah [in order to read it], there is a difference of opinion between two *Tanna'im*.[47] One declared that he should open it, look [for the passage which is to be read], roll it up and then say the benediction;[48] but the other declared that he should open it, look [for the required passage] and say the benediction.[49] What is the reason?[50] Because it is written, *And when he opened it, all the people stood up;*[51] and what follows? *And Ezra blessed*[52] *the Lord, the great God.*[53] Whereby did he proclaim His greatness?[54] Rab said: He proclaimed His greatness by pronouncing the Ineffable Name.[55] Raba said: He proclaimed His greatness by the recital of the prescribed benediction.

What is the form of the benedictions?[56] In an assembly of ten[57] one says, 'Bless ye the Lord Who is to be blessed'.[58] In the

(43) The ancestor of the people who were the first to attack Israel after their exodus from Egypt. (44) The last four words come from Prov. XVI, 18. The translation of the paragraph embodies most of GRA's emendations. (45) Esth. IX, 9. (46) i.e. the *waw* must be longer than the other letters. The ruling is quoted from Meg. 16b (Sonc. ed., p. 99). The river has not been identified. (47) On the question whether the prescribed benedictions should be said while the scroll is open or rolled. (48) Were one to say it while the scroll is open, people might erroneously assume that the benediction is written in the Torah (Meg. 32a, Sonc. ed., pp. 192f). (49) Because nobody could be so ignorant as to be unaware that the benedictions do not form a part of the text of the Torah (Meg. *loc. cit.*). (50) That the scroll must be open when the benediction is said. (51) Neh. VIII, 5 referring to the scroll of the Torah. (52) i.e. he said the prescribed benedictions. (53) *ibid.* 6. As Ezra *opened* the scroll and *blessed the Lord,* so everyone who reads the Torah must have the scroll open when the benedictions are said. (54) As implied in the words *the great God.* (55) The Tetragrammaton. (56) Before and after the reading in the Torah. (57) A minimum of ten males over the age of thirteen is required for congregational worship. (58) And then follow the benedictions given later for an individual in private reading.

case of an individual, when he rises early to read in the Torah, he says, 'Blessed art Thou, O Lord our God, King of the universe, Who hast given us a Torah from heaven, everlasting life from the heights. Blessed art Thou, O Lord, Who givest the Torah'. Then[59] he rolls up the scroll[60] and says, 'Blessed art Thou, O Lord our God, King of the universe, Who hast given us a Torah of truth and hast planted everlasting life in our midst. Blessed art Thou, O Lord, Who givest the Torah'.[61]

RULE 9. Similarly when one reads from the Prophets,[62] a benediction is said as follows: 'Blessed art Thou, O Lord our God, King of the universe, Who hast chosen good prophets, and hast found pleasure in their words which were spoken in truth. Blessed art Thou, O Lord, Who hast chosen the Torah and Moses Thy servant, and Israel Thy people, and the prophets of truth and righteousness'.[63]

RULE 10. And at the end [of the reading of the portion from the Prophets], one says the following benedictions: 'Blessed art Thou, O Lord our God, King of the universe, Rock of all worlds, righteous through all generations, O faithful God, Who sayest and doest, Who speakest[64] and fulfillest, all Whose words are truth and righteousness'. The people forthwith stand and say:[65] 'Faithful art Thou, O Lord our God, faithful are Thy words, ever faithful, living and enduring are Thy name and remembrance; and do Thou reign[66] continually over us for ever and ever'. This point[67] is one of the disagreements between the scholars of the East and West; the former give the

59) At the conclusion of the reading. (60) This is a unanimous ruling. It is upheld even by the Rabbi who maintained that the scroll must be open when the first benediction is said. (61) The benedictions now in use are shorter (P.B., p. 147). (62) The *hafṭarah* which is read after the conclusion of the prescribed section of the Torah. (63) *Wehaẓẓedeḳ*, the noun being preceded by *he*, the definite article. This is the version adopted by the Sefaradim, while the Ashkenazim omit the article (cf. P.B., p. 149). (64) V reads *medabber*, without the article, as in the current version (P.B., *loc. cit.*). (65) This is not the present usage when the reader proceeds to say the benedictions mentioned in Rule 11. (66) So GRA. V reads 'He will reign', H 'Thou wilt reign'. (67) Whether the benediction is to be said while sitting or standing.

response[68] while sitting and the latter while standing. But wherever two *Tanna'im* or two *'Amora'im* differ, and we are not certain with whom the *halakah* agrees, we follow him who maintains the stricter view. How much more then must we, in regard to the praise[69] of the Life of all the worlds,[70] which is matter of the heart,[71] teach our disciples as the rule to be practised that the *halakah* is in agreement with him who upholds the stricter view;[72] as Scripture states, *The Lord hath made every thing for His own purpose.*[73]

RULE 11. After that[74] the *mafṭir* resumes his recital[75] and says, 'Faithful art Thou, O Lord our God, and faithful are Thy words, and not one of Thy words shall return void, for Thou art a faithful[76] God and King. Blessed art Thou, O Lord, the God Who art faithful in all Thy words'.

RULE 12. 'Comfort,[77] O Lord our God, Zion Thy city, for it is the home of our life, and save her that is grieved in spirit speedily, even in our days. [40*b*] Blessed art Thou, O Lord, Who makest Zion joyful through her children.'

RULE 13. 'Gladden us, O Lord our God,[78] with Elijah the prophet, Thy servant, and with the kingdom of the house of David, Thine anointed. Soon may he come and rejoice our hearts. Suffer not a stranger to sit upon his throne, nor let others any longer inherit his glory; for by Thy holy name Thou didst swear unto him, that his light should not be quenched for ever. In his days Judah shall be saved, and Israel shall dwell safely; and this is his name whereby he shall be

(68) To the reader, with the benediction. (69) The benedictions. (70) [On this designation of God, cf. Marmorstein, *The Old Rabbinic Doctrine of God*, I, p. 85.] (71) V reads *galuī* (revealed), M and H *taluī* (dependent). (72) Following the emended text of GRA. (73) Prov. XVI, 4. There is consequently all the more reason why the stricter view should be followed, viz. that the blessings and praises of God be said while standing. (74) After the people have concluded their benedictions (see the preceding Rule). (75) lit. 'subject'. (76) The current version adds 'and merciful' (P.B., p. 149). (77) This is the continuation of the benedictions after the *hafṭarah*. The version now in use (P.B., *loc. cit.*) reads 'have mercy' instead of 'comfort' (GRA emends accordingly), and 'O Lord our God' and 'Thy city' are omitted. (78) From 'with Elijah' to 'swear unto him' is represented in V by 'etc.' M and H cite the benediction in full.

called: the Lord is our righteousness.[79] Blessed art Thou, O Lord, Who causest the horn of salvation to flourish for Thy people Israel.'[80]

RULE 14. 'For the Torah, [for the divine service],[81] for the prophets and for this holy[82] . . . which Thou, O Lord our God, hast given us for holiness and for rest, for honour and for glory. For all these things, O Lord our God, we thank Thee, and continually bless[83] Thy name, O God of our salvation. Blessed art Thou, O Lord, Who sanctifiest Israel and such and such a day.'[84]

An exception is made on the Sabbath when 'Israel' is not mentioned in the conclusion but only 'Who sanctifiest the Sabbath'; because the Sabbath preceded Israel, as it is written, *For in six days the Lord made heaven and earth, and on the seventh day He ceased from work and rested,*[85] and it is further said, *See that the Lord hath given you the sabbath,*[86] which implies that the Sabbath had already been in existence.

(79) 'In his days . . . righteousness' is a quotation from Jer. XXIII, 6 and is now omitted from the benediction. (80) The present custom (in accordance with Pes. 117b, Sonc. ed., p. 603) is to conclude, 'Blessed art Thou, O Lord, the Shield of David'. (81) M and H insert this phrase which is included in P.B. (82) The 'Sabbath' or the name of the Festival is inserted here; and when a Festival coincides with the Sabbath both are mentioned. (83) The P.B. version reads, 'Thee, blessed be Thy name by the mouth of every living being continually and for ever'. (84) For 'such and such a day' the name of the Festival is inserted. (85) Ex. XXXI, 17. (86) *ibid.* XVI, 29. The Sabbath was instituted at the creation of the world, and the use of the definite article in the second quotation indicates that it was a well-known institution at the time. The Festivals, on the other hand, were ordained after the people of Israel came into existence.

CHAPTER XIV

RULE 1. And why did [the Rabbis] enact all these [benedictions]?[1] In order to establish a correspondence between the seven benedictions [of the *hafṭarah*] and the seven readers.[2] You may also similarly explain the reason for the twenty-two verses read in the [Book of a] Prophet: twenty-two corresponding to the seven readers, each of whom must read [a minimum of] three verses, and one corresponding to the superintendent of the Synagogue services.

RULE 2. All that had been said[3] applies only where the text was neither translated nor expounded; but where it was translated or expounded[4] the *mafṭir* reads three, five or six verses in the Prophet, and this suffices.[5]

RULE 3. In the case of Ruth, the Song of Songs, Ecclesiastes,[6] Lamentations and Esther,[7] it is necessary to say the benediction, 'Concerning the reading of the *Megillah*',[8] although it is included in the Hagiographa.

RULE 4. One who reads in the Hagiographa must say, 'Blessed art Thou, O Lord our God, King of the universe, Who hast sanctified us by Thy commandments and hast given us command to read in the Holy Writings'.

RULE 5. [The Rabbis] enacted that, as regards [the reading of]

(1) For the *hafṭarah* as specified in the previous chapter. (2) The minimum number who must be called to the reading of the Torah every Sabbath. (3) In the preceding Rule concerning the minimum number of verses to be read in the Prophet. (4) So that much of the time of the worshippers was taken up by the translation or exposition. (5) The reading is curtailed for the convenience of the congregation. (6) Inserted by GRA and H. (7) These books are read respectively on Pentecost, Passover, Tabernacles, the Fast of Ab and *Purim*. (8) The full benediction is: 'Blessed art Thou, O Lord our God, King of the universe, Who hast sanctified us by Thy commandments, and hast given us command concerning the reading of the *Megillah*' (P.B., p. 276). The present custom is to say the benediction for the scroll of Esther only. The others are read usually from a printed book without a benediction.

the scroll of Esther, the benediction on the 'season' must be said;[9] and after the conclusion of the reading the reader must say, 'Blessed art Thou, O Lord our God, King of the universe, O God Who dost plead our cause, judge our suit and avenge our wrong, Who redeemest and savest us from the hand of all tyrants. Blessed art Thou, O Lord our God, Helper and Saviour'.[10] The benediction is said[11] on account of the humiliation of the Torah, while others maintain that it is said on account of the humiliation of Israel.[12]

RULE 6. [The Rabbis] further laid down that it is also necessary to offer praise and thanksgiving [in the benediction] for the redemption and release.[13] Then one concludes: 'Blessed art Thou, O Lord, God of vengeance, Who dost requite enemies according to their deeds, art a Shield to the righteous, and savest Thy people from the hands of their adversaries'. After that the righteous are lauded: 'Blessed be Mordecai, blessed be Esther, blessed be all Israel'. Rab, however, declared that it is necessary to say, 'Accursed be Haman and accursed be his sons'. R. Phinehas said: It is necessary to say, 'Harbonah be remembered for good'.[14]

RULE 7. R. Berekiah, quoting R. Jeremiah who had it from R. Ḥiyya, who reported it in the name of R. Joḥanan, said: When R. Jonathan came to the verse, *Whom Nebuchadnezzar . . . had carried away,*[15] he used to exclaim, 'O the wicked Nebuchadnezzar, may his bones be crushed! the good is rewarded[16]

(9) Like the benediction in the preceding note it begins with 'Blessed art Thou . . . universe' and concludes with 'Who hast kept us in life, and hast preserved us, and enabled us to reach this season'. (10) Cf. the version in P.B., p. 276. (11) The reason for the benediction is given to explain why it must begin with 'Blessed art Thou', although it would appear to be a continuation of the benediction for the *Megillah* which includes this beginning. (12) Whose vindication is celebrated. As it is independent of the *Megillah,* it must consequently begin again with the usual formula. For 'Torah', M and H read 'the Divine Presence' affronted by Haman's plot against God's people. (13) From threatened destruction. (14) He contributed to Haman's downfall (cf. Esth. VII, 9). For the version now in use, cf. P.B., p. 277. (15) Esth. II, 6. (16) lit. 'to mix' (drinks), hence 'to serve drinks' and, metaphorically, 'retribution, recompense'.

according to his goodness and the wicked according to his wickedness, as it is stated, *The memory of the righteous shall be for a blessing; but the name of the wicked shall rot*'.[17]

RULE 8. The *maftir* recites also the parts of the *Shema*'.[18] Of what *Shema*' has this been said?[19] Of the one [recited when] the scroll of the Torah [is taken from the ark].[20] How does one begin?[21] *Happy are they that dwell in Thy house.*[22] Then the *maftir* stands and recites, *There is none like unto Thee among the gods, O Lord; and there are no works like Thine.*[23] *Who is like unto Thee, O Lord, among the mighty? Who is like unto Thee, glorious in holiness, fearful in praises, doing wonders?*[24] *Thy kingdom is a kingdom for all ages, and Thy dominion endureth throughout all generations.*[25] *The Lord is King, the Lord hath reigned, the Lord shall reign for ever and ever.*[26] *The Lord was pleased, for His righteousness' sake, to make the teaching great and glorious.*[27] *The Lord will give strength unto His people; the Lord will bless His people with peace.*[28] *Thou art the Lord, even Thou alone; Thou hast made heaven, the heaven of heavens, with all their host, the earth and all things that are therein, the seas and all that is in them and Thou preservest them all; and the host of heaven worshippeth Thee.*[29]

RULE 9. Thereupon[30] the *maftir* steps forward,[31] takes the scroll of the Torah and says, *Hear, O Israel,* chanting the first verse,[32] and the people say it after him in response.

RULE 10. [The *maftir*] then elevates the Torah scroll and says: 'One is our God, great is our Lord, holy and revered is His name for ever and ever'.[33] Then he repeats: 'One is our God, great is our Lord, holy is He. One is our God, great is our Lord, holy and revered is His name'. [This is said three times] correspond-

(17) Prov. X, 7. This verse justifies the execration of Nebuchadnezzar and (in Rule 6) of Haman. (18) This is explained below. The recitation of the *Shema*' is deemed to be a great honour which compensates for the lesser dignity conferred by the reading of the *hafṭarah*. (19) The *Shema*' is recited several times during the service. (20) Cf. the next Rule. (21) The collection of Biblical verses recited when the Torah scroll is taken from the ark. (22) Ps. LXXXIV, 5. (23) *ibid.* LXXXVI, 8. (24) Ex. XV, 11. (25) Ps. CXLV, 13. (26) Compounded from Ps. X, 16, XCIII, 1 (E.V. *reigneth*) and Ex. XV, 18. (27) Isa. XLII, 21. (28) Ps. XXIX, 11. (29) Neh. IX, 6. (30) lit. 'immediately'. (31) lit. 'enters'. (32) i.e. the whole of Deut. VI, 4. (33) This is the reading of GRA. V, M and H omit the sentence.

ing in number[34] to the three patriarchs; others hold that it corresponds to the three *kedushshoth*.[35]

RULE 11.[36] '*Thy righteousness also, O God, reacheth unto high heaven; Thou Who hast done great things, O God, who is like unto Thee?*[37] *O Lord, Thy name endureth for ever; Thy memorial, O Lord, throughout all generations.*[38] Let all ascribe strength to God and give honour to the Torah. *O magnify the Lord with me, and let us exalt His name together.*'[39] The Torah scroll must be elevated at *Hear, O Israel,* at the threefold declaration of the unity of God, and at *O magnify the Lord with me.*[40]

RULE 12. One must also say:[41] 'Magnified and hallowed,[42] praised and glorified, exalted and extolled, uplifted, honoured and adored[43] above all be the name of the supreme King of kings, the Holy One, blessed be He, in the worlds which He hath created, this world and the world to come, in accordance with His desire and the desire of all His people, the house of Israel. May His kingdom be revealed and made visible unto us speedily and at a near time; and may He build His house in our days, and be gracious unto our remnant and unto the remnant of His people Israel in His mercy and in the abundance of His lovingkindness, in peace and grace, kindness and compassion. May the Omnipresent do all this for us for the sake of His great name; and say ye, Amen'.[44]

RULE 13. After that he elevates the Torah scroll and says: 'One is our God, great is our Lord, holy and revered is His name for ever and ever'. Then he begins to chant, 'The Lord is God, the Lord is His name'. The congregation says it after him in response; then he repeats it twice and the congregation responds twice.[45]

(34) The three repetitions of 'one is our God', etc. (35) lit. 'sanctifications', i.e. 'Holy, holy, holy' with suitable introductions said three times in the morning service (cf. P.B., pp. 39, 45 and 73). (36) This is a continuation of the verses begun in Rule 8. (37) Ps. LXXI, 19. (38) *ibid.* CXXXV, 13. (39) *ibid* XXXIV, 4. (40) For the modern ritual, cf. P.B., p. 145. (41) In concluding the verses and prayers cited in the preceding Rules. (42) This word is included by GRA and H. (43) V adds in parenthesis 'honoured and revered' (so also M). (44) Cf. the version in P.B., pp. 145f. (45) This Rule is enclosed in round brackets in V. It appears to be a duplicate of Rule 10, but both M and H include it.

RULE 14. The scroll of the Torah is immediately unrolled a space of three columns and is elevated so as to show the face of the script to the people standing on the right and on the left. Then it is turned round towards the front and towards the rear; for it is a precept for all men and women to see the script,[46] to bend their knees and exclaim, '*And this is the Torah which Moses set before the children of Israel.*[47] *The Torah of the Lord is perfect, restoring the soul*'.[48] The *mafṭir* then hands it over to the superintendent of the Synagogue services who returns it to the first[49] of those who are to be called to the reading, because it is not an honour for the Torah to be left alone.[50] Similarly it is not proper for the precentor to stand alone before the reading-desk; so [two persons] should stand with him, one on his right and the other on his left, [the number] corresponding to that of the patriarchs.[51] The pure-minded men of Jerusalem acted in this manner: When the Torah scroll was taken out of the ark and when it was returned they followed it as a mark of respect.

RULE 15. A minor[52] may read in the Torah and translate it, but he may not read the parts of the *Shema'*[53] by reciting 'Who formest light';[54] nor may he stand before the reading-desk,[55] nor lift up his hands.[56] A *poḥeaḥ*, that is one whose knees are exposed or whose clothes are torn, or one whose head is

(46) Before it is read. The ritual here described is followed by the Sefaradim. The Ashkenazim elevate the scroll after the conclusion of the reading (cf. P.B., p. 148). (47) Deut. IV, 44. For other verses which are now added, cf. P.B., *loc. cit.* (48) Ps. XIX, 8. This verse is not included now. (49) lit. 'the head' (so GRA). V has 'to cover the heads', which is obscure. (50) lit. 'single'. It is therefore necessary for the *mafṭir*, the superintendent and one of the congregation who is to read a portion to accompany the scroll. (51) V inserts in parenthesis a ruling which seems displaced although it is included by GRA, M and H. It reads: 'Some say that [the *mafṭir*] recites the *Shema'* with the benediction "Who formest light" (P.B., p. 128) and "Holy" (p. 131) because of the benediction which he says "For the Torah, for the divine service", etc. (pp. 149f)'. (52) The age is defined in Rule 17. (53) Cf. X, 7, p. 258 nn. 24ff. (54) The first of the benedictions before the *Shema'* (cf. P.B., pp. 37f). (55) lit. 'pass before', etc., to act as reader of the prayers for the congregation. (56) To pronounce the priestly benediction if he is a *Kohen* (cf. P.B., p. 238a).

uncovered, may read the parts of the *Shema*'. Others say that if a person's knees [are exposed] or his clothes torn he may read the parts of the *Shema*', but one may not do so when his head is uncovered, since it is not permitted to utter the divine names [with uncovered head]. In either case he may translate, but not read in the Torah, nor stand before the reading-desk, nor lift up his hands.

RULE 16. A blind man may read the parts of the *Shema*' and translate. R. Judah said: One who has never seen the light may not read the parts of the *Shema*'.[57]

RULE 17. The minor of whom the Rabbis spoke[58] is one who is under twelve years of age. A person who is above that age may read the parts of the *Shema*', but may not stand before the reading-desk nor lift up his hands[59] until he is twenty years of age and bearded. If he has no beard, although he is twenty years of age, he is forbidden to do so because[60] he looks like an eunuch. Others say that even an actual eunuch is permitted [to perform these acts]. If, however, a person has grown a beard even from the age of eighteen, he may stand before the reading-desk and lift up his hands.

RULE 18. As regards the scroll of Esther, all are qualified to read it except a deaf person, an imbecile and a minor. R. Judah declared a minor to be qualified. R. Levi said: The scroll of Esther must be read [on *Purim*] at night and repeated in the day-time, as it is stated, *So that my glory may sing praise to Thee*—i.e. by night, *and not be silent*[61]—i.e. by day. (Therefore it is customary to read it at the termination of the Sabbath of two [successive weeks].)[62] [41*a*] When R. Meir once passed by a Synagogue he heard the reading of[63] a section [of the scroll of Esther].[64] 'How long,' he said to them, 'will you be cutting up the Torah[65] into

(57) Since it contains thanksgivings for the creation and enjoyment of light. (58) In Rule 15. (59) So GRA. V, M and H read: 'and he who stands before the reading-desk and he who lifts up his hands'. (60) So GRA. V, M and H read 'although' for 'he is . . . because'. (61) Ps. XXX, 13. (62) It is later explained that there was an ancient practice for the congregation to read the Book of Esther on the two Saturday evenings before *Purim*. (63) lit. 'the voices'. (64) On a Saturday night. (65) Which, in its wider sense, includes the Book of Esther.

sections?'[66] ['We do it'], they replied, 'on account of *my glory may sing praise unto Thee*', and he allowed them [to continue the practice]. People have adopted the practice of reading it on two[67] Saturday nights of *Adar* until fifteen days of the month have elapsed. In what manner is it read? At [the termination of] the first Sabbath of *Adar* the people read together up to *In that night,*[68] and on the next Saturday night they read from *In that night* up to *and speaking peace to all his seed.*[69]

In the case of the Song of Songs, it is read on the last [two] nights of the [Passover] Festival,[70] half of it on the first night and the other half on the second night.

Ruth [is read] on the termination of the first day of Pentecost to [the end of] its [first] half, and concluded on the termination of the last day of the Festival. Others hold that with all the Festivals, we begin to read [the respective scrolls] on the Saturday night preceding them. People have also adopted the following procedure, viz. that no ruling is authoritatively laid down unless a custom[71] had been definitely established.[72] As regards the saying of the Rabbis that 'a custom cancels a ruling',[73] it applies to a custom of the pious men of old; but a custom which has no support from the Torah is only like an error of judgment.[74]

RULE 19. As we read [the weekly portion] from the Torah and the *haftarah* from the Prophet in daytime, so it is obligatory to read the scroll of Esther in daytime;[75] as it is stated, *In the day that the enemies of the Jews hoped,*[76] on which it was taught in the Mishnah:[77] The whole of the day is a proper time for the reading of the scroll of Esther.

(66) lit. 'making the Torah callings up, callings up'. (67) Inserted by GRA. (68) Esth. VI, 1; half the book. (69) To the end of the book. (70) So one MS. quoted by M. V and others add 'of the exile', which cannot be justified since only the last day of Passover is a 'Festival of the exile'. (71) On which it is based. (72) So GRA. V, M and H read: 'unless it is a custom'. (73) [Cf. j.B.M. VII, 1, 11b.] (74) lit. 'weighing of an opinion'. (75) This is a repetition of R. Levi's teaching quoted in the preceding paragraph, except that it is more specific. The word *welishnothah* (translated 'repeated') might be mistranslated as 'the study of the Mishnah' on the *Megillah*. The wording here precludes such a rendering. (76) Esth. IX, 1. (77) Meg. II, 5 (Sonc. ed., p. 124).

RULE 20. There is no difference between scrolls [of Scripture] and *tefillin* and *mezuzoth* save that the scrolls,[78] etc. If a *tefillah* had worn out, no *mezuzah* may be made of it;[79] but if a *mezuzah* had worn out it may be made into *tefillin*,[80] because in sacred matters ascent to a higher degree of sanctity is allowed but not descent to a lesser degree.

(78) The subject is continued in XV, 1. (79) A *mezuzah* is deemed to be of a lesser degree of sanctity. (80) If the margins are still in a good condition and fit for the purpose.

CHAPTER XV

RULE 1. There is no difference between scrolls [of Scripture] and *tefillin* and *mezuzoth* save that the scrolls may be written in any language,[1] whereas *tefillin* and *mezuzoth* may only be written in the Assyrian script.[2] Rabban Simeon b. Gamaliel said: Even scrolls [of Scripture] were permitted by the Rabbis to be written only in Greek.[3]

RULE 2. Although Rabban Simeon b. Gamaliel[4] said, 'Even scrolls [of Scripture] were permitted by the Rabbis to be written only in Greek', the Sages did not agree with him. For Rabbi related:[5] It once happened that Rabban Simeon b. Gamaliel was standing at the side of a building [in course of construction] on the Temple Mount, when a Targum of the book of Job was brought before him. He ordered the builder, 'Bury it under the course of stones'. But the Sages also maintained their ruling, because we have learned in the Mishnah:[6] All holy writings[7] may be saved from a fire[8] irrespective of whether they are used in public reading[9] or not;[10] and although they are written in any language, they must be stored away.[11]

(1) For use in the Synagogue. Two such official translations are known: one in Aramaic, the Targum Onḳelos, and another in Greek made by Aquila under Rabbinic supervision. (2) The Hebrew square characters are described as 'Assyrian' because they came into common use for religious writings after the return from the Babylonian exile (cf. Sanh. 21b, 22a, Sonc. ed., pp. 119ff and notes). (3) [For the reason, cf. Meg. 9b (Sonc. ed., p. 50).] (4) An eminent authority. (5) Quoted in V, 15 (p. 236). The following statements in the name of Rabban Simeon b. Gamaliel and the Sages respectively prove that both maintained their views. (6) Shab. XVI, 1 (Sonc. ed., p. 563). (7) The Pentateuch, Prophets and Hagiographa. (8) On the Sabbath by being removed from one domain to another, although this is not permitted with ordinary objects. (9) Such as the Prophets from which the *hafṭarah* is selected. (10) viz. the Hagiographa. (11) When they are worn out and no longer fit for use. Sacred writings must never be destroyed.

And why do we not read [some of these scrolls]? On account of [possible] neglect of the House of Study.[12]

The sheath of a scroll may be saved[13] together with the scroll, and the *tefillin* bag together with the *tefillin*, although they contain money.[14] To what place may one rescue them? To a closed alley.[15] Ben Bathyra said: Even into an open alley.

RULE 3. Although the Sages have said that [some of] the Holy Writings may only be read from [the Sabbath] afternoon service onwards,[16] yet they may be studied and expounded. If it is necesssary [to refer to] a word,[17] one may take a scroll and examine it. As regards secular documents, however, although they have ruled lines,[18] it is forbidden to read them [on the Sabbath].

RULE 4. Benedictions,[19] in which many passages of the Torah were quoted,[20] must not be saved from a fire [on the Sabbath].[21] Hence it was declared: They who write down benedictions are like those who burn the Torah.[22]

It was related of a man who wrote benedictions that R. Ishmael went to examine him. As soon as he heard the sound of R. Ishmael's steps, he seized a bundle of written sheets[23] and threw it into a bowl of water. In the following words [did R. Ishmael] address him, 'The punishment for the latter act[24] is greater than for the former'.[25]

(12) On the Sabbath when lectures are delivered in the Houses of Study. By engaging in the reading of the books mentioned the public would neglect the lectures. (13) From a fire on the Sabbath. (14) Which otherwise would not be permitted to be moved. (15) Where movement on the Sabbath is less restricted than in the public domain. (16) When there are no public lectures in the Houses of Study (cf. Shab. 116b, Sonc. ed., p. 572). (17) In Shab. *loc. cit.* the reading is 'a verse'. (18) Like sacred scrolls, and one is less likely to forget the Sabbath and insert notes or corrections. (19) Such as those of the '*Amidah* (P.B., pp. 44-53) and the like. (20) lit. 'written'. (21) They do not possess the same degree of sanctity as the scrolls of Scripture. (22) Since these could not be saved if a fire broke out on the Sabbath. (23) Containing benedictions and selections from the Torah. (24) Destruction of the sheets containing sacred texts by water. (25) Writing benedictions which included passages from Scripture.

RULE 5. Why did he[26] so address him? On account of the passages from the Torah which were quoted in them.[27]

For[28] R. Simeon b. Yoḥai taught: He who occupies himself with [only the study of] Scripture indulges in an indifferent practice;[29] with Mishnah it is a practice for which a reward is conferred; as for one who occupies himself with *Shas*,[30] there is no worthier practice, provided he had first studied Scripture and Mishnah.[31]

RULE 6. Always run to the Mishnah more than to the *Shas*. R. Jose b. Abin said: [The preceding Rule only applies to the time] before Rabbi had edited[32] the *Mishnayoth*, but now that Rabbi has edited the *Mishnayoth* run to the Mishnah more than to the *Shas*.[33]

RULE 7. [The Sages], however, said: Scripture has been compared to water, the Mishnah to wine, and the *Shas* to spiced-wine. The world cannot exist without water, it cannot exist without wine, and it cannot exist without spiced-wine; but a rich man enjoys all three of them. So, too, it is impossible for the world to exist without Scripture and without Mishnah, but it can never exist without the *Shas*.[34]

RULE 8. The Torah[35] has also been compared to salt, the Mishnah to pepper, and the *Shas* to spices. The world cannot exist

(26) viz. R. Ishmael. So N.Y.; V reads 'they'. (27) i.e. the benedictions; and could not, therefore, be saved from a fire on the Sabbath. (28) The following reason has no connection with the beginning of Rule 5. It refers back to Rule 2 above which lays down that one must not read certain books of the Scripture during the hours when lectures are delivered in the Houses of Study (N.Y.). (29) lit. 'a measure and no measure'. (30) The Heb. letters *shin samek*, pronounced *Shas*, stand for ששה סדרים 'the six orders' of the Mishnah or of the combined Mishnah and Gemara. Here it evidently refers to the Gemara only. The corresponding passage in B.M. 33a (Sonc. ed., p. 206) reads 'Gemara'. It has been suggested that the proper reading is 'Talmud' (cf. B.M. *loc. cit.*, n. 6). (31) It is accordingly proved that the study of Mishnah and Gemara, which necessarily includes the Scriptures, is of far higher importance than of Scripture only. (32) lit. 'sunk', an unusual verb in such a connection. [Instead of שקע, H mentions a MS. variant קבע (fixed).] (33) So N.Y. as required by the context. V, M and H read: 'run to the *Shas* more than to the Mishnah.' (34) Which includes all. (35) The term here embraces the whole of the Scriptures.

without salt, without pepper and without spices; but the rich man enjoys all three. So, too, it is impossible for the world to exist without Scripture, without Mishnah and without the *Shas*.

RULE 9. Happy is the man whose labour is in [the study of] the *Shas*. Not that he should skip Scripture and the Mishnah and come [direct] to the *Shas*; but he should learn Scripture and Mishnah with the object of coming to the *Shas*. Of such a person it is stated, *The rich man's wealth is his strong city, and as a high wall in his own conceit.*[36]

RULE 10. Abba Gurion of Ẓadian[37] said in the name of Abba Guria:[38] A man should not teach his son to be an ass-driver,[39] sailor, waggoner, shepherd[40] or shop-keeper,[41] because their occupations are robbery.[42] R. Judah,[43] however, quoting him,[44] said: Ass-drivers are mostly wicked, but sailors are mostly pious.[45] The best of physicians are [destined] for Gehinnom[46] and the most worthy of butchers is Amalek's partner.[47] Bastards are mostly keen-witted,[48] slaves are mostly arrogant,[49] the children of reputed parents are mostly bashful, and children usually resemble the mother's brother.

R. Simeon b. Yoḥai taught: Kill the best of the heathens in

(36) Prov. XVIII, 11. (37) i.e. Bethsaida in Galilee. (38) So GRA in agreement with Ḳid. 82a (Sonc. ed., p. 423). V reads 'said' after the first 'Gurion' and a second 'Gurion' for 'Guria'. (39) These, when sent on a long journey, hire themselves to others and so make a profit by using the time which belongs to the original employer. (40) He feeds his flock in other persons' fields. (41) He gives false measure or sells adulterated goods. (42) The descriptions are no doubt a reflection of the standards of the time. (43) Differing from Abba Gurion. (44) Abba Guria. (45) The perils of the sea turn their thoughts to God. (46) Because they may be guilty of causing loss of life through neglect or over-confidence; or, by trusting too much in their own skill, they deny the power of God [with this passage, cf. ARN XXXVI, 5, and notes]. (47) In his desire to avoid financial loss, he sells unwholesome meat and thereby spreads disease. 'Amalek' is the type of Israel's enemies. (48) They are like their cunning fathers who enticed their mothers. (49) Reading גאים with GRA. V, M and H have נאים, 'beautiful', an improbable reading.

time of war;[50] crush the brain of the best of serpents. The most worthy of women indulges in witchcraft. Happy is he who does the will of the Omnipresent.[51] [*41b*]

(50) [For the various forms of this saying, cf. Bacher, *Ag. d. Tannaiten*, II, p. 86, n. 3. The qualifying phrase 'in the time of war' he regards as a later addition to soften the harshness of the utterance. It was called forth in a time of bitter oppression and is not to be taken as typical of Jewish ethics. On the subject, cf. J. S. Bloch, *Israel and the Nations*, pp. 204ff.] (51) Because he is delivered from all worldly temptations.

CHAPTER XVI

RULE 1. R. Nehorai said: I abandon all professions in the world and teach my son only Torah,[1] because a man enjoys part of its reward in this world while the principal remains intact for the world to come. The other professions, however, are not so. For should a person come to sickness, old age or suffering and is unable to carry on his work, he would die of starvation; whereas with the Torah it is not so, but it protects him from all evil in his youth and gives him a future and hope in his old age. What does it say in Scripture of his youth? *But they that wait for the Lord shall renew their strength.*[2] And what does it say of his old age? *They shall still bring forth fruit in old age.*[3]

RULE 2. R. Joshua b. Levi said: With regard to the *'aggadta,*[4] he who writes it down has no share in the world to come,[5] he who expounds it[6] is cursed,[7] while he who listens to it receives no reward.

R. Ḥinnena b. Papa taught:[8] *The Lord spoke with you face to face*[9]—*face* implies two,[10] *to face* also implies two, thus providing four expressions of 'face' [alluding to] Scripture,[11] Mishnah, *halakoth* and *'aggadoth;*[12] an awestruck face for Scripture, a neutral face for Mishnah, a friendly[13] face for *Shas*[14] and a smiling[15] face for *'aggadta.*

(1) Inserted by GRA in agreement with Ḳid. 82a (Sonc. ed., p. 423). (2) Isa. XL, 31. (3) Ps. XCII, 15. In Ḳid. *loc. cit.* the Mishnah adds: 'And thus it is said of our father Abraham, *And Abraham was old . . . and the Lord blessed Abraham in all things* (Gen. XXIV, 1)'. (4) So M and H. V has "*aggadta* written in it'. (5) *'Aggadta* must only be taught and learned orally. (6) From a written text; similarly with 'he who listens to it'. (7) lit. 'blessed', a euphemism. (8) So GRA and M. V reads, 'but did not . . . teach?', but there is no answer in the text. (9) Deut. V, 4. (10) The Heb. *panim* (face) is a singular noun with a plural form and is homiletically treated as denoting not less than two. (11) This and the following three words are inserted by GRA and omitted by V. (12) This refers to *'aggadoth* which have not been committed to writing. (13) So GRA, lit. 'a making clear'; V reads 'smiling'. (14) Here it stands for *halakah* which is its main contents. (15) So GRA; V 'friendly'.

RULE 3. R. Nehemiah, in the name of R. Jacob b. Jannai, remarked on the text, *As in water face answereth to face:*[16] It is customary to have a master who desires to teach and a student who does not want to learn, or a student who desires to learn and a master who does not want to teach him; but in this case[17] the Master desires to teach and the student to learn.[18]

RULE 4. R. Isaac Nappaḥa began his discourse as follows: *Stay me with dainties*[19] refers to the well-founded[20] *halakoth; refresh me with apples* refers to the *'aggadoth*[21] whose fragrance is pleasant like that of apples. *For I am love-sick*—R. Isaac said: In the past when money was plentiful[22] one longed to hear a word of the *halakah*,[23] but now that money is scarce[24] one longs to hear[25] a word of *'aggadah*.[26]

RULE 5. R. Tanḥum b. Ḥanilai said: If the Torah had been given as a clear-cut code,[27] no judge would have a *locus standi*[28] in laying down a ruling;[29] but now a judge has a *locus standi*,[30] for if he declares a thing to be clean there are [authorities] who declare a thing in a similar condition to be unclean, and if he decides that it is unclean there are [authorities] who declare a thing in a similar condition to be clean.[31]

RULE 6. R. Jannai said: The Torah which the Holy One, blessed be He, gave to Moses was delivered to him in forty-nine aspects of uncleanness and forty-nine aspects of cleanness,[32] as it is

(16) Prov. XXVII, 19. (17) viz. of God and Moses. (18) V adds in parenthesis 'Scripture and Mishnah, Gemara and *'aggadah*'. The words are included in M and H. (19) Cant. II, 5, Heb. באשישות. (20) מאושות, meaning 'strong, firm'. (21) Inserted by GRA; not in V. H reads: 'these are the words of Torah'. (22) And people enjoyed leisure and an easy existence. (23) Which requires time for concentration of thought and serious application of the mind. (24) And there is a hard struggle to earn a livelihood. (25) So GRA. V omits 'but now . . . hear'. [The reading of H is: 'but now that money is scarce, and especially when we are oppressed by (lit. sick from) the government, one longs to hear a word from Scripture and a word of *'aggadah*'.] (26) Which is easy, consoling and entertaining. (27) lit. 'cut'. (28) lit. 'standing of feet', reading with M and H עמידת for עומדות. (29) Since he could not use his discretion and reasoning power. (30) The clause 'but . . . *standi*' is inserted by GRA. It is lacking in V, M and H. (31) He can always find authority in support of his view. (32) i.e. of prohibition and permissibility respectively.

stated, *And his banner*[33] (*wediglo*), the numerical value of its letters being forty-nine.

RULE 7. R. Abahu said in the name of R. Joḥanan: R. 'Aḳiba had a distinguished[34] disciple who knew how to interpret the Torah in forty-nine aspects of uncleanness and forty-nine aspects of cleanness, not one reason being the same as another.[35] Consequently[36] if those who rule a thing to be unclean are in the majority it is unclean, and if those who rule a thing to be clean are in the majority it is clean.[37] Whence [did he learn] all these? [From his extensive studies], because he was learned in the Scriptures, expert in the Mishnah, distinguished in Talmud and brilliant[38] in *'aggadah.*

RULE 8. It was related of R. Joḥanan b. Zakkai that he did not neglect the study of a single passage of the Torah.[39] He also studied [all] Scripture,[40] Targum, Mishnah, *halakoth* and *'aggadoth.*[41] He learned everything. It was also related of him that he declared, 'If all the heavens were sheets, all the trees quills and all the seas ink, they would not suffice for recording my wisdom which I acquired from my masters; and yet I have gained[42] no more of the wisdom of the Sages than a fly [acquires] which dips in the great sea and deprives it of the tiniest drop'.[43]

RULE 9. From whom did he[44] receive the Torah? From Hillel and Shammai. It was said of Hillel that he had not omitted to study any of the words of the Sages, even all languages, even the speech of mountains, hills and valleys, the speech of trees and herbs, the speech of wild beasts and cattle, the speech of

(33) Cant. II, 4, the continuation of the verse being *over me is love*. The verse is interpreted of the Torah, which is God's *banner*, entrusted to Israel as a mark of His love. Each Heb. letter denotes a number. (34) Or, 'religiously scrupulous and meek' (Rashi). (35) Cf. the note of GRA. (36) Since, according to R. 'Aḳiba's disciple and R. Tanḥum (in Rule 8), the interpretations are as many on one side as on the other. (37) Because, in addition to their majority, they also have as many ancient authorities on whom to rely as their opponents. (38) lit. 'bright, intelligent, a reasoner'. (39) i.e. the Pentateuch. (40) Including the Prophets and the Hagiographa. (41) M has 'proverbs about foxes'; V and H insert 'and proverbs'. (42) lit. 'set apart'. (43) [Cf. ARN XXV, 3, p. 126.] (44) Rabban Joḥanan b. Zakkai. Cf. for the eulogy, Suk. 28a (Sonc. ed., p. 123).

demons[45] and parables. Why [did he study] all these? Because it is stated, *The Lord was pleased, for His righteousness' sake, to make the teaching great and glorious.*[46]

RULE 10. R. Joshua b. Levi said: I have never looked into a book of *'aggadta* except once when I looked and found written therein that the one hundred and seventy-five sections of the Torah,[47] in which occurs any expression of speaking, saying or commanding, correspond to the number of years of our father Abraham;[48] for it is written, *Thou hast ascended on high, Thou hast led captivity captive; Thou hast received gifts*[49] *for the sake of the man,*[50] and it is also written, *The greatest man*[51] *among the Anakim.*[52] On this account the Rabbis instituted one hundred and seventy-five orders in the Torah [to be read in public worship] every Sabbath[53] [as regularly as the] continual burnt-offering.[54]

RULE 11. The hundred and forty-seven psalms[55] included in the Book of Psalms correspond to the number of years of Jacob.[56] This is intended to teach you that all the praises which Israel offer to the Holy One, blessed be He, correspond to the number of years of our father Jacob. What is the reason?[57] [Scripture states,] *Yet Thou art holy, O Thou that art enthroned upon the praises of Israel.*[58]

RULE 12. The hundred and twenty-three times that Israel respond with *Halleluyah*[59] correspond to the number of years

(45) [For *shedim* (demons), H quotes a MS. variant שירים (songs).] (46) Isa. XLII, 21. (47) i.e. the Pentateuch. (48) Abraham lived 175 years (Gen. XXV, 7). (49) Explained as the Torah given to Moses as a gift from God. (50) viz. Abraham. Ps. LXVIII, 19, E.V. *among men.* (51) Also explained of Abraham. (52) Josh. XIV, 15. (53) Completing the entire Pentateuch in 175 weeks, or three and a half years: fifty orders or sections in one year. This was the Jerusalem practice. In Babylon and at the present time the Pentateuch is completed every year. (54) Cf. Num. XXVIII, 10. (55) The number of Psalms in the Heb. Bible is 150; but, according to Rabbinic opinion, I and II, IX and X, CXXXIV and CXXXV are each reckoned as one Psalm. (56) Cf. Gen. XLVII, 28. (57) GRA inserts the question. (58) Ps. XXII, 4. Israel is synonymous with Jacob. (59) Not all these are to be found in M.T. or Psalms, but many such and other responses and refrains were frequently made orally. Cf. my articles on 'Antiphony in Ancient Heb. Poetry' (*Jewish Quarterly Review*, New Series, XXVI, pp. 199-219), 'The Text and Ancient form of Recital', etc. (*Journal of Biblical Literature*, LI, pp. 214-226), 'Long and Shorter Versions of Ancient Heb. Poems' (*American Journal of Semitic Languages and Literatures*, XLIX, pp. 15-31).

of Aaron.[60] What is the reason?[61] [Scripture states,] *Halleluyah, praise God beḳodsho,*[62] which [is interpreted as] 'with His holy man', i.e. Aaron, the holy man of God.

Nevertheless[63] I was afraid at night.[64]

[65]A minor who is not allowed to read portions of the *Shema'*[66] must not say 'Holy'[67] in the benediction *Yoẓer* privately;[68] but with a congregation he may respond together with the others. An adult, however, who reads portions of the *Shema'* may say 'Holy' because it is in the order [of the Biblical text];[69] but as for the 'Holy' of the '*Amidah,*[70] since he would have to say 'We will reverence and sanctify Thee',[71] it is not proper for him to say it if less than ten adults are present. A minor, furthermore, may not be counted in the quorum of ten[72] for *Bareku,*[73] the reading of the Torah and *ḳaddish* until he is thirteen years of age; but no examination[74] is carried out in such cases.[75].

(60) Cf. Num. XXXIII, 39. (61) The question is inserted by GRA. (62) Ps. CL, 1, E.V. *in His sanctuary*. (63) Although R. Joshua b. Levi only once looked into a written book of *'aggadta*. This remark refers back to Rule 10. (64) The lapse continued to worry him. (65) In V and M this is preceded by a parenthesis which virtually is a repetition of part of Rule 7, 'R. 'Aḳiba had a distinguished disciple', etc. (66) Cf. XIV, 15, p. 280. (67) Cf. P.B., p. 39. (68) *Yoẓer* (Who formed) designates the first benediction before the *Shema'*, beginning 'Blessed' (P.B., p. 37) and ending with 'Creator of the luminaries' (p. 39). The first *ḳedushshah* of the morning service is included in it. (69) He may therefore read it, not as a part of the divine service but as a passage of Scripture. (70) P.B., p. 45. (71) Which is a part of the congregational service (P.B., p. 160). This form, now used in the *ḳedushshah* for the Sabbath *musaf,* was used formerly, and in certain congregations to-day, on week-days. (72) Being the minimum number of adult males required for a congregational service. (73) 'Bless ye', etc. (P.B., p. 37). (74) As to whether the boy has also grown two pubic hairs. (75) The age of 13 is sufficient to establish puberty. 'No examination . . . cases' (GRA) corrects *nidbaḳin* (cleaved) in V to *nibdaḳin*.

CHAPTER XVII

RULE 1. *The words of the wise are as goads . . . they are given from one shepherd;*[1] and one Shepherd[2] has uttered them. Therefore they must be saved from a fire.[3] A book of the *'aggadta,* although not allowed to be written, must nevertheless be saved from a fire. What is the reason? *It is a time to work for the Lord; they have made void Thy law.*[4]

RULE 2. [The sequence of the Sabbath readings] is interrupted[5] for New Moons, *Ḥanukkah, Purim,* fasts, *ma'amadoth* and the Day of Atonement.[6]

RULE 3. In what manner are the interruptions made if the New Moon or the days of *Ḥanukkah* fall on a Sabbath? [In the former case] seven persons read the regular Sabbath section while the eighth reads that of the New Moon, viz. the two portions[7] *And on the sabbath day*[8] and *And in your new moons;*[9] and if the first day of *Ḥanukkah*[10] falls on a Sabbath, seven read [the section] of the Sabbath while the eighth reads, *And it came to pass on the day that Moses had made an end*[11] up to *so he made the candlestick.*[12]

RULE 4. [42*a*] What[13] is the procedure on *Purim?* If *Purim* falls on a Sabbath, seven read [the section] of the Sabbath while the eighth reads *Then came Amalek.*[14] The three fast days[15] are not observed on consecutive days but are separated [and observed]

(1) Eccles. XII, 11. (2) [i.e. God; cf. ARN XVIII, 3, p. 105.] (3) Even on the Sabbath. (4) Ps. CXIX, 126, E.V. *for the Lord to work.* This implies that when the welfare of the people or the preservation of the Faith requires it, a law may be temporarily suspended. (5) To make room for the special reading for the particular occasion which replaces it, or is added to it, as explained below. (6) In the afternoon service, even when it falls on a Sabbath. (7) So GRA. V and M read 'breaks'. (8) i.e. the passage Num. XXVIII, 9f which begins with these words. (9) The passage *ibid.* 11-15. (10) Or any of the other days. Unlike our present custom, they read the same portion on the Sabbath irrespective of which day of *Ḥanukkah* it was. (11) Num. VII, 1. (12) *ibid.* VIII, 5. (13) From here to *Then came Amalek* is the reading of GRA. (14) Ex. XVII, 8-16. (15) In commemoration of the three days of fasting ordained by Mordecai and Esther (Esth. IV, 16).

on Monday, Thursday and Monday. Our Rabbis in the land of Israel had the custom of fasting after *Purim*[16] on account of [the victory over] Nicanor and his associates,[17] and also because the commemoration of sad events is postponed rather than antedated.

RULE 5. [What was the procedure in the case of] *ma'amadoth?* As it was taught:[18] The men of the *ma'amadoth* used to fast [as follows]: On every Monday for the sake of those who sail on the sea, as it is written, *And God said: Let there be a firmament in the midst of the waters;*[19] on Tuesdays for the sake of wayfarers, as it is written, *And God said: Let the waters under the heaven be gathered together;*[20] on Wednesdays for the sake of children that they should not be attacked by croup, as it is written, *And God said: Let there be lights,*[21] the written form being defective;[22] on Thursdays they fasted for the sake of pregnant women and nursing mothers that they should not lose their children, as it is said, *And God said: Let the waters swarm with swarms.*[23] On the Sabbath eve and at the conclusion of the Sabbath[24] they did not fast from respect for the Sabbath. Some declare[25] that at the twilight of the Sabbath eve an additional soul is given to every Israelite, and after the Sabbath it is taken from him.[26] Another reason[27] is that Christians[28] should not say, 'Because we rejoice on the Sunday they fast on it'. The Sages, however, said: In the period of the *ma'amadoth* they were not concerned with the hatred of

(16) Not, as others, before it. (17) This occurred on the thirteenth of Adar, the day before *Purim* [cf. 1 Macc. VII, 49; 2 Macc. XV, 36; Josephus, Antiq. XII, x, 5], on account of which fasting was prohibited. Nicanor was a Syrian commander who fell in the Maccabean war in the battle of Adasa in 161 B.C.E. (18) [Cf. Ta'an. 27b (Sonc. ed., p. 145).] (19) Gen. I, 6. The mention of *water* is a call to prayer on behalf of those who sail over the sea. (20) *ibid.* 9, which is followed by *And let the dry land appear.* (21) *ibid.* 14, children being to the home what the heavenly luminaries are to the world. (22) A *waw* is missing in the noun מארת (lights). (23) *ibid.* 20, followed by *living creatures* (*ibid.*). (24) i.e. Sunday, as explicitly mentioned in Ta'an. 26a (Sonc. ed., pp. 136f). (25) As a reason why they did not fast on Sundays. (26) The body is then weakened, and fasting is held to be too great a hardship. (27) Why there was no fasting on Sunday. (28) So M and H. V has 'worshippers of stars', an alteration made because of the censor.

the Christians, but the reason is that it is written *He ceased from work wayyinnafash,*[29] [which is homiletically interpreted] *wai 'al nefesh,* 'Woe for [the loss of the additional] soul'.

RULE 6. On Passover we read from the section of the Festivals in Leviticus;[30] on Pentecost *Seven weeks;*[31] on New Year *In the seventh month on the first day of the month;*[32] on the Day of Atonement *After the death.*[33] On the first day of Tabernacles we read from the section of the Festivals in Leviticus,[34] and on the other days of Tabernacles the section of the offerings of the Festival.[35]

RULE 7. On *Ḥanukkah* we read the section of [the dedication of the altar by] the princes;[36] on *Purim, Then came Amalek;*[37] on the New Moon, *And in your new moons;*[38] at the *ma'amadoth* the account of the creation.[39] On the fast days of the Ninth of *Ab* and the last seven days in connection with droughts,[40] we read the section of the blessings and curses;[41] but on other fast days *And Moses besought,*[42] and we read as the *hafṭarah Seek ye the Lord.*[43] Some say that no *hafṭarah* is to be read, but the people have adopted the custom of reading the *hafṭarah.*[44] There must be no break in the section of curses because it is not proper to end with curses and to begin with curses.[45]

RULE 8. On Mondays and Thursdays and at the Sabbath afternoon service the regular portion of the week is read, and this is not reckoned as a part of the reading [for the succeeding Sabbath].[46] [The reason[47] is] because it is stated, *And Moses declared unto the children of Israel the appointed seasons of the Lord,*[48] which implies that it is an ordinance that each [appointed section]

(29) Ex. XXXI, 17, E.V., *and rested.* (30) Lev. XXII, 26—XXIII, 44. (31) Deut. XVI, 9ff. The present practice is to read *ibid.* XV, 19—XVI, 17 on the second day of Pentecost; and if it falls on a Sabbath to begin from XIV, 22. (32) Lev. XXIII, 23ff. (33) *ibid.* XVI. (34) *ibid.* XXII, 26—XXIII, 44. (35) Num. XXIX, 12ff, on each day the corresponding offering. (36) Num. VII. On the first day verses 1-17 are read; on the next six days the corresponding offerings; and on the eighth day VII, 54—VIII, 4. (37) Ex. XVII, 8-16. (38) Num. XXVIII, 11-15. (39) Gen. I, 1—II, 3, because it is on account of the Temple service that the heaven and earth were created. (40) lit. 'the shutting up of the rains'. (41) Lev. XXVI, 3-46. (42) Ex. XXXII, 11-14, XXXIV, 1-10. (43) Isa. LV, 6—LVI, 8. (44) So GRA. V, M and H omit 'but' and 'of reading the *hafṭarah*'. (45) Cf. above XII, 1. (46) When it must be repeated. (47) For the various readings prescribed above. (48) Lev. XXIII, 44.

shall be read in its season. Hence [the Rabbis] said: [The sequence of the readings] is interrupted for them all—for New Moons, *Ḥanukkah, Purim,* fasts, *ma'amadoth* and the Day of Atonement,[49] irrespective of whether these occur on a Sabbath, a Monday or Thursday, on which days there exists a regular sequence of readings.[50] This sequence is interrupted[51] and the [special sections] are read. You cannot, however, say of fasts or *ma'amadoth*[52] that they would fall on a Sabbath in order [to lay down the rule that] the normal sequence of the Sabbath [readings] is interrupted on their account. [For these can interrupt the sequence] of a Monday or Thursday only.

RULE 9. When a New Moon falls on the Sabbath, the eighth person who has to read *And on the sabbath day* and *And in the beginnings of your months*[53] also reads, as the *hafṭarah, Thus said the Lord God: The gate of the inner court that looketh toward the east.*[54] If [the New Moon] falls on a Sunday, he[55] reads on the Sabbath preceding the New Moon *And Jonathan said unto him: To-morrow is the new moon.*[56] On the New Moon itself, three persons read the section of the continual offering. The first person reads, *And . . . spoke,*[57] *Command,*[58] *And thou shalt say.*[59] The second person reads, *The one lamb,*[60] *And the tenth part,*[61] *It is a continual burnt-offering,*[62] *And the drink-offering thereof,*[63] *And the other lamb.*[64] The third person repeats and reads, *It is a continual burnt-offering, And the drink-offering, And the other lamb, And on the sabbath day,*[65] *This is the burnt-offering of every sabbath.*[66] [The reason for this arrangement is] because [the Rabbis] ruled that it is not permitted to read

(49) Cf. Rule 2. (50) lit. 'which they read according to order'. H (so N.Y.) has 'on which they do not read', etc., changing *shehem* to *she'ain.* (51) lit. 'that they interrupt'. (52) Which can never occur on the Sabbath. (53) Cf. Rule 3. (54) Ezek. XLVI, 1. The present custom is to read Isa. LXVI. The *hafṭarah* prescribed here is included in that of *parashath haḥodesh,* which is read only once a year, on the Sabbath of the New Moon of *Nisan* or, if that falls on a week-day, on the Sabbath preceding it. (55) The eighth person called to the reading. (56) 1 Sam. XX, 18-42. (57) Num. XXVIII, 1. (58) *ibid.* 2. (59) *ibid.* 3. (60) *ibid.* 4. (61) *ibid.* 5. (62) *ibid.* 6. (63) *ibid.* 7. (64) *ibid.* 8. This verse is included by GRA and M. (65) *ibid.* 9. This and the following verses are added by GRA. (66) *ibid.* 10.

less than three verses in a section nor[67] is it permissible to leave unfinished less than three verses at the end of a section.[68]

RULE 10.[69] If two verses were read,[70] and another section was begun,[71] there must be no stop before three verses of the latter were read. And since [the third person] reads, . . . *burnt-offering, And the drink-offering thereof, And the other lamb, And on the sabbath day, This is the burnt-offering of . . . sabbath,*[72] it follows that the third person reads five verses,[73] while [the next] one reads the whole section of the New Moon, *And in the beginnings of your months.*[74]

RULE 11. On the New Moon it is necessary to say after *May the glory*[75] the following: *The Lord reigneth,*[76] *O sing unto the Lord a new song;*[77] and after that, *O give thanks unto the Lord, call upon His name*[78] and the six daily psalms;[79] for[80] R. Jose said, 'May my lot be among those who include in their daily prayers[81] those six psalms'. It has also been stated: Why did David mention Abraham, Isaac and Jacob[82] in the psalm beginning, *O give thanks unto the Lord, call upon His name?* Because it has to be said daily.

(67) So GRA. V, M and H read 'and some say'. (68) The sections under discussion are the following: Num. XXVIII, 1-8, 9f, 11-15. (69) The text according to GRA is followed. (70) As with the section, *And on the sabbath day* (Num. XXVIII, 9f), which consists of only two verses. (71) e.g., *And in the beginnings of your months* (*ibid.* 11-15). (72) *ibid.* 6-10. (73) So GRA. V, M and H have 'four'. (74) *ibid.* 11-15. (75) Ps. CIV, 31. The reference is to the collection of verses beginning with these words (cf. P.B., pp. 28f) or to the whole of Ps. CIV which is added now to the daily Psalm at the end of the morning service of the New Moon. (76) Ps. XCIII. (77) Ps. XCVIII. From 'on the New Moon' to 'a new song' is the reading of GRA. V, M and H begin with 'but', omit 'on the New Moon', and conclude with 'according to the words of the Scribes'. (78) I Chron. XVI, 8-36. (79) Pss. CXLV to CL. (80) So according to M. V and H read 'and'. (81) lit. 'those who pray'. (82) So GRA. V, M and H read 'priests, Levites and Israelites'.

CHAPTER XVIII

RULE 1. Why has it been ordained that the psalms[1] [prescribed for the Temple service] are to be said[2] on every New Moon?[3] [This is done in accordance with the view of] R. Simeon b. Laḳish. He enquired of R. Joḥanan whether it was permissible to recite the psalms[4] in the absence of libations, and he replied, 'We may deduce the answer from the following statement: On this and that [occasion][5] the Levites stood on the platform[6] and recited, *And He hath brought upon them their own iniquity*'.[7] R. Simeon b. Laḳish asked him, 'Which is first, the psalm[8] or the additional sacrifice?'[9] He replied,[10] 'It is obvious that the psalm is read first'.[11] For this reason[12] the people have adopted the custom of saying psalms[13] at their proper times;[14] as we have learned in the Mishnah:[15] 'These were the psalms which the Levites used to recite in the Temple: On Sunday[16] they used to

(1) So H while M has the singular; it is lacking in V. (2) At the present time when no sacrifices are offered. (3) As in Temple times when they were recited while the continual sacrifice was being offered. (4) lit. 'song'. (5) The destruction of the first and second Temples. (6) On the Sunday immediately following the respective destructions ('Arak. 11b, Sonc. ed., p. 65). (7) Ps. XCIV, 23. As this Psalm was prescribed normally for Wednesdays (in connection with the sacrifices and libations of the day) but was said on these two occasions on the Sunday (for which a different Psalm had been arranged), it follows that the recital of a particular Psalm is independent of the sacrifices or libations of the day. It was ordained, therefore, that the Psalm for the New Moon, originally prescribed for the Temple service, should also be said at the present time (cf. N.Y.). (8) Which was said in connection with the morning continual offering. (9) Of the New Moon, if the Psalm had been delayed until the time of the additional sacrifice had arrived. (10) Inserted by GRA. (11) Since it belongs to the earlier part of the service. (12) Because of the ruling above that the Temple Psalm of the New Moon should continue to be said even at the present time. (13) As in the Temple, although no sacrifices are now offered. (14) As prescribed for the Temple service. (15) Tamid VII, 4 (Sonc. ed., pp. 37f). (16) lit. 'the first day'. Monday is called 'the second day' and so on.

recite, *The earth is the Lord's, and the fulness thereof; the world, and they that dwell therein.*[17] On Monday, *Great is the Lord, and exceedingly to be praised,*[18] etc. On Tuesday, *God standeth in the congregation of God,*[19] etc. On Wednesday, *O Lord, Thou God to whom vengeance belongeth,*[20] etc. On Thursday, *Sing aloud unto God our strength,*[21] etc. On Friday, *The Lord reigneth; He is clothed in majesty.*[22] On the Sabbath, *A psalm, a Song. For the sabbath day,*[23] [which is the psalm and song also][24] for the hereafter, for the day which will be wholly a Sabbath and [will bring] rest in life everlasting'. For whoever makes mention of a Biblical verse at its proper time is regarded [by God] as though he had built a new altar and offered a sacrifice upon it.

RULE 2. On *Ḥanukkah* [the psalm is] *I will extol Thee, O Lord.*[25] On *Purim* it is *Shiggaion of David,*[26] but others say it is *O God, keep not Thou silence.*[27] On the first day of Passover it is, *Praise ye the name of the Lord,*[28] and the same [is said during] the intermediate days of the Festival; but on the first [two] days of Passover one must [also] say *May the glory of the Lord,*[29] while all the people stand. Then[30] they sit and say all the prescribed psalms[31] up to *And blessed be His glorious name for ever;*[32] but on the last day of Passover the Great *Hallel* is said. And what is the Great *Hallel?* [*42b*] *O give thanks unto the Lord, for He is good . . . O give thanks unto the God of gods.*[33] The people have adopted the custom of saying the Great *Hallel,* although this is not the proper thing to do.[34]

RULE 3. On the Feast of Weeks[35] [the psalm is] *Ascribe unto the*

(17) The quotation represents Ps. XXIV, and the following quotations denote the respective Psalms in which they occur. (18) Ps. XLVIII. (19) Ps. LXXXII. (20) Ps. XCIV. (21) Ps. LXXXI. (22) Ps. XCIII. (23) Ps. XCII. (24) So in Tamid *loc. cit.*, but omitted in V. (25) Ps. XXX. (26) Ps. VII. (27) Ps. LXXXIII. This is inserted by GRA but lacking in V, M and H. (28) Ps. CXXXV. V, M and H quote as an alternative Ps. LXXXIII. (29) Ps. CIV, 31. The reference is to the collection of verses beginning with these words (cf. P.B., p. 28). (30) From 'Then' to 'for ever' is the reading of GRA. The order of the words in V, M and H is confused. (31) P.B., pp. 20-33. (32) Ps. LXXII, 19; but the reference is to the doxology (P.B., p. 33) which concludes the morning Psalms. (33) Ps. CXXXVI. (34) The proper time to say it is 'when the appetite is satisfied and the stomach is full' (Ta'an. 26a, Sonc. ed., p. 135) and not in the morning service before food has been tasted. (35) Pentecost.

Lord, O ye sons of might.[36] On the ninth day of *Ab* [the reading consists] of four verses of Jeremiah, *Hast Thou utterly rejected Judah?* to *For Thou hast made all these things,*[37] and the following two psalms, *O God, the heathen are come into Thine inheritance*[38] and *By the rivers of Babylon.*[39] Although it is usual[40] to give precedence to the Holy Words[41] over the words of [prophetical] traditions,[42] in this case the latter[43] takes precedence over the former.[44]

RULE 4. Some [congregations] read the Book of Lamentations in the evening[45] while others postpone it to the [following] morning after the reading of the Torah, when the reader[46] stands up, his head covered with ashes, his clothes torn,[47] and reads it with weeping and lamentation. If he is able to translate it, well and good; but if he is unable he entrusts it to one who knows how to translate properly and [that person] does the translation, so that the rest of the people, the women and children may understand it; women being under the obligation to listen to the reading of the Book the same as men, and much more so male persons.

Women have similarly the duty to read the *Shema'*, the ['*Amidah*] prayer and the Grace after meals, and to have a *mezuzah* [on their doors]. But if they are not acquainted with the holy tongue they are to be taught [to say them] in any language which they can understand and master. From this it was deduced that the man who recites the benedictions[48] must raise his voice for the benefit of his young sons, his wife and daughters. It is, therefore, a logical deduction that every section of the Torah and the Prophet [prescribed for the readings] of the Sabbath should be translated for the people, the women and the children after the reading of the Torah. This is why it was ruled: On the Sabbath the people come [to the Synagogue] early and depart late. They come early to

(36) Ps. XXIX. (37) Jer. XIV, 19-22. (38) Ps. LXXIX. (39) Ps. CXXXVII. (40) lit. 'in every place'. (41) lit. 'words of holiness', the Hagiographa. (42) The Prophets forming the second division of the Scriptures. (43) Jeremiah, although it is included in the Prophets. (44) The Psalms, which are included in the Hagiographa. (45) Of the Ninth of *Ab*. (46) GRA. (47) Like a mourner, the mourning being for the destruction of the Temples. (48) In his home.

read the *Shema'*, like the pious men of old, with the first glimpse of the sun; and they depart late to listen to the interpretation of the weekly section. On a Festival, however, they come late, because they have to prepare the food for the day;[49] and they hasten to depart because it is unreasonable to interpret [the Torah or the Prophet] for them, it having been stated: Rab did not appoint an interpreter from [the beginning of the first day of] the Festival to the conclusion of the second day.[50]

RULE 5. There was likewise a beautiful custom in Jerusalem to train[51] their young sons and daughters to afflict themselves on a fast day:[52] at the age of eleven to the middle of the day, at the age of twelve the full day, and at the age of thirteen [the boy] was taken round[53] and presented to every elder to bless him and pray for him that he may be worthy to study the Torah and engage in good deeds. In like manner,[54] everyone who had a man superior to him in the town would rise from his place and go and bow down to him [requesting] that he pray on his behalf. This is meant to teach us that they[55] were splendid men and their deeds were splendid, and that their hearts [were directed] towards Heaven. Furthermore, they did not leave their young children behind but took them to the Synagogue to encourage them in the performance of the precepts.

RULE 6. On the day when R. Eleazar b. 'Azariah was appointed head of the academy, he began his discourse by saying: *Ye are standing this day all of you . . . your little ones, your wives*,[56] the men came to listen, the women came to receive a reward for their

(49) Which is permitted on a Festival when not the Sabbath. (50) lit. 'its companion'. Rab's reason was that, owing to the legitimate indulgence on the Festival days, his mind might not be clear to impart the proper instruction or to give the necessary guidance to the public through the interpreter. Similarly it is implied that, in order to enable the people to enjoy the festivities of the day, they are given the opportunity of departing at an earlier hour. (51) Inserted by GRA, M and H. (52) Although the duty of fasting the whole day did not apply to them. (53) So GRA. V, M and H read 'and after that he carried him'. (54) This is an insertion of GRA, omitted in V, M and H. (55) The men of Jerusalem. (56) Deut. XXIX, 9f.

journey,[57] but why did the little ones come? That a reward may be given to those who bring them. From this the young daughters of Israel learnt the practice of coming to the Synagogue so that a reward may be granted to those who bring them while they would [in due course][58] also receive their reward.[59]

RULE 7.[60] The reader on the Ninth of *Ab*[61] says,[62] 'Blessed . . . the true Judge'.[63] Some place the Torah scroll[64] on the ground in a black wrapping and say, *The crown is fallen from our head.*[65] The reading and the lamentations are carried out as with a man whose dead lies before him. Some change their [customary] places [in the Synagogue]; others descend from their benches, and all of them roll in ashes and do not greet one another throughout the night and also throughout the day until the people have finished their lamentations. During the recital of the lamentations it is forbidden to speak [any irrelevant] word, or to go outside [the Synagogue], lest one's mind be diverted from the mourning; and it is obvious that no conversation with a Gentile is permitted.[66]

RULE 8. In the evening service[67] no one can hear the other, because all pray in a whisper;[68] therefore we say neither 'Bless ye'[69] nor '[Blessed] be the name'.[70]

(57) lit. 'steps'. Even if the women did not understand the discourse, they were entitled to reward for their attendance and bringing their children with them. The corresponding passage in Ḥag. 3a (Sonc. ed., p. 9) reads 'men came to learn, women came to listen'. (58) When they reach womanhood. (59) As the result of their early training and practice. In childhood one is subject neither to reward nor punishment. (60) This is the continuation of Rule 4 above. (61) Inserted by M and H, omitted in V. (62) Before the reading of the Book of Lamentations, or before the reading of the section of the Torah. (63) Cf. P.B., p. 292. This blessing is said on a calamity or hearing bad news. (64) M reads 'the case of the Torah'. (65) Lam. V, 16. (66) Since the conversation would have no relevance to the destruction of the Temples. (67) On the ninth of *Ab*. (68) As a mark of mourning for the destruction. (69) 'Bless ye the Lord Who is to be blessed' which is addressed to the congregation at the beginning of the evening service (cf. P.B., p. 96). (70) Which was exclaimed before 'Bless ye' but is not now said.

CHAPTER XIX

RULE 1. In the morning service,[1] however,[2] after the psalms and the Scriptural verses, [the reader] in the *Yoẓer* benediction[3] says 'Bless ye' in a low voice; but neither 'Holy'[4] nor *ḳaddish* is to be recited. In the afternoon prayer, however, both 'Holy'[5] and *ḳaddish* are said.

RULE 2.[6] And on the New Year we say, *O clap your hands, all ye peoples;*[7] on the Day of Atonement *Bless the Lord, O my soul*[8] and *Out of the depths have I called Thee, O Lord;*[9] on the Festival of Tabernacles *In Judah is God known;*[10] on the Eighth Day [of Solemn Assembly] *For the Leader . . . on the Sheminith.*[11] If one is not conversant with these psalms, he says *I will give thanks unto the Lord with my whole heart,*[12] and that suffices.

RULE 3. On Passover, both in the ['*Amidah*] prayer[13] and over the cup of wine[14] one must mention 'On this Festival of holy convocation, this day of the Festival of Unleavened Bread'; and during the intermediate days of the Festival 'This Festival of Unleavened Bread'.[15] On the seventh day one says[16] 'On the Seventh Day of Solemn Assembly', but no mention is made of 'Festival' since it is not an independent Festival.[17]

RULE 4. On the Feast of Weeks[18] one says 'On this Festival of holy convocation and this day of the Feast of Weeks'. The evening, morning and afternoon services consist of the same prayers.[19]

(1) Of the ninth of *Ab*, the services of which were treated in the previous chapter. (2) The contrast is with the ruling in XVIII, 8 where it was stated that in the evening service 'Bless ye' is not said. (3) Cf. P.B., p. 37. (4) The *ḳedushshah*, 'Holy, holy', etc. (P.B., p. 39). (5) P.B., p. 94c. (6) This and the following Rule continue the interrupted regulations on the selection of psalms for various occasions begun in XVIII, 2f. (7) Ps. XLVII. (8) Ps. CIV. (9) Ps. CXXX. (10) Ps. LXXVI. (11) Ps. VI. (12) Ps. IX. (13) P.B., p. 228. (14) The *Ḳiddush*, P.B., pp. 230f. (15) So GRA and H. V and M read 'this so and so Festival'. (16) In the '*Amidah* and *Ḳiddush*. (17) The seventh day is part of the Passover. (18) Pentecost. (19) As on Passover except for the change in the name of the Festival.

RULE 5. On the New Moon of *Nisan*[20] one must mention[21] 'On this day of the New Moon'; and on the New Year 'On this Festival of holy convocation,[22] this day of the New Year, this Day of Memorial, a day of blowing the *Shofar*', concluding with[23] 'King over all the earth, Who sanctifiest Israel and the Day of Memorial and the Seasons'.[24]

RULE 6. On the Day of Atonement no mention is made[25] of 'on the Festival Day', because there is no Festival on a fast day; but one says, 'On this day of holy convocation, on this day of the Fast of the Tenth,[26] on this day of pardoning of iniquity', concluding with[27] 'pardonest and forgivest our iniquities and the iniquities of Thy people Israel in mercy, and grantest remission for their transgressions, King over all the earth, Who sanctifiest Israel and the day of the Fast of Atonement, and the Seasons and the holy convocation'; but no mention is made of Festival and joy since there is no joy without partaking of food.

RULE 7. As we laud [God] on the first day, the intermediate days and the last day[28] of the Festival, so we laud Him [on the other] Festivals in the morning,[29] afternoon and evening prayers.[30] And how is He lauded? 'Our God and the God of our fathers, do Thou make the glory of Thy kingdom manifest upon us'.[31] This is followed by, 'We pray Thee, O Lord our God,[32] may . . . rise and come,[33] etc. Bestow upon us';[34] and the conclusion of the prayer is, 'Blessed art Thou Who sanctifiest Thy people Israel, the Festival of joy, the Seasons and the holy convocation'.

(20) And similarly on the other New Moons. *Nisan* is named because it is the first of the months of the year. (21) In the '*Amidah* (P.B., p. 50). (22) V, M and H add 'and on this day of New Moon'. GRA omits because this addition is no longer customary. (23) The benediction (P.B., p. 242). (24) So GRA. The reading in V is confused. (25) In the '*Amidah*. (26) The Day of Atonement is observed on the tenth of *Tishri*. (27) Cf. P.B., p. 258. (28) Added by GRA; omitted in V and M. The reading of H is: 'As we laud Him on the New Year and Day of Atonement, so we laud Him on the Festivals'. (29) In the *Yoẓer* prayer which begins the morning benedictions before the *Shema*'. (30) In the '*Amidah*. (31) Cf. P.B., p. 234. (32) So H. V reads 'our God name'. (33) Cf. P.B., p. 228. (34) *ibid.*, p. 229.

RULE 8. As the concluding words [of the benedictions] of the New Year and the Day of Atonement are different from those of other Festivals, so are the prayers of these days; and we do not include 'remembrance'[35] either in the first three[36] or last three[37] [benedictions of the '*Amidah*] except only on the two Festival days of the New Year and Day of Atonement[38] and, even with these, permission was given with difficulty.[39] If the New Year falls on a Sabbath, one does not say 'A day of blowing the *Shofar*' but 'a day of remembrance of blowing the *Shofar*', because the blowing of the *Shofar* does not take precedence of the Sabbath in country towns,[40] this being a preventive measure.[41]

RULE 9. On the New Moon,[42] the associations of elders, leaders and students were assembled in session[43] from the time of the afternoon service onwards until the sun had set and the moon appeared in the night [sky].[44] It is necessary to say [after the ceremonial meal] in the benediction over the wine,[45] 'Blessed art Thou, O Lord our God, King of the universe, Who createst the fruit of the vine. Blessed art Thou, O Lord our God, King of the universe, Who hast revealed the secret of the renewal of the moon, Who didst instruct and teach us[46] the [courses of] the seasons, New Moons and Festivals[47] and Who didst

(35) 'Remember us unto life', etc. (P.B., p. 239). (36) 'Blessed art Thou . . . the holy God' (*ibid.* pp. 44f). (37) 'Accept O Lord . . . with peace' (*ibid.* pp. 50-54). (38) Cf. *ibid.* pp. 239, 256. (39) Because, as a rule, no break is allowed in these benedictions. (40) Outside Jerusalem. This was permitted in the Temple only (Rashi). According to Maimonides the permissibility extended to all Jerusalem. (41) One might carry the *Shofar* on the Sabbath through a public domain to an instructor to take lessons in the art of blowing it. (42) Which occurred on the 31st day of the preceding month. The New Moon was celebrated either on the 30th day of the preceding month (if witnesses testified in time that they saw the new moon in the evening sky) or on the 31st if no reliable witnesses were forthcoming. (43) V inserts in brackets 'on the first day'. They assembled in the academy where a ritual feast was held in honour of the declaration and sanctification of the New Moon. (44) So GRA. V, M and H omit 'and the moon . . . sky'. (45) A cup of wine was used for the Grace after meals. (46) lit. 'them'. (47) The translation follows the version of GRA. The text in V is confused and varies with that of M and H which also disagree with each other.

appoint men of understanding who determine the times [of the New Moons and Festivals]. Thou, our Rock, hast weighed and calculated the minutest divisions of time whereby those New Moons and Festivals are determined, as it is written, *Who appointedst the moon for seasons; the sun knoweth his going down,*[48] and it also states, *For as the new heavens and the new earth, which I will make'*;[49] and one concludes with 'Blessed art Thou, O Lord, Who sanctifiest Israel and the New Moons'. [Then one says,] 'O give thanks unto the Lord for He is good; on this day we all in Jerusalem rejoice and are happy in the All-present. May Elijah the prophet soon come to us; may the king Messiah cause to spring forth in our days the [happy] time like the years[50] when the Temple will be rebuilt, and may joyous occasions multiply in Israel'; and the people answer and say 'Amen'. [The prayer is then continued,] 'May good tidings multiply in Israel, may happy days multiply in Israel, may disciples of the Torah multiply in Israel. Consecrated is the New Moon, consecrated at the beginning of the month, consecrated in its proper time, consecrated in its intercalation,[51] consecrated according to[52] the Torah, consecrated according to the *halakah*, consecrated in the celestial regions, consecrated in the terrestrial regions, consecrated in the land of Israel, consecrated in Zion, consecrated in Jerusalem, consecrated in all the habitations of Israel, consecrated by the order of our Rabbis, consecrated in the House of Assembly. O give thanks unto the Lord for He is good'. Then [the reader] says, 'You are all blessed'. After every benediction, moreover, [the reader] says, 'O give thanks unto the Lord for He is good', except after the benedictions of the Levites.[53]

(48) Ps. CIV, 19. (49) Is. LXVI, 22. (50) So M; V wrongly 'in the years'. H reads: 'that he may appoint the days like the years'. (51) i.e. the addition of the 30th day to the preceding month by declaring the 31st day to be the New Moon and the first day of the new month. (52) So M and H. V wrongly 'in'. (53) Who omitted 'for He is good' (cf. its omission in 2 Chron. XX, 21). GRA reads 'the mourners' instead of 'the Levites' (cf. Rule 12 below). N.Y. also had this reading but considers the phrase 'except after', etc., superfluous.

RULE 10. When he[54] sings the praises of God he does so in the presence of the twelve notable men[55] of the town and twelve *ḥaberim*[56] corresponding to the twelve tribes, the twelve months and the twelve constellations.

RULE 11. Although [in the Grace after meals the prayer] 'May . . . rise and come'[57] has been said in [the benediction concluding with] 'rebuildest Jerusalem' and all[58] the benediction of *zimmun* has been said over the cup[59] [of wine], that cup being passed on to one's wife[60] to fulfil that which is stated, *To cause a blessing to rest on thy house,*[61] nevertheless another cup of wine is brought over which is said the benediction 'Who createst the fruit of the vine' and afterwards 'Who didst reveal', etc.[62] The same rule also applies[63] to the benediction of bridegrooms and the benediction of mourners,[64] because two sanctifications[65] must not be pronounced over the same cup. Our Masters have adopted the practice of saying the benediction of bridegrooms[66] in the morning over a cup of wine in the presence of ten men; and [in the presence of] new guests all the seven days;[67] and similarly in the evening after[68] the meal.

RULE 12. With regard to the benediction of mourners on the Sabbath, when mourning is suspended, it is said after the statutory service in the presence of the worshippers over a cup

(54) i.e. the one who presides over the assembly which is consecrating the new moon. (55) lit. 'good'. (56) Members of an association scrupulously observant of the laws concerning ritual purity. The translation accords with the text of GRA and H. (57) P.B., p. 282. (58) lit. 'and he finishes'. (59) So M and H. V reads 'all the cup'. (60) To partake of its contents. (61) Ez. XLIV, 30. Cf. 'his house is his wife' (Yoma I, 1, Sonc. ed., p. 1). The wife is the mainstay of the home. (62) As in Rule 9 above (GRA). V has the meaningless text: 'which is a circle all of it'. (63) lit. 'and so you say'. (64) These benedictions, too, must be said over a cup of wine other than the one used for the Grace after meals. (65) The benedictions whereby the sanctifications are declared: that for the Grace after meals, on the one hand, and the benedictions mentioned on the other. (66) V adds 'and the benediction of mourners', which is omitted by M and H. The benediction of mourners is dealt with in Rule 12 below. (67) Of the wedding festivities. If no new guests arrive, the benedictions are said only on the first day. (68) So GRA. V, M and H read 'before'.

of wine; for R. Eliezer b. Hyrḳanos said:[69] Solomon saw the greatness[70] of those who bestow lovingkindness, and built two gates for Israel, one for bridegrooms and the other for mourners and excommunicated persons. On the Sabbath the inhabitants of Jerusalem used to congregate, ascend the Temple Mount and take their seats between these two gates to show kindness to these persons. Since the Temple was destroyed it was enacted that bridegrooms and mourners should go to the Synagogue so that kindness could be shown to them: to bridegrooms by recounting their praises and escorting them to their homes. To mourners [by comforting them as follows:] After the reader finishes the *musaf*, everyone goes behind the doors of the Synagogue, which are in front of[71] the Synagogue, and there meet the mourners and all their relatives. The benediction[72] is said followed by *ḳaddish*. The version 'In the world that will be renewed in the time to come'[73] is only said after the study of[74] the Talmud and a Rabbinic discourse.[75]

(69) This follows GRA. V, M and H read: 'in the evening after the prayer in the presence of the worshippers over a cup on the Sabbath when mourning in public is suspended according to R. Eliezer b. Hyrḳanos who said'. The text is clearly out of order. (70) lit. 'power'. (71) So GRA. V omits 'everyone' and inserts 'or' before 'in front'. [H has the reading *pinnath*, 'the corner of'.] (72) For the mourners. (73) This is an enlarged *ḳaddish* which is now recited by sons after the interment of a parent (P.B., pp. 321f). (74) lit. 'over'. (75) lit. 'exposition'.

CHAPTER XX

RULE 1. The benediction over the moon must not be said except at the conclusion of the Sabbath when one is in an exhilarated mood[1] and well dressed. [43*a*] He directs his eyes towards the moon, places his feet together and pronounces the benediction 'Who[2] didst create the heavens by Thy word and all their hosts by the breath of Thy mouth. Thou didst set for them a fixed law and time that they should not change their ordained task. They are glad and rejoice to perform the will of their Possessor.[3] They act loyally, for their[4] action is truth. To the moon Thou didst say that it should renew itself with a precious light and a diadem of beauty for those who have been sustained from the womb[5] who, like it, will be renewed in the future and glorify their Creator for the majesty of His kingdom. Blessed art Thou, O Lord, Who hallowest the New Moons'.[6]

RULE 2. Then one says three times, 'An auspicious omen, an auspicious omen, shall it be for all Israel. Blessed be He Who formed thee, blessed be Thy Maker, blessed be thy Possessor, blessed be thy Creator'. Turning in the direction of the moon,[7] he jumps three times and exclaims three times, 'As I jump towards thee but do not[8] touch thee, so if others should jump against me to hurt me may they not touch me. Let terror and dread fall upon them and may this be retrospective, Amen, Amen, Selah. Praise ye the Lord'. He then says 'Peace' three times to his fellow and goes home with a cheerful heart. That

(1) After the happiness of the Sabbath day. (2) Preceded, as all benedictions, by 'Blessed art Thou, O Lord our God, King of the universe'. (3) Inserted by GRA and M; omitted by V. H adds it in the textual notes. (4) So GRA, M and H. V has 'for his'. (5) A reference to Israel (cf. Is. XLVI, 3). (6) H reads 'hallowest Israel and the New Moons'; the reading of GRA is 'Who renewest the months'. (7) lit. 'towards it'. (8) M reads 'and cannot' which is the reading in the ritual.

is [the conclusion of the regulations] concerning the interruptions for New Moons.[9]

RULE 3. What are the regulations respecting *Ḥanukkah?*[10] The Rabbis said: On the twenty-fifth day of *Kislew*[11] the *Ḥanukkah* lamp is kindled,[12] and it is forbidden to use an old lamp;[13] but if a person has only an old lamp, he must thoroughly heat it in fire;[14] nor may [the *Ḥanukkah* lamp] be moved[15] from its place before it is extinguished.[16]

RULE 4. The commandment to kindle it extends from sunset until the last person has left[17] the street.[18] And, although there is no actual proof,[19] there is an allusion to it: *The pillar of cloud by day [and the pillar of fire by night,] departed not.*[20] If it was lit in daytime, one must derive no benefit from it, nor may the benediction be said over it; for so [the Rabbis] said: No benediction is to be pronounced over the lamp before one enjoys its light. There is no need, however, to be concerned about changing the wick before it has been used up.

RULE 5. It is a religious precept to place the *Ḥanukkah* lamp by the door which is near to the public domain,[21] in such a manner that the *mezuzah* should be on the right hand and the *Ḥanukkah* lamp on the left, to fulfil what is stated, *How fair and*

(9) Cf. XVII, 2f where the regulations for the New Moon began and, with many interruptions, insertions and amplifications, continued to the end of this Rule. (10) lit. 'how do we interrupt for *Ḥanukkah*', a reference to XVII, 2 where *Ḥanukkah* was first introduced in this set of regulations with the statement, 'The sequence . . . is interrupted for . . . *Ḥanukkah*'. (11) The ninth Heb. month on the twenty-fifth of which the Festival begins. (12) This takes place on the preceding evening, the night belonging to the following day. (13) If it is an earthen lamp, because the burnt oil renders it unsightly. (14) To burn away the old oil, after which the lamp may be used. (15) lit. 'lifted'. (16) Carrying the lamp about while it is burning might cause suspicion that one is making a profane use of it; but the *Ḥanukkah* light, commemorating the miracles which led up to the celebration (cf. Rule 5), is sacred, is only to be looked at and must not be used for any other purpose. (17) lit. 'the foot ceases from'. (18) The light is intended to serve as a public demonstration, but at such a late hour there are no passers-by to see it. (19) That the lighting must take place after sunset. (20) Ex. XIII, 22, which indicates that the pillar of fire which, like the *Ḥanukkah* lamp, was intended to shed light, appeared in the night only. (21) So that the light is seen from the street.

how pleasant art thou[22]—*how fair* with the *mezuzah* and *how pleasant* with the *Ḥanukkah* lamp. The number[23] of lights [for each night] is in accordance with the ruling of the School of Hillel,[24] because in sacred matters one should proceed to a higher grade[25] but not descend to a lower one,[26] [and also because the number of lights should] correspond to the days [of the Festival] as they pass.

RULE 6. In what manner are the benedictions[27] said? On the first day, the person who kindles [the lamp] says three benedictions while the onlooker says two. The person who kindles says, 'Blessed art Thou, O Lord,[28] Who hast sanctified us by Thy commandments and hast given us command to kindle the light of *Ḥanukkah*'. Then[29] he says, 'We kindle these lights on account of the deliverances and the miracles and the wonders which Thou didst work for our fathers, by means of Thy holy priests.[30] During all the eight days of *Ḥanukkah* these lights are sacred, and it is not permitted to make any profane use of them but we are only to look at them, in order that we may give thanks unto Thy name for thy wonders, Thy miracles and Thy deliverances'. [The third benediction is] 'Blessed art Thou, O Lord, Who hast kept us in life'.[31] [Before this] he says, 'Who wroughtest miracles for our fathers'.[32] These benedictions are for the person who kindles the lights, but the onlooker says on the first day only two benedictions: 'Who hast kept us in life' and 'Who wroughtest miracles'. From that day onwards the person who kindles the lights says, 'To kindle'

(22) Cant. VII, 7. (23) Inserted by GRA, wanting in V, M and H. (24) One light on the first night, two on the second, and so on, until eight lights burn on the eighth and last night of the Festival. (25) Adding lights on the succeeding nights. (26) As would happen if the number were to be reduced from eight on the first night to one on the last in accordance with the view of Beth Shammai. (27) Over the *Ḥanukkah* lights. (28) Inserting after 'Lord', as in all benedictions, 'our God, King of the universe' (P.B., p. 274). (29) After the three benedictions: the one just given and the two mentioned below. (30) The Maccabees who were a priestly family. (31) Concluding 'and hast preserved us, and enabled us to reach this season' (P.B., p. 274). (32) Beginning, as usual, 'Blessed art . . . universe' and concluding 'in the days of old at this season' (P.B., p. 274).

and 'Who wroughtest', while the onlooker only says 'Who wroughtest miracles'.

RULE 7. The precentor must say, 'Thou art holy'[33] on the eight days[34] of *Ḥanukkah,* and similarly on New Moons and on the intermediate days of a Festival,[35] because *beside*[36] *the continual burnt-offering*[37] is written in connection with them. And R. Hiyya learnt: On any day on which there is a musaf *ḳedushshah* is said except on *Ḥanukkah* on which *ḳedushshah* is said although there is no *musaf* on it, because *Hallel* is included [in the service]. Some maintain [that it is said] on *Purim* also, because the scroll of Esther is read on it.

RULE 8. In the benediction for Thanksgiving[38] we include [on *Ḥanukkah*] 'and thanks for the wonders and salvation of Thy priests which Thou hast wrought in the days of Mattathias, son of Joḥanan, High Priest, and the Hasmoneans his sons. So also, O Lord our God and God of our fathers, perform for us miracles and wonders, and we will give thanks unto Thy name for ever. Blessed art Thou, O Lord, Who art all-good'.[39] The miracles [of the days] of Mordecai and Esther are also mentioned [on *Purim*] in the benediction for Thanksgiving. Both[40] are likewise mentioned in the Grace after meals.[41]

RULE 9. The whole *Hallel*[42] is recited during all the eight days of *Ḥanukkah.* During [the recital of] the first two[43] chapters one may not return greetings, and there is no need to say that one must not give greetings. During [the recital of] the last two

(33) i.e. the *ḳedushshah*. It appears that, instead of beginning with 'We will sanctify' (P.B., p. 45) or 'We will reverence' (P.B., p. 160), there was a custom to begin with 'Thou art holy' on Sabbath and Festivals. Rule 7 extends this practice to some of the less important days as specified below. It has also been suggested to read, instead of *'attah ḳadosh* ('Thou art holy') *'eth haḳḳedushshah* ('the *ḳedushshah*'). (34) So GRA. V, M and H read 'in the eighteen [benedictions]'. (35) viz. Passover and Tabernacles. (36) Inserted by GRA, omitted by V, M and H. (37) Num. XXVIII, 15 (on the New Moon); *ibid.* 24 (on the intermediate days of Passover); and *ibid.* XXIX, 19, 22, 25, 28, 31, 34 (on those of Tabernacles). (38) Beginning 'We give thanks' (P.B., p. 51). (39) The present version of this form of thanksgiving is longer and differs in wording (P.B., p. 52). (40) Those for *Ḥanukkah* and *Purim.* (41) In the second benediction (P.B., p. 281). (42) Including Pss. CXV, 1-11 and CXVI, 1-11 (P.B., pp. 220f). (43) So GRA. V, M and H read 'three'.

chapters one may give greetings out of fear;[44] during the two middle chapters[45] [greetings may be given] for the sake of peace or out of respect. The following are the first two chapters: *Praise, O ye servants of the Lord*[46] and *When Israel went forth.*[47] The two middle ones are: *Not unto us*[48] and *I love.*[49] The last two are: *O praise the Lord*[50] and *O give thanks unto the Lord.*[51] It is also necessary to say a benediction[52] before them and read them melodiously. For R. Simeon b. Jehoẓadaḳ said:[53] On eighteen days and one night the individual reads the whole *Hallel* and they are: the eight days of *Ḥanukkah,* the eight days of Tabernacles,[54] the Festival of Solemn Assembly, the first Festival day of Passover and the night preceding it.[55] In the Diaspora[56] [the whole *Hallel* is read on] twenty-one days and two nights. The most proper way of performing the commandment is to read the *Hallel* psalms on the two nights [of Passover] in the Diaspora in the Synagogue,[57] to say the benediction over them, and to recite them melodiously to fulfil what is stated, *And let us exalt His name together.*[58] When, however, one reads [the *Hallel*] at home,[59] there is no need to say the benediction because it has already been said in the congregational service.[60]

(44) To a person who can cause harm in his resentment at not having been greeted. (45) The reading of GRA. V and M have 'and return greetings for the sake of peace and out of respect'. H omits the text of V and GRA. (46) Ps. CXIII. (47) *ibid.* CXIV. V, M and H adds Ps. CXV as the third. (48) *ibid.* CXV; 'the two middle . . . *us*' is the reading of GRA. (49) *ibid.* CXVI. (50) *ibid.* CXVII. (51) *ibid.* CXVIII. (52) 'Blessed art Thou . . . to read the *Hallel*' (P.B., p. 219). (53) So GRA. V, H and M read 'learnt' using a term which refers to a Mishnah, whereas the quotation is from the Gemara in Ta'an. 28b (Sonc. ed., pp. 150f). (54) Omitted by V and M, but added by GRA and H in agreement with Ta'an. *loc. cit.* (55) [Cf. Pes. V, 7 (Sonc. ed., p. 327) where it is described how the *Hallel* was recited during the sacrifice of the Paschal lamb on the eve of Passover.] (56) i.e. all countries outside the land of Israel where two days are observed as holy instead of the first day of Tabernacles, two days for the Festival of Solemn Assembly, and two days each for the first and seventh day of Passover. (57) In addition to reading them at home in the course of the *Seder* ritual. 'In the Synagogue' is inserted by GRA but omitted by V, M and H. (58) Ps. XXXIV, 4. (59) During the *Seder*. (60) lit. 'among many'. The Service in Synagogue precedes the *Seder* in the home.

RULE 10. A scroll[61] is then taken out[62] and we read in the section of the princes,[63] *And he that presented his offering the first day was;*[64] and likewise for each day [the corresponding section of the offering] of that day,[65] until the eighth day. On the Sabbath [during *Ḥanukkah*] one reads, *And it came to pass on the day that Moses made an end*[66] up to *so he made the candlestick.*[67] On the eighth day he reads from *On the eighth day*[68] through all the sections[69] until *so he made the candlestick.* On the Sabbath[70] one also reads as the *haftarah, Thus all the work . . . was finished.*[71]

RULE 11. During the eight days of *Ḥanukkah* we read the following one day earlier:[72] *On the second day,*[73] *On the third day,*[74] *On the fourth day,*[75] *On the fifth day,*[76] *On the sixth day,*[77] *On the seventh day,*[78] *On the eighth day,*[79] so as to complete ten verses.[80]

RULE 12. When the New Moon of *Ṭebeth*[81] falls on a Sunday, three persons read on the first day[82] in the passage of the New Moon first, while the fourth reads the passage of *Ḥanukkah,* because that which is more frequent takes precedence,[83] and so [the reading for the New Moon] precedes the other. On the second day, however, the order is not the same, but three persons read the passage of *Ḥanukkah* while the fourth reads that of the New Moon, because on the previous day the section

(61) M and H read 'a scroll of the Torah'. (62) In the Synagogue Service during *Ḥanukkah.* (63) Num. VII. (64) *ibid.* 12-17. (65) lit. 'and so for each day its day', the number of the *Ḥanukkah* day corresponding to the respective number of the days of the offerings of the princes. (66) Num. VII, 1. (67) *ibid.* VIII, 4. (68) *ibid.* 54. (69) Of the offerings of all the princes. (70) So GRA. V and M read: 'and so on the eighth day until *And this was the work of the candlestick* (Num. VIII, 4) all the verse'. H has a different text. (71) i.e. in the passage I Kings VII, 51—VIII, 21. (72) lit. 'we advance to say'. To the prescribed reading of the day that of the following day is added. (73) Num. VII, 18-23. This is added to the reading of the first day and then repeated on the second, and similarly with the rest. (74) *ibid.* 24-29. (75) *ibid.* 30-35. (76) *ibid.* 36-41. (77) *ibid.* 42-47. (78) *ibid.* 48-53. (79) *ibid.* 54-59. (80) Which is the minimum required for the reading of the three persons who are called to the Torah each day of *Ḥanukkah.* (81) Which always occurs during *Ḥanukkah.* (82) Of the New Moon, which is observed sometimes on one day and sometimes on two. (83) The New Moon occurs every month, *Ḥanukkah* once a year.

of the New Moon had been read first.[84] [This is the procedure] because R. Isaac Seḥorah asked R. Isaac Nappaḥa, 'Which do we read [first][85] when the New Moon of *Ṭebeth* falls on a Sabbath?' [He replied,] 'In the section of *kalloth Mosheh,*[86] while the *maftir* reads[87] the passages relating to the Sabbath and the New Moon.[88] If it falls on a week-day, on the first day [of the New Moon] three persons read [the passage] for the New Moon, the fourth reading that of *Ḥanukkah;* because that which is more frequent takes precedence. As, however, the section of the New Moon was read first,[89] three persons are to be called up on the second day for the reading of the *Ḥanukkah* section,[90] while the fourth reads[91] the section of the New Moon, viz. *And in your new moons* to the end of the section.[92] Why is this so?[93] Because it is only on account of the *musaf* of New Moon[94] that a fourth person is added.[95] Behold [we have concluded the regulations respecting] the interruption which is made for the sake of *Ḥanukkah.*[96]

(84) So GRA. V, M and H read: 'because the reckoning of the month is from the second day only when the years are regular'. (85) In the second and third scrolls of the Torah. In the first the regular portion of the week is read. (86) E.V. *Moses had made an end* (Num. VII, 1). The extent of the reading is given in Rule 10 above. (87) In the third scroll. (88) Num. XXVIII, 9-15. (89) On the first day of New Moon. (90) In the first scroll. Only two scrolls are taken out on the week-days of *Ḥanukkah*. (91) In the second scroll. (92) Num. XXVIII, 11-15. (93) Why is the order of the reading reversed on the second day as compared with the first? (94) On the other week-days of *Ḥanukkah* there is no *musaf*. This argument cannot be applied to the first day of New Moon because it is the second day which begins the month, the first being the last day of the old month. (95) Rule 12 incorporates nearly the whole of XII, 7. (96) Cf. XVII, 2f.

CHAPTER XXI

RULE 1. [Reverting to the sequence of the readings which] is interrupted for *Purim*.[1] It is[2] the custom of our Rabbis in the West to afflict themselves by fasting the three days of the fast of Mordecai and Esther[3] intermittently, viz. after *Purim* on the Monday, Thursday and Monday.

RULE 2. And why do we not fast in the month of *Nisan?* Because on the first of *Nisan* the Tabernacle was erected[4] and twelve princes offered their sacrifices during [the first] twelve days, a day for each tribe,[5] and everyone held a festival on his day.[6] Furthermore, in the time to come the Sanctuary will be rebuilt in *Nisan,* to confirm what is stated, *There is nothing new under the sun.*[7]

RULE 3. For this reason[8] no supplications[9] are offered on any of the days of *Nisan* and there is no fasting until *Nisan* has passed. The only exception is [the fast of] the firstborn who fast on the eve of Passover.[10] The very pious also fast on that day on account of the unleavened bread, in order that they shall begin to eat it[11] with relish.[12] Scholars fast on Mondays and

(1) Cf. XVII, 2 where the subject was begun. Having been suspended in favour of other Festivals, it is here resumed. (2) So GRA and H. V and M read 'according to'. (3) Cf. Esth. IV, 16. (4) Cf. Ex. XL, 2. (5) Cf. Num. VII, 1ff. (6) Between the twelfth of *Nisan* and the fifteenth, on which Passover begins, only two days intervene; therefore they, too, are regarded as festival days. The Passover ending on the twenty-first (in the land of Israel) or on the twenty-second (in the Diaspora), only eight or nine days of the month remain. As by far the greater part of the month was made up of festival days, the entire month is treated as a festival season in which fasting is prohibited. (7) Eccl. I, 9. (8) That most of the month contained festival days. (9) This refers in particular to the prayer, 'And He, being merciful', etc. (P.B., pp. 57-65). (10) In thanksgiving for the deliverance of the Israelite firstborn on Passover eve when Egypt's firstborn perished (Ex. XII, 29). (11) On the evening preceding the fifteenth of *Nisan*. Lit. 'that they shall enter it'. (12) In honour and appreciation of the commandment.

Thursdays [throughout the year] on account of the desecration of the name of God[13] and for the honour of the Temple which was burnt.

RULE 4. To what does the foregoing apply? To fasting in private, but it is forbidden to proclaim a public fast until *Nisan* has passed.

On the first day of *Adar* a public proclamation is made regarding the shekels.[14] Why on the first of *Adar?* Because it was foreseen, revealed and known before Him Who spoke and the world came into being that Haman would in time to come weigh [shekels] against Israel.[15] He, therefore, forestalled him and instructed Moses that the shekels of Israel should precede Haman's. It is required that Israel shall give their shekels before [43*b*] the Sabbath of Remember;[16] and it is forbidden to say of them[17] that they are 'for a ransom' [but must be given] for a freewill-offering. From the proceeds water and food should be supplied for their poor brethren on account of a sacrifice[18] and gifts to the poor.[19] Some supply bread and wine, others supply bread and fish; in any event not less than two gifts[20] should be given, although they consist only of wheat and beans.

RULE 5.[21] In villages and towns [the *Megillah*] is read on the fourteenth [of *Adar*], and in walled cities[22] on the fifteenth of the month.

RULE 6. We read[23] from *Then came Amalek;*[24] and although it

(13) By the heathens who destroyed Jerusalem. (14) Every adult had the obligation to give one half-shekel as a contribution to the Temple. (15) Cf. Esth. III, 9. (16) The Sabbath before *Purim* when the *mafṭir* reads the passage beginning *Remember* (Deut. XXV, 17-19). (17) The half-shekels. (18) Reading *ḳorban* with GRA. V has 'on account of complaints' (*ḳoblin*). [M has *ḳislin* which Krauss, *Lehnwörter,* p. 531, renders 'feast'.] (19) Cf. Esth. IX, 22. (20) Since Esth. *loc. cit.* speaks of *gifts,* in the plural, which indicates not less than two. (21) The translation of this Rule follows the reading of GRA. V, M and H read: 'On the fourteenth and fifteenth of Adar, tables of *ḥaberim* ("associates", i.e. men who observed levitical purity) were set up (for changing foreign currency into half-shekels); in the villages on the fourteenth and in the walled cities on the fifteenth'. (22) Those that, like Jerusalem, had been walled in the days of Joshua the son of Nun (cf. Meg. I, 1). (23) On *Purim* in the morning service. (24) Ex. XVII, 8-16.

consists of only nine verses,[25] we do not begin[26] *Now Jethro . . . heard,*[27] but the first [to be called up] reads three verses, viz. *Then came Amalek . . . And Moses said . . . So Joshua did;*[28] the second reads *And it came to pass, when Moses held up his hand . . . But Moses' hands . . . And Joshua discomfited;*[29] the third reads *And the Lord said . . . And Moses built . . . And he said: The hand upon the throne of the Lord: the Lord will have war.*[30] The scroll of the Torah is then put back in its place, and *Blessed be the name of the Lord from this time forth and for ever*[31] and *ḳaddish* are said;[32] because neither on New Moons, nor fast days, nor Mondays and Thursdays, nor on the intermediate days of a Festival, nor the eight days of *Ḥanukkah,* nor *Purim* is *ḳaddish* said until after the Torah scroll had been restored to its place, while the people stand and respond 'Amen, let His great name', etc.,[33] with devotion and [still] standing. Furthermore, you have no reading that requires a *ḳaddish* before [the scroll] is put back except that of Sabbath and Festivals alone, [when it is said] before the *hafṭarah* is read in the Prophet.

RULE 7. R. Huna said: For three readings in the Torah[34] not less than ten verses must be allotted.[35] Hezekiah[36] explained [the reason:[37] The number] corresponds to the Ten Commandments. But have we not learned in a Mishnah:[38] 'On Sunday [the men of the *ma'amad* read] *In the beginning*[39] and *Let there be a firmament*'[40] although they contain not more than eight

(25) While the general rule is that a reading must consist of not less than ten verses (cf. Rule 7). (26) For the third person called to the Torah. (27) Ex. XVIII, 1, etc., which follows the section beginning *Then came Amalek.* (28) *ibid.* XVII, 8-10. (29) *ibid.* 11-13. (30) *ibid.* 14-16. (31) Ps. CXIII, 2. (32) V inserts here in parentheses, as also M and H, 'For there is no reading [of the Torah] which requires *ḳaddish* until after he restores [the scroll in the ark] except that of the Sabbath alone on account of the *mafṭir* and over the Prophet. After the scroll of the Torah is put in its place one says *ḳaddish;* and why *ḳaddish?* Only to teach'. GRA transposes this to the end of the Rule in an emended version. (33) Cf. P.B., p. 75. (34) i.e. when only three persons are called up to the reading of a section, viz. on a Monday or Thursday or at a Sabbath afternoon service. (35) Three verses for each of the first two and four for the third. (36) A Rabbi of that name. (37) Why ten verses are required. (38) Ta'an. IV, 3 (Sonc. ed., p. 137). (39) Gen. I, 1-4. (40) *ibid.* 5-8.

verses?[41] R. Iddi said: Kahana and Ashë differ [on the method of procedure],[42] one holding that [the reader] goes back, and the other maintaining that he cuts.[43] According to him who holds that '[the reader] goes back', he repeats two verses;[44] and according to him who maintains that 'he cuts', *And there was evening and there was morning*[45] is a verse on its own.[46] But have we not learned in [the same] Mishnah: 'On Monday [the reading of the *ma'amad* was] *Let there be a firmament*[47] and *Let the waters . . . be gathered together*'?[48] Now, according to him who holds that '[the reader] goes back', he goes back over two verses, but according to him who maintains that 'he cuts', even if he does so, there are not ten[49] verses![50] R. Polippa b. R. Pariṭ raised an objection before R. Jonah,[51] 'Behold the section of Amalek!'[52] 'This is different', he replied, 'since[53] it is the prescribed portion for the day'.[54] R. Eliezer b. R. Maḳom raised an objection:[55] [It has been taught,] 'He who reads the *hafṭarah* from the Prophet shall read not less than twenty-one verses',[56] but [if R. Huna's

(41) How then could R. Huna rule that a minimum of ten verses was required? (42) As how to make ten verses out of eight. (43) This is explained in the continuation. (44) The second person repeats the last two of the three verses which the first had read. The two, together with the eight, make up the minimum of ten verses. (45) The second part of each of verses 4 and 8 of Gen. I. (46) So that verses 4 and 8 represent two verses each, bringing the number to ten. (47) Gen. I, 6-8, three verses. (48) *ibid.* 9-13, five verses. (49) Added by GRA, omitted by V, M and H. (50) There would only be nine, since *And there was evening,* etc., forms the whole of verse 13 and cannot be reckoned as two verses as in the case of verses 5 and 8. (51) To R. Huna's ruling. (52) Ex. XVII, 8-16, read on *Purim,* which consists only of nine verses. (53) So GRA, M and H. V reads: 'he said, No, it is taught, it'. (54) This reply could also have been given to the preceding objection, since in Gen. I, 6-13, if only verse 8 is divided into two, there would be nine verses, as in the section of Amalek. (55) To R. Huna's ruling. (56) Meg. 23a (Sonc. ed., p. 140). From 'but [if R. Huna's ruling . . . to the last one]' is added by GRA. V omits it but inserts in brackets: 'It is permitted to skip in a Prophet but not in the Torah, because if [a reader] skipped even one verse by not reading it, and restored the scroll [to the ark] and recited *ḳaddish,* he must unroll it again, say the benedictions, and read that verse and the two verses which follow it'. This is a repetition of XI, 2, 6.

ruling] is valid, twenty-three verses should be required, ten for the first three,[57] ten for the second three, and three for the last one![58]

RULE 8. Where the custom is to read the *Megillah* on two days[59] it should be so read, [and where it is customary to read it] in the night and in the day, it should be so read; all depends on the practice of the country. Furthermore, all Israel must read it in the holy tongue.[60]

RULE 9.[61] *The greatest man among the Anakim*[62]—*among the Anakim* refers to our father Abraham whose height was equal to that of seventy-four men; his eating and drinking were of a similar proportion, equal to those of seventy-four men; so too his strength. What did he do?[63] He removed the sixteen[64] sons of Keturah, built for them a walled city of iron and settled them in it. The sun never penetrated into it because it was exceedingly high, so Abraham handed to them disks of precious stones and pearls of which use will be made[65] in the hereafter when the Holy One, blessed be He, will cause the sun and moon to be confounded, as it is written, *When the moon shall be confounded, and the sun ashamed,*[66] because use will be made of these [disks as luminaries].

Og[67] is identical with Eliezer,[68] and [he was so huge that] he could hide Abraham's feet in the palm of his hand. Once he

(57) In accordance with R. Huna's ruling above that 'for three readings . . . no less than ten verses must be allotted'. (58) Since a minimum of three verses must be read for each person who is called up. No reply is given to the objection, but it is possible to provide the following explanation: Only when no more than three persons are called up is it necessary to allot ten verses, but when the number of persons is more than three, as, e.g., on the Sabbath when not less than seven persons must be called to the Torah, three verses for each person or twenty-one in all are sufficient. (59) The fourteenth and fifteenth of *Adar*. (60) In Hebrew. (61) From this point to the end of the tractate is an aggadic addendum. (62) Josh. XIV, 15. (63) This is probably a reference to Gen. XXV, 6, *But unto the sons of the concubines . . . Abraham gave gifts; and he sent them away . . . eastward, unto the east country*. (64) So GRA in accordance with Gen. XXV, 2-4. V, M and H incorrectly 'seventeen'. (65) So GRA. V, M and H read, 'and they will be used'. (66) Is. XXIV, 23. (67) King of Bashan; Deut. III, 11. (68) Abraham's servant; cf. Gen. XV, 2, XXIV, 2ff.

was rebuked [by Abraham] and from fright his tooth fell out. Abraham picked it up and made ivory beds of it in which he slept. Others say that he made of it a chair which he used[69] all his life. Who gave him to Abraham? Nimrod.[70] Og went and built sixty cities, the smallest of which was sixty miles high, as it is stated, *Threescore cities, all the region of Argob.*[71] And what did he eat? A thousand oxen and the same [number of] other animals, and his drink consisted of a thousand measures. A[72] drop of his semen weighed thirty-six pounds.[73]

It was taught: What did our father Jacob do when his sons brought him the coat [stained] with blood?[74] He did not believe them at all. Whence do we infer this? For it is written, *But he refused to be comforted,*[75] because no consolations are acceptable for a living person. One, however, who is dead passes naturally from the mind,[76] as it is stated, *I am forgotten as a dead man out of mind.*[77] What then did he do? He proceeded to make a test with sheaves,[78] writing upon them the respective names of the tribes, their constellations and the months, and said to them, 'I order you to prostrate yourselves before Levi because he wears the Urim and Thummim',[79] but they did not stand up. 'Before Judah who is king', but they did not stand up; but when he mentioned Joseph to them, they all stood up and bowed before Joseph. But it was not yet quite clear that he was alive. So Jacob went to the mountains, hewed twelve stones, arranged them in a row, and wrote on each the name of its tribe, the name of its constellation and the name of its month. On one stone he wrote 'Reuben, lamb, *Nisan*'[80] and similarly on every stone. He began from Simeon and said to them, 'I order you to stand up for Reuben', but they did not stand up. 'For Simeon', but they did not stand up. 'For every

(69) lit. 'and sat in it'. (70) Mentioned in Gen. X, 8ff. (71) Deut. III, 4. (72) So GRA. V, M and H read 'and what was the'. (73) V and H add 'and so for all generations', which makes no sense. (74) Cf. Gen. XXXVII, 31ff. (75) *ibid.* 35. (76) lit. 'he is forgotten from the heart of his own accord'. (77) Ps. XXXI, 13. (78) GRA transposes the order of V, M and H by putting the test of the sheaves before that of the stones, and omits 'according to the first opinion'. (79) Cf. Ex. XXVIII, 30. (80) The name of the tribe, constellation and month.

tribe', but the stones did not stand up. As soon, however, as he mentioned the name of Joseph to them, they stood up at once and bowed before Joseph's stone.[81] For this reason, all the tribes were written on Joseph's stone. Similarly, all Israel are called by Joseph's name, as it is stated, *Thou that leadest Joseph like a flock*.[82] So also all the heads of the families of the priests and Levites, [e.g.] *Eliashib*,[83] because of the phrase *lahashibo 'el 'abiw*;[84] *Elkanah*,[85] because Potiphar had bought him [as it is stated,] *And Joseph was brought down to Egypt, and Potiphar . . . bought him*.[86]

When Rebekah left her father's house[87] she was three years old,[88] because it is customary among kings, when a daughter is born to them, to hear of it after three days;[89] but as her father did not hear [of her birth] he did not defile her up to that time; and now a miracle happened to her in that her father died so that he should not defile her, as it is written, *Neither had any man known her*,[90] and by *man* only her father could be meant,[91] for such was the practice of the Arameans to lie with their virgin daughters after they were three years of age,[92] and then to give them away in marriage.[93]

Dinah was six years old when she bore Asenath from [her association with] Shechem,[94] corresponding to[95] the six years

(81) The translation follows the text of GRA. (82) Ps. LXXX, 2 where *Joseph* is a synonym of all Israel. (83) Neh. III, 1. (84) In the story of Joseph (Gen. XXXVII, 22), E.V. *to restore him to his father*. The name Eliashib is broken up in three parts corresponding in sound and meaning to these three Heb. words. From 'For this reason' to *'abiw* is the reading of GRA. V and H have instead: 'but from the *mishmaroth*, Eliashib the priest'. (85) Connected with *kanah*, 'he bought'. (86) Gen. XXXIX, 1. V inserts in parentheses, *And Pharaoh called Joseph's name Zaphenath, paneah*, etc. (*ibid*. XLI, 45), which has no relevance to the subject. (87) Cf. *ibid*. XXIV, 59ff. (88) V, M and H add 'and three days'. (89) H reads 'after three years and three days'. (90) Gen. XXIV, 16. (91) From 'he did not' to 'meant' is GRA's reading. V, M and H read: 'therefore a miracle happened to her that she should not be defiled'. (92) 'After . . . age' is inserted by GRA; omitted in V, M and H. (93) V, M and H add: 'on account of that which is written, *Neither had any man known her*, and by *man* only her father could be meant'. (94) Cf. Gen. XXXIV. (95) lit. 'the number of'.

which Jacob served Laban in payment for the flock,[96] thus completing[97] the twenty years of his service. [The Archangel] Michael then descended and took her away to the house of Potiphar.

From here onward let the man of understanding increase knowledge.[98]

(96) *ibid.* XXXI, 41. (97) lit. 'until'. (98) From 'completing the twenty years' to 'knowledge' is GRA's text. V and M have instead: 'and he added twenty years, because he died. From this point onwards let the man of understanding increase knowledge. And Michael descended and led her to Potiphar's house'.

'EBEL RABBATHI

NAMED

MASSEKETH SEMAḤOTH

TRACTATE ON MOURNING

TRANSLATED INTO ENGLISH
WITH INTRODUCTION
AND NOTES

BY

RABBI DR. J. RABBINOWITZ
B.A., PH.D.

CONTENTS

INTRODUCTION

Semaḥoth (lit. 'Joys') is a euphemistic term for the older name of the tractate, *'Ebel Rabbathi* (lit. 'Great Mourning'). A tractate of this name is cited in the Talmud, M.Ḳ. 24a, 26b (Sonc. ed., pp. 148, 172) and Keth. 28a (Sonc. ed., p. 153), but is not completely identical with the present work.

The original *Semaḥoth* consisted of a collection of *Baraithoth* dealing with the laws of mourning for the dead prescribed by Judaism, compiled in Palestine by R. Eliezer b. Ẓadoḳ (first cent. C.E.). Later it was amplified and embellished by R. Ḥiyya, a Babylonian of the second century. It took its present form probably in the middle of the eighth century.

The tractate consists of fourteen chapters and, in addition to the laws of mourning, includes much aggadic material and several stories, e.g. the death of the Ten Martyrs (ch. VIII) and the son of R. Ḥanina b. Teradion (ch. XII). It opens with an aggadic passage of a less gloomy character, the compiler apparently feeling it desirable to begin on a brighter note.

Semaḥoth prescribes the regulations to be observed during the closing hours of a person's life, from the time he is dying until after the burial, and the ceremonial mourning to be kept by his nearest kin during the seven and the thirty days which follow. The tractate may therefore be described as 'The Mourner's Manual'.

I venture the suggestion that, because mourners were forbidden to study the Torah during the seven days of strict mourning, the tractate with its aggadic embellishments served as a suitable text for reading and meditation.

I have to acknowledge my indebtedness to M. Higger's invaluable edition of *Semaḥoth* which was of great help in the preparation of this work.

J. RABBINOWITZ.

PROEM[1]

And it came to pass at midnight, that the Lord smote all the first-born in the land of Egypt,[2] etc.; and it is written, *For all the first-born among the children of Israel are Mine, both men and beast; on the day that I smote all the first-born in the land of Egypt, I sanctified them for Myself.*[3] R. Joḥanan said: Although He smote them with the plague of death at midnight, the souls writhed within them until morning. A common proverb says, 'If you give a morsel of bread to a child, inform his mother'.[4] Likewise, the Holy One, blessed be He, said, 'I will inform My children of the death by choking[5] of which their enemies are dying. Let their souls await the morning [before expiring], so that My children shall look upon [the fate of] their enemies'.

(1) The introductory passage bears no relation to the subject-matter of the tractate. The reason which the compiler may have had in mind in using it as a preface is mentioned in the Introduction. Higger (Introduction to his ed., p. 24) has demonstrated that this passage was originally the conclusion of *Soferim* which, in most MSS., preceded *Semaḥoth*. The tractate *Soferim* ends with an unpleasant subject and the author, following an ancient practice, added an aggadic passage of a more cheerful nature (cf. the repetition in the Bible of the penultimate verse of the books of Malachi, Lamentations and Ecclesiastes). The Proem is to be found in *Pesiḳta Rabbathi* XVII, ed. M. Friedmann, pp. 87a, b. Owing to the juxtaposition of the two tractates, it was erroneously attached to *Semaḥoth*. (2) Ex. XII, 29. (3) Num. VIII, 17. (4) Cf. Beẓah 16a (Sonc. ed., p. 81) where it is quoted, not as a proverb, but as a saying of Rabban Simeon b. Gamaliel. (5) GRA's emendation of a verb in the text meaning 'which silences'.

SEMAḤOTH

CHAPTER I

RULE I. A dying man[1] is regarded as a living entity in respect of all matters in the world: he holds [his brother's wife] tied to the leviratical marriage,[2] he frees [his mother] from the obligation of a leviratical marriage[3] and enables her to eat *terumah*,[4] and he [may also] disqualify her from eating *terumah;*[5] he inherits and transmits;[6] if one of his limbs is severed, it is regarded as a limb cut off from the living;[7] if [part of his] flesh [is severed], it is regarded as flesh cut off from the living;[8] and the blood of his sin-offering and guilt-offering is sprinkled for him until the time he dies.[9]

(1) Heb. *gosēs,* the term applied when the rattle in the throat indicates that a person is at the point of death. (2) Cf. Deut. XXV, 5ff. Should the brother die while he himself is dying, the former's widow is precluded from marrying until she is released by the latter from his obligation to wed her (cf. Ohol. I, 6, Sonc. ed., pp. 151f). (3) If his father died and left no other children, his mother is free to remarry because the dying man is regarded as living. Even a child who survives one day frees his mother from the levirate. Cf. Nid. 43b (Sonc. ed., p. 303). (4) If his mother is the daughter of a lay-Israelite married to a *kohen,* she may continue to eat *terumah* so long as he remains at the point of death. (5) If she is the daughter of a *kohen* married to a lay-Israelite, she may not eat of the *terumah* belonging to her father which, on the death of her husband, she is permitted to eat when she returns to his home (cf. Lev. XXII, 12f). The reason is that, since her son is regarded as living, it would be contrary to the stipulation in Lev. *and have no child.* (6) i.e. an estate. On inheritance and transmission, cf. B.B. 108a (Sonc. ed., p. 448). (7) There is a legal difference if it is a limb severed from a living or dead body. If it was from a dead body, a piece of flesh from it, even the size of an olive, communicates defilement; but if from a living body it does not. Therefore, if one of the dying man's limbs is severed, flesh from it does not defile because he is considered a living being. (8) Flesh not necessarily from a severed limb. (9) Where a man who brought a sin- or guilt-offering died before it was sacrificed, the animal for the former had to be killed and the latter turned into the fields to graze until it died naturally. But with a dying man who brought an offering, the ritual connected with his sacrifice was carried out completely.

RULE 2. We do not tie up his cheek-bones,[10] or stop up his apertures,[11] or place a metal vessel or anything which chills on his navel;[12] as it is stated, *Before the silver cord is snapped asunder and the golden bowl is shattered, and the pitcher is broken at the fountain.*[13]
RULE 3. We may not move him, or place him on sand or salt[14] until he dies.[15]
RULE 4. We may not close the eyes[16] of a dying man. Whoever touches and moves him is a murderer. For R. Meir used to say: He can be compared to a lamp which is dripping;[17] should a man touch it he extinguishes it. Similarly whoever closes the eyes of a dying man is considered as if he had taken his life.
RULE 5. We do not rend the garments or bare the shoulder,[18] or deliver a memorial address, or bring the coffin into the house until he dies.[19]
RULE 6. We do not summon the people[20] or recount his good deeds. R. Judah said: If he is a scholar we recount his good deeds.[21]

(10) To prevent the jaw from dropping; cf. Shab. 151a (Sonc. ed., p. 771). (11) To prevent air from entering. (12) Shab. *loc. cit.* reads 'on his stomach', that it should not swell. (13) Eccl. XII, 6. None of these acts may be done because they hasten death. (14) For 'salt' GRA reads 'a vessel that chills'; cf. Tosiftha Shab. XVIII, 18. (15) So that the body should keep cool and not swell. (16) Shab. *loc. cit.* (Sonc. ed., p. 772). Closing the eyes of a corpse is a very ancient practice. According to Ibn Ezra the custom is alluded to in Gen. XLVI, 4, *and Joseph shall put his hand upon thine eyes* (cf. his commentary *ad loc.*). The custom was current among the ancient Greeks and Romans and is practised by the Egyptians [cf. Seyffert, *Dictionary of Classical Antiquities*, p. 101b, and Lane, *Manners and Customs of the Modern Egyptians*, ch. XXVIII]. A man, at the moment of death, was believed to behold the Divine Presence (cf. Job XIX, 27) and therefore it was unfitting that after that vision his eyes should look at anything mundane. Cf. A. Bender in *Jewish Quarterly Review*, VII (1895), pp. 102f. (17) Shab. *loc cit.* reads 'a lamp that is going out'. (18) Cf. Rashi to M.Ḳ. 22b (Sonc. ed., p. 140). R. Meir of Rothenberg explains the word *ḥolezin* in the usual sense of 'removing the shoes'. (19) These things should be avoided so as not to frighten the dying person. (20) Cf. 1 Sam. XV, 4, XXIII, 8 for this usage of the Heb. verb. Brüll adds the word *'ayaroth* (cf. Sanh. 47a, Sonc. ed., p. 311), 'We do not summon the people of the townships'. (21) Because he is accustomed to have his praises sung and it would not distress him in the circumstances.

RULE 7.[22] In the town people do not greet each other.[23] This applies only in a village,[24] but in a large city it is permissible.
RULE 8. We do not carry out the mourning rites for one who came out [at birth] by pieces or with feet foremost, or for one born prematurely[25] at eight months[26] alive or at nine months dead.
RULE 9. For a non-Jew or a slave we do not occupy ourselves with his funeral rites, but we exclaim of him, 'Alas lion![27] alas mighty man!'. R. Judah said: [We, for instance, exclaim], 'Alas, Ṭabi![28] alas, faithful man who ate[29] of his labour!'. They said to him,[30] '[If so], what have you left [to be said] of worthy men [who are not slaves]?' He replied, 'If he was worthy, why should we not say it of him, since[31] we do not receive condolence for [the loss of] male or female slaves?'
RULE 10. It is related that when R. Eliezer's female slave died, his disciples came to comfort him. He entered the courtyard [to avoid them], but they followed him; he went into the house, but they followed him. He said to them, 'I imagined that you would be scalded with tepid water, but now you are not even scalded with hot water.[32] Have [the Sages] not said:[33] We do not receive condolence for slaves because they are reckoned as animals?'[34]
RULE 11. And when Ṭabi the slave of Rabban Gamaliel died, he received condolence for him. They asked him, 'Master, have

(22) This Rule is not connected with the preceding, but speaks of a case where there is a dead person in the town. (23) Because all must share in the mourning, and greeting is not permitted to a mourner. (24) Where all learn quickly of the death. (25) Heb. *nefel,* a child who dies within thirty days of birth. (26) And cannot therefore survive. (27) So H; V repeats 'lion'. (28) The faithful slave of Rabban Gamaliel (cf. Ber. 16b, Sonc. ed. p. 96). (29) In Ber. 'who worked for his living'. (30) To R. Jose who, in Ber. (Sonc. ed., p. 97), suggested the praise to be made over a faithful slave. (31) So H; V lacks 'since'. (32) The meaning is, I made it clear to you that I did not want to receive your condolence; cf. Ber. *loc. cit.* (33) In Ber., 'Have I not taught you', etc. (34) The text in Ber. reads: What do we say over them? As we say to a man on the death of his ox or ass, 'May the Omnipresent repair thy loss', so we say to a man on the death of his slaves, 'May the Omnipresent repair thy loss'.

you not taught us that we do not receive condolence for slaves?' He replied, 'My slave Ṭabi was unlike all other slaves; he was a worthy man'.

RULE 12. He also permitted Ṭabi to put on the *tefillin*. They said to him, 'Master, have you not taught us that slaves are exempt from [the precept of] *tefillin?*' He replied, 'My slave Ṭabi was unlike all other slaves; he was a worthy man'.

RULE 13. We do not call male and female slaves 'Father So-and-so, Mother So-and-so'. Those of the house of Rabban Gamaliel, however, were called 'Father Ṭabi' and 'Mother Ṭabitha'.[35]

RULE 14. We confine the term 'our father' to the three Patriarchs,[36] and the term 'our mother' to the four Matriarchs.[37]

(35) Quoted from Ber. *loc. cit.* [The female slave Ṭabitha is mentioned in j.Nid. I, 4, 49b.] (36) Abraham, Isaac and Jacob. (37) Sarah, Rebekah, Rachel and Leah. This Rule is also culled, in a slightly different form from Ber. *loc. cit.*

CHAPTER II

RULE 1. We do not occupy ourselves in any respect with the funeral rites of one who committed suicide wilfully. R. Ishmael said: We exclaim over him, 'Alas for a lost[1] [life!] Alas for a [lost] life!' R. 'Akiba said to him, 'Leave him unmourned; speak neither well nor ill of him'.[2]

We do not rend garments for him,[3] bare the shoulder, or deliver a memorial address over him. We do, however, stand in a row[4] for him and recite the benediction of mourners[5] for him, from respect of the living [relatives]. The general rule is: With anything that makes for respect of the living we occupy ourselves, but with anything that does not make for the respect of the living, the public do not in any way occupy themselves.

RULE 2. Who [comes within the category of] 'one who committed suicide wilfully'? He does not who climbed to the top of a tree and fell down and died, or he who went up to the top of the roof and fell down and died.[6] But he who calls out, 'Look, I am going to the top of the roof or to the top of the tree, and I will throw myself down that I may die' [comes within the category]. When people saw him go up to the top of a tree or roof [for the purpose] and he fell down and died, he is presumed to have committed suicide wilfully; and with the person who commits suicide wilfully we do not occupy ourselves in any respect.

(1) Heb. *niṭṭelah*, '[a life] carried away'. H reads *nishlah* with a similar meaning (cf. *God taketh away [yeshel] his soul,* Job XXVII, 8). GRA emends to *nithlah*, 'hanged'. (2) lit. 'do not bless him and do not curse him'. (3) According to the *Ṭur* Y.D., §345, near relatives do not rend their garments. (4) At the cemetery after the funeral those present divide themselves into two rows and the mourners pass between them to receive condolences. (5) The condolence ended with the words, 'Blessed be He Who comforteth the mourners' (Keth. 8b, Sonc. ed., p. 40). Hence the term 'benediction of mourners'; cf. J. Rabbinowitz, *Mishnah Megillah*, p. 119. (6) It may have been an accidental fall.

RULE 3. If a person was found strangled or hanging from a tree or lying dead on a sword, he is presumed not to have committed suicide wilfully, and none [of the rites] are withheld from him.
RULE 4. It is related of the son of Gorgias[7] of Lydda that he ran away from school and his father pointed to his ear.[8] In fear of his father he went and destroyed himself in a pit.[9] They went and inquired of R. Ṭarfon who ruled: We do not withhold anything from him.[10]
RULE 5. It is related of a child in Benë Beraḳ[11] that he broke a bottle on the Sabbath and his father pointed to his ear. In fear of his father he went and destroyed himself in a pit. They inquired of R. 'Aḳiba who ruled: We do not withhold anything from him.
RULE 6. Hence the Sages ruled: A man should not point at the ear of a child, but either punish him immediately or keep silent and say nothing to him.

R. Simeon b. Eleazar said:[12] With human nature,[13] a child and a woman, the left hand should repulse them but the right hand bring them back.[14]
RULE 7. With those executed by a Court we do not occupy ourselves in any respect. Their brothers and relatives come and greet the witnesses and judges[15] [as if to say], 'We have no [ill feelings] against you in our hearts because you gave a true judgment'. They observe no [public] mourning[16] for them but grieve, since grief is felt only in the heart.
RULE 8. R. Nathan said: There is no difference between silence and mourning.[17]

(7) A variant is Gornos. [He is not mentioned elsewhere in Rabbinic literature.] (8) i.e. he threatened to punish him. (9) So GRA and H. V wrongly 'with a garment'. (10) He is buried with full rites. (11) A town near Jaffa. (12) Sanh. 107b (Sonc. ed., p. 736), Soṭah 47a (Sonc. ed., p. 246). (13) Heb. *Yeẓer*, which means human instinct; cf. Lazarus, *Ethics of Judaism*, II, pp. 106f. (14) One should not be too severe with them, not suppressing their desires but disciplining them. (15) Cf. Sanh. 46a (Sonc. ed., p. 305). (16) i.e. the seven days, thirty days and the twelve months. (17) i.e. the silence of the mourners is itself a form of mourning. Hence the persons mentioned in the previous Rule must not even grieve. It is suggested that R. Nathan's statement was originally a marginal note which found its way into the text.

RULE 9. The 'meal of comfort'[18] is not eaten in their case, as it is stated, *Ye shall not eat* [anything] *with the blood.*[19]

[The judges of] a Court who ordered the execution of a man used not to eat anything on that day.[20]

[The condemned] are allowed to converse with their brothers and relatives; and not to delay matters[21] they are given to drink wine containing frankincense[22] so that they should not feel grieved. They are urged[23] to confess, because he who confesses has a portion in the World to Come. We find it so with Achan to whom Joshua said, *My son, give, I pray thee, glory to the Lord, the God of Israel, and make confession unto Him; and tell me now what thou hast done; hide nothing from me. And Achan answered Joshua, and said: Of a truth I have sinned against the Lord, the God of Israel, and thus and thus have I done.*[24] What is the meaning of *and thus and thus?* It teaches that he violated the ban twice.[25] [44*b*] *I have sinned,* i.e. I and not my household, I and not my children. This teaches that he truthfully[26] confessed. And whence do we know that his confession made atonement for him? As it is stated, *And Joshua said: Why hast thou troubled us? The Lord shall trouble thee this day*[27]—*this day* art thou to be troubled but thou shalt not be troubled in the World to Come; and it states, *And the sons of Zerah: Zimri, and Ethan, and Heman, and Calcol and Dara: five of them in all.*[28] Do we not know that there were *five of*

(18) The first meal partaken by the mourners on their return from the funeral is termed 'the meal of comfort [*habra'ah*]'; cf. 2 Sam. III, 35, *to cause David to eat bread* (*lehabroth*). It was prepared by friends and consisted of lentils and eggs (cf. Sanh. 63a, Sonc. ed., p. 430, n. 6) the round shape of which being a reminder of the revolving wheel of fortune. (19) Lev. XIX, 26. This is homiletically interpreted to mean: where blood is shed (i.e. an execution has taken place) no ceremonial meal of mourners should be eaten. Cf. Sanh. *loc. cit.* (20) Sanh. *loc. cit.* (21) i.e. to avoid giving the appearance that the execution of justice is unduly protracted. (22) To numb the senses; cf. Sanh. 43a (Sonc. ed., p. 279). (23) lit. 'they teach them'. (24) Josh. VII, 19f. (25) By taking from the devoted things on two occasions. Sanh. 43b (Sonc. ed., p. 284) explains that he took of the ban three times, twice in the days of Moses and once at Jericho. (26) *Of a truth* (*'omnam*) is explained as *be'emunah* ('truthfully'). (27) *ibid.* 25. (28) 1 Chron. II, 6.

them in all?[29] It teaches that Achan will be with them in the world to come.[30]

Similarly one who steals the tax[31] or anything devoted [to the Sanctuary] is as if he shed blood; and not only is he as if he shed blood, but he is also as if he worships idols, was guilty of immorality and desecrates the Sabbath.[32]

RULE 10. We do not occupy ourselves with those who separated themselves from the community[33] in any respect. Their brothers and relatives clothe themselves in white, wrap themselves in white and eat and drink and rejoice because an enemy of the All-present perished; as it is stated, *Do not I hate them, O Lord, that hate Thee? And do not I strive with those that rise up against Thee? I hate them with utmost hatred; I count them mine enemies.*[34]

RULE 11. We do not withhold mourning rites from those executed by the Government.[35]

When do we begin to count [the days of mourning] for them?[36] From the time that [the relatives] despaired in their appeal [for the body to be delivered to them for burial], but not [given up the hope] of stealing it. For he who steals is as if he shed blood, and not only is he as if he had shed blood, but also as if he worshipped idols, etc.[37]

RULE 12. Mourning rites are not withheld in any respect from one who fell into the sea, or was washed away by a stream, or killed by a wild beast. When do we begin to count [the days of mourning] for such as these? From the time that hope of

(29) Since five names are specified. (30) Cf. Sanh. 44b (Sonc. ed., p. 291). Zimri, according to a tradition, is identical with Achan. As Achan is mentioned together with the other four, who are considered to be worthy men, it is an indication that his confession was accepted and with them he shared in the World to Come. (31) i.e. eludes the customs; cf. B.Ḳ. 113a (Sonc. ed., p. 663), Tosiftha B.Ḳ. X, 8. (32) [On this passage, cf. Büchler, *Studies in Sin and Atonement*, p. 198n.] (33) According to Maimonides (*Hil. 'Ebel*, I, 5, cf. *Ṭur* Y.D., §345) the reference is to those who discarded all the religious precepts and ceremonies of Judaism. (34) Ps. CXXXIX, 21f. (35) i.e. the occupying power, viz. the Romans. (36) Usually this begins from the moment the grave is filled in, but here the body of the victim was not handed over to the family for burial. (37) This sentence is repeated from the last clause of Rule 9 and has no relevance to the present context.

finding them has been given up. If they found a body limb by limb, we do not count [the days of mourning] until the head and greater part [of the torso] is found. R. Judah said: The spine and skull constitute the greater part [of the torso].

RULE 13. If one's husband, wife, father or mother had been impaled[38] in his city, one should not continue to reside there[39] unless it is a city as big as Antioch.[40] [Even then] one should not reside in the same side of the city but in another part. Until when is one so forbidden? Until the flesh is completely decomposed and the identity[41] unrecognizable from the bones.

RULE 14. [Beth Shammai said:][42] If a man divorced his wife, he should not live in the same alley or courtyard as she.[43] If the alley belonged to both of them, he transfers the door [of his house] to another side; and if the courtyard belonged to both of them, one vacates it on account of the other, and the woman vacates it on account of the man. This rule only applies if she has remarried[44] and in the case of the [divorced] wife of a *kohen* even if she has not remarried.[45] It further applies only if she is divorced after marriage and not after betrothal.[46] Likewise one who has freed his sister-in-law from the levirate marriage[47] does not vacate on account of her, because he does not feel attracted to her.

(38) By the Roman authorities. Impaling was not a form of execution carried out by the Jews. (39) On seeing him, people will recall the impaling of his relative, and that would be a slight on the memory of the victim. (40) The ancient capital of Syria. Since it is a large city, the fact might not be generally known. (41) lit. 'the form'. (42) GRA omits. For what follows, cf. Keth. 27b, 28a (Sonc. ed., p. 152). (43) Lest he be tempted to cohabit with her. (44) So GRA; V 'they have married'. After remarriage with another she can never return to her first husband (cf. Deut. XXIV, 3f). (45) A *kohen* may not marry a divorced woman, not even his divorced wife (Lev. XXI, 7). (46) Cf. Kallah I, n. I. (47) Cf. Deut. XXV, 5ff.

CHAPTER III

RULE 1. A child who lived only one day counts to his father and mother as a fully-grown man.[1] [The words] 'who lived only one day' are not to be taken as an [irreducible] limit;[2] even if only his head and the greater part of his body came out viable [he is so counted, but in their formulation of the law] the Sages speak of what actually happens.

RULE 2.[3] [An infant] who is carried in the arms[4] is buried by one woman and two men.[5] Abba Saul said: [The burial may be done] by one man and two women. [The Sages] said to him: One woman may be alone with two men, but one man may not be alone with two women.[6]

[The people at the burial] do not stand in line on account of him and they need not recite the mourner's benediction on account of him unless he was thirty days old. If he was thirty days old, he is accompanied [to the grave] by men and women and is carried in a case upon the arms[7] up to the age of twelve months. If he was twelve months old, he is accompanied by men and women and is carried in a case on the shoulder up to the age of three years. R. Judah said: Should his father desire to honour him, they take him out in a coffin to the cemetery even before[8] he is three years old.

RULE 3. If three years old he is taken out on a bier. R. 'Aḳiba said: If he is three years old but his limbs are [developed] like those of an infant two years old,[9] or if he is two years old but

(1) With respect to mourning; cf. Nid. 44a (Sonc. ed., p. 303). The phrase *ḥathan shalem,* lit. 'a complete bridegroom', is based on *ḥathan damim, a bridegroom of blood* (Ex. IV, 25). For the idea that circumcision makes one 'complete', cf. Ned. 31b (Sonc. ed., p. 93). (2) lit. 'the end of the matter'. (3) Cf. M.Ḳ. 24a (Sonc. ed., p. 151). (4) lit. 'goes out in the bosom'. (5) For reasons of propriety. GRA inserts 'but not by one man and two women'. (6) A quotation from Ḳid. IV, 12 (Sonc. ed., p. 413). (7) Cf. M.Ḳ. 24b (Sonc. ed., pp. 151f). Apparently not a full-sized coffin is meant. (8) So GRA; V 'until'. (9) V wrongly in brackets 'he is not carried on a bier'.

his limbs are like those of an infant three years old, he is carried on a bier. Simeon the brother of Azariah said: For anyone who is taken out on a bier the people show their distress.[10] R. Meir said in the name of R. Eleazar b. Azariah: If he is known to the public at large they participate in connection with him [at the funeral], but if not, they do not participate in connection with him.

RULE 4. R. Judah said in the name of R. Eleazar b. Azariah: For the purpose of a memorial address it is sufficient that his neighbours [know him]. In the case of the poor a memorial address is delivered for a child of three,[11] and in the case of the rich for a child of four. R. 'Aḳiba said: In the case of the poor, for a child of six and in the case of the rich for a child of seven. The children of the rich are like the children of scholars and the children of scholars like the children of kings.[12]

RULE 5. In the case of a child of developed intelligence[13] we dwell [in the memorial address for him] on his own [good] deeds, but if he has no such deeds we dwell on the deeds of his parents; and if his parents have no such deeds we dwell on the deeds of his relatives. In the case of a bride we dwell on the honour of her father or father-in-law, because she rises [in esteem] with him[14] but does not fall with him. We may not ascribe merits to one who has none,[15] but we may magnify those which he possessed.[16]

RULE 6.[17] In Jerusalem there was a saying, 'Perform actions [which can be lamented] in front of your bier',[18] and in Judea

(10) [Heb. *meḳallesin* which in Rabbinic Heb. means 'stamp with the foot' as a sign of mourning (cf. Ezek. VI, 11).] The Talmud, which gives the name of the Rabbi as Simeon b. Eleazar, uses a different verb; cf. M.Ḳ. 24b (Sonc. ed., p. 151, n. 9). (11) The child being a greater joy to poor parents who have few pleasures in life, and so his death is a greater loss. (12) The children are praised in the memorial address to honour the parents. (13) lit. 'he knows how to transact [his affairs]'. (14) viz. her father-in-law. The reading of GRA and H is adopted. (15) lit. 'we do not add from the start'. Cf. Ber. 62a (Sonc. ed., p. 390), 'As the dead are called to account [for their deeds], so are funeral orators [who exaggerate the merits of the dead]'. (16) lit. 'we may add to the stock'. (17) Cf. Shab. 153a (Sonc. ed., p. 781). (18) Apparently the place of the people in a funeral procession differed according to local custom. In Jerusalem they walked in front of the bier, in Judea behind it. Cf. Tosiftha Pes. II, 16.

there was a saying, 'Perform actions [which can be lamented] behind your bier'. For in Jerusalem they recounted in front of a dead man's bier only the merits which he possessed; but in Judea they recounted merits which he possessed and did not possess. They, however, who walked behind the bier only repeated after them the merits which he possessed.[19]

[One who dies] between the ages of three and thirty [is mourned] like a bridegroom;[20] between thirty and forty like a brother;[21] between forty and fifty like a father.[22]

RULE 7. R. Simeon b. Eleazar said: Between thirty and forty, if he has children or the majority of his own age have children, [he is mourned] like a father; if not, like a brother. Between forty and fifty, if he has children or the majority of his own age have grandchildren, [he is mourned] like a grandfather, if not like a father.[23]

RULE 8.[24] If one dies under fifty, that is death by *kareth*;[25] at fifty-two, that is the death of Samuel of Ramah; at sixty, that is the death referred to in the Torah, as it is stated, *Thou shalt come to thy grave in ripe age*;[26] at seventy, that is the death of the hoary head, as it is stated, *The days of our years are threescore years and ten*;[27] at eighty, that is the death of a vigorous old man,[28] as it is stated, *Or even by strength fourscore years*.[29] More than this is a life of trouble, for so[30] *Barzilai the Gileadite said to David, I am this day fourscore years old; can I discern between good and bad?*[31]

RULE 9. If one dies after [an illness of] one day, that is a death by [divine] wrath;[32] after two days, it is a precipitous death;

(19) The emended text of GRA and H is followed. (20) Since he may be unmarried. (21) He may be married but childless. (22) As one mourned by his children. (23) So GRA. V and H read: 'have children [he is mourned] like a father; if not like a brother'. (24) Cf. M.Ḳ. 28a (Sonc. ed., p. 182). In j.Bik. II, 1, 64c there are variants in the enumeration. (25) Cf. J. Rabbinowitz, *Mishnah Megillah*, p. 54. (26) Job V, 26; *in ripe age* is בכלח in Heb., the numerical value of the letters being sixty. Cf. M.Ḳ. *loc. cit.* (27) Ps. XC, 10. (28) lit. 'of strength'. (29) *ibid.* (30) This is GRA's reading; V and H have 'and likewise Barzilai' and insert 'more than this is a life of trouble' after the quotation. (31) 2 Sam. XIX, 36. (32) In M.Ḳ. 28a (Sonc. ed., p. 181) the reading is 'a death by being hustled away'.

after three days, it is a death by pestilence; after four days, it is a hurried death; after six days, it is the death decreed in the Torah;[33] after seven days, it is a death of [divine] love; after a longer period, it is a death of suffering.

RULE 10. R. Ḥanina b. Antigonos said: An old man who eats forbidden fat[34] or one who desecrates the Sabbath dies by *kareth*. And what is there to show us that they died by *kareth?* But he who dies after [an illness of] three days dies by *kareth;* after four by a hurried death; after six, it is the death decreed in the Torah; after seven it is a death of [divine] love; after a longer period it is a death by suffering.

R. Judah said:[35] The pious men of former times used to suffer with stomach trouble for about twenty days before death in order to be cleansed of everything, so that they should come pure[36] into the World to Come;[37] as it is said, *The refining pot is for silver, and the furnace for gold, and a man is tried by his praise.*[38] [45a].

(33) A normal death. M.Ḳ. *loc. cit.* has 'five' instead of 'six', quotes Deut. XXXI, 14, *Behold thy days approach that thou must die* and explains: *behold* accounts for one (cf. Sonc. ed., *loc. cit.*, n. 6), *thy days* accounts for two more, *approach* gives a further two, which makes five. (34) Cf. Lev. III, 17. (35) Cf. Midrash Rabbah, Genesis, LXVI, 2 (Sonc. ed., p. 549) and Shab. 118b (Sonc. ed., p. 583). (36) So GRA; V and H 'innocent'. (37) [For the thought, cf. ARN I, 1, p. 1, n. 5.] (38) Prov. XXVII, 21. [H quotes *ibid.* XVII, 3 as the proof-text.]

CHAPTER IV

RULE 1.[1] For all [the nearest of kin] for whom a *kohen* defiles himself as commanded in the Torah[2] [a mourner must observe mourning], viz. for his father, mother, son, daughter, brother, sister and wife.[3] R. 'Aḳiba said: For relatives in the second degree[4] he observes the periods of mourning and grieves,[5] [but should he be a *kohen*] he does not defile himself.

RULE 2. R. Simeon b. Eleazar said: He mourns for his father's father and son's son.[6] But the Sages said: For whomsoever he mourns he should mourn with, and for whomsoever he does not mourn, he does not mourn with.[7] If there is a doubt whether [the deceased] is a brother or not[8] or whether he is his son or not, he mourns and grieves for him, but [if he is a *kohen*] he does not defile himself for him.

RULE 3. For his betrothed wife one does not mourn, grieve,[9] or [if a *kohen*] defile himself.[10] For his divorced wife, although he had children by her, he does not mourn, grieve, or [if a *kohen*] defile himself.

(1) Cf. M.Ḳ. 20b (Sonc. ed., p. 130). (2) Lev. XXI, 2f. (3) So GRA and H. V reads 'wife and sister'. (4) i.e. his grandfather, grandchildren and nephews (Rashi to M.Ḳ. *loc. cit.*). In Sonc. ed., p. 130, n. 7 the enumeration is grandfather, grandmother, grandchildren and the brothers and sisters of parents. (5) While waiting for the funeral to take place; cf. Rule 19 below. (6) R. Simeon either interprets that R. 'Aḳiba excludes the daughter's son and the sister's son, or differs from him in that he holds that one mourns only for these two relatives in the second degree. (7) As one mourns in sympathy with one's father on the death of his father, so should a father mourn with his son on the death of the latter's son. (8) Where the identity of the child at birth or in infancy became confused. j.Yeb. XI, 7, 12a cites an actual case. (9) 'Or grieve' is added by GRA and H. (10) The duty of mourning, etc., for a wife devolves upon the husband only when she can be termed *his kin* (Lev. XXI, 2). The betrothed woman does not come in this category and the divorced wife has lost that status (cf. Sanh. 28b, Sonc. ed., p. 171). See also Yeb. 22a (Sonc. ed., p. 132), 29b (Sonc. ed., p. 183).

RULE 4. Which is [the period of] 'grieving'? From the day of the death until the day of the burial, according to R. Meir; but the Sages said: 'Grieving' is only for one day.[11]

If a High Priest is married to a widow or an ordinary *kohen* to a divorced woman or one freed[12] from levirate marriage, he mourns and grieves for her but does not defile himself.

RULE 5. For his betrothed sister, R. Meir said that [a *kohen*] defiles himself. R. Judah and R. Simeon said that he does not.[13]

RULE 6. For [his sister who was] 'wounded',[14] R. Judah said that [a *kohen*] defiles himself. R. Meir and R. Simeon said that he does not. For a woman who was raped or seduced, all agree that [a *kohen*] does not defile himself. For an adolescent,[15] all agree that he defiles himself.

RULE 7. The general principle laid down by R. Simeon is: He defiles himself for any one who is eligible [to marry] a High Priest, but may not defile himself for one who is not eligible [to marry] a High Priest.

RULE 8. Of all those regarding whom they said that a *kohen* defiles himself, the defilement is not voluntary but obligatory. R. Simeon said: It is voluntary. R. Joshua said: It is obligatory.[16]

RULE 9. It is related of Joseph, a *kohen*, that his wife died on the eve of Passover and he would not defile himself for her. His colleagues pushed him[17] and defiled him forcibly. Defilement is not voluntary but compulsory.

RULE 10. Until how long is it one's duty to defile himself for

(11) Cf. Zeb. 100b (Sonc. ed., pp. 483f). (12) Although such marriages are forbidden (Lev. XXI, 7, 14, the levirate woman being treated in Rabbinic law as a divorced woman), yet if contracted they are valid; but being irregular, they come under the prohibition of *ibid.* 2 (priests in general) and *ibid.* XXI, 11 (the High Priest). Cf. Yeb. 90b (Sonc. ed., p. 616), 'but he may not defile himself for his unlawful wife'. (13) Lev. XXI, 3, *and for his sister a virgin*, betrothal being a form of marriage; cf. Yeb. 60a (Sonc. ed., pp. 400f). (14) lit. 'struck by wood', viz. one who lost her hymen as the result of a blow; Yeb. *loc. cit.* (15) i.e. over the age of twelve years and six months. (16) The phrase *for her he defiles* [E.V. *may he defile*] *himself* (Lev. XXI, 3) is to be understood as an obligation; cf. Zeb. 100a (Sonc. ed., p. 480). (17) He forced him to make contact with the corpse; Zeb. *loc. cit.*

her? R. Meir said: The whole of that day;[18] R. Judah said: Up to three hours. R. Judah said in the name of R. Ṭarfon: Until the top stone closes the grave.[19]

RULE 11. It is related that when R. Simeon b. Yehoẓadaḳ died in Lydda, his brother Joḥanan came from Galilee to defile himself for him after the top stone had closed the grave. They went and inquired of the Sages who said: He may not defile himself, but open the grave for him that he may view [the body].

RULE 12. It is related[20] of a boy[21] that he willed away his property to strangers and left his family out. They protested saying, 'Let [his body] be examined'.[22] They went and inquired of the Sages who said, 'The body may not be examined; after the top stone has closed the grave, a corpse may not be moved from his place'. Another explanation is: Since he is dead, his hair has undergone change.[23]

RULE 13. An ordinary *kohen* who defiled himself for his near kin may not defile himself for strangers even on the same day.[24] This rule applies only when there are sufficient to carry the bier and bury him, but if there are not sufficient to carry the bier and bury him, then he must defile himself.[25] Should he have defiled himself and sufficient people come to carry the bier and bury, he must withdraw to a place of cleanness.

RULE 14. Should there be two roads [for his return from the cemetery] one short but [ritually] unclean and one long but [ritually] clean, if the other persons take the longer road he should go with them; and if they do not, he should take the unclean road out of respect for the people.[26]

RULE 15. While he stands and buries his dead he may, during

(18) i.e. of the death. The funeral generally took place on the same day. (19) Cf. Nazir, Sonc. ed., p. 202, n. 5. (20) Cf. B.B. 154a (Sonc. ed., p. 669). (21) A minor under thirteen years and one day, who could not legally dispose of his property. (22) i.e. let the body be exhumed and his age ascertained from the presence or absence of signs of puberty. (23) Therefore the examination cannot produce decisive evidence of age. (24) Cf. Nazir 42b (Sonc. ed., pp. 154f). (25) Then it is a case of *meth miẓwah* (v. Glos.). (26) This is the reading of H. V has 'respect for the Name'.

the time he is standing in the grave, receive [a body] for burial from others;[27] but once he has withdrawn from the grave he may not defile himself.

RULE 16. If he defiles himself [for a stranger] on the same day [as for another], R. Ṭarfon deems him culpable, but R. 'Aḳiba frees him from culpability. If he defiles himself the next day, all are agreed that he is culpable, because he has rendered one day [of his mourning] void.[28]

RULE 17. A *kohen* must defile himself for his near kin even when they have a disqualification;[29] for his son and daughter who are *Nethinim*[30] or illegitimate;[31] for his brother and sister who are *Nethinim* or illegitimate; but not for any issue he may have from a slave or a non-Jewess (nor from the issue he may have from another source).[32]

RULE 18. If there is a doubt whether [the deceased] is his brother or not or whether he is his son or not, he mourns and grieves but [if a *kohen*] he does not defile himself.[33]

RULE 19. How long is [the period of] 'grieving'? From the day of the death until the day of the burial, according to the view of R. Meir; but the Sages said: 'Grieving' is for one day only.

RULE 20. A High Priest who defiles himself for the dead, lets the hair of his head go loose, or rends his garments,[34] receives forty lashes.[35]

RULE 21. Any defilement contracted by a Nazirite from the dead and for which he must shave his head,[36] if contracted by a High Priest he receives forty lashes for it; but [for those defilements for which] the Nazirite has not to shave his head,

(27) As he is engaged in burying his dead, the new burial merely prolongs his uncleanness; cf. Nazir 42b (Sonc. ed., p. 155). (28) i.e. he has to begin afresh the seven days of mourning. (29) If they are his children by marriage to a divorced woman, etc. (cf. Lev. XXI, 7). (30) The name given to the descendants of the Gibeonites whom Joshua made hewers of wood and drawers of water (Josh. IX). (31) The issue of an incestuous marriage. (32) The clause in brackets is omitted by GRA. It may, however, refer to the issue of one who left the community. (33) Repeated from the latter part of Rule 2, and Rule 19 is repeated from Rule 4. (34) Cf. Lev. XXI, 10. (35) Cf. Tosiftha Mak. IV, 17. (36) Cf. Num. VI, 9.

[if contracted by a High Priest], he does not receive forty lashes.[37]
RULE 22. A High Priest[38] who defiles himself or enters a cemetery receives forty lashes.
RULE 23. If [a *kohen*] entered[39] the residence of non-Jews[40] or the territory of Gentiles[41] or a *beth happeras*[42] or goes outside the land [of Israel],[43] he receives punishment for disobedience.[44]
RULE 24. If he enters a field wherein [the location of] a grave had disappeared, he is not culpable unless he traverses the whole of it.[45]
RULE 25. A *kohen* may defile himself by going outside the land [of Israel] for the purpose of [dealing with a non-Jewish Court in] a civil suit or a capital charge, to announce the new moon or intercalate the year, or to rescue his field from a non-Jew, even if he only goes to protest [against his taking possession of it].[46]
RULE 26.[47] [He may go outside the land of Israel] to study Torah or to take a wife. R. Judah said: If he has nowhere else to study he may so defile himself, otherwise he may not. R. Jose said: Even though he has elsewhere to study he may defile himself, because no one is so meritorious as to be able to learn Torah from any man. It is related of Jose the Babylonian that he defiled himself by going outside the land [of Israel to study Torah] with R. Jose in Zidon.[48]
RULE 27.[49] A *kohen* must defile himself for [the burial of] a bone

(37) Cf. Nazir 49b (Sonc. ed., p. 184). If, e.g., the Nazirite came in contact with a corpse or the flesh of a corpse of the size of an olive. (38) This Rule virtually repeats Rule 20 and is deleted by GRA. (39) So GRA and H. V reads 'although they entered'. (40) Who do not conform to the laws of uncleanness and he is therefore liable to contract defilement. (41) i.e. a district in Palestine which is inhabited only by non-Jews. (42) The noun *peras* denotes 'half' the length of a furrow. A *beth happera* is defined by Jastrow as 'an area of a square *peras*, especially a field, of a square *peras*, declared unclean on account of crushed bones carried over it from a ploughed grave'. (43) Where the laws of uncleanness are not observed by the inhabitants. (44) Unlike the forty stripes which is the punishment for certain offences, this penalty is left to the discretion of the Court and is consequently a Rabbinical form of punishment. (45) Then he must have come in contact with it. (46) Cf. 'A.Z. 13a (Sonc. ed., p. 66). (47) *ibid.* (48) In Phœnicia. (49) The text of this Rule is in disorder and the translation follows the text of GRA.

from his father's [corpse] of the size of a barleycorn,[50] but he may not defile himself for a limb severed from a living person be it even that of his father. R. Judah said: At first [a *kohen*] may not defile himself for a limb severed from a corpse, be it even that of his father.

RULE 28. It is related of Joseph [the son of] Piskas[51] who had a swelling on his foot that a doctor came to remove it. He said to him, 'When you have left as much as a single hair, tell me'. He cut the abscess, and when he had left only as much as a single hair,[52] he informed him. He called his son Neḥunia and said to him, 'My son, until now it was your duty to attend to me, but now go your way; for the Sages said, "One must not defile himself for a limb that was severed from a living person, even if it be his father's" '.[53] When the Sages heard of it they said, 'Of such a man as he it has been stated, *My soul is continually in my hand; yet have I not forgotten Thy law;*[54] [and it further states,] *There is a righteous man that perisheth in his righteousness*[55] *and there is a wicked man that prolongeth his life in his evil-doing.*'[56]

RULE 29. If he found a *meth mizwah,* he must attend to him and bury him. Which is a *meth mizwah?* When [he who finds the body] cries out and the inhabitants of the city cannot hear his voice; but if they can hear his voice, it is not a *meth mizwah.*[57]

RULE 30. [The body remains] a *meth mizwah* until sufficient people arrive to carry the bier and bury him; but once there are sufficient to carry the bier and bury him it is no longer a *meth mizwah.* [45*b*]

RULE 31. If a High Priest[58] and a Nazirite [found a *meth mizwah*], R. Eliezer said that the High Priest should defile himself and not the Nazirite, because the latter must offer a sacrifice on his defilement[59] whereas the former does not. But the Sages said:

(50) Cf. Nazir 43b Sonc. ed., p. 159, n. 2). (51) Cf. j.Nazir VII, 1, 55d. The text here is corrupt and the reading of GRA which agrees with the Talmud is followed. (52) i.e. the swelling was hanging from the foot as by a hair. (53) Joseph was a *kohen*. (54) Ps. CXIX, 109. (55) Although Joseph was in danger of dying under the operation, he remembered to warn his son of the law of defilement which devolved upon a *kohen*. (56) Eccl. VII, 15. (57) Yeb. 89b (Sonc. ed., p. 610), Nazir 43b (Sonc. ed., p. 158). (58) So GRA in agreement with Nazir VII, 1 (Sonc. ed., p. 177). (59) Num. VI, 9ff.

The Nazirite should defile himself even if he has to bring a hundred sacrifices, and let not the High Priest[60] defile himself, because the one is consecrated from the womb and the other is not,[61] and the consecration of the one is temporary[62] and that of the other permanent.

RULE 32.[63] All are agreed that [in the case of the High] Priest anointed with the oil of anointing[64] and [the High Priest robed] in many vestments,[65] the latter must defile himself.[66] As between a [High Priest robed] in many vestments and a deputy [High Priest] who had been anointed,[67] the latter must defile himself. As between a deputy [High Priest] and a *memunneh,*[68] the latter must defile himself. As between a *memunneh* and a *kohen* anointed for war,[69] the latter must defile himself. As between a *kohen* anointed for war and an ordinary *kohen,* the latter must defile himself.[70] As between an ordinary *kohen* and a Levite, the Levite must defile himself.[71] As between a

(60) So H; V reads 'an ordinary *kohen*'. (61) A man becomes a Nazirite by choice. (62) For the term of his vow. (63) For the varying degrees of sanctity indicated in this Rule, cf. Nazir 47a (Sonc. ed., p. 177). The translation follows the emended text of GRA. (64) All High Priests, beginning with Aaron, were consecrated with oil. During the reign of Josiah this ceremony ceased because the king had concealed the flask of special oil used for the ceremony (Hor. 12a, Sonc. ed., p. 85). (65) During the Second Temple the High Priest was not anointed, and was only distinguished from the ordinary priests by wearing a larger number of vestments when officiating, eight as against their four. Hence he was designated 'in many vestments'; cf. J. Rabbinowitz, *Mishnah Megillah,* p. 64. (66) He being of lower sanctity, the duty of attending to a *meth mizwah* devolves upon him. (67) A *kohen* who acted as deputy of the High Priest when disqualified by uncleanness to officiate. When the High Priest returned to duty, the deputy did not revert to the rank of ordinary priest but retained the status of a High Priest with all the privileges of that office with two exceptions (cf. Meg. I, 9, Sonc. ed., p. 51). He was known as *kohen she'abar*. See J. Rabbinowitz, *Mishnah Megillah,* p. 65. (68) Superintendent of the Temple Service, identified with the *Segan,* the deputy High Priest; cf. Sanh. 19a (Sonc. ed., p. 97, n. 1). (69) A priest appointed to accompany the army into battle (Deut. XX, 2; cf. Soṭah VIII, 1, Sonc. ed., p. 207). (70) Because the law against defilement exempts him in other contingencies (Lev. XXI, 2f). (71) Because the Levite is under no restriction in this matter.

Levite and a lay-Israelite, the latter must defile himself.[72] If, however, the two [who find a *meth miẓwah*] are of equal status, the quicker of the two must defile himself; and if the two of them are [equally] quick, then whichever of them wishes to do so should defile himself.

RULE 33. If they found [the body] between a ploughed field and a fallow field, they bury him in the fallow field;[73] between a ploughed field and a field sown with seeds, they bury him in the ploughed field; between a field sown with seeds and an orchard, they bury him in the field sown with seeds; between an orchard and a vineyard,[74] they bury him in the orchard. If both are alike, they bury him in the nearer of the two; and if they are equidistant,[75] they bury him in whichever of them they desire.

RULE 34. R. 'Aḳiba said: This was the beginning of my ministration[76] before the Sages. I once went out early and found the body of a man who had been killed. I took charge of him for a distance of three Sabbath-limits[77] until I brought him to a place of burial and buried him. When I came and discussed the matter before the Sages, they said to me, 'For each step you took it will be accounted to you as if you had committed murder'.[78] I then argued from the less to the greater as a result of my experience:[79] if when I intended to perform a meritorious act I rendered myself culpable, how much more so if I had not intended to perform a meritorious act!' Whenever a person repeated this incident before R. 'Aḳiba, he exclaimed, 'This was the beginning of my ministration [before the Sages]'.

(72) Since the Levite would be precluded from attending to his duties in the Temple for a period. (73) To interfere as little as possible with agriculture (B.Ḳ. 81b, Sonc. ed., pp. 463f). (74) *Kerem* is the reading of GRA and H in agreement with j.Nazir VII, 1, 56b. (75) So H; V incorrectly 'and if they are not alike'. (76) H in conformity with j.Nazir VII, 1, 56a reads *tashmishi*. (77) A Sabbath-limit is two thousand cubits. (78) He should have buried the corpse on the spot; B.Ḳ. 81a (Sonc. ed., p. 459). (79) The next sentence is translated from the text of j.Nazir *loc. cit.*, and the last word of the chapter is again changed to *tashmishi*. The text of V is in disorder.

CHAPTER V

RULE 1. A mourner is forbidden to do work[1] throughout the seven days[2] [of mourning], he, his sons and daughters,[3] his male and female slaves and his cattle; and as he[4] is forbidden to do work, so too others are forbidden to do work for him.
RULE 2. They may do work for him in connection with perishable things; they may gather his harvest for him, operate his wine-press for him and bung[5] his casks. If his olives had been turned,[6] R. Judah says that he may put on the first[7] beam and after his mourning he completes the work. R. Jose said to him, 'But they are perishable things! He may complete [the whole operation in his mourning]'.
RULE 3. With regard to his flax [which is ready] for lifting from the retting and his wool [ready] for lifting from the dye-bath, if there are others [to do the work] they should lift it,[8] but if not he may lift it in private.[9]
RULE 4. If his cask [of wine] is [ready] for bunging, R. Judah says that they cover it with shingles[10] and after the mourning he completes [the work]. R. Jose said to him, 'But it is perishable! He[11] may complete [the whole operation in his mourning]'.
RULE 5. They may besprinkle his white field[12] but may not[13]

(1) Cf. M.Ḳ. 15b (Sonc. ed., p. 92) where by an interpretation of Amos VIII, 10 and by the process of analogy this rule is arrived at. (2) Cf. *ibid.* 21b (Sonc. ed., p. 135) where the reading is 'the first three days'. See, however, Tosafoth *ad loc., s.v. mikk'an,* where it is explained that this refers only to a very poor man. (3) If they reside with him and are dependent upon him (Nachmanides). (4) The reading of GRA and H. (5) Reading *gafin* with H. (6) For maturing before pressing or milling. (7) i.e. press them once. (8) GRA reads *'otho* for V's *'immo.* (9) M.Ḳ. 11b (Sonc. ed., p. 63). 'In private' means behind closed doors. (10) To prevent the wine from turning sour. (11) So GRA for V's 'they'. (12) i.e. a bright, shadeless vegetable or grain field, the opposite of an orchard (Jastrow). (13) H reads שלו for שלא, 'his white field in order to sow it'. GRA emends: 'but do not sow; and they may sow a field of flax for him in his turn for watering rights, according to R. Judah', reading (so also H) רביעה for רביעית. Farmers took turns in drawing on the water-supply.

sow it; they may sow for him a strip [of field] for a crop of flax when his turn for watering rights comes, according to R. Eliezer; but the Sages said: If he had not already sown it with flax, he should sow it with another kind [of crops], and if he does not sow it that week, he can sow it the following week.[14]

RULE 6. If he is a baker in the town and there is no other, he may do the work in private out of respect[15] for the public.

RULE 7. R. Simeon b. Yoḥai[16] said: If he is a hair-dresser or a bath-attendant in the service of the public, and a Festival is close at hand, he may do the work in private out of respect for the public.

RULE 8. If he is engaged in cutting a person's hair and people come and tell him, 'Your father is dead', he should complete the work; this applies whether he is the hair-dresser or he is having his hair dressed. Workmen who have undertaken to do work for a mourner are forbidden to do it in his house but may do it in their own. R. Simeon b. Yoḥai[17] said: A workman hired by the day is forbidden[18] to do work in either [place]; a workman on a contract basis[19] is forbidden [to do it in the mourner's] house, but may do it in his own home. If it is work in connection with objects attached to the ground, it is forbidden [to do the work in either place];[20] in another town it is permitted in either case.[21]

RULE 9. A mourner overtaken by his days of mourning[22] may ease [his hair] with a shearing-knife or a clipping-tool,[23] but not with a scissors; and if his clothes are soiled he may wash them in cold water but not in urine.[24]

(14) GRA reads: 'if he cannot sow it on this watering turn, he can sow it on the next'. The Sages differ from R. Eliezer on both points, viz. they forbid the sprinkling of a white field and sowing flax during the mourning. (15) GRA reads צורך, 'needs' instead of כבוד, 'respect of'. (16) GRA reads 'Gamaliel' in agreement with M.Ḳ., *loc. cit.* (17) GRA reads 'Eleazar'. (18) Because he has the right to repudiate his bargain at any time. (19) i.e. a piece-worker. (20) Because it is generally known that they are working for the mourner. (21) It is not generally so known. (22) i.e. he suffered one bereavement immediately after another. (23) GRA reads 'or with a razor' in accordance with M.Ḳ. 17b (Sonc. ed., p. 112). These instruments remove only a little of the hair and are not usually employed for hair-cutting. (24) Used as a bleaching agent.

RULE 10. A mourner and an excommunicated person who are travelling on the road are permitted to wear their shoes, but as soon as they reach a city they must remove them. The same rule applies [to everybody] on the Ninth of *Ab*[25] and on a public fast day.[26]

RULE 11. An excommunicated person who died has to be 'stoned'[27]—not that they place a high heap of stones upon him, as in the case of Achan[28]—but the messenger of the *Beth Din* takes a stone and places it on the coffin in order to fulfil the duty of 'stoning' in his case.[29]

RULE 12. An excommunicated person may not read a passage of Scripture to others nor may others read it to him; he may not teach nor may others teach him; but he may read Scripture and study for himself so as not to forget his learning.[30]

RULE 13. He may be hired to work and others may hire themselves to him for work; not for his profit, but in order not to close the door before him.[31]

RULE 14. One who is placed under excommunication by his city is not[32] considered to be under it in another city; [46*a*] one under the ban to the disciples is not under the ban to the Sages; one under the ban to the Sages is under the ban to the disciples; one under the ban to all the people is not under the ban to the *Nasi'*;[33] one under the ban to the *Nasi'* is under the ban to all the people.

RULE 15. If one of those who had placed a person under the ban dies, should he have given authority to his colleagues [to annul the ban], they free him, otherwise they do not.[34]

RULE 16.[35] No ban holds for less than thirty days, and no 'reproof'[36] for less than seven days.

(25) The day of mourning for the destruction of the Temple when every Jew has to regard himself as a mourner. (26) Proclaimed in a time of drought. (27) Cf. M.Ḳ. 15a (Sonc. ed., p. 88). (28) Cf. Josh. VII, 26. (29) Cf. M.Ḳ. *loc. cit.*, and 'Eduy. V, 6 (Sonc. ed., p. 35) in the case of Eliezer b. Ḥanok. (30) Cf. M.Ḳ. 15a (Sonc. ed., p. 90). (31) 'Not' is added by GRA and H; i.e. to encourage him to amend his ways to enable him to live. (32) GRA and H insert 'not'. (33) The President of the Grand Sanhedrin. (34) Cf. M.Ḳ. 16a (Sonc. ed., p. 99). (35) *ibid.* (36) As in the case of Miriam (Num. XII, 14f). 'Reproof' is a sharp reprimand; e.g. 'How impudent is that fellow!', cf. M.Ḳ. 16b (Sonc. ed., p. 102).

RULE 17. Rabban Gamaliel said: Any one against whom the Sages pronounce excommunication,[37] even if they later received him back, does not leave the world in peace.[38]

(37) lit. 'stretch forth'; GRA and H insert 'hand' after the verb. (38) Cf. *ibid.* 17b (Sonc. ed., p. 110), 'Whenever the Sages set their eyes against one [the result was] either death or poverty'.

CHAPTER VI

RULE 1.[1] A mourner is forbidden to read the Pentateuch, Prophets and Hagiographa;[2] he is also forbidden to study Mishnah, Talmud, *halakoth* and *'aggadoth*. He is under the prohibition to bathe, anoint [the body], put on sandals[3] and cohabit. He is obliged to cover his head and overturn his couch.[4]

It is related of Rabban Gamaliel[5] that when his wife died he bathed on the first night. His disciples said to him, 'Master, have you not taught us that a mourner is forbidden to bathe?' He replied, 'I am not like other men, I am delicate'.

RULE 2.[6] If people greet him, he should say to them, 'I am a mourner'. On the first day and on the second day he should say to them, 'I am a mourner', but on the third day he may return their salutation in a low voice, although he may not greet them.[7]

RULE 3. On the first day he does not put on the *tefillin*;[8] on the second day he puts them on and if people come to comfort him he takes them off, according to the view of R. Eliezer.

(1) For a full discussion of what is prohibited to a mourner, cf. M.Ḳ. 15a, b and 21a, b (Sonc. ed., pp. 90ff, 133ff). The law is based on Ezek. XXIV, 17, 23 where the prophet is warned not to observe the usual rites of mourning. (2) Because the study of the Torah is a joy. (3) These and covering the head are signs of mourning; cf. 2 Sam. XV, 30, Jer. XIV, 3f, Esth. VI, 12. (4) Cf. M.Ḳ. 15a, b (Sonc. ed., p. 92): God says, 'I have set the likeness of Mine image on them and through their sins have I upset it; let your couches be overturned on account thereof'. According to A. Marmorstein the rite served the purpose of warning the mourners against sexual intercourse which is forbidden in the days of mourning; cf. j.Ber. III, 1, 6a. (5) Cf. Ber. 16b (Sonc. ed., p. 96). (6) From this point V does not divide the chapters into Rules and the division of H is adopted. (7) Cf. M.Ḳ. 21b (Sonc. ed., p. 135). The reading of GRA is: 'On the first, second and third days, he says to them, "I am a mourner", but from the fourth day onwards he returns their salutation'.

R. Joshua said: On the first and second day he does not put on the *tefillin*;[8] on the third day he puts them on and if people come to comfort him he takes them off.[9]

RULE 4. If [another] death took place in that city, on the first and second day [of his own mourning] he does not go out with [the other mourners],[10] but on the third day he goes out with them and stands in the line to receive condolence but not to offer comfort to the others. This only holds good when there are sufficient people to carry the bier and do the burial, but if there are not sufficient he goes out with them even on the first day.[11]

RULE 5. If he came from another district to his relatives, on the second and third day he completes [the days of his mourning] with them, but from the fourth day he counts [the remaining period of mourning] on his own.[12] R. Simeon b. Eleazar said: If he found them still sitting [as mourners] even if it is the seventh day[13] he completes [the period] with them; and if he did not find them sitting [as mourners] even if it be the second day he counts on his own.

RULE 6. On the first and second day, he may not do work even if he is in receipt of charity.[14] On the third day he may[15] work but in private.

RULE 7.[16] He may not work in a field adjoining the city or the road, but he may work privately in his own garden. Likewise a woman may not work on top of the roof or within the courtyard, but she may work privately in her house so long as she is not overlooked by her neighbours.[17]

RULE 8. [The period of] three days applies to a dog which devoured [some of] the flesh of a corpse and entered a house.

(8) *ibid.* 21a (Sonc. ed., p. 134). GRA transposes the names of the two Rabbis in agreement with the Talmud. (9) GRA reads: 'he does not take them off'; H adds at the end 'all the seven days'. (10) To the cemetery to attend the funeral. (11) Cf. M.Ḳ. 21b (Sonc. ed., p. 135). (12) *ibid.* (Sonc. ed., p. 138). So GRA; V reads 'on the fourth and fifth'. (13) So GRA according to M.Ḳ. *loc. cit.* V wrongly 'third day'. (14) Heb. תמחוי, the daily distribution of food to the poor supplied by contributors. (15) GRA omits 'go out and' which is in V. (16) H inserts 'on the first and second day'. (17) Cf. M.Ḳ. 21b (Sonc. ed., p. 135).

If this happened after three days the house is clean, if less it is unclean.[18]

RULE 9. [The period of] three days[19] applies to any of the five species[20] [of grain] sown; [if three days] before Passover it is permitted [to be eaten], if less than this it is prohibited.[21]

RULE 10. One should not go out with a caravan less than three days before the Sabbath.

One may not go out to war,[22] if it is of a voluntary nature,[23] less than three days before the Sabbath. One may not set out on a ship less than three days before the Sabbath.[24]

RULE 11. On the first and second day [of mourning] he may not enter the Temple Mount; on the third day he may enter but must go round to the left.[25] These are they who must go round to the left: a mourner, an excommunicated person, one who has a sick person in his house, and one who lost an object. [When asked,] 'Why do you[26] go round to the left?' [he answers,] 'Because I am a mourner'. They reply, 'May He Who dwells in this House comfort you'. [If he says,] 'Because I am under a ban', [they reply,] 'May He Who dwells in this House put it into their heart to draw you near'; so said R. Meir. R. Jose said to him, 'You make out as if they [who banned] passed a wrong judgment on him; but [what they say

(18) Ohol. XI, 7 (Sonc. ed., p. 198), Shab. 155b (Sonc. ed., p. 796). Three days is deemed to be sufficient time for the dog to have digested the flesh of the corpse, and therefore there is no longer a question of uncleanness being conveyed by the dog into the house. This and the other extraneous matter which follows is introduced here because of the 'three days' which is the time factor. (19) Cf. Ḥallah I, 1f (Sonc. ed., pp. 317f), Men. 70a (Sonc. ed., p. 414). Grain sown three days before Passover is deemed to have taken root. Hence the Omer brought on Passover renders them permissible to be eaten any time after Passover. But if sown less than three days, it is no longer considered the present year's produce when it ripens and may not be eaten until the Omer of the following year is brought. (20) Wheat, barley, rye, oats and spelt. (21) The last clause is added by GRA. (22) Cf. Tosiftha 'Erub. IV, 7, Shab. 19a (Sonc. ed., p. 79). The translation follows H's reading, יוצאין, V has מוציאין which means 'we do not lead [troops] out'. (23) i.e. a war of conquest, the opposite of 'a war of obligation', viz. a war commanded to Israel by God. (24) Cf. Shab. *loc. cit.* (25) Since he is forbidden to bring an offering (Deut. XXVI, 14); cf. Mid. II, 2 (Sonc. ed. p. 6). (26) Reading with GRA and H מה לך for V's מהלך.

is,] "May He Who dwells in this house put it into your heart to hearken to the words of your colleagues so that they may draw you near" '. To one who has a sick person in his house they say, 'May He Who dwells in this House have mercy upon him'; and if he is barely living[27] [they say,] 'May He have mercy upon him immediately'. It is related of a certain woman whose daughter was ill that she ascended the Temple Mount and went round it, and did not move from there until they came and told her, 'She is cured'.

To one who lost some object they say, 'May He Who dwells in this House put it into the heart of the finder to return it to you at once'. It is related of Eleazar b. Ḥananiah b. Hezekiah b. Gorion that he lost a scroll of the Torah which he had bought for one hundred *minas*. He ascended [the Temple Mount], went round it and did not move from there until they came and told him, 'The scroll of the Torah has been found'.

RULE 12. From the beginning Solomon built the Temple only on condition that anyone in trouble would come there and pray; as it is stated, *If there be in the land famine, if there be pestilence, if there be blasting or mildew, locust or caterpillar; if their enemy besiege them in the land of their cities; whatsoever plague, whatsoever sickness there be; what prayer and supplication soever be made by any man.*[28] I have here only the case of an individual; whence do we know that it also holds good of a community? The text continues, *Of all Thy people Israel.* Whence do we know that it holds good of the non-Jew? The text states, *Moreover concerning the stranger that is not of Thy people Israel.*[29] From the words *be made by any man* you might think that it holds good of one who wants children or possessions which will not be for his welfare; hence Scripture states, *For Thou, even Thou only, knowest the hearts of all the children of men*[30]—what is good for him do Thou give to him. And whence do we know that this holds good only if they do not continue in their rebellion? As it is stated, *Who shall know every man the plague of his own heart, and spread forth his hands toward this house.*[31]

(27) lit. 'son of existence', far gone in his illness. (28) I Kings VIII, 37f. (29) *ibid.* 42. (30) *ibid.* 39. (31) *ibid.* 38.

CHAPTER VII

RULE 1. The Sabbath enters into the number of the days of mourning[1] but does not interrupt;[2] Festivals interrupt[3] but do not enter into the number.[4] R. Eliezer said: Since the destruction of the Temple, '*Aẓereth*[5] is reckoned as the Sabbath [during the period of mourning]. Rabban Gamaliel[6] said: New Year and the Day of Atonement are [in this respect] like the Festivals; but the Sages say: The rule is according to the view of neither, but '*Aẓereth* is like the Festivals and the New Year and Day of Atonement are like the Sabbath.

RULE 2. If a man suffered a bereavement one day before a Festival, he interrupts [his mourning] throughout the Festival and counts six days [of mourning] after the Festival; if three days before the Festival he does not need to overturn his couch[7] [after the Festival] according to R. Eliezer;[8] but the Sages said: Even one day, or even one hour [before the Festival]. R. Eliezer b. R. Simeon said: These are the very words of Beth Shammai, and also the very words of Beth Hillel; because Beth Shammai said, 'Three days before a Festival' and Beth Hillel said, 'Even one day and even one hour'. [46*b*]

RULE 3. Abba Saul said: If one buried his dead three days before a Festival, the restrictions[9] appertaining to the seven

(1) Cf. M.Ḳ. 19a (Sonc. ed., p. 121). (2) Although all mourning is suspended on the Sabbath it is yet reckoned as one of the seven days, and the remaining days of mourning continue after the Sabbath. (3) Cancel the rest of the days of mourning. (4) If the burial took place during the Festival. (5) lit. 'solemn assembly', the name given in Rabbinic literature to Pentecost. The Rabbis regarded this Festival as the complement of Passover in the same way that *Shemini 'Aẓereth* (cf. Num. XXIX, 35) is the complement of Tabernacles. (6) So GRA; V has 'Rabban Simeon b. Gamaliel'. (7) The remaining days are cancelled. (8) The translation follows the text as emended by GRA in agreement with M.Ḳ. 20a (Sonc. ed., p. 126). (9) Heb. *gezeroth*, 'restrictive measures', i.e. the prohibitions of a mourner as enumerated in the preceding chapters.

days' mourning cease to apply to him; if eight days before a Festival, the restrictions of the thirty days cease to apply[10] (and the ruling is in accordance with this statement).[11]

RULE 4. [Should the death occur] eight days before a Festival, if he wishes to cut his hair or wash his clothes on the eve of the Festival he may do so; if he did not cut his hair or wash his clothes on the eve of the Festival, he may not do so until the thirty days are completed.

RULE 5. [If the death occurs] two days within the Festival,[12] he interrupts [the mourning] for all the Festival and counts seven [days] after it, and people occupy themselves[13] with him for the five days after the Festival. [If the death occurs] seven days within the Festival, he interrupts [the mourning] for all the Festival and counts [seven days] after the Festival, and the community do not occupy themselves with him at all after the Festival.[14]

RULE 6. On the days which he counts after a Festival, neither his slave nor his cattle need abstain from work; only he and his near kin conduct themselves like mourners.

RULE 7. A Festival is reckoned for the mourner into the count of the thirty [days][15] but not into the count of the seven [days]. A mourner is regarded on a Festival as if he were no mourner, but in matters of a private nature he does observe mourning. The general rule is: as regards any [mourning rite] in the carrying out of which others are associated with him,[16] a Festival is taken into account with the seven days,[17] otherwise it is not taken into account with them.

(10) Cf. M.Ḳ. 19b (Sonc. ed., p. 122). By then he has sufficiently done his duty to the dead. (11) GRA deletes this clause which is printed by V in brackets. (12) Passover or Tabernacles. (13) People came to offer him condolence. (14) It is presumed that they had done so during the Festival, visiting mourners being then permitted. (15) If the seven days ended before the conclusion of the Festival, the Festival interrupts the thirty days; if the funeral took place during the Festival, although the seven days have to be observed after the Festival, for the purpose of the thirty days the period of the Festival is taken into account. (16) e.g. consolation of the mourners. (17) Hence when the burial took place during the Festival, people come to condole for four days only or not at all.

RULE 8. Thirty are the days of mourning.[18] For thirty days he may not put on pressed clothes[19] or cut his hair. Thirty days are allowed for the collection of debts; thirty days must elapse before a captive woman of 'goodly form'[20] may be taken to wife; thirty days in the case of betrothal; thirty days in the case of marriage; thirty days within which a charge of lack of virginity can be made; thirty days are granted to a widow about to remarry to make her preparations; thirty days for a sister-in-law [after her levirate marriage to declare, 'He has not cohabited with me']. If a man forbade his wife by vow to have any benefit from him [the prohibition lasts] thirty days. The vow of a Nazirite of unspecified duration [remains in force] for thirty days.

RULE 9. Whence [thirty days] for mourning? As it is stated, *And the children of Israel wept for Moses in the plains of Moab thirty days.*[21]

RULE 10. How is it with pressed clothes? It is forbidden [for a mourner] to don pressed clothes, i.e. those that came from the press.[22] This is the view of Rabbi [Judah the Prince]; the Sages said: [It refers] to dyed but not white garments. R. Meir said: White but not dyed, new but not worn garments. He may put on his money-belt,[23] girdle,[24] felt-shoes[25] and turban.[26] It is permitted to take garments to be pressed within thirty days.[27]

RULE 11. How is it with cutting the hair? [A mourner] is forbidden to remove the hair whether of the head or of his [upper] lip, or of the beard or of the hair on any part of him. A woman is permitted to remove hair[28] after the seven days.

RULE 12. How is it with the collection of debts?[29] If a person

(18) All the points mentioned in this Rule are discussed in the continuation. (19) i.e. clothes ironed or pressed smooth of creases; cf. Krauss, *Talmudische Archäologie*, I, p. 581, n. 375. (20) Cf. Deut. XXI, 11. (21) *ibid.* XXXIV, 8. (22) After bleaching, the clothes were put in the press; M.Ḳ. 23a (Sonc. ed., p. 145, n. 5). (23) A hollow belt in which money was carried. (24) A band or fillet worn by women over the breast. (25) Or, felt hat. (26) Although they are pressed, they are not regarded as garments. (27) In readiness for wear after the thirty days. (28) The translation follows the text of GRA and H. (29) Cf. Mak. 3b (Sonc. ed., p. 11).

lends his friend money without specifying a date [for repayment], he may not demand it of him until thirty days are completed.

RULE 13. How is it with a woman of 'goodly form'? [It is stated,] *And thou hast a desire unto her, and wouldest take her to thee to wife; then thou shalt bring her home to thy house; and she shall shave her head, and pare her nails.*[30] [This means that] she shall shave her head and cut her nails, so the view of R. Eliezer;[31] R. 'Aḳiba [takes the meaning to be,] she lets the hair of her head grow long and lets her nails grow. R. Eliezer said: An act is mentioned in respect of the head[32] and an act is mentioned in respect of her nails;[33] as the former signifies removal of the hair so the latter signifies removal of the nails. R. 'Aḳiba said: An act is mentioned in respect of the head and an act is mentioned in respect of the nails; as disfigurement is the purpose of the former so is disfigurement the purpose of the latter. There is a support for R. Eliezer [in the verse], *And Mephibosheth the son of Saul came down to meet the king; and he had neither dressed his feet, nor trimmed his beard.*[34] There is a support for R. 'Aḳiba [in the verse], *Till his hair was grown like eagles' feathers, and his nails like birds' claws.*[35]

And she shall put the raiment of her captivity from off her.[36] If she wore white garments and they were comely for her, black garments and they were comely for her,[37] bracelets, nose-rings or rings, they are taken away from her so that she should sit and appear in her disfigurement. *And she shall remain in thy house:*[38] so that while she remains in his house he enters and sees her in her disfigurement. *And bewail her father and her mother:*[39] this means her actual father and mother, in the view of R. Eliezer; but R.

(30) Deut. XXI, 11f; cf. Yeb. 48a (Sonc. ed., p. 316). (31) The text is so corrected by GRA and H in accordance with Yeb. *loc. cit.* The Heb. verb, the meaning of which is disputed, is lit. 'do'. (32) *She shall shave her head.* (33) *And 'do' her nails.* (34) 2 Sam. XIX, 25, where the word for *trimmed* is lit. 'done'. (35) Dan. IV, 30. The 'support' is here not the usage of the verb but the idea that letting the nails grow is a disfigurement. (36) Deut. XXI, 13, i.e. waits before he may marry her. (37) H reads: 'If she wore beautiful garments she is clothed in black garments; if she had on . . . taken away from her to make her look ugly'. (38) Deut. *ibid.* (39) *ibid.*

'Aḳiba explains that *her father and her mother* refers to the idols [which she worshipped], as it is stated, *Who say to a stock: 'Thou art my father', and to a stone: 'Thou hast brought us forth'.*[40]

A month of days[41]—i.e. thirty days. R. Simeon b. Eleazar said: [It means] three months, as it is stated, *And bewail her father and her mother a month,* i.e. one month, *of days* signifies [with the former] two months, *and after that* [is added in the text] to include the third month, [the purpose being] that the holy seed shall not be mingled with that of other peoples. When does this apply? Only if she does not wish to become a proselyte; but if she is willing to become a proselyte, he has her immersed [in the ritual bath] and emancipates her, and is permitted to marry her forthwith. R. Simeon b. Eleazar said: Even if she is not willing[42] at first, he has her immersed as a handmaid, emancipates her and may marry her forthwith. Why all this [procedure]? In order that the holy seed should not be mingled with that of other peoples.[43] It is better for Israelites to eat the flesh of animals about to die, yet ritually slaughtered, than the flesh of dying animals which definitely perished.[44]

RULE 14. How is it with betrothal? It is forbidden to hold a betrothal feast within the thirty days [of mourning].[45]

RULE 15. How is it with marriage? It is forbidden to hold a marriage feast within the thirty days [of mourning], but if his meat is prepared[46] and his father or mother-in-law[47] died, he brings the bride into the bridal chamber, performs the act of consummation and then separates himself from her [until] after the seven days.[48] When does this apply? Only if his father

(40) Jer. II, 27. (41) Deut. *ibid.*, E.V. *a full month*. The translation follows the emended text of GRA. (42) Added by GRA. (43) The question and answer are deleted by GRA. (44) And were not ritually slaughtered. The intention is that the procedure is based on the principle of the lesser evil. It is better for the man to be married to the woman rather than just cohabit with her (cf. Ḳid. 21b, 22a, Sonc. ed., p. 104). The last word of the sentence should be read as בודאי (definitely) instead of לבדה (alone). (45) Cf. M.Ḳ. 23a (Sonc. ed., p. 145). (46) Cf. Keth. 4a (Sonc. ed., p. 11). (47) So GRA instead of V 'father-in-law', and again later in this paragraph. (48) Only in an extreme contingency like this is a mourner permitted to hold the marriage-feast.

or mother-in-law died; but if his wife died, he is forbidden to remarry until three Festivals have gone by. R. Judah said: Until two Festivals have gone by, and he brings [her into the marital chamber] on the third. When does this apply? Only if he has children, but if he has no children or his children are young, it is permitted for him to remarry within thirty days.[49] It happened that R. Ṭarfon's wife died, and he said to her sister within the days of mourning, 'Be my wife and bring up your sister's children'. Nevertheless he did not cohabit with her until after the thirty days.

RULE 16. How is it with virginity? Within thirty days he may make a plea of the absence of virginity,[50] but after thirty days he cannot.

RULE 17. How is it with a widow?[51] If the man [to whom she is betrothed] claims her [in marriage] and she holds back, we allow her thirty days to make provision for herself; and as we allow [that period] to the woman, so too we allow it to the man.[52]

RULE 18. How is it with a sister-in-law?[53] If a sister-in-law declared within thirty days [after the levirate marriage], 'I have had no cohabitation',[54] [the levir] is compelled to give her *ḥaliẓah*, but [if her declaration was made] after thirty days, he is not compelled[55] to give her *ḥaliẓah*.

RULE 19.[56] Should a man forbid his wife by vow to have any benefit from him, [if the prohibition is to last] not more than thirty days he must appoint a steward,[57] but if for a longer period he must divorce her and give her [the amount stipulated in] her *kethubah*.[58]

RULE 20. [How is it with a Nazirite whose vow is of unspecified duration?][59] The vow of a Nazirite which is of unspecified

(49) Cf. M.Ḳ. *loc. cit.* (50) Deut. XXII, 13ff; Yeb. 111b (Sonc. ed., p. 780). (51) Cf. Keth. 57a (Sonc. ed., p. 337). (52) i.e. the same time is allowed to a widow and to a man to make preparation for the wedding. (53) Cf. Yeb. *loc. cit.* (54) And he denies her allegation. (55) GRA reads with Yeb. *loc. cit.*, 'he is requested to give her *ḥaliẓah*'. (56) Cf. Keth. 70a (Sonc. ed., p. 433). (57) To provide maintenance for his wife. (58) If the woman demands a divorce. (59) Cf. Num. VI, Nazir 5a (Sonc. ed., p. 16).

duration [remains in force] thirty days.[60] Whether he declared, 'Behold I am a Nazirite' without qualification, or he declared, 'Behold I am a Nazirite for one day', his status as a Nazirite lasts thirty days.[61] If he completed his period as a Nazirite outside the land of Israel[62] and later returned there, [47a] Beth Shammai said that he remains a Nazirite for thirty days, and Beth Hillel said that he [reverts to the] beginning of his status as a Nazirite.[63]

RULE 21. One who resides in the land of Israel thirty days is under the obligation to affix a *mezuzah*, and he who rents a house must do so forthwith;[64] but he who resides outside the land of Israel is exempt. One who rents a house for thirty days[65] and one who resides in an isolated place[66] for thirty days is under the obligation to affix a *mezuzah*.

RULE 22. If one buys newly born cattle from his neighbour, [he may retain the dam] to suckle them, in the case of small cattle[67] for thirty days and in the case of large cattle[68] for fifty days. R. Jose said: In the case of small cattle for three months because they need much attention.[69] As for attending to the first-born of cattle[70] [before handing them over to the *kohen*], in the case of small cattle the period is thirty days and for large cattle fifty days. R. Jose said: In the case of small cattle the period is three months because they need much attention.

RULE 23. Beth Shammai[71] declared an old *Sukkah* to be invalid; Beth Hillel pronounced it valid (but he must add something new to it).[72] What is 'an old *Sukkah*'? One which was made thirty days before the Festival [of Tabernacles]; but should he have made it for the purpose of [being used on] the Festival, even [if erected] at the beginning of the year, it is valid.

(60) The period of thirty days is based on the numerical value of the word *yihyeh, he shall be* [*holy*] in Num. VI, 5. (61) So GRA. (62) Where the laws incumbent on a Nazirite cannot be carried out effectively. (63) i.e. he has to start afresh; cf. 'Eduy. IV, 11 (Sonc. ed., p. 28). (64) Cf. Men. 44a (Sonc. ed., p. 266). (65) So GRA; V and H 'fifty days'. (66) A halting-place for travellers (Jastrow). (67) Sheep, goats, etc. (68) Of the bovine species. (69) Cf. B.M. 69a (Sonc. ed., p. 402). (70) Ex. XIII, 12, cf. Bekoroth 26b (Sonc. ed., p. 170). (71) Cf. Suk. 9a (Sonc. ed., p. 32). (72) The words in brackets are added by GRA and H from j.Suk. I, 2, 52b.

RULE 24.[73] Rice, millet, panic and sesame which took root before the New Year are tithed[74] as belonging to the previous year[75] and are permitted in the seventh year;[76] but if they did not [take root before the New Year] they are forbidden in the seventh year and are tithed as belonging to the next year.[77] R. Simeon of Shezur said: Egyptian beans sown from the outset for the purpose of seeds[78] are treated in a like manner. R. Simeon said: Large beans are treated in a like manner if they formed pods[79] before the New Year. Shallots[80] and Egyptian beans which have not been watered within thirty days of the New Year are treated as if a year had passed[81] and may be retained in the seventh year; otherwise they are not considered as such and may not be retained in the seventh year. RULE 25.[82] If one plants, bends over[83] or grafts a tree within thirty days of the New Year, a year has passed for him [by the New Year][84] and he may preserve the growth during the seventh year; otherwise a year has not passed for him and he may not preserve the growth in the seventh year. R. Judah said: Any grafting which does not take root within three days will never do so. R. Simeon and R. Jose said: Any grafting which does not take root within two weeks is no grafting. The fruit of such a planting is forbidden until the fifteenth of *Shebaṭ*.[85]

(73) Cf. Shebi. II, 7 (Sonc. ed., p. 152). (74) In an ordinary year. (75) If the previous year was the first, second, fourth or fifth of the seven-year cycle the tithe is termed 'the second tithe'; if it was the third or sixth it is termed 'the poor man's tithe'. (76) Those that took root in the seventh year are unaffected by the incidence of the sabbatical year. (77) They are treated like the produce of the sabbatical year and not subject to the tithe. (78) And not for food. (79) When beans grow hard and appear as in a pod they are liable to the tithe. (80) lit. 'onions which produce no seeds'. (81) i.e. for the purpose of the tithe they are treated as last year's produce. (82) Cf. Shebi. II, 6 (Sonc. ed., p. 151). (83) viz. a branch from a tree and plants it in the ground without separating it from the parent tree. (84) i.e. the thirty days count as a full year of the three years in connection with *'orlah;* cf. Lev. XIX, 23ff. (85) 'The New Year for trees', although the three years of *'orlah* are reckoned to have been completed by the previous New Year.

CHAPTER VIII

RULE 1. We go out to the cemetery and examine[1] the dead within three days and do not fear [of being suspected of] superstitious practices.[2] It once happened that [a man who was buried] was examined [and found to be living], and he lived for twenty-five years and then died. Another[3] [so examined lived and] begat five children before he died.

RULE 2. We erect a canopy[4] for bridegrooms and brides [who died before marriage] and suspend from it articles which have and have not reached the edible stage; this is the opinion of R. Meir. R. Judah[5] said: We only suspend from it articles which have not reached the edible stage.[6] These are what are suspended from it: Nuts which have not reached the edible stage,[7] loaves of bread which are not edible,[8] strips of purple wool, flasks of perfumed oil. And these are the articles which may not be suspended from it: Nuts which have reached the edible stage, pomegranates which have reached the edible stage, loaves of bread which are edible, and flasks of sweet oil. The general rule is: no benefit may be derived from anything that is suspended from the canopy.

RULE 3. We scatter before bridegrooms and brides strings of fish[9] and pieces of meat in summer but not in winter; but not pieces of cooked fish, mushrooms, truffles or sesame both in

(1) To see if by chance there is life in them. This was the practice in ancient times when the dead were buried in caves and it was only necessary to lift the lid of the coffin to make an inspection. Cf. *Ṭur* Y.D., §394. (2) lit. 'the ways of the Amorites'. For examples of such practices, cf. Shab. 67a, b (Sonc. ed., pp. 320ff). (3) According to the reading of the *Ṭur* which omits 'another', this refers to the same man. (4) Not to deprive them of the ceremony of which they were deprived by death. (5) GRA reads 'the Sages'. (6) Because such fruit will become prohibited and therefore wasted, and to waste food is not permitted. (7) GRA and H insert 'pomegranates' to make this list conform to the next sentence. (8) i.e. burnt or mouldy.

summer and winter; but one takes roasted ears of corn and nuts and throws them. The general rule is: we may not scatter before them anything that is perishable.

RULE 4. We may let wine and oil flow through pipes[10] before bridegrooms and brides and we do not fear [of being suspected] of superstitious practices; nor do we fear of sinning by putting food to shame.[11] It is related that Judah and Hillel, the sons of Rabban Gamaliel, came to Ben Zakkai at Kabul[12] and the citizens let wine and oil flow through pipes [in their honour].

RULE 5. We may burn [articles][13] at the funerals of kings and mutilate [their animals], and we do not fear [of being suspected] of superstitious practices. Any mutilation which disqualifies the animal as food makes it forbidden to be eaten, but benefit may be derived from it; and when the mutilation does not disqualify the animal it may be eaten and obviously benefit may be derived from it. Which mutilation disqualifies it? From the knee downwards.[14]

RULE 6. We may burn articles at the funeral of kings but not at the funeral of princes.[15] When Rabban Gamaliel the Elder died, the proselyte Onḳelos burnt after him more than eighty Tyrian *minas*. They asked him, 'What was your purpose in doing this?' He replied, 'It is written, *Thou*[16] *shalt die in peace; and with the burnings of thy fathers, the former kings that were before thee, so shall they make a burning for thee.*[17] And is not Rabban Gamaliel worth more than a hundred useless kings?'

RULE 7. We cover the hair of [dead] brides, uncover the face of [dead] bridegrooms,[18] and place ink and pen at their

(9) Fish strung on a line; cf. B.M. II, 1 (Sonc. ed., p. 130). (10) Cf. Ber. 50b (Sonc. ed., p. 306). According to Büchler, this was done for the purpose of diffusing a sweet odour and do honour to distinguished guests (M.G.W.J., XLIX, pp. 12ff). (11) i.e. wasting it. So GRA, V has 'their prohibition'. (12) A town S.E. of Akko in northern Palestine. (13) So that others may not use them; cf. 'A.Z. 11a (Sonc. ed., p. 57). (14) Corrected in agreement with Ḥul. 76a (Sonc. ed., p. 419). V and H read 'upwards'. (15) Cf. 'A.Z. *loc. cit.* GRA reads: 'As we burn articles at the funeral of kings, so do we likewise at the funeral of princes'. (16) Addressed to Zedekiah, king of Judah. (17) Jer. XXXIV, 5. (18) As a sign of grief.

side,[19] and we do not fear [of being suspected] of superstitious practices.

[20](When Rabban Gamaliel the Elder entered [the meeting place of the Rabbis to intercalate the year], he found eight [present]. He asked, 'Who is it that entered without permission?' Samuel the Small arose and said, 'Rabbi, I entered only to inquire about the law [of intercalation]'.[21] He answered, 'O Eldad and Medad,[22] all Israel know that if I had ordered that only two should enter, you would have been one [of them] to enter'.)[23]

We suspend the key and writing-tablet of a dead man from his coffin from grief of soul. When Samuel the Small died, they suspended his key and writing-tablet from his coffin because he had no son, and when Rabban Gamaliel the Elder and R. Eleazar delivered their funeral oration over him, they exclaimed, 'For this one it is fitting to weep, for this one it is fitting to mourn. When kings die they leave their crowns to their sons; when wealthy men die they leave their riches to their children; but Samuel the Small has taken away with him all the desirable things in the world and has departed'. And thus he[24] spoke at the time of his death, 'Simeon [b. Gamaliel] and Ishmael [the son of Elisha the High Priest][25] are destined for the sword and the rest of the people for spoliation; great distress will befall [Israel] after them'. He uttered these words in Aramaic.

RULE 8.[26] When R. Simeon b. Gamaliel and R. Ishmael came [to be tried], it was decreed against them that they should be

(19) As if to say that had the bridegroom lived he would have written a *kethubah* for his bride. (20) GRA deletes this paragraph which is printed by V in brackets. It has no relevance to the context and is derived from Sanh. 11a (Sonc. ed., p. 44). The text is in great disorder. (21) And not to take part in the proceedings without invitation. (22) Cf. Num. XI, 26. They were worthy that the Spirit of God should alight upon them. (23) So highly was Samuel the Small esteemed. (24) i.e. Samuel the Small under the influence of the Holy Spirit. (25) They met their death after the capture of Jerusalem. (26) [Cf. ARN XXXVIII, 3, above pp. 191ff.] (27) A title of honour (cf. Gen. XLI, 43). It was interpreted by the Rabbis as the initial letters of the Heb. phrase, 'father in wisdom though tender in years'; cf. Midrash Rabbah, Genesis, XC, 3 (Sonc. ed., p. 829).

put to death. Whereupon R. Ishmael broke into tears; and R. Simeon said to him, '*Abrek,*[27] why do you weep? Two steps more[28] and you will be in the bosom of the righteous, and yet you weep!' He replied, 'Do I then weep because we are about to be executed? It is because we are about to be executed [in the same way] as murderers and desecrators of the Sabbath'. He said to him, 'Perhaps you were having a meal or you were sleeping when a woman came to ask [a ruling] concerning her ritual impurity or her cleanness, and your servant told her that you were asleep. And the Torah states, *Ye shall not afflict*[29] *any widow or fatherless child. If thou afflict them in any wise—for if they cry at all unto Me, I will surely hear their cry.*[30] And what is written after this? *My wrath shall wax hot, and I will kill you with the sword*'. Some say that it was [47b] R. Simeon b. Gamaliel who was weeping and R. Ishmael who answered him in these words.

When R. Simeon and R. Ishmael were executed and the report reached R. 'Aḳiba and R. Judah b. Baba, they arose, girded their loins with sackcloth, rent their garments and exclaimed, 'Our brother-Israelites, if good were destined to come to the world, at first none would receive it but R. Simeon and R. Ishmael; but now that it is revealed before Him Who spake and the universe came into being that eventually great punishments will come upon the world, they have consequently been taken out of the world; [as it is stated,] *The righteous perisheth, and no man layeth it to heart,*[31] and it continues, *He entereth into peace, they rest in their beds*'.[32]

RULE 9. When R. 'Aḳiba was executed in Caesarea and the news reached R. Judah b. Baba and R. Ḥanina b. Teradion, they arose, girded themselves in sackcloth, rent their garments and exclaimed, 'Our brethren, hearken unto us! R. 'Aḳiba was not executed for robbery or because he did not labour in the Torah with all his strength. He has only been put to death as a sign,[33] as it is stated, *Thus shall Ezekiel be unto you a sign; according to all that he hath done shall ye do; when this cometh, then shall ye know*

(28) i.e. immediately. (29) Keeping an anxious woman waiting is a form of affliction. (30) Ex. XXII, 21f. (31) Isa. LVII, 1. (32) *ibid.* 2. (33) Of great misfortunes to come.

that I am the Lord God.[34] Within a short while there will be no place found in the land of Israel where no [slain] will be cast forth, as it is stated, *Speak: Thus saith the Lord—And the carcasses of men fall as dung upon the open field, and as the handful after the harvestman, which none gathereth'.*[35] It is reported that it was not long before war came and disturbed the world, and within twelve months the municipalities[36] in Judea ceased; as it is stated, *Tremble, ye women that are at ease; be troubled, ye confident ones:*[37] *Ye women that are at ease* refers to the municipalities in Judea, *ye confident ones* refers to the fortified towns.[38] *Confident ones* is nothing else than a term for walled cities.[39] It is reported that twelve months had not passed before what had been said was fulfilled.

RULE 10. R. Meir illustrated it by a parable. To what is the matter like? To a king who prepared a banquet and invited guests without fixing a time when they should leave. The shrewd among them left at the ninth hour,[40] returned home and went to bed while it was still light; others left at sunset while the shops were still open and the lamps burning, entered their homes and went to bed by the light of the lamps; still others left at two or three hours in the night when some shops were open and some shut, some with their lamps alight and some with their lamps extinguished, entered their homes and went to bed in the dark. Those remaining at the banquet became intoxicated, and wounded and killed each other; as it is stated, *I saw the Lord standing beside the altar; and He said: Smite the capitals, that the posts may shake; and break them in pieces on the head of all of them; and I will slay the residue of them with the sword.*[41]

RULE 11. When R. Ḥanina b. Teradion was arrested[42] on the

(34) Ezek. XXIV, 24; verses 15-27 describe the symbols of Ezekiel's bereavement. (35) Jer. IX, 21. (36) Heb. *bula'oth,* the Greek for 'senate, city-council'. Büchler, *The Economic Conditions of Judaea,* p. 28, n. 2, defines the term as 'open places as opposed to fortified towns'. (37) Isa. XXXII, 11. (38) Cf. Büchler, *loc. cit.* (39) Heb. *ṭeraksin* which Jastrow takes to be a corruption of *kerakim,* 'walled cities'. [The sentence is apparently a marginal note, and it is difficult to see how a common word should have been misread as an unusual one. Krauss, *Lehnwörter,* pp. 274f, more probably 'enclosures'.] (40) i.e. 3 p.m. (41) Amos IX, 1. (42) So GRA and H; V has 'entered'.

charge of heresy,[43] [the Romans] sentenced him to be burnt, his wife to be executed and his daughter to be consigned to a brothel. He asked, 'What have they decreed against that poor woman?' They replied, 'She is to be executed'. Thereupon he recited of her the verse, *The Lord is righteous in all his ways.*[44] She asked, 'What have they decreed against the Rabbi?' They replied, 'He is to be burnt'. Thereupon she recited of him the verse, *Great in counsel, and mighty in work.*[45]

When they burnt him, they wrapped him in a scroll of the Torah and burnt him. His daughter wept, wailed and threw herself before him. Whereupon he exclaimed, 'My daughter, if for me you weep, if for me you throw yourself down, it were better that a fire which [a man] has fanned should consume me and not one which [a man] has not fanned;[46] as it is stated, *A fire not blown by man shall consume him.*[47] If, however, you threw yourself down because of the scroll of the Torah, behold, the letters are flying upwards and only parchment is being consumed. For even great servants of the king are punished by inferior servants, [as it is stated,] *Therefore have I hewed them by the prophets, I have slain them by the words of My mouth*'.[48]

RULE 12.[49] R. 'Aḳiba said: A king had four sons. One was silent when punished, another protested when punished, another begged for mercy when punished, and another when punished said to his father, 'Go on punishing me'. Abraham remained silent when punished, as it is stated, *Take now thy son, thine only son, whom thou lovest, even Isaac . . . and offer him there for a burnt-offering.*[50] He could have argued, 'Yesterday You said to me, *For in Isaac shall seed be called to thee!*'[51] Then it is stated, *And Abraham rose early in the morning.*[52] Job protested when punished, as it is

(43) His heresy consisted in occupying himself with the Torah when it was forbidden by the Romans. Cf. 'A.Z. 17b (Sonc. ed., p. 90), Sifrë, §307. (44) Ps. CXLV, 17. (45) Jer. XXXII, 19. (46) i.e. the fires of Gehinnom. (47) Job XX, 26. (48) Hos. VI, 5. The prophets, the servants of God, endeavoured to hew Israel into shape but the people ill-treated them. (49) H transposes the two paragraphs. [On this passage, cf. Büchler, *Sin and Atonement*, pp. 165ff and his comment upon the use of the verb *ba'aṭ*, lit. 'kick' in the sense of 'protest'.] (50) Gen. XXII, 2. (51) *ibid.* XXI, 12. (52) *ibid.* XXII, 3. He submitted to God's decree in silence.

stated, *I will say unto God: Do not condemn me; make me know wherefore Thou contendest with me.*[53] Hezekiah besought God for mercy when punished, as it is stated, *Then he turned his face to the wall, and prayed unto the Lord, saying,*[54] etc. Some say that Hezekiah protested when he was punished since he later added, *And have done that which is good in Thy sight.*[55] David [when punished] said to his Father, 'Continue to punish me', as it is stated, *Wash me thoroughly from mine iniquity, and cleanse me from my sin.*[56]

RULE 13. We do not interrupt the study of the Torah until the soul departs from the dying man.[57] When R. Simeon, the son of R. 'Aḳiba, fell ill, the latter did not interrupt his expositions in the Academy but made inquiries after him through a messenger. The first messenger came and reported, 'He is very ill'. He said to [his disciples], 'Continue to ask questions'. Then a second came and reported, 'He has grown worse'. R. 'Aḳiba resumed the study of the Torah. A third came and reported, 'He is dying', and he said [to his disciples, 'Continue] to ask questions'. A fourth came and reported, 'He is dead'.[58] Whereupon he arose, removed the *tefillin,*[59] rent his garments and said to them, 'Our brother-Israelites, hearken! Until now we had the duty to study the Torah; but from now onward we have the duty to occupy ourselves with honouring the dead'.

A large assembly gathered to bury R. 'Aḳiba's son, and he said to them, 'Bring a bench[60] for me to the cemetery'. He stood[61] upon it and expounded, 'Our brother-Israelites, hearken! Not because I am a scholar [have you come here], there being greater scholars here than I; not because I am a rich man [have you come here], there being richer men here than I; the men of the Darom[62] know R. 'Aḳiba, but how

(53) Job X, 2. (54) 2 Kings XX, 2. (55) *ibid.* 3. The verse, in which he claimed innocence, is understood as a protest against his fate. (56) Ps. LI, 4. David interpreted his suffering as purification of his sin and asked God to do it *thoroughly*. (57) What follows is also related in M.Ḳ. 21b (Sonc. ed., pp. 135f). [For the variations in the two versions, cf. Bacher, *Ag. d. Tannaiten*, pp. 298f.] (58) lit. 'he has completed [his life]'. (59) Pious men wore them throughout the day. (60) To improvise a rostrum. (61) GRA reads 'stood'. (62) Southern Palestine.

should the men of Galilee know him?[63] Men know him, but how should women and young children? I know, however, that your reward is great because you have only taken the great trouble to come here for the honour of the Torah and for the sake of the commandment [to attend the dead to the grave]. I should be comforted though I had seven sons whom I [now] buried. Not that a man desires to bury his children, but I know that my son is destined for the World to Come because he caused the many to be righteous, and[64] whoever causes the many to be righteous, sin occurs not through him, and whoever causes the many to sin, they do not afford him the faculty to repent. Moses was righteous and caused the many to be righteous, [therefore] the righteousness of the many was [considered] dependent on him, as it is stated, *He executed the righteousness of the Lord, and His ordinances with Israel.*[65] Jeroboam, the son of Nebat, sinned and caused others to sin, [therefore] the sin of the many was [considered] dependent on him, as it is stated, *For the sins of Jeroboam which he sinned, and wherewith he made Israel to sin'.*[66]

RULE 14. Further [R. 'Aḳiba] sat on the bench [and taught]: Good things are brought about through the agency of good men.[67] Even if Moses and Aaron had not arisen, Israel would still have been worthy to be redeemed from Egypt,[68] as it is stated, *And afterward shall they come out with great substance.*[69] Had not Moses and Aaron and the Generation of the Wilderness arisen, Israel would still have been worthy to receive the Torah, as it is stated, *He layeth up sound wisdom for the upright.*[70] The section of 'the judges'[71] would have been worthy to be promulgated even if Jethro had not arisen. The section of 'the smaller Passover'[72] would have been worthy to be promulgated even

(63) A gibe at the Galileans who were not careful to reproduce the traditions which they received from their teachers and their inability to retain their learning. On Judeans and Galileans, cf. 'Erub. 53a (Sonc. ed., pp. 370f). (64) From here to the end of the paragraph is quoted from Aboth V, 21 (Sonc. ed., V, 18, p. 71). (65) Deut. XXXIII, 21. (66) I Kings XV, 30. (67) Cf. Shab. 32a (Sonc. ed., p. 146). (68) Because of the promise God made to Abraham. (69) Gen. XV, 14. (70) Prov. II, 7, *sound wisdom* being a synonym for the Torah and *the upright* for Israel. (71) Ex. XVIII, 21-23. (72) Num. IX, 1-14, also known as the 'second Passover'.

if the 'unclean' had not arisen, as it is stated, *We are unclean by the dead body of a man; wherefore are we to be kept back, so as not to bring the offering of the Lord in its appointed season among the children of Israel?*[73] The section of 'inheritance'[74] would have been worthy to be promulgated even if the daughters of Zelophehad[75] had not arisen. The Temple would have been worthy to be built even if David and Solomon had not arisen, as it is stated, *The sanctuary, O Lord, which Thy hands have established.*[76] Israel would have been worthy to be redeemed in the days of Haman even if Mordecai and Esther had not arisen, as it is stated, *And yet for all that, when they are in the land of their enemies, I will not reject them, neither will I abhor them, to destroy them utterly,*[77] etc.

Israel were destined to be enslaved even if Pharaoh had not arisen in Egypt, as it is stated, *And* [they] *shall serve them; and they shall afflict them four hundred years.*[78] Israel were destined to serve idols even if Jeroboam, the son of Nebat, had not arisen, as it is stated, *And this people will rise up, and go astray after the foreign gods of the land.*[79] The section of 'the blasphemer'[80] and of 'the gatherer of sticks'[81] would have been worthy to be promulgated even if the son of the Israelitish woman and the gatherer of sticks had not arisen. Israel would have been destined to be destroyed by the sword even if so and so[82] had not arisen, as it is stated, *All the sinners of My people shall die by the sword;*[83] and it declares, *By sword and famine shall they be consumed.*[84] Israel would have deserved to be destroyed even if Nebuchadnezzar and his companions had not arisen, as it is stated, *Therefore shall Zion for your sake be ploughed as a field, and Jerusalem shall become heaps, and the mountain of the house as the high places of a forest.*[85]

RULE 15. And further [he expounded]: Reward is brought about through persons of merit and punishment through persons of guilt. [86]When Trajan was about to execute Pappus and his brother Lulianus in Laodicea, he said to them, 'If you are of

(73) *ibid.* 7. (74) *ibid.*XXVII, 6-11. (75) *ibid.* 1-5. (76) Ex. XV, 17. (77) Lev. XXVI, 44. (78) Gen. XV, 13. (79) Deut. XXXI, 16. (80) Lev. XXIV, 10ff. (81) Num. XV, 32-36. (82) i.e. nations hostile to Israel. They were so many that they are not specified. (83) Amos.Cf. IX, 10. (84) Jer. XIV, 15. (85) Micah III, 12. (86) E.V. *those prophets be consumed.* Cf. IX, 10. Ta'an. 18b (Sonc. ed., p. 89).

the people of Hananiah, Mishael and Azariah, let your God come and deliver you from my hands, in the same way as He delivered Hananiah, Mishael and Azariah [from Nebuchadnezzar]'. They replied, 'Hananiah, Mishael and Azariah were worthy men and Nebuchadnezzar was a worthy king, and it was fitting that a miracle should be wrought through their agency; but you are a wicked king and are not worthy that a miracle should be wrought through your agency. As for us, we deserve death at the hand of God, and if you do not slay us, the Omnipresent has many other agents of death; He has many demons, many bears, many leopards, many snakes, many venomous serpents, many scorpions which will come and attack us; but when we die you will learn that we are the descendants of Hananiah, Mishael and Azariah'. It is reported that before they died they witnessed his eyes gouged out.[87]

RULE 16. The allegorical interpreters[88] of Scripture said: *And ye shall break down their altars:*[89] wherein have the trees and the stones sinned?[90] Because they were a stumbling-block to man Scripture decreed, *And ye shall break down.* This is an argument from minor to major: if with trees and stones, which are capable neither of merit nor guilt, neither of good nor evil, because they were a stumbling-block to man the Torah declared, *And ye shall break down,* how much more [will a man be punished] who causes his neighbour to sin and turns him away from the way of life to the path of death! Similarly, *And if a woman approach unto any beast, and lie down thereto, thou shalt kill the woman, and the beast.*[91] If a human being sinned, how has the animal offended?[92] Because evil came to a human being through it, and so that the animal shall not pass through the

(87) The parallel passage in Ta'an. reads, 'two officials arrived from Rome and split his skull with clubs'. (88) lit. 'expounders of jewels', i.e. precious ethical principles. These interpreters stressed the idea behind the law and not its fulfilment. This type of interpretation was a product of Alexandria and was strongly opposed by the Talmudical Rabbis. Cf. Lauterbach, *Jewish Quarterly Review* (new series), I, pp. 503ff. (89) Deut. XII, 3. (90) Cf. Sanh. 55a (Sonc. ed., p. 374). (91) Lev. XX, 16. (92) Sanh. 54a (Sonc. ed., p. 367).

street and people say, 'This is the animal on account of which So-and-so was stoned'. This is an argument from minor to major: if with an animal, which is capable neither of merit nor guilt, neither of good nor evil, because it was a stumbling-block to a human being the Torah declared, *It shall be stoned,* how much more [will a man be punished] who causes his neighbour to sin and turns him from the way of life to the path of death!

Similarly Scripture declares of the stones of the altar, *Thou shalt lift up no iron tool upon them,*[93] and elsewhere it states, *For if thou lift up thy tool upon it, thou hast profaned it.*[94] Wherein is iron different from all other metals to be unfit for [the building of] the altar? Because the sword is a symbol of curse and the altar an agent of atonement; so we remove the symbol of curse on account of the agent of atonement. This is an argument from minor to major: if with the stones of the altar which do not see and speak, eat or drink, because they make peace between Israel and their Father in heaven the Torah declared, *Thou shalt lift no iron tool upon them,* the children of the Torah,[95] who are an atonement for the world, how much more [should they not lift an iron tool against each other!] Similarly Scripture declares, *Thou shalt build the altar of the Lord thy God of unhewn stones*[96]—stones that bring peace to the world. This is an argument from minor to major: if with stones which do not see or hear, speak or eat or drink, because they make peace between Israel and their Father in heaven they must be 'whole' [48*a*] before [the Holy One, blessed be He], how much more the children of the Torah, who are an atonement for the world, must be 'whole' before the Holy One, blessed be He!

(93) Deut. XXVII, 5. (94) Ex. XX, 22. (95) The people of Israel. (96) Deut. XXVII, 6.

CHAPTER IX

RULE 1. One does not rend [his garments] for the dead[1] except for his teacher who taught him wisdom.[2] R. Simeon b. Eleazar said: When a Sage dies, all present at his death rend [their garments] for him, but all those who are not present do not rend them.

RULE 2. For a Sage who died[3] one bares the right [shoulder]; for an *'Ab Beth Din* who died one bares the left [shoulder]; for a *Nasi'* who died one bares both shoulders.[4] It is related[5] that when R. Eliezer died, R. 'Aḳiba bared both shoulders and kept on beating his heart[6] until the blood flowed, and he cried out, '*My father, my father, the chariots of Israel and the horsemen thereof!*'[7]

RULE 3.[8] One does not bare [the shoulder] for the dead in general but only for his father and mother; and if they are not worthy,[9] he does not rend even for his father and mother. It is related that when R. 'Aḳiba's father died, those present bared [the shoulder], but he did not.

RULE 4. For the dead in general one rends [the garments] with a knife,[10] but for his father and mother he does not rend with a knife.[11]

RULE 5. For the dead in general one does not bare his chest, but for his father and mother he bares it.[12]

RULE 6. For the dead in general one does not divide[13] the [upper] selvage-border [of his garment],[14] but for his father and mother he does divide it. R. Judah said: Any rending [of

(1) If they are not his near of kin. (2) i.e. Torah. Cf., however, M.Ḳ. 25a (Sonc. ed., p. 154), Shab. 105b (Sonc. ed., p. 509) where it is taught that one rends the garments on the death of any worthy man. (3) M.Ḳ. 22b (Sonc. ed., pp. 143f). (4) lit. 'hands'. (5) Sanh. 68a (Sonc. ed., pp. 463f). (6) For 'heart' Sanh. reads 'his flesh'. (7) 2 Kings II, 12. (8) M.Ḳ. 22b (Sonc. ed., p. 140). (9) e.g. if the son is a distinguished scholar, as it would be undignified for him to be seen with bared shoulders; cf. *Ṭur* Y.D., §340. (10) M.Ḳ. 22b (Sonc. ed., p. 143). (11) But with the hand. (12) M.Ḳ. *loc. cit.* (Sonc. ed., p. 142). 'Chest' is lit. 'heart'. (13) *ibid.* (14) i.e. about the neck and shoulders.

a garment] which does not divide the selvage-border is mere make-believe. R. Judah said:[15] Any initial rending must be [to the extent of] three fingers, while the extension may be as small as he cares.[16] One only rends as far down as the region of the navel.[17] In the case of children, others rend for them.[18] One who rends [not as a relative but] from respect [for the dead] may stitch [the edges] forthwith. The rending of one's undershirt is not indispensable.[19] R. Benjamin said in the name of R. 'Aḳiba: One must rend the undershirt.

RULE 7.[20] For the dead in general one rends only the uppermost [garment], but for his father and mother he must rend [all] even though he be wearing a hundred. A woman only rends her uppermost [garment]. R. Judah said: A woman rends her undergarment, turns it front to back, and then rends the remaining [garments].[21]

RULE 8. For the dead generally one tacks[22] the rent together after seven days, and [completely] restitches [the edges] after thirty; but for one's father and mother one never restitches [the edges]. A woman tacks the rent together after seven [days] and restitches [the edges] after thirty. R. Judah said: A woman tacks the rent together immediately[23] and restitches [the edges] after seven [days].[24]

RULE 9.[25] For the dead generally one expedites[26] the bier and does not occupy himself unduly with their affairs;[27] but in the case of his father and mother, whoever greatly occupies himself with their affairs and does not expedite the bier is praiseworthy. But if time is pressing, or the Sabbath-eve is

(15) M.Ḳ. 26b (Sonc. ed., p. 169). (16) lit. 'whatever it be', i.e. when the tear is extended for another death. (17) If a succession of deaths occurs, that is the limit to which the tear may extend. (18) The reading in M.Ḳ. is 'children are made to rend'; not that they are under the obligation to do so, but in order to arouse sadness in those who witness it. (19) Cf. M.Ḳ. 22b (Sonc. ed., p. 142). (20) *ibid.* (21) So as not to expose her chest. (22) With large basting stitches. (23) From a sense of self-respect (M.Ḳ. *loc. cit.*). (24) So GRA and H; V reads 'three'. (25) Cf. M.Ḳ. 22a (Sonc. ed., p. 140). (26) i.e. hastens the interment. (27) viz. their business affairs before the funeral (Rashi). R. Ḥananel, on the basis of a passage in j.M.Ḳ. III, 8, 83d, explains 'reduces the funeral expenses and the lament to a minimum'.

approaching, or rain falls, he may expedite the bier for his father and mother and does not unduly occupy himself with their affairs.

RULE 10. For the dead in general it is forbidden to wear pressed clothes until thirty days [are completed], but in the case of his father and mother it is forbidden until the [next] Festival occurs and then only if his companions rebuke him.[28]

RULE 11.[29] For the dead generally it is forbidden to trim one's hair until thirty days are completed; but in the case of his father and mother, one lets the hair grow long until his companions rebuke him.

RULE 12. For the dead generally one is forbidden to engage in trade[30] until thirty days are completed; but for one's father and mother until his companions rebuke him and say to him, 'Come out with us'.

RULE 13.[31] For the dead generally it is forbidden to go to a house of feasting until thirty days are completed; but for one's father and mother, all the twelve months unless it is for a sacred cause.[32]

RULE 14. If news reached him that his father died and he rent, but [in fact] it was his mother, he has done his duty.[33] [If news reached him that] his mother died, but it was his father and he rent, he has done his duty. [If news reached him that] his father died and he rent, but it was one of his near relatives, he has done his duty. [If news reached him that] one of his near relatives died, but it was his father, he has not done his duty.[34]

RULE 15. If one's father and mother died [at the same time], he makes only one rent for the two of them.[35] R. Judah b. Tema said: He rends for each separately. If one's ten children died at the same time, he makes one rent for all of them.

[36]If after he had made a rent [for another] news reached him

(28) On his untidy appearance. (29) M.Ḳ. 22b (Sonc. ed., p. 141). (30) Not ordinary trade which is permissible after seven days of mourning, but to set out on a business journey to distant lands, because that might be interpreted as an indication of callousness. (31) Cf. M.Ḳ. *loc. cit.* (32) e.g. a wedding. (33) He has not to rend again. (34) He has to rend again. (35) Cf. M.Ḳ. 26b (Sonc. ed., p. 170). (36) *ibid.*

that his son died, he continues to rend until it [reaches down] to the navel; when it has reached the navel he turns [the garment] front to back.

If his son died and he rent [and news of another death reached him], he leaves a space of three fingers and again rends.

RULE 16.[37] The rent must be made only between the two borders;[38] one who makes the rent along the border or at the side has not done his duty.[39] R. Judah said: He has done his duty. R. Judah said: It happened in the days of Ḥarsum[40] that people used to make the rent at the lower end [of the garment] and at the side. His colleagues retorted, 'No proof may be adduced [from a practice adopted] in a time of danger'.

A man dressed in torn garments does not rend.[41] R. Judah said: One who rends a cloak of *Birrus,*[42] a Brundisian cloak,[43] a *Paenula,*[44] a stitched garment or a veil,[45] has not done his duty.[46] One who rends a basted garment[47] has done his duty. What constitutes a basted garment? [When its tear] has been completely basted.

RULE 17. These are the rents which may not be basted: [When it was done] for his father or mother, for his teacher who instructed him in wisdom, for a scroll of the Torah which has been burnt, for the ruined Temple, for evil tidings, [on hearing] the Divine Name blasphemed, on seeing Jerusalem from Mount Scopus,[48] and [on the death of] a *Nasi*'. Some add: [On the death of] a High Priest, a prophet, or an *'Ab Beth Din.* As

(37) The text is corrupt, and the translation follows the version of Nachmanides (cf. N.Y.). (38) On either side of the front opening of the shirt or tunic. (39) Because the rent is hidden. (40) The name of a High Priest who lived in a time of persecution. GRA reads *ḥerum* which means 'prohibition to travel', e.g. in a time of war. (41) Since his garments are already torn, the new rent will not be distinguishable. (42) 'A cloth named after a Celtic people, Burri' (Krauss); 'a cloak of thick woollen material' (Jastrow). (43) A cloak thicker than the previous material (Jastrow); a cloth named after a Celtic people, the Burridens (Krauss). (44) A travelling cloak (Jastrow). (45) Jastrow emends חרויד to רדיד, a garment of fine texture. (46) These materials are either too thick or too fine for the rent to be distinguishable. (47) i.e. one sewn with large stitches. (48) Because from there the ruins of Jerusalem are visible.

regards the burning of a scroll of the Torah, [the garment is rent] not on hearing of this happening but only when he stands by while it burns. As for the ruined Temple, [he rends his garment] even if he heard that it has been destroyed; similarly with evil tidings because they are as grievous as the destruction of the Temple.

One who sees Jerusalem from Mount Scopus must rend; when he enters [the city] he extends the rent, and if he goes up [again to Jerusalem] he must extend it further. 'If he goes up again'—this is to teach that he is obliged to make a rent every time he goes up [to Jerusalem] during each period [of thirty days].[49] If he came up [to Jerusalem] and settled there, he rends once and has thereby done his duty.

RULE 18. One who buys a tunic which has been rent [by a mourner] from[50] his companion may not baste it unless he knows that the rent is of the kind which may be basted. One who sells a tunic which has been rent [by a mourner] to his companion must inform him whether the rent is of the kind which may be basted or not.[51] All rent [garments] which may not be basted must not be sold to non-Jews[52] or stitched together or be reversed from top to bottom, according to the view of R. Simeon; but R. Eliezer permits it to be done. [53]One who borrows a tunic from his companion to go and visit his father and when he arrives finds that his father died, he rends it, bastes it and returns it to his companion. If, however, he borrowed it without specifying for what purpose he needed it, he is not permitted[54] to rend it.

RULE 19.[55] One who goes out before the bier of the dead with a garment already rent robs the dead [of his due]. More grievous is the robbing of the dead than robbing the living, because one who robs the living can appease him by making restitution,

(49) [The meaning is illustrated by j.Ber. IX, 2, 13d: R. Simeon Ḳamṭraya asked R. Ḥiyya b. Abba, 'Since I am an ass-driver and go up to Jerusalem throughout the year, how is it about rending my garment?' He replied, 'Within thirty days [after a visit] it is unnecessary for you to rend'.] (50) So GRA and H; V has 'for'. (51) Cf. M.Ḳ. 26b (Sonc. ed., p. 169). (52) Lest they resell it to a Jew. (53) Cf. M.Ḳ. *loc. cit.* (Sonc. ed., p. 172). (54) This is the reading of GRA and H. (55) Cf. M.Ḳ. *loc. cit.*

but one who robs the dead cannot appease him by making restitution.

[56]Likewise you may say: One who honours his father and mother after their death[57] is as if he honoured them in their lifetime, since one who honours them while they are alive may do so from fear or for the sake of an inheritance; but he who honours them after their death does so in the name of Heaven only.[58]

RULE 20. He who made a rent for one [presumed] dead and he revived, if he dies immediately afterwards [the man who made a rent] has fulfilled his duty, but if [death occurred] after some time he has not done his duty.[59]

RULE 21. Whosoever rescues garments from the dead[60] robs the dead. There are times when a man may rescue them and times when he may not. [48*b*] If the garments have not touched the bier he may rescue them, but if they have touched the bier he may not. We, however, instruct people not to seize them.[61] And whoever piles up garments on the dead commits a transgression because of the law which forbids wilful destruction,[62] according to the view of R. Meir. R. Eliezer b. Ẓadoḳ said: It disgraces him. Rabban Gamaliel said: He causes maggots to breed upon [the dead]. R. Nathan said: The garment which goes down with him to the grave will come back with him in the time to come,[63] as it is stated, *It is changed as clay under the seal; and they stand as a garment.*[64]

(56) This sentence and the next Rule are transposed in accordance with GRA. A better sequence is thereby obtained. (57) Cf. Ḳid. 31b (Sonc. ed., p. 154). (58) To fulfil God's command and without a motive of self-interest. (59) Cf. Ned. 87a (Sonc. ed., p. 268). (60) Cf. Sanh. 48a, b (Sonc. ed., pp. 321f). If parents piled on the bier garments belonging to their child as an expression of grief and as a sign that they renounced everything that belonged to him. Saving the garments constituted an act of returning lost property; but when the articles touched the bier they were regarded as designated for the dead. (61) V inserts 'but did not [the Sages] say' which GRA deletes. (62) The Rabbis derived a law against the wanton destruction of articles from Deut. XX, 19; cf. Shab. 129a (Sonc. ed., p. 644, n. 1). (63) In the Resurrection; cf. j.Keth. XII, 3, 35a, Sanh. 90b (Sonc. ed., p. 607). (64) Job XXXVIII, 14; לְבוּ׳שׁ, *a garment*, is homiletically read as לְבוּ׳שׁ, 'as he is dressed'.

CHAPTER X

RULE 1. A mourner, as long as his dead is lying before him,[1] is exempt from reading the *Shema'* and *Tefillah* and from all the commandments prescribed in the Torah. Even if he desires to place himself under greater restrictions [than the law requires] he should not do so out of respect for the dead.

RULE 2.[2] When the time comes for reading the *Shema'*, all the people [present] read it but he remains silent; when they stand to read the *Tefillah*, all read it but he justifies for himself the divine decree. What does he say? 'Sovereign of all the universe, I have sinned before Thee; I have repaid but few of my obligations; I merit much more punishment than this; may it be Thy will to repair our breaches and to comfort us'. R. Simeon b. Eleazar said: He also prays for all the needs of the dead person.

RULE 3.[3] A mourner eats [his meal] in the house of his neighbour, and if he has no neighbour he eats it in another room; and if he has no other room [than that in which the dead is lying], he puts up a partition and eats; and if he is not able to put up a partition, he turns his face away from the dead and eats. But he must not eat in a reclining posture,[4] eat as much food as he needs, eat meat or drink wine. He is not included in the *Zimmun*, others do not say Grace on his behalf, and we do not request him, 'Say Grace'.[5] When does this apply? On week-days, but on the Sabbath[6] he eats as much as he needs,

(1) i.e. before the burial for which he has to make arrangements; cf. Ber. 18a (Sonc. ed., p. 106). (2) Cf. Ber. 19a (Sonc. ed., p. 116). (3) *ibid.* 17b-18a (Sonc. ed., p. 102), M.Ḳ. 23b (Sonc. ed., p. 146). (4) At meals people usually reclined on the left elbow on a couch as a mark of ease. (5) This means to lead the company in Grace after meals; but the Gemara, Ber. 17b (Sonc. ed., p. 107), reads 'and he does not say a blessing [over food]', which Rashi interprets as referring to Grace before meals. (6) When there is no outward mourning.

he may eat meat and drink wine, and is included in the *Zimmun*. Rabban Gamaliel said: A mourner [is regarded] on the Sabbath as if he were not a mourner.

RULE 4. We do not remove the body [for burial] near [the time of] reading the *Shema'*, unless it is an hour before.[7]

RULE 5.[8] Once the bearers of the bier have carried [the body] out—such as are before the bier[9] and such as are behind it[10]—those who are before the bier, whose services are still needed, are exempt from reading the *Shema'* and are forbidden[11] to wear shoes. All alike are exempt from the *Tefillah* and from putting on the *tefillin*.

RULE 6.[12] Having buried the dead and returned [from the graveside], if they are able to begin and complete [the reading of the *Shema'*] before arriving at the row,[13] they read[14] it and afterwards stand in the row; but if not, they stand in the row and afterwards read [the *Shema'*] and the *Tefillah*.

RULE 7.[15] The inner row [of the comforters] who can see the mourners is exempt [from reading the *Shema'*], but the outer row is under the obligation. R. Judah said: Even if there be [only] one row, those who stand for the sake of [comforting] the mourner are exempt, but those who stand for the sake of [their own] honour[16] [are under the obligation].[17] If they came to the memorial address,[18] those who can see the mourners are exempt and those who cannot see them are under the obligation.

RULE 8. R. Simeon b. Eleazar said: Rabban Gamaliel had a

(7) V and H add 'or they postpone it for an hour' which GRA deletes. (8) Cf. Ber. 17b (Sonc. ed., p. 106). (9) Awaiting their turn to relieve the bearers. (10) These have already carried the coffin and so have done their duty. (11) V has 'permitted'; but GRA emends: 'are forbidden to wear shoes; but as for those who are behind the bier whose services are no longer required, they are obliged to read the *Shema'* and, permitted to wear shoes'. (12) Ber. *loc. cit.* (13) To offer condolence to the mourners. (14) The text is corrupt, and the translation follows the reading of GRA and H. (15) Cf. Ber. 19b (Sonc. ed., p. 117). (16) Ber. *loc. cit.* reads 'for their own purposes', i.e. to see the crowd. (17) The words in brackets are added by H. (18) So H; GRA reads 'to comfort'. The word in V is corrupt.

borrowed grave[19] in Jabneh where they brought the dead and locked the door behind it. Men came, stood in the row and comforted the mourners and the public was thereby exempt [from this duty]. Later [the bodies] were conveyed to Jerusalem [for burial].

RULE 9. After [the tomb] was closed with the top stone, [the mourner] muffles his head.[20] Should he take his stand in the row,[21] he unmuffles his head and exempts others [from standing in the row for him]. When he leaves the row he muffles his head. After he has entered his house, should others come to comfort him, he unmuffles his head and exempts them.

RULE 10.[22] When a Sage or a disciple suffers bereavement, people come and sit down before him and discuss the laws relating to mourners. Should they make a mistake he corrects them in a low tone, but he does not ask questions.[23] If he so desire he may speak personally to them, and if not he appoints someone to be his spokesman. It is related that when his son died, R. Judah appointed someone to be his spokesman. It is related that when his son died, R. Jose the Galilean appointed someone to be his spokesman. It is related that when his son died, R. 'Aḳiba continued his discourse all the day.[24] The same is also reported of Rabbi [Judah the Prince]; he continued his discourse all the day.

RULE 11.[25] In the first week a mourner does not enter the Synagogue; in the second week he enters but does not sit in his [usual] place; in the third week he enters and sits in his [usual] place but does not speak; in the fourth week he is like any other person. R. Simeon said: In the first week[26] people come up to him to comfort him; the second week is treated

(19) It is not mentioned elsewhere in Rabbinic literature and what it denotes is uncertain. It probably means a sepulchre owned by Rabban Gamaliel which was lent for the purpose described when it was required. (20) As a sign of mourning; cf. M.Ḳ. 15a (Sonc. ed., p. 88). (21) When present at another funeral before returning home. (22) This is Rule 11 in H. (23) On the laws of mourning, because that would be studying Torah which is forbidden to a mourner. (24) Cf. above VIII, 13ff. (25) Cf. M.Ḳ. 23a (Sonc. ed., p. 144). This is Rule 12 in H. (26) V adds in brackets 'and the second week'.

like the first, the third like the second, and in the fourth week he is like any other person. R. Meir said: In the first and second week he does not enter the Synagogue, in the third he enters and sits in his [usual] place, and in the fourth he is like any other person. To what does this apply? To a Synagogue, but as for a House of Study he may enter it even in the first week.

[27]On the Sabbath-eve at dusk he unmuffles his head; at the termination of the Sabbath he muffles it again. On the Sabbath-eve at dusk he turns back [the garment which is] rent; at the termination of the Sabbath he turns it to the front.

RULE 12.[28] When a Sage dies, his *Beth Hammidrash* goes into vacation and all the others change their place. When an *'Ab Beth Din* dies, all the other Houses of Study in his city go into vacation and the others change their place. When a *Nasi'* dies, all the Houses of Study go into vacation; people do not walk about in the street but enter [their homes] and sit in silence overcome by distress like men without a leader. When the time of rising arrives, they stand up and reduce their affairs to a minimum. The people of the Synagogue enter the Synagogue [on the Sabbath] and seven persons read the weekly portion of the Torah and go away.

RULE 13.[29] Neither *Halakah* nor *'Aggada* should be expounded in the *Beth Hammidrash* of a mourner. Should a question be raised, they begin with the laws relating to mourners, pass on to other themes and revert to and end with the laws relating to mourners.

[30]R. Ḥanina b. Gamaliel said: We may discourse upon an aggadic theme in the *Beth Hammidrash* of a mourner. In Judea they greeted mourners [on the Sabbath] on their entry and departure to indicate that there is no mourning on the Sabbath.

(27) This paragraph is Rule 10 in H in a fuller form. (28) This is Rule 13 in H. The text here is in disorder and the translation follows the emendation of GRA; cf. M.Ḳ. 22b (Sonc. ed., p. 144). (29) Cf. M.Ḳ. 23a (Sonc. ed., p. 144). This is Rule 14 in H. (30) This is Rule 15 in H in a different form.

CHAPTER XI

RULE 1. In a city where there are two dead, they take out the first[1] [for burial]; and if[2] they keep the first overnight[3] they take out the second, because [the Sages] said, 'Whoever keeps the dead overnight disfigures him'.[4] But if [the delay] is to dig a grave for him, or to procure shrouds for him, or to enable his relatives to come from another place, he may be kept overnight and there is no wrong done.[5]

When a Sage and a disciple die, they first take out the Sage [for burial]; a disciple and an *'am ha'areẓ*, they first take out the disciple. If both were Sages or disciples or an *'am ha'areẓ* they take out the one who dies first. If a man and a woman [died], they first take out the woman because a woman is apt to become disfigured more quickly.[6]

RULE 2. The differences between man and woman[7] are: [the bier of] a man is set down in the broadway[8] but not that of a woman;[9] for a man they go up with the *ḥeber 'ir*[10] but not for a woman; for a male [mourner] the mourners' meal[11] is

(1) i.e. the one who died first and then the second. (2) So GRA and H. V reads 'and they do not'. (3) For reasons which follow. (4) Sanh. 46b (Sonc. ed., p. 307) reads 'transgresses a negative commandment on account of him', and GRA corrects accordingly. (5) lit. 'and there is nothing in it'. (6) Cf. Rashi on the Mishnah M.Ḳ. 27a. (7) In respect of funeral rites. (8) lit. 'an open space' in the city where the bier was set down for the delivery of the memorial address. There, too, the 'benediction of the mourners' was recited on the return from the cemetery (cf. Keth. 8b, Sonc. ed., p. 37). According to Krauss, *Synagogale Altertümer*, p. 297, it was the open space in front of the Synagogue, but this definition is disputed; cf. J. Rabbinowitz, *Mishnah Megillah*, p. 88. (9) 'For the sake of propriety', M.Ḳ. 27a (Sonc. ed., p. 177). (10) This term may signify a Rabbi who took a leading part in town affairs, or 'a group' denoting either a town council similar to the Roman Collegia or an official communal religious or charitable organization (Meg. 27b, Sonc. ed., p. 164, n. 1). The assembly was usually headed by the Rabbi, and it was considered undignified for him to do so for a woman. (11) Cf. above II, 9, p. 332, n. 18.

provided but not for a female [mourner].[12] R. Judah said: If she has young children, a meal is provided [for her] together with them.

RULE 3. If they have taken out the first [body] and buried him, they do not stand in the row for him, nor do they recite for him the benediction of mourners until they have taken out the second and buried him. When they have taken out the second and buried him, people come and stand in the row and comfort [the mourners], and they thereby exempt the community [from their duty in this matter]. We do not offer consolation to two mourners[13] at the same time unless they are of equal status.

RULE 4. We do not take out two dead on one bier unless they are of equal status and [merit] equal praise. It is related of a certain man in Usha[14] that the house collapsed on his two sons and daughter. People went and inquired of R. Judah [49*a*] who said, 'Take out the three of them at the same time'.[15] They placed the bridegrooms[16] at one end [of the bier] and the bride[17] at the other and they lamented, 'Alas, alas, bridegrooms! Alas, alas, bride!'

RULE 5. We do not deliver two memorial addresses [at the same time] in one city unless there are sufficient to attend each. We do not bewail two brides [at the same time] in one city unless there are sufficient to attend each. R. Simeon b. Eleazar said: Even then it is forbidden because of ill-feeling.[18]

RULE 6. When a dead person and a bride are being honoured and [the two processions] approach one another, we cause the funeral procession to make way for the bridal procession,[19] because the honour of the living takes precedence over the honour of the dead. In the case of a royal procession and a bridal procession, the latter makes way[20] out of respect for the king. King Agrippa made way for a bride and the Sages praised

(12) Out of propriety and in order to avoid suspicion of any irregular conduct. (13) Unless they are both related to the dead person. (14) In Galilee. (15) On one bier. (16) i.e. the sons who but for the accident would later be bridegrooms. (17) i.e. the dead daughter. (18) People should not fall out in their choice of which to attend. (19) Cf. Keth. 17a (Sonc. ed., p. 94). (20) *ibid.*

him. They asked him, 'What was your reason for doing this?' He replied, 'I wear a crown every day but she wears a crown for one hour only'.

RULE 7. We do not[21] interrupt the study of the Torah for the sake of a funeral or bridal procession. Abba Saul said: [Good] deeds[22] take precedence of the study of the Torah. R. Judah acted as follows: Whenever he saw a dead person or a bride being honoured, he used to look at his disciples and exclaim, 'Deeds before study'.

RULE 8.[23] A woman who is bereaved of her father-in-law or any of her husband's relatives may not paint her eyelids with kohl or adorn herself, but conducts herself as [her husband] does.[24] Likewise if [her husband] is bereaved of his father-in-law or any of his wife's relatives, he cannot compel her to adorn herself but conducts himself as she does.

RULE 9.[25] Sweeping the floors, washing dishes and making beds do not constitute work for a mourner.[26]

RULE 10.[27] A *dargesh*[28] is tilted up[29] and not overturned. R. Simeon b. Eleazar said: He loosens its step[30] and leaves it as it is.

RULE 11. Should five brothers eat at their father's table and he dies, if each of them [usually] goes to his own home to sleep, he overturns [the bed] in his house; but if not, he overturns it only in the house which is used [for sleeping].

RULE 12. If a man possesses five houses, should he be making use of all of them he overturns [the bed] in all of them; if not, he does not overturn it in all of them but only in the house which is used [for sleeping].

(21) [A less strict ruling is given in ARN IV, 1ff, above pp. 35ff. The probability is that the negative אין is to be deleted. Cf. Büchler, *Types of Jewish-Palestinian Piety*, p. 86, n. 2.] (22) i.e. honouring the dead or the bride. (23) Cf. M.Ḳ. 20b (Sonc. ed., p. 131). (24) i.e. she observes mourning with him. (25) Cf. M.Ḳ. 27a (Sonc. ed., p. 177). (26) They are permissible. (27) The text is in disorder and is corrected according to j.M.Ḳ. III, 5, 83a. (28) An elaborate couch, described in M.Ḳ. 27a (Sonc. ed., pp. 174f). (29) To make it uncomfortable for sleeping or sitting on it. (30) Jastrow defines the word as the 'step placed before a bed'. The reading in M.Ḳ. is "[In the case of] a *dargesh* [it is enough if] he unfastens the inner bolster-frame and lets it down'.

RULE 13. If one resides with his friend as a guest, should he be very intimate with him he overturns [the bed there], and if not he does not overturn it.

RULE 14. If one is on a journey and news reaches him that he suffered a bereavement, should he be able to overturn [the bed] with the consent of others he overturns it, and if not he does not overturn it.

RULE 15. One overturns his bed [which is laid] on two benches or on four stones even if there be five mattresses on it, and even though it be [only] four handbreadths[31] above the ground, so long as its legs are tilted upwards.

RULE 16. So long as his dead is lying before him, a mourner may not sleep on a bed [in an erect position] or on an overturned bed.

RULE 17.[32] One who sleeps on a bench or on a bench for water-jugs[33] is subject to the duty of overturning.[34] If he declares, 'I will not overturn the bed but sleep[35] on the bench', we do not listen to him but say, 'It is subject to [the law of] overturning'.

RULE 18. The bed has to be overturned six times, five times, four times [or] three times, neither less nor more. How is this? If the death took place close to dusk,[36] [it is done] six times; if close to dusk on the Sabbath-eve five times; if a Festival occurs on the day following the Sabbath four times; in the case of the two days of the New Year [after a Sabbath] three times.[37]

RULE 19.[38] When does one overturn the bed? From the time

(31) H reads 'cubits'. (32) Cf. M.Ḳ. 27a (Sonc. ed., p. 175). (33) Emend to *'uryani*, 'the Roman *urnarium*, a long oblong bench or kitchen table used for keeping near to hand urns, water vessels and other earthenware utensils and out of the way of being broken' (M.Ḳ., Sonc. ed., p. 175, n. 8). The words *meṭalletha dekarma*, 'a watchman's hut in the vineyard' is an incorrect marginal gloss on *'uryani* which crept into the text. (34) Since it is a bed so far as he is concerned. (35) The translation follows the text of H (cf. the comment in N.Y.). (36) And the burial has taken place so that at nightfall one day of mourning has already gone. (37) There being no mourning on Sabbaths and Festivals. (38) M.Ḳ. 27a (Sonc. ed., p. 173).

the corpse is taken out through the door of the house, according to the view of R. Eliezer. R. Joshua said: From the time the slab closes the tomb. It is related that when Rabban Gamaliel the Elder[39] died, as soon as he was taken out through the door of his house, [R. Eliezer] said to them,[40] 'Overturn your beds'; and when the slab closed the tomb R. Joshua said, 'Overturn your beds'. They replied, 'We have already overturned them by order of the Elder'.[41]

(39) Rabban Gamaliel was R. Eliezer's brother-in-law. (40) To his wife Imma Shalom, Rabban Gamaliel's sister and others in the house; cf. M.Ḳ. *loc. cit.* (41) viz. R. Eliezer.

CHAPTER XII

RULE 1.[1] The day of hearing[2] [the news of the death] is regarded as the day of burial[3] for rending [garments], mourning and the observance of the seven [days] and thirty [days]; but as for eating sacred flesh[4] he is only regarded as one who gathers bones.[5] Both of them may not eat sacred flesh.[6]

RULE 2. R. Eliezer said: [On receiving] 'near tidings',[7] [that is to say, if news reached him] within thirty days [of the death], one observes [mourning] for seven [days] and thirty [days]; [if the news reached him] later than this he observes [mourning] for only one day. R. 'Aḳiba said: On receiving 'near tidings' [that is to say, if news reached him] within twelve months [of the death], one observes [mourning] for seven [days] and thirty [days]. The Sages said: Whether it be 'near tidings' or 'distant tidings',[8] he observes [mourning] for seven [days] and thirty [days]. It is related that when R. Ẓadoḳ's father died at Ginzaḳ[9] in Media and the news reached him after three years, he observed [mourning] for seven [days] and thirty [days].

RULE 3. Any [dead person] for whom one rends [the garments] on his death, one also rends for him when his bones are gathered. For [a dead person] for whom one may not baste [the edge of his garments] on his death, one may not baste them when his bones are gathered.

RULE 4. The gathering of bones must be done only during one

(1) Cf. Zeb. 100b (Sonc. ed., p. 482). (2) If within thirty days of the death. (3) i.e. his full mourning begins then. (4) i.e. of sacrifices if he is a *kohen*. (5) A corpse was first buried temporarily in a cave and later transferred to a permanent burial-place in the family tomb. This is termed 'gathering the bones'; cf. M.Ḳ. I, 5 (Sonc. ed., pp. 40f). By Rabbinical law a man gathering the bones of his father or mother is regarded as a mourner during that day. (6) On that day only. (7) Cf. M.Ḳ. 20a (Sonc. ed., p. 127). (8) After thirty days. (9) Gazaka, a city in North Media; according to Rawlinson it is Shiz, near lake Urmia (M.Ḳ., Sonc. ed., p. 128, n. 5).

day; therefore one only gathers them towards dusk.[10] If he gathered them throughout the day and[11] it became dark, it is permissible [to continue] on the following day. We do not stand in the row for them, nor do we recite over them the benediction of mourners, nor offer consolation to the mourners[12] [in public], but we may do so in private. We do not hold an assembly for them in the broadway,[13] but we do bring the mourners' meal into the mourner's home.[14] R. Simeon b. Eleazar said: During the day he lies[15] on an overturned bed and at dusk he straightens it.

RULE 5. The following was the practice of the Brotherhoods[16] in Jerusalem: Some went to the house of mourning, others to the house of feasting,[17] some went to a circumcision[18] and others to gather bones. [In the choice between going] to the house of mourning and the house of feasting, the house of feasting takes precedence; to a circumcision and to gather bones, the circumcision takes precedence. The pious men of olden days, however, gave precedence to the house of mourning over the house of feasting, for it is stated, *It is better to go to the house of mourning, than to go to the house of feasting; for that is the end of all men, and the living will lay it to his heart.*[19] Whoever follows the bier should say, 'I, too, will follow this one [to the grave]'.

RULE 6. We do not break the bones nor sever the sinews [of a corpse] unless the bones were already broken of their own accord and the sinews severed of their own accord.

RULE 7. A man may gather all bones except those of his father and mother,[20] in the view of R. Joḥanan b. Nuri. R. 'Aḳiba

(10) To reduce the period of mourning. (11) The words that follow are based on the reading of GRA and H. (12) By paying a eulogy to the dead. (13) Cf. XI, 2, p. 384, n. 10. (14) But not in public as is done after a funeral. (15) The translation follows the emended text of GRA and H. (16) Associations organized for the purpose, *inter alia,* of attending to the dead and mourners. Cf. Krauss, *Talmudische Archäologie,* II, p. 63 and p. 480, n. 459. (17) A marriage feast. (18) lit. 'the week of the son', a disguised term for the circumcision ceremony which was adopted during the Hadrianic persecution when the rite was prohibited; cf. B.B., Sonc. ed., p. 246, n. 8. (19) Eccl. VII, 2. (20) But others gather them for him.

said: Bones may not be gathered until the flesh dissolves; once the flesh is dissolved the appearance [of the person] is no longer recognizable.[21]

RULE 8. One may gather the bones of two dead persons at the same time; he then places one collection at one end of the sheet [49*b*] and the other at the other side of it, in the view of R. 'Aḳiba. R. Joḥanan b. Nuri said: [If this is done] the sheet may in the end decay and the bones be mixed together; so we gather them and place them [separately] in cedar[22] [boxes].

RULE 9. We sprinkle wine and oil upon [the bodies], in the view of R. 'Aḳiba; R. Simeon b. Nanos said: Oil but not wine because wine causes deterioration;[23] and the Sages said: Neither oil nor wine because they breed wood-worms,[24] but we place dry clods of earth upon them. R. Eliezer b. Ẓadoḳ said: When my father was dying he gave me this instruction, 'On my death bury me first in a valley, and later gather my bones and place them in a cedar[25] coffin, but do not gather them with your hands'. And I did so for him. R. Joḥanan entered [the cave] and spread a sheet over [the bones]; then I entered, rent [my garments] and spread dry clods of earth [over the bones].[26] As [my father] did for his father so I did for him.

RULE 10. A man bandages[27] and binds [the limb] of a man but not of a woman; a woman bandages and binds both a man and a woman. A man attends to a man suffering from disease of the bowels but not to a woman;[28] a woman attends both to a man[29] and a woman suffering from disease of the bowels.

RULE 11. Abba Saul b. Bothnith[30] used to say to his sons, 'Bury me at the feet of my father and remove the thread of blue from [the *ẓiẓith* of] my cloak'.

RULE 12.[31] One may enter a [public] bath with all except[32] his

(21) Consequently there is no disrespect to a dead parent if the son gathers the bones. (22) According to the text emended by GRA and H. (23) It is not permitted to hasten their disintegration. (24) So GRA. V is in disorder. (25) As emended by GRA. (26) GRA reads 'and spread a linen sheet over them'. (27) Correcting מברך to מכרך. (28) From modesty. (29) A woman is assumed to be less liable to prurient thoughts. (30) So H for the unintelligible reading of V. (31) Cf. Pes. 51a (Sonc. ed., pp. 248f) where the text adds 'brother-in-law'. (32) For reasons of modesty.

father, father-in-law, stepfather and his teacher who taught him wisdom. R. Judah said: If his father is old or ill, he may enter and bathe him because that is a way of honouring him.[33] RULE 13. We do not take out [the dead on] a bier unless his head and the greater part of his body are there. R. Judah said: The spinal column and the skull constitute the greater part. It is related of the son of R. Ḥanina b. Teradion that he took to evil ways and robbers seized and killed him. After three days his swollen body was found; they placed him in a coffin,[34] set him on a bier, took him into the city and paid him a eulogy[35] out of respect for his father and mother. His father quoted over him the verse, *And thou moan, when thine end cometh, when thy flesh and thy body are consumed, and say, 'How have I hated instruction, and my heart despised reproof; neither have I hearkened to the voice of my teachers, nor inclined mine ear to them that instructed me! I was well nigh in all evil in the midst of the congregation and assembly.'*[36] When he had finished he went back to the beginning of the verse. His mother quoted over him the verse, *A foolish son is the vexation to his father, and bitterness to her that bore him.*[37] His sister quoted over him the verse, *Bread of falsehood is sweet to a man; but afterwards his mouth shall be filled with gravel.*[38]

(33) By attending to his needs. (34) According to an emended reading. (35) For the parallel to this story, cf. Midrash Lamentations III, 6 (Sonc. ed., p. 195). (36) Prov. V, 11-14. (37) *ibid.* XVII, 25. (38) *ibid.* XX, 17.

CHAPTER XIII

RULE 1. One who gathers or guards bones is exempt from reading the *Shema'*, the *Tefillah*, from *tefillin* and all the commandments prescribed by the Torah. Should he desire to impose a strict view upon himself, he may not do so because of the honour of the bones.[1] R. Joḥanan b. Nuri said: He should withdraw a distance of four cubits and read [the prayers]. R. Simeon b. 'Azzai said: If he was travelling on a ship with the bones, he should remove them to another part [of the vessel] and read.[2] R. Isaac said: If they are the bones of a near relative he is exempt, but if of strangers he is under obligation. R. Simeon said: On the Sabbath he is under obligation,[3] but on week-days he is exempt. R. Nathan said:[4] If the bundle [containing the bones] is with him, he is not exempt[5] because the obligation of guarding [the bones] rests upon him but not the obligation of guarding the bundle.

RULE 2. One who is removing bones or sacred books from one place to another may not place them on a wagon or a ship or an animal and[6] sit on them; but if it is for their benefit[7] or to escape paying ransom to robbers it is permissible.[8]

(1) His obedience of laws, from which he is exempt, would result in delay in the burial of the bones. (2) The text is in disorder and the translation follows the version of GRA. (3) Because if he does not read the prayers he would appear to be mourning on the Sabbath which is not permitted. (4) The text is corrupt and emended by GRA. R. Nathan agrees with the ruling that one who guards bones is exempt from the *Shema'*, etc., because his concern about their safety may not allow him to concentrate on his religious devotions; but where he carries them in a bundle the question of their safety does not arise and he should be able to concentrate. (5) In his note on the text GRA reads 'is exempt', but in his annotation to Y.D. ch. 403 he rules that, in the circumstances here described, the man is obliged to read the prayers, etc. (6) So GRA and H. V has 'and not sit'. (7) i.e. for the protection of the bones. (8) V inserts here a sentence in brackets which is irrelevant to the subject and is omitted by GRA and H.

RULE 3. If one passes through graves he should not wear the *tefillin* or carry sacred books in his hand, because it is disrespectful [to the dead].[9]

RULE 4. If one is constructing a burial chamber[10] [in a cemetery] and the time for reading the *Shema'* arrives, he should not read the *Shema'* or the *Tefillah* but withdraw to a clean place and read; after that he re-enters [the chamber].

RULE 5. If one finds a dead body in a grave he may not move it from its place,[11] unless he knows that the place was lent to it.[12]

RULE 6. If one finds bones in a grave he should place them in mounds,[13] in the view of R. 'Aḳiba; but the Sages said: He should not move them from their place. If he found them in a burial chamber or in a cedar-wood coffin,[14] he should not move them from their place.

RULE 7. We may not transfer a dead body or bones from one place of honour to another, or from a place of shame to a place of honour,[15] and needless to say from a place of honour to a place of shame; but within [the dead person's] property it is permissible [to transfer] even from a place of honour to a place of shame, because it is to his honour.[16]

RULE 8. We do not bury two dead bodies in close proximity to each other, or a dead body in close proximity to bones, or bones in close proximity to a dead body. R. Judah said: Whoever sleeps with him in his lifetime[17] is buried with him in his death.[18]

(9) In Ber. 18a (Sonc. ed., p. 108) he is said to transgress the teaching, *Whoso mocketh the poor blasphemeth his Maker* (Prov. XVII, 5), because the dead are 'poor' in that they cannot acquire merit by the study and performance of the Torah. (10) Vaults were made in the graves for receiving the dead; cf. Ber. 14b (Sonc. ed., p. 85). (11) The dead acquire possession of the spot wherein they are buried. Cf. Sanh. 47b (Sonc. ed., p. 316). (12) Cf. above X, 8. The word 'lent' is according to the text of GRA and H. (13) Reading מהמורות defined as 'mounds used as burying places of executed criminals' (Jastrow). GRA reads: 'One who finds bones in mounds should place them in a grave'. (14) So Jastrow. GRA has 'or in a ravine'. (15) The translation follows GRA who alters the text in agreement with j.M.Ḳ. II, 4, 81b. (16) To be buried within his own property. (17) i.e. young children. (18) i.e. in close proximity to him.

RULE 9. One may derive benefit from a grave which has been cleared,[19] but he may not turn it into a magazine for straw, a stable, a store for wood or a depot. If one clears a burial chamber he may not make use of it [for any other purpose]. If one prepares a grave for a living person[20] he may sell it; but if he prepared it for the dead he may not sell it. Stones which were hewn[21] for one still living may be sold, but if for the dead they may not be sold. If one clears a coffin he may not make use of it; but if it was made of stone or earthenware it must be broken up, and if of wood it must be burnt. If one finds boards in a cemetery[22] he may not move them from their place.

(19) Since it is no longer considered the possession of the dead. (20) In preparation for his death. (21) To be used for a sepulchre. (22) So emended by GRA. V reads 'if one carries out boards to a cemetery'.

CHAPTER XIV

RULE 1. A watercourse should not be diverted through cemeteries,[1] a path should not be cut through them, cattle should not be grazed on them, one should not take a walk there[2] for pleasure, and one should not gather wood or grass from there. If he gathered them he may not make use of them, and if he gathered them for the benefit [of the cemetery][3] he burns them on the spot.

RULE 2. Inherited lands may be conveyed from one [party] to another or alienated from one family to another, but a grave cannot be so conveyed or alienated.[4]

RULE 3. A new cemetery[5] may be measured[6] and sold or divided;[7] an old one may not be measured, sold or divided. A new cemetery may sometimes be regarded as old and an old one as new. An old cemetery in which ten bodies have been buried without the consent of the owners is regarded as new; it may be measured, sold or divided. A new cemetery in which one premature child[8] lies buried with the consent of the owners is regarded as old; it may not be measured, sold or divided.[9]

RULE 4. No right of legal ownership can be claimed in respect of a cemetery of exiles;[10] in time of pestilence or war no right of legal ownership can be claimed in respect of cemeteries.[11] Rabban Simeon b. Gamaliel said: Premature children do not acquire possession of their grave.[12] One who has buried without

(1) Out of respect for the dead; cf. Meg. 29a (Sonc. ed., p. 177). (2) It should not be used as a short cut. (3) To clear the ground for more graves. The words in brackets are inserted by GRA and H. (4) Cf. below, §11. (5) In which only a few have been buried. (6) To find out how much land had already been used for burials as a guide for further interments. (7) Among heirs. (8) Under thirty days old; how much more an adult! (9) 'Or divided' is added by GRA and H. (10) Who in time of pestilence or war move from place to place. (11) This clause is explanatory of the preceding. (12) If buried without the consent of the owners.

the consent [of the owner of the land] possesses no right of legal ownership.

RULE 5. A woman who inherited a grave-space is buried therein as also her issue, in the view of R. Meir; R. Judah said: She [is buried there] but not[13] her issue. R. Judah admits that any offspring whom she saw in her lifetime are buried with her [if they die] after her death.[14]

RULE 6. If her father says, 'Let her be buried by my side' and her husband says, 'Let her be buried [50a] by my side', she is buried by the side of her father; but if she had children, she is buried by her husband's side, and if she says, 'Bury me by the side of my children', she is buried by their side.

RULE 7. If her father says, 'She is not to be buried by my side' and her husband says, 'She is not to be buried by my side', she is buried by the side of her husband because her husband has the obligation to support her, redeem her [from captivity],[15] bury her and provide all that is necessary[16] for her funeral, [for example,] a bier, pipers[17] and wailing women.[18] Where it is customary to have a memorial address, he has a memorial address delivered over his wife. If her husband does not attend to her [burial, her father] attends to it and the expenses are recovered from [the husband] by force.

RULE 8.[19] Consequently you say that there are three kinds of graves: a grave which has been found may be cleared,[20] and

(13) So GRA and H. V reads 'and all' incorrectly. (14) But not a posthumous child. V has 'on her death' and the reading of H is adopted. (15) Cf. Keth. 46b (Sonc. ed., p. 266). (16) So GRA. (17) To play at the funeral; cf. B.M. VI, 1 (Sonc. ed., p. 437, n. 3). (18) Cf. M.Ḳ. III, 9 (Sonc. ed., p. 185). They are mentioned in Jer. IX, 16. (19) The text is in disorder. The translation follows the emendation of GRA on the basis of Sanh. 47b (Sonc. ed., p. 316). Higger (Introduction, pp. 49f) points out that the text is not in agreement with the parallel passage in Tosiftha Ohol. XVI, 9 or with the Babylonian Talmud *loc. cit.* or with the Jerusalem Talmud, Nazir IX, 3, 57d. He suggests that the compiler of *Semaḥoth* must have had before him various passages dealing with the uncleanness of the grave and the prohibition of using graves and he mixed them up. The introductory phrase 'consequently you may say' points to the fact that there must have been a discussion on the subject and the statement in the text sums up the conclusion arrived at. (20) i.e. the bones are transferred to another place. A person had been buried there without the knowledge and consent of the owner.

if cleared its site is [ritually] clean and it is permitted to make use of it. A known grave may not be cleared,[21] and if cleared its site is [ritually] unclean and it is forbidden to make use of it. A grave which injures the public[22] may not be cleared, and if cleared its site is [ritually] clean but it is forbidden to make use of it.

RULE 9. As regards a cemetery which is enclosed by a city on three sides or on two opposite sides, if it is more than fifty cubits distant from one side [of the city] and more than fifty cubits distant from the other side, it is not[23] cleared and if less it may be cleared.

RULE 10.[24] All graves may be cleared except that of a king or a prophet. R. 'Aḳiba said: The grave of a king or prophet may also be cleared. R.'Aḳiba was asked, 'Were not the graves of the house of David and of Huldah the prophetess[25] [situated] in Jerusalem and no man ever touched them?' He replied, 'Can you adduce a proof from [Jerusalem]? There was an underground passage there and the uncleanness was conveyed to the brook of Kidron'.[26]

RULE 11. If one sells to another the path [leading] to his grave, this is no sale.[27] If one sells to another his place of mourning,[28] it is no sale. If one sells[29] to another his halting place,[30] the elders of the *'Ab Beth Din* estimate it as an area of four *ḳab*.[31] A private path [has a width] of four cubits, a public road [a width] of sixteen cubits, the king's highway has no limits. The path of a funeral

(21) As a precautionary measure against persons contracting defilement. (22) Reading המזיק, i.e. a grave which lies in a public thoroughfare and so communicates uncleanness to people who are overshadowed by something which also overshadows it. (23) The negative is inserted by GRA and H. (24) The text is reconstructed in agreement with Tosiftha B.B. I, 11. (25) Cf. 2 Kings XXII, 14. (26) East of Jerusalem. (27) Because the sale is a slight on his family; cf. B.B. 100b (Sonc. ed., p. 420). (28) When, on the return from the cemetery, the cortège halts and the mourners receive condolence; cf. B.B. Sonc. ed., p. 416, n. 8. (29) V reads 'buys' which is corrected by GRA. (30) Where, on returning from the funeral, ceremonial halts were made to offer consolation to the mourners. (31) An area sufficient for sowing four *ḳab* of seed.

cortège has no limits.[32] and the path of [a place of] mourning has no limits.

RULE 12.[33] One who sees a mourner within the thirty days speaks to him words of consolation but does not inquire after his welfare; after thirty days he inquires after his welfare but does not speak to him words of consolation; within the twelve months he inquires after his welfare and then speaks words of consolation to him; after twelve months he speaks to him words of consolation and then inquires after his welfare.

R. Meir said: One who sees a mourner within the thirty days speaks to him words of consolation and then inquires after his welfare; after thirty days but within twelve months he inquires after his welfare and then speaks to him words of consolation; after twelve months he makes no reference at all [to the bereavement]. For R. Meir illustrated the matter by a parable. To what may it be compared? To one who has a wound and was cured of it, and a physician came and said to him, 'Pay me a fee and I will lance your wound and cure you'. Likewise, whoever reminds a mourner after twelve months [of his bereavement] is accounted as if he had stirred up his wound again. Rabban Simeon b. Gamaliel said: To one whose wife died and he remarried within twelve months we speak words of consolation in the street but not in his home.[34]

RULE 13. All bring to the house of a mourner loaves of white bread, meat and fish, and where an assembly in the broadway[35] is held also vegetables, peas and fish. Rabban Simeon b. Gamaliel said: Where it is customary also cooked dishes.[36]

RULE 14.[37] Ten cups of wine are drunk in the house of a mourner: two before the meal, five during the meal and three after the meal, namely one for the benediction of mourners,[38] one for the consolation of the mourners and one [in honour

(32) The followers may even tread upon cornfields if there is no room for them on the public highway. (33) Cf. M.Ḳ. 21b (Sonc. ed., p. 136). (34) Not to embarrass his second wife. (35) Cf. XII, 4, n. 13. (36) Cf. B.B. 16b (Sonc. ed., p. 84). When Abraham died, Jacob made a broth of lentils to comfort his father Isaac. (37) Cf. Keth. 8b (Sonc. ed., p. 42), j.Ber. III, 6a. The text here is similar to that of the Jerusalem Talmud. (38) The Jerusalem Talmud reads 'for the Grace after meals'.

of] charity.[39] Three more [cups of wine] were added later, namely, one for the Chief of the Synagogue,[40] one for the Synagogue attendant[41] and one for Rabban Gamaliel.[42] When, however, the *Beth Din* found that people became intoxicated they restored the *status quo*.[43]

RULE 15. He who recites the Grace after meals in the house of a mourner does not say the fourth benediction,[44] in the view of R. Jose the Galilean; R. 'Aḳiba said: [He recites] 'Who art kind and dealest kindly'; the Sages said: [The benediction to be recited is, 'Blessed art Thou] Who art the true Judge, Who rulest over Thy works, Judge of all generations in righteousness, Whose people and servants we all are; and for all this it is our duty to thank and bless Him'.

RULE 16.[45] He who sees a place where miracles were wrought for Israel says, 'Blessed be He Who wrought miracles for our fathers in this place. *O give thanks unto the Lord, for He is good*'.[46]

(39) i.e. in honour of those who came to comfort the mourners and performed a pious act. (40) An official who administered the external affairs of the Synagogue (cf. Yoma VII, 1, Sonc. ed., p. 322, n. 2). (41) An official who seems to have been next in rank to the Chief of the Synagogue. (42) Who introduced a simple style for funerals to lessen the expense and relieve poor mourners; cf. M.Ḳ. 27b (Sonc. ed., p. 178), Keth. 8b (Sonc. ed., p. 43). (43) i.e. that ten cups only should be drunk. (44) Cf. P.B., p. 283. In Ber. 46b (Sonc. ed., p. 281) the decision is that the benediction is not omitted. (45) Cf. Ber. 54a (Sonc. ed., p. 327). (46) Ps. CVII, 1.